Calculations

Calculations

Net Assessment and the Coming of World War II

Edited by

Williamson Murray
and
Allan R. Millett

THE FREE PRESS
A Division of Macmillan, Inc.
NEW YORK
Maxwell Macmillan Canada
TORONTO
Maxwell Macmillan International
NEW YORK OXFORD SINGAPORE SYDNEY

The Free Press
A Division of Macmillan, Inc.
866 Third Avenue, New York, N. Y. 10022

Maxwell Macmillan Canada, Inc.
1200 Eglinton Avenue East
Suite 200
Don Mills, Ontario M3C 3N1

Macmillan, Inc. is part of the Maxwell Communication
Group of Companies.

Printed in the United States of America

printing number
1 2 3 4 5 6 7 8 9 10

Library of Congress Cataloging-in-Publication Data

Calculations: net assessment and the coming of World War II / edited
   by Williamson Murray and Allan R. Millett.
         p. cm.
   Includes bibliographical references (p.   ) and index.
   ISBN: 1-4165-7684-3
   ISBN-13: 978-1-4165-7684-6

      1. Military planning—History—20th century.   2. Military
readiness—History—20th century.   3. Military planning—Europe—
History—20th century.   4. Military planning—United States—
History—20th century.   5. Military planning—Japan—History—20th
century.   6. Europe—Armed Forces—History—20th century.   7. United
States—Armed Forces—History—20th century.   8. Japan—Armed
Forces—History—20th century.   9. World War, 1939–1945—Causes.
I. Murray, Williamson.   II. Millett, Allan Reed.
U150.C35 1992   91-20672
355'.033'0043—dc20   CIP

In memory of
Stanley J. Kahrl
our good friend and colleague

Contents

Calculations

1

Net Assessment on the Eve of World War II

Williamson Murray and Allan R. Millett

SHORT OF THE COSTLY and perilous audit of war itself, the problem of estimating the likely performance of one's armed forces against one's potential enemy is the most intractable problem of defense planning. The process is not new—at least in its unstructured form—but in Western parlance it has now become known as "net assessment." In Soviet usage it is part of evaluating "the correlation of forces." Writing in the fourth century B.C., the Chinese philosopher of warfare Sun Tzu described the assessment process:

> Now if the estimates made in the temple before hostilities indicate victory, it is because calculations show one's strength to be superior to that of his enemy; if they indicate defeat, it is because calculations show that one is inferior. With many calculations, one can win; with few one cannot. How much less chance of victory has one who makes none at all?

> By this means I can examine the situation and the outcome will be clearly apparent.[1]

The translator of Sun Tzu, however, adds that this passage escapes easy translation and that the methods Sun Tzu suggests for estimates are unclear, even though Sun Tzu cites them by inference throughout *The Art of War* and implies that the process is rational, structured, comprehensive, in part quantified, and explicit about assumptions and data. Modern net assessment follows Sun Tzu's principles, if not his confidence in outcomes. The important allusion is to "the temple" and the role of faith.

The process of net assessment has been integral to relations between states whether one talks about war or periods of peace. Yet the processes by which statesmen and strategists weigh the balance and calculate the risks of the international arena have received relatively little attention from both political scientists and historians. The former have focused on the general relationships between players or "actors" on the international scene; the latter have generally satisfied their curiosity with studies that lay out in excrutiating detail one side of the story or the other. Policy-makers have reinforced the inclinations of these disciplines. On the one hand they have used history, if at all, to elucidate "lessons" rather than ambiguities; on the other, they have found political science with its artificial clarity and quantifications both alluring and attractive. Whether it has been useful is another matter.[2]

An additional complication has been the natural tendency of academic analyses to focus on intelligence rather than net assessment. Two factors help explain this. First, formal net assessment has only recently made its appearance (1972) as a coherent, disciplined effort to address problems inherent in achieving meaningful measures of the international balance. Even historians with documents on both sides of international conflicts and crises have proved surprisingly unwilling to attempt balance analyses. It is not difficult to estimate the balance of forces in May 1940; the wreckage of French and British armies in northern France would seem to make the balance in that month quite clear. Yet unless one accepts Calvinistic or Marxist predestination, an understanding of the shifting military and strategic balances through the 1930s, both real and in terms of perceptions of statesmen and military leaders, is crucial in judging how the international arena worked.[3] Unfortunately, historians have tended to center analyses on single nations; consequently, convinced by the weight of one nation's documentary evidence, they have barely moved beyond the perceptions of those who weighed the risks under the pressures of time and incomplete information.[4] As a result, balance assessments by historians have consisted mostly of simple "bean counts" of units available on opposing sides.[5] Besides, historians have frequently confused assessment with intelligence, thus reducing the complexities and ambiguities of national balance analysis to intelligence organizations and their products.[6] Net assessment, however, has aimed at achieving a different picture of the world from that proposed by intelligence organizations either past or present.[7]

Another argument that bedevils the process of net assessment is debate about organization. Although it is a truism that organization can or, more emphatically, will influence process and analytic outcomes, net assessment is not just a problem in bureaucratic politics. Nevertheless, as net assessment increases its influence on the defense decision-making process—as it has in the United States—it becomes increasingly subject to territorial disputes over the nature and dependability of data and the appropriateness of method. One might argue that heightened political influence turns what should be a non-zero-sum game into a zero-sum game, for personal and organizational fates do indeed rest on whose analysis eventually triumphs and whose does not. Those outside of government tend to see territorial problems as simply matters of bureaucratic self-interest that can be cured by reorganization. Such positions undervalue the problems of net assessment that adhere to the intellectual enterprise itself. The cry for reorganizing the process begs many of the problems that defy reorganization. A corollary to the question of process change is the "Rockefeller solution," that is, to throw enough assets at a problem so that it eventually is crushed by the weight of the investment—or at least changes its nature. Such an approach, which might be called "the American way of success," surely has outlived its usefulness in defense decision-making. The efficacy of net assessment depends upon factors that cannot be accommodated simply by increasing budgets and rearranging organizational relationships, but instead requires educating decision-makers on the value of the intellectual enterprise of defining options and unmasking the unknowns as well as thinking about the known factors. Clarifying difficult choices is not a happy function in government, regardless of its form. It is, however, essential to rational decision-making.

While net assessment is a relatively recent concept, statesmen and military leaders have engaged in serious attempts to weigh national power within the international arena whether in peace or at war. Admittedly these efforts have been somewhat ill-formed. As Paul Kennedy has suggested about British leadership before the outbreak of World War I:

> In fact, the very concept of "the balance of power" was never deeply explored, in either the political or military sense. As an expression, it was, of course, much employed: in early August 1911 [Sir Henry] Wilson noted that it was "an axiom that the policy of England is to prevent any Continental Power from attaining a position of superiority that would allow it to dominate and to dictate to the rest of Europe." One can concede that certain Britons who studied German advances in industry and technology (say, James Louis Garvin, Leo Amery, Eyre Crowe) became alarmed at the prospect of this new and formidable economic might being at the disposal of the Prusso-German elite; yet did this reasoning move those many other Britons, especially the military, who took little interest in economic matters?[8]

Kennedy's description of the international arena confronting Britain in the first decade of this century fits most other periods and nations. The fog of war is only one reflection of the general ambiguities of human affairs. Statesmen operate in a milieu in which calculations of even their own national power are intrinsically unsure. If it is difficult to calculate one's own strength, then how much more difficult is it to calculate the strengths of others whose culture, language, and nationality are so different?

NET ASSESSMENT: A HISTORICAL PERSPECTIVE

This book examines the problems posed by net assessment in the 1930s. The seven separate essays investigate the processes by which the major powers (Great Britain, Germany, Italy, France, the Soviet Union, the United States, and Japan) carried out and were affected by the processes of national net assessment in the decade preceding World War II. This task poses some unusual difficulties for the historian, not the least of which is that few of these countries possessed formal net assessment organizations.

The purpose of this study is to examine how the process of net assessment worked in the late 1930s. While no explicit organizations existed in this period to assess the shifting net balance among the powers, government leaders had little choice but to move beyond the elementary data provided by their intelligence agencies and, for better or worse, to make the best net assessments they could. Given the absence of formal net assessment organizations and processes, the task of the historians in this project was to piece together the often implicit, informal, or even unconscious ways in which judgments about military balances were reached. A historical examination of the process of net assessment should *not* aim at creating a neat model or framework for explaining events. Rather it should uncover the complexities and ambiguities involved in the net assessment process.

The essays, therefore, analyze the failures as well as the successes in national net assessment efforts during the 1930s as a basis of addressing larger questions. What were (and are) the pitfalls in making national net assessments? Why did they tend to miss the mark? What were the elements in the process that might have been corrected, and what lay beyond the reach of policy-makers? The important factors in net assessment, whether in the 1930s or 1990s, multiply as one examines the phenomenon. The intelligence portion of the process is itself complex, even if one assumes that the only function of military intelligence agencies is to describe and (usually with great reluctance) assess the forces of one's allies and potential enemies. First, someone must decide what the important questions of capability are and design a collection effort to provide the relevant data, in itself no mean feat. The collection effort is never complete and often far short of satisfactory, but commanders cannot wait, and they demand assessment. They often are unsatisfied with descriptions of capability or organizational orders-of-battle and want some analysis of enemy intentions as well, even though this process is perilous at best. Examples of purposeful fabrication, delusion, and ambiguity characterize the history of intelligence agencies in the twentieth century.

The process of net assessment, however, also demands an accurate assessment of one's own forces and their likely performance in war. This exercise is no less fraught with miscalculation since it must include educated guesses about the quality of leadership; the likely performance of untested weapons and other military equipment like communications systems and transport; the appropriateness of force organization for varied missions; morale; the physical condition of personnel; and the forces' state of training. These judgments cannot be made inside some bubble of "objectivity" called "military science," because they invariably are influenced by personality, organizational roles, the assessment process itself, and deeply held (if often unarticulated) beliefs about national military "traits," traditions, and other culturally driven attitudes.[9]

Net Assessment and the Road to World War II

In order to evaluate the organization, process, and results of net assessment by the seven major belligerents of World War II, one must begin with World War I and its legacy. By the 1930s three participants in the earlier war had endured fundamental changes in regimes that placed ruthless dictators in control of revolutionary political parties and the formal governments. Two of these nations had been losers in World War I (Germany and Russia), and the other, Italy, might as well have lost, given the costs of its war. In the case of Japan, success in World War I had been forfeited (in the eyes of Japanese imperialists and militarists) in the negotiations that began at Versailles and ended with the Washington treaties of 1922. By the 1930s, largely through their use of intimidation (including assassination) and the intrinsic appeal of their plan to make Manchuria and China economic colonies, the Japanese imperialists had eliminated much of the traditional nobility, the business leadership, and the civilian party politicians from the design of Japanese foreign policy. The four non–status quo nations— Germany, Italy, the Soviet Union, and Japan—formed governments dedicated to an aggressive foreign policy that assumed a high risk of war.

Three future belligerents maintained the same forms of government with which they had waged World War I. Britain remained a constitutional monarchy with the effective reins of government in Parliament and the ministries (staffed by members of the parliamentary majority and the career civil service) and the military staff system that culminated in the Committee of Imperial Defence. The French Third Republic, staggered by the national hecatomb on the Western Front, also remained a parliamentary democracy with the Prime Minister at the apex of the three military ministries and a ministry of foreign affairs, supported by civilian ministers and an elaborate military staff system largely dominated by army officers. Although they would have been loath to admit it, the British and French governments had much in common in both the form and the substance of the management of defense policy-making. They also shared a common memory of the effect of the World War upon their economies, their social fabric, and their eroded ability to rule their global empires. The United States had also preserved its democratic form of government despite the disappointments of its timid experiment with collective security (the League of Nations) and the psychological and social demoralization of the Great Depression, an experience it shared with all the other Great Powers and many lesser ones. Only the Soviet Union had avoided the collapse of the world industrial system in the 1930s, largely because civil war, collectivization, and the Stalinist purges had produced the same results without foreign assistance. The American government, however, organized its national defense structure in accordance with a Constitution that separated the executive and legislative branches to a degree unknown in Great Britain and France. The President of the United States could shape policy without the same degree of direct accountability that a British or French Prime Minister assumed as the leader of the parliamentary majority. Nevertheless, the annual budget process and substantive legislation (like the Neutrality Acts) assured a congressional role, however tumultuous.

All seven governments had ample experience in World War I upon which to build organizational lessons about the process of assessing their own and others' military capabilities. Gauging political intentions remained basically the responsibility of the heads of government and their Foreign Ministers. None of the heads of government lacked for relevant, if incomplete, information about their potential enemies and allies. To be sure, the more secretive governments, characterized by censorship and the restricted distribution of military data, had an advantage in that they could deny democratic governments access to much information about their own military capability. Nevertheless, the military intelligence organizations of the 1930s could and did piece together relatively sound descriptions of the Great Powers' military order-of-battle, at least in the static sense of numbers of operational units, the technological performance of weapons systems, and the relevant operational doctrine adopted by the armed forces. In fact, four of the powers had conducted major military operations before the war assumed its final form in 1940–41. The Japanese had been at war in China since 1937 and had fought the Soviet Union first at Changkufeng in 1938 and then at Nomonhan in 1939. The Italians had fought in Africa, and the Italians, Germans, and Russians had intervened in the Spanish Civil War. The German army had deployed twice to occupy Austria and Czechoslovakia. The Russians had invaded Finland in 1940, and both the Russians and the Germans had attacked Poland in 1939.

Although all the implications of these operations may have eluded military analysts, the military intelligence communities showed a high degree of energy, assiduousness, cleverness, and professional competence in collecting information by open means (military observers and attachés) and covert methods (agents and electronic intelligence). The basic organizational problem of the seven nations' intelligence agencies was not the collection of data or even the challenge of expert capability analysis, but credibility within the highest levels of military planning and political assessment.

There is, however, one characteristic in the military intelligence effort that has organizational implications. When the armed forces of the industrialized powers created military intelligence agencies in the nineteenth century, these agencies grew as part of service staffs and reflected their parent services' concern about their like services in other countries. Armies fought armies; navies fought navies; and, later, air forces fought air forces. The tridimensional concept of military operations eroded some in World War I, but not to the degree that it disappeared in World War II. None of the World War II belligerents foresaw the interrelationship of land, naval, and air forces that characterized that war or predicted the considerable effect that one-service strategic approaches (for example, strategic bombing, submarine commerce-raiding) could have on the course of all military operations, if only in the area of opportunity costs.

Nor did intelligence agencies, established on service lines and loyalties, provide sound appreciations of what the combination of tactical aviation and mobile land forces might do to the conventional concepts of land warfare. Although it is now fashionable to describe the doctrinal and operational flaws in Blitzkrieg, which surely existed and cannot be camouflaged by postwar German and British apologists, it is also true that no military intelligence organization in the 1930s predicted that the Wehrmacht had mastered an operational approach to warfare that could restore the initiative to an army that accepted the perils of the offensive. As an institution, the Soviet army might have reached the same conclusions as the Germans did—driven in part by the inherent Russian problem of defending indefensible terrain with mobile forces—but Stalin's decapitation of the Red Army's leadership made it unfashionable to follow German military doctrine. Even when there were modest tests of mechanized warfare, as there were in Spain and Outer Mongolia, the limited use and special operational circumstances tended to dilute the intelligence analysis of these operations. Although individual officers like Charles de Gaulle, Percy Hobart, and

Adna R. Chaffee, Jr., might have understood the potential of mechanized warfare, only the German officer corps (and then only part of it) appreciated the full potential of mobile operations, and they did so through their own maneuvers, not intelligence activities. Foreign military staffs did not miss the creation of panzer formations, but they could not predict the panzers' performance with sufficient alarm to galvanize the reform of their own armies.[10]

At the level of intelligence evaluation, then, the major organizational weakness was the absence of interservice military intelligence organizations that could examine military capability across service lines and develop detailed appreciations of enemy strengths and weaknesses in joint and combined operations. Where military intelligence staffs attempted such assessments, they did so as *ad hoc* committees formed for the special purpose of making a single assessment, not for continuing analysis and collection of relevant data. Moreover, military intelligence staffs did not have sufficient information or authority even to do force-on-force comparisons. Planning staffs demanded intelligence assessments from their intelligence sections, but they did not provide friendly force information either to their intelligence sections or to an independent evaluation group. The German armed forces probably did the best job of structured operational assessment because of their dedication to war-gaming. Nevertheless, the Germans did not evaluate the likely course of a strategic bombing campaign—either one mounted against Great Britain or one directed at the Third Reich—or investigate the long-term demands of submarine commerce-raiding against Allied antisubmarine-warfare countermeasures. Military staffs could do and did regular evaluations of their own forces' performance in maneuvers and exercises, but they did not do operational-capability net assessment, which clearly rested within their domain.[11]

Although the organization for strategic appraisal differed from country to country, all seven of the Great Powers shared common problems and experiences that could not have been easily corrected by organizational reform alone. All the nations (with the exception of the United States) eventually created elaborate interdepartmental organizations to fuse diplomatic assessment, military evaluation, and domestic political considerations. As in most complex bureaucracies—as all these governments surely were—formal and informal lines of influence and communication influenced net assessment, but all the responsible heads of government (with the possible exception of the Japanese Prime Ministers until Tōjō Hideki) had adequate access to a wide range of advisers with the relevant expertise about their own countries' strengths and weaknesses and those of their allies and potential adversaries. All the nations but Japan had the recent experience of World War I with which to define their strategic problems. In the realm of economic mobilization, for example, governments had a respectable grasp of their own manpower resources, raw materials, industrial plant capacity, fiscal and monetary condition, transportation systems, agricultural productivity, and export–import balances. They understood the relevance of statistics and statistical trends even if they could not always be sure about the interrelationship of important economic variables. They may have been more uncertain about other nations' economic condition, and they may have too often seen other economic systems as similar to their own, but the economic foundations for strategic assessment were sound enough for informed decision-making. The same may be said for the organized reporting of foreign and domestic political trends, technological developments in armaments, scientific research, and public opinion.

From the perspective of organizational theory, which stresses the importance of timely and accurate information flow to responsible decision-makers, the one government that could have used more organizational structure was the United States, which had no analogy to the cabinet governments of Great Britain and France. The French, however, fretted about the adequacy of their organization for strategic appraisal—almost to the point of paralytic obsessiveness—while the British chose not to tinker with reorganization as a cure for unpalatable facts. Even the autocratic regimes had agencies for strategic appraisal: the Russians the Council of People's Commissars and the Main Military Council, the Italians the Supreme Defense Commission, the Germans the Oberkommando der Wehrmacht, and the Japanese (who prized collegial and consensual decision-making beyond Western norms) the Imperial Privy Council. An organizational theorist could find much to change in any of these arrangements to ensure a more rational and efficient flow of factual analysis and the structured development of policy options, but none of the seven major belligerents of World War II flirted with catastrophe or suffered ultimate defeat because of formal governmental organization. The flaws in strategic net assessment had deeper and more persistent roots.[12]

With the exception of the Japanese militarists, whose grip on the Japanese people was complete by 1937, the governments of the Great Powers could not escape the fact that strategic net assessment bore within it the seeds of regime destruction, and they did their best to curb any internal challenge to national security policy that might overturn the government.

For the three Western democracies, the problem had predictable links to elections and party politics, although in truth none of the opposition parties in the United States, France, and Great Britain offered a real alternative to the policies of appeasement and crisis-avoidance that characterized those three nations after 1937. Franklin D. Roosevelt, for example, managed national security issues the same way he handled any public policy issue, which was to rely on personal advisers, to discount bureaucratic analysis, to keep power within the executive branch diffused and authority uncertain, and to deal with Congress and the American people with a degree of indirection and ambiguity that bordered on duplicity. Perhaps he had learned too much from Woodrow Wilson, whom he had observed closely from his position as Assistant Secretary of the Navy during World War I. In Wilson's case, however, presidential confusion was honest; in Roosevelt's case, indecision was calculated since the President probably concluded as early as 1937 that Germany, Japan, and Italy had embarked on policies of aggression that endangered America's future. Roosevelt's problem was not the strategic net assessment process, but how to educate the American people on perils they felt less acutely than did he.

For Neville Chamberlain in Great Britain and Léon Blum and Edouard Daladier in France, the basic challenge was to examine the condition of the armed forces and the risk of war within the normal (that is, restricted) governmental forums like the Committee of Imperial Defence and the Comité Permanent de la Défense Nationale without revealing too much of their deliberations to the Germans and Italians and their domestic political critics, who tended to be skeptical individuals rather than whole parties. The processes of strategic assessment posed some problems: the intricate system of drafting collective documents, the arguments about data and analysis that plagued the intelligence services, and the tortuous and time-consuming requirement to reach consensus within the foreign policy and military bureaucracy before Cabinet consideration. Both Great Britain and France had difficulty appraising the Luftwaffe, and at critical times in their diplomacy with Hitler they miscalculated the threat of German air power. Nevertheless, the respective roles the participants expected to play in the process (political leader, military adviser, civilian expert) were played by the rules of democratic political culture and ensured that responsible political leaders dominated the policy process through setting procedures and framing the questions for evaluation. The process probably did not allow adequate airing of dissent among the expert advisers, and it tended to mute pessimistic advice, but on the whole the British and French governments understood their strategic dilemmas. Their basic mistake was more devastating: They believed (or hoped) that Adolf Hitler felt the same pressures and responsibilities that they did.

The process of net assessment in Germany, Italy, and the Soviet Union had eccentricities related to the personalities of Adolf Hitler, Benito Mussolini, and Josef Stalin and to the one-party dictatorships they led. From their personal military experience none of three dictators had any real competence above the role of squad leader, but their fear of their nations' traditional military officer corps (and the military's assumed longing for its lost monarchical legitimacy) compelled them to inflict their personal biases upon the strategic net assessment process. All three eventually assumed the functions of head of the armed forces in both military (commander-in-chief) and civilian (defense minister) roles. Their functional responsibilities as party leaders made it essential that they also dominate those portions of the government (the military and the police) that performed the intimidation and actual violence upon which dictators depend to silence opposition. The dictatorships found themselves in a dilemma they richly deserved. The popular appeal of National Socialism and Fascism rested in part on the promise of a "greater" Germany and "greater" Italy, which implied an imperialist program that risked war. Yet the megalomania, paranoia, and political survivalism that characterized Hitler, Mussolini, and Stalin dictated a form of government that made it difficult to evaluate the likely behavior of other states and—more importantly—their own. For one thing, all three nations developed two governments, the party structure and the traditional ministerial organizations they inherited. Although the Bolsheviks did the most thorough job in bringing revolution to the bureaucracy, they did not entirely replace (or kill) it, and thus the sensible thing for any dictator to do was to produce a party structure that carried on the same policy-advising and assessment functions as the government. For example, V. M. Molotov, Joachim von Ribbentrop, and Geleazzo Ciano might serve as foreign ministers, but in the end they depended upon their personal relationship with Stalin, Hitler, and Mussolini for their power, not an independent power base in either the party or the government. Essentially, the dictators ran a court, not a government, a court of privileges granted and patronage voided (unto the point of death) that

Niccolò Machiavelli would have recognized in an instant. Such a system was unduly sensitive to personal whim in the assessment process.

The fundamental nature of dictatorships and the national goals of Germany, Italy, and the Soviet Union in the 1930s determined that strategic net assessment would be adulterated by the conspiratorial, personalist nature of the three regimes. For example, all three dictators argued that only they understood one another or truly saw the weak, compromising Western democratic leaders for the cowards they were. In military matters, Hitler and Mussolini had a strong tendency to dismiss reports of systemic problems and to reduce critical issues to matters of technology, tactical trivia, and will power. Stalin showed a greater willingness to trust the military staff's strategic net assessment system—after, of course, he had purged the Soviet officer corps of virtually all its senior commanders and replaced them with his own generals. The dictators played the services off against each other and exploited all the personal rivalries they could. They reduced anyone else's capacity for independent strategic analysis. Mussolini could not rid himself of the one effective focus of opposition, King Vittorio Emanuele III with his trusted advisers, Marshal Pietro Badoglio and Marshal Emilio de Bono. With deep contacts throughout the Italian government, these three men remained aware of the facts that belied Fascist romanticism, and they eventually unseated Mussolini in a coup in 1943, with a mighty push from the Allies. Hitler and Stalin scored higher successes at regime-dominance, but they so intimidated their advisers that only sycophants like Martin Bormann could survive. Stalin, it is true, made his peace with his surviving senior officers, but only for the duration of the war. Had the marshals of the Red Army not emerged victorious national heroes from the Great Patriotic War, they would have proceeded to the wall or the gulag, as had their predecessors in the 1930s. Certainly such was the fate of their contemporaries in Germany, especially the conspirators of July 1944. Such poisonous civil–military relations are not likely to ensure that strategic discourse is influenced by frank discussions of operational feasibility, the essential contribution of military professionals to net assessment.

The Japanese did things differently. With the cabinet and ministries under military domination in the 1930s, the Japanese imperialists had no reason to fear either the cowed political parties or the general population, who had no historical experience with democratic opposition. Instead, the Japanese military wanted to ensure that the Emperor and his personal advisers had no opportunity to challenge the military's definition of Japan's long-term economic vulnerability and the immediate strategic opportunities to create an autarkic empire. The Japanese military integrated two powerful weapons: an organizational structure that could provide Western-style staff assessments (which reflected the intellectual debt to the German army and the British navy) and a cultural claim of moral oneness with the Emperor and the Supreme Deity that had created the *yamato,* or "chosen people." Facts and feelings made a powerful combination in defining "the Imperial Way."

On the other hand, the military's self-assumed mission to save the *yamato* and the overpowering pressure from group consensus prevented any searching discussion of worst-case strategic assessments. It was no novelty for Axis generals and admirals to enter World War II with grave personal doubts about the eventual outcome, but in the case of the Japanese military, the senior officers bore a degree of responsibility for the decision for war not shared by their German and Italian colleagues. If the German and Italian assessments contained too much politics, the Japanese assessment process allowed for too much strategy.

For those powers that sought to revise the international balance of power by force (Germany, Italy, and Japan) and those that pursued peace at almost any cost (France, Great Britain, and the United States), the organization and process of net assessment produced some common problems. Even for the one nation in an intermediate position, the Soviet Union, which combined small wars with Japan, Finland, and Poland with big appeasement (the Molotov–Ribbentrop Agreement of 1939 and the Neutrality Pact with Japan of 1941), the problem of strategic net assessment proved no less slippery and led to the ultimate disaster of Barbarossa. The experience of these seven nations provides some cautionary lessons for future practitioners of net assessment.[13]

The most important issue is the dynamic relationship between political judgment and strategic evaluation. Heads of government reach the pinnacle of power through their mastery of their own political culture, and they do not abandon what works for them when they begin to operate in the international arena. Until the widespread use of public opinion polling and the quantitative analysis of voter behavior, domestic political planning had virtually no empirical basis. Of course, even where public opinion means something and voting is significant, these contributions to rational assessment often take a back seat to political intuition. Politicians pride themselves on being creatures of instinct, and they have a notorious aversion to accepting collective bureaucratic analyses at face value. At the same time they are not normally the product of long careers as diplomats and military officers, which reduces their capacity to judge the likely behavior of their opposite numbers from other political cultures. Compensating for culture bias is difficult enough in evaluating military capability and operational doctrine. In the murky margins where international diplomacy merges with strategic assessment, the task of differentiating between one's judgments about how others (enemies or allies) *should* behave and how they *might* behave becomes even more challenging. To seek and accept expert opinion, whether it comes from intelligence professionals, military planners, or diplomats, is an act of moral courage that comes hard for heads of government, because such advice in content and form often conflicts with the assumptions about human behavior that political leaders prize. The issue, then, is far more complex than just defining civil–military relations and the functional domains of decision-makers and their advisers. Successful net assessment is a continuing educational process in which the assessors bear the delicate burden of providing tutorials on strategic analysis for their political masters. In the status quo democracies of the 1930s, this responsibility was at best difficult, and for the autocracies, it became virtually impossible as the likelihood of war increased.

Another continuing problem is the timing of assessments and the time period for which assessments are supposed to be valid. In each successive crisis of the 1930s the political leaders asked their advisers whether the armed forces were ready *now* for a variety of possible conflicts; the answer was consistently "no," with various qualifications and degrees of uncertainty. The focus of these assessments—such as they were—bore on questions not about the course of a war, but about the likely course of a specific campaign that would initiate a war or respond to an enemy offensive. Like the planning that preceded the outbreak of war in 1914, the time period covered by the assessment was limited to months, not years, and assumed some sort of rapid resolution to the conflict, whether the resolution came in the form of a dictated or a negotiated termination of hostilities. Unlike the period before 1914, however, the assessments of the 1930s did provide analysis of long-term demographic and economic trends that might influence the generation of military capability from total national mobilization. In a technical sense, most of these long-war assessments were remarkably accurate. The difficulty is that politicians are steeped in the contingent nature of governmental behavior, true believers in the role of what Machiavelli called *fortuna*. The appeasers of the 1930s, for example, entertained the hope that if they could at least postpone war, something would turn up. The aggressor states (especially Germany and Japan) assumed that the inherent fragility of their rivals—whether they were capitalist democracies or Communist dictatorships—made long-war calculations irrelevant. What no one apparently examined in any detail was a strategic "black hole" that might occur between the transition from short war to long war, the period of extemporization in which the belligerent military establishments would fight a "broken-back" war with forces that survived the initial onslaught, but which did not yet include forces created after war began. Where in Axis planning (or Allied planning, for that matter) does one find an analysis of the likelihood or results of the Russian, Mediterranean, or South Pacific campaigns of 1942–43, all of which produced a substantial (if selective) attrition of Axis military capability?

The last major problem inherent in strategic net assessment is that political leaders and military advisers approach the intellectual enterprise of planning the pursuit of national goals with military force from opposite perspectives. The political leaders address strategic issues in Clausewitzian terms, whether they realize it or not. In the 1930s they attempted to foresee how war would influence their vision of their nations' well-being, but they did so (with the possible exception of the Japanese) without a very firm grasp of the operational capabilities of their national forces or those of their allies. The military leaders, on the other hand, tended to project operational capabilities into campaign planning and to frame strategic issues in operational terms. In itself, this predisposition is both understandable and professional, but it also tends to exclude some issues of logistical sustainability, doctrinal adaptiveness, enemy behavior, operational timing, and technological innovation. As the belligerents of World War II discovered, the soundest of strategic decisions still required operational effectiveness, but that operational skill could not redeem flawed strategy. Even if strategy remained essentially dependent upon the political goals that drove decision-making, strategic planning could not be simply defined as the aggregation of tactical capabilities and the extension over time and space of operational considerations.

In summary, the experience of the major World War II belligerents suggests that the organization of net assessment may be important, but only if it provides the fullest amount of relevant information about military capability, presented in force-on-force comparisons that are tested to the degree possible by appropriate analysis like free-play exercises, weapons effects, quantitative modeling, war-gaming, doctrinal exegesis, and leadership and organizational behavior. Net assessment should be conducted in some organizational framework that has access to timely and definitive political guidance as well as military advice. The process should ensure that organizational and personal bias—of whatever sort—is reduced, if not eliminated. The process should also provide for assessments that identify problems in terms of immediate, midrange, and long-term significance. When political leaders face military capability assessments, they should have the expertise (probably from a personal staff) to dig into the methods and assumptions that drive the analysis. It is a truism that military capability should not be viewed as an infallible indicator of political intent, but it is equally true that political intent alone does not produce appropriate military capability. Political leaders may be responsible for providing guidance to military planners, but that does not spare them the parallel responsibility of educating themselves on the substantive issues of military planning and organizational effectiveness.

The experience of the nations that eventually fought one another in World War II has relevance for the 1990s. As the nuclear dominance of the United States and the Soviet Union becomes less awesome, especially to other states, the importance of conventional force net assessment increases, a development hastened by the fragmentation of the two dominant alliance systems on the Eurasian continent. Depending upon the nature and location of real or possible conflict, the combinations of potential participants appear—if not infinite—far more complex than the alliance systems forged by the United States and the Soviet Union after World War II. The proliferation of modern weapons makes net assessment more important, especially since so many newly industrialized nations have shifted weapons procurement from foreign to domestic sources, a development that complicates the intelligence process at the very least. As the influence of the United States and the Soviet Union over their formal or *ad hoc* alliance partners and surrogates declines, the importance of national military "ways of war" increases. The most important variant to Western-style warfare in the postwar period was "people's war," the Maoist-style population-based insurgency, but at least this approach to war could be analyzed (if not always overcome) on the assumption that one side had dramatic technological inferiority. Such is no longer likely to be the case, even if operational doctrine and tactical practices may still vary widely. For example, the availability of hand-held surface-to-air missiles can transform peasant guerrillas in the 1990s into a far different force from what they would have been in the 1960s.

In any event, the difficulties of net assessment in the 1930s cannot be dismissed simply because the Great Powers lacked formal organizations dedicated to the task. Even Great Britain, which used the system of military evaluation most like that of other nations after World War II, made serious miscalculations. One cannot insist, moreover, that the judgments about military capability were irrelevant to nations led by appeasers, megalomaniacs, imperialist romantics, or defeatists since perceptions of likely military performance inevitably fed the political decisions of the 1930s. If war remains an extension of politics, then net assessment remains the handmaiden of political and strategic calculation.

2

British "Net Assessment" and the Coming of the Second World War

Paul Kennedy

THE BRITISH SYSTEM of "net assessment" in the 1930s was elaborate, relatively sophisticated, and bureaucratically well developed yet also flexible and truly global in nature. Compared with this model, the strategic assessment structure elsewhere in that period appears splintered, provisional, and parochial.[1] Yet for all its *relative* sophistication, British net assessment often did not manage to "get it right," with the result that many early wartime campaigns (Norway, France, Greece, Malaya) were disasters compensated for only by the fact that the larger global balances were steadily swinging against the Axis. The reasons—personal, institutional, and contextual—for those defective assessments will be analyzed below; what is simply pointed out here is that even the most developed structures and procedures provide no guarantee either that correct judgments are being made, or against future conflicts unfolding in unanticipated ways.

The British system of net assessment in the 1930s was both well developed bureaucratically *and* global in its range because of two major influences: a Cabinet-cum-committee structure of executive government and the fact that those who made decisions were aware that they had inherited a worldwide empire of territories, interests, and obligations. While these are quite separate points,* they are worth linking at this early stage because both elements—the organizational, and the spatial/contextual—were critically concerned with the task of relating ends to means. Simply put, both elements involved the ordering of priorities and the striking of balances.

British governmental structures consisted of a strong central executive, which, while accountable to Parliament (on a regular sessional basis) and to the country at large (at general elections), was nonetheless able to decide upon and implement national policies without much outside interference. Moreover, those "decisions" were made not by a powerful individual alone, as was the case with Stalin, Hitler, and, to some degree, even Roosevelt, but on a *collective* basis, in Cabinet or in Cabinet subcommittees, and then executed by senior civil servants and/or military advisers who themselves had usually played some part in the assessments. Even the briefest perusal of the records of Cabinet debates, of the memoranda and position papers laid before the ministers, or of a policy document that proceeded ever upward (from a subcommittee to the Committee of Imperial Defence, and then to the Cabinet itself) is likely to leave the reader with an impression of an extraordinarily well-oiled and elaborate machine—and to give the historian the illusion that in Britain's case it is possible to connect policy "inputs" with policy "outputs" in straightforward fashion.

And much of that is an illusion, created by the neatness of the minute-taking and memo-filing machine of Sir Maurice Hankey, the long-serving Secretary to the Cabinet and to the Committee of Imperial Defence (CID). Even at its late-Victorian best, it is hard to recognize Robinson and Gallagher's idealized portrait of the British "Official Mind" at work. In that portrait, Government ministers, briefed by their permanent officials, were able to sit in Cabinet, "consciously above and

---

*The committee system could exist without an empire—as is the case today; and the empire could have existed without a Cabinet system of government—as was true of most other empires.

outside" the day-to-day political pressures; their system permitted them to "assemble and weigh all the factors," so that in fact they "registered and balanced all the contingencies."[2] Yet issues such as Irish Home Rule, tariff reform, and higher taxation all disrupted this picture of Olympian detachment. Moreover, in the shadows cast by the Great War, the coming of full parliamentary democracy, and the impact of the post-1929 economic crisis, ministers were ever more conscious of "background influences on British external policy."[3] In addition, personal and practical factors also impinged upon the decision-making process: Some departments, such as the Treasury, were much more important than others, and of course the power and opinion of the Prime Minister meant that his views carried tremendous weight. If the Prime Minister was opposed to a certain proposal, neither it nor its backers were likely to get very far. This was not a gathering of philosopher-kings.

Nonetheless, the Prime Minister was not an autocrat. While someone like Neville Chamberlain heavily shaped British policies during his premiership, he did it as part of a *deliberative* process, in Cabinet itself or in some ministerial committee. Decisions were *shared* decisions, in which senior ministers such as Halifax (Foreign Secretary, 1938–40) also had great weight. The simple organizational fact that a group of fifteen or so ministers would spend an entire morning discussing a paper on policy options—which itself was probably the product of an interdepartmental committee or working party—meant that decisions were rarely eccentric or impromptu. This had both advantages and disadvantages. It was scarcely likely, for example, that the British people would wake up one morning to find themselves on the brink of war with other powers as a consequence of actions taken by *their* leaders. On the other hand, this system of rational discussion, bureaucratic compromise, referral to specialist committees, and the like tended to delay action, even when swift measures were called for; and the very continuity of this urbane manner of Cabinet discourse and "parliamentary behavior" into the Fascist era may have obscured perceptions of the transformations that had taken place in global politics and ideology since Mr. Gladstone's day. All this will be returned to later, for mentalités are probably the most difficult and important part of the process of net assessment to be recovered.

The other factor that made for a "process" was Britain's global-imperial position. Ever since 1880 (that is to say, the Carnarvon Report),[4] British politicians and officials had engaged in a form of net assessment. The happy combination of geographical and technological circumstances that had made mid-nineteenth-century Britain the leading naval, imperial, commercial, and industrial nation in the world was then eroding. Rising new powers were beginning to assert themselves. Britain's economic lead was cut back, and then overtaken; its market shares declined, and its industries struggled to compete. Joseph Chamberlain's purple description of "the Weary Titan, staggering under the too-vast orb of its own fate" was overly dramatic, but his general argument was true. The gap between Britain's global obligations and its national capacities had become dangerously large and was likely—since other countries were still growing faster—to get larger.[5]

All this in turn led to a series of strategical reassessments by British ministers and their armed services; it produced that system of interdepartmental committees to examine "imperial" defense as a whole (as opposed to "colonial" defense, which was merely local), and to offer broad-ranging reviews: of the Cardwell reinforcement system, the deployments of the Royal Navy's fleets, the development of empire communications, logistics, and (with the Dominions) even "burden-sharing." While this restructuring helped to produce a more centralized and efficient imperial "command and control," it could not recover for Britain the position it had held in Palmerston's time. It was not, in other words, an *alternative* to that parallel process of measuring the dangers and requirements across the globe and deciding which colonies should have smaller or larger garrisons, which oceans needed more or less battleships. That in turn involved political assessments of which foreign countries posed the greatest dangers to British interests (France in Africa? the United States against Canada? Germany in Europe?), and whether diplomatic compromises might be made with the less threatening Powers.

This process of global-strategical assessment had been accelerated by the shocks of the Boer War of 1899–1902, which led to the establishment of the Committee of Imperial Defence, and then had been made even more necessary by the test of World War I, which produced the War Cabinet machinery and subcommittees administered by Hankey and his assistants. Further institutional refinements occurred later—thus, the Chiefs of Staff Sub-Committee was a consequence of the Chanak crisis of 1922, and in 1936 it was decided to establish a Minister for the Coordination of Defence[6]—but the basic point remains. Since the premiership of Arthur Balfour, and perhaps earlier, the British had been obliged to carry out a rough-and-ready form of strategical assessment, and on a world scale.

DEPARTMENTAL CONCERNS AND COLLECTIVE
COMPROMISES

In order better to illustrate this process of net assessment, this chapter will examine in some detail one of the major British strategical surveys of the 1930s, the 91-page document known as the *European Appreciation, 1939-40*, produced by the Chiefs of Staff Sub-Committee early in 1939. As this is done, the reader will be able to comprehend the genesis, the development, and the consequences of strategic assessment in the British system. More important still, an analysis of a specific (albeit typical) document offers perhaps the best way to understand what the planners themselves did, or did not, regard as important, which in turn gives us considerable insight into the strengths and the weaknesses of this particular assessment process.

Although it was external events (the Nazi seizure of power, the Abyssinian crisis) that prompted the British to reassess their strategic requirements, the first stages in the actual process inevitably had to begin in the service departments themselves. The pattern was for the political leadership to request the Chiefs of Staff to prepare new strategical surveys, lists of comparative force strengths, estimates of the services' prospects in the event of war, and—if those estimates were gloomy (which they often were)—submissions for additional resources.[7] This then caused the generals, admirals, and air marshals to assemble their data for the requested submission. In so doing, the service departments not only *selected* what they judged to be most relevant but also suggested conclusions that might be drawn—as to strengths and weaknesses, opportunities and dangers, the balance of risks, the optimal allocation of forces, the need for improvements.

Even before the departments engaged in this task, an earlier form of "assessment" had already taken place, namely that done by British service attachés and diplomats stationed abroad whose task it was to send regular reports on the strategical *power* of the country in question. While other, less regular sources (occasional radio decrypts, accounts by visiting businessmen, reports from secret agents) supplemented this information, it was the attachés who provided the most systematic and authoritative flow of data about foreign armed forces that Whitehall "consumed" during the 1930s.[8] In all cases, the British attachés were long-serving career officers with a gift for languages and considerable experience of foreign travel and cultures. Coming from typical middle- or upper-class "service" families who provided the overwhelming bulk of the officer corps of the interwar British armed forces, they reflected the values and assumptions of those to whom they reported. That same background usually allowed them to establish good personal relations with members of the officer corps of the country in which they were serving and thus to glean additional information from social contacts. There is no doubt, therefore, of their overall value.

Yet considerable difficulties prevented them from acquiring a fully objective picture of what was going on. The first of these was simply the physical and political obstacles thrown up by the secretive and totalitarian regimes in which the attachés were stationed. Time and again, they confirmed in their reports to London that they had been shown only the outside of *static* models of German tanks or that their visits to a Japanese dockyard were consumed by formalities, introductions, and other diversions.[9] Being so restricted in the access to verifiable data, they often had to fall back upon rumors, tips, anecdotal evidence, and fleeting impressions.

Above all they fell back upon their own cultural, racial, and ideological prejudices, which, given the socially homogeneous nature of the services they represented, Whitehall was unlikely to challenge. Indeed, it was likely to be seen as *confirming* already existing assumptions about other countries and their armed services. Thus, the reportage upon the Reichsheer in the early to mid-1930s by the British military attaché in Berlin, Colonel Thorne, suggested that the German army was an independent and "moderate" instrument in the Nazi state, thereby reinforcing London's belief that an accommodation with Germany was feasible; while, at the other side of the globe, the British naval attaché, Captain Vivian, offered a view of the Japanese character—unimaginative, deferential, imitative, lacking initiative—which then permitted the Admiralty to regard Japan as a "less than first-class" power.[10]

Such information from abroad would already exist in the files at the time when the Cabinet or Committee of Imperial Defence would ask the Joint Chiefs of Staff for a strategical assessment. Normally, the Chiefs would delegate the initial research and drafting to their respective staffs, who would then attempt to "fit together" their individual departmental visions so as to present a common overview to the political leadership. The years of experience of civil–military relations, together with the constricting socio-economic circumstances that prevailed in interwar Britain, meant that the papers the armed services offered to the Cabinet were usually cautious, restrained, balanced—in a word, conservative. Any other style or form would have been counterproductive.

Few of the early judgments and proposals of the Chiefs of Staff survived unscathed: As will be noted later, most of the army's draft suggestions in the 1930s were likely to be severely reduced, whereas the Royal Air Force's schemes would at times be augmented, but not necessarily in accordance with Air Staff preferences. In addition, there was the predictable impact of tacit interservice bargaining, whereby a branch's requests (and strategic assumptions) were not seriously contested by the other services provided their own requests (and strategies) were also conceded in the main. But whatever partial amendments and compromises occurred *en route,* the implications of this mode of proceeding for the general theory and process of "net assessment" are important. It meant that, for the most part, political decision-makers confronted an amalgam of service-generated data and assumptions that it was difficult for busy Cabinet ministers to challenge. Even the creation of the post of Minister for the Coordination of Defence early in 1936 did not fully grapple with this fundamental problem, that the "building blocks" of information and judgment did *not* come from objective, independent sources. To be sure, the Minister could often recommend to the Cabinet spending priorities as between the various services' bids, but it was much more difficult to contest the Admiralty's assessment of the fighting power of the Japanese navy, say, or the army's plans to deal with the Wehrmacht on the battlefield. Those were internal matters on which the military was virtually unchallengeable. The implication was that the Cabinet had to take on trust a service's assessment of the military power of other countries, as well as that same service's opinion that it was, or was *not,* ready and able to go to war. Since each of the services had a *different* strategic concern, causing them to "buy time" for further rearmament, their pre-1939 reports tended to be a conflation of their worst-case assumptions—although in Chamberlain's case the generally pessimistic strategical assessments of the British services fitted in nicely with his own predilections toward appeasement.

Another important implication was that, however sophisticated the *overall* strategic surveys might be, they could not anticipate which way *individual* campaigns would go, whether in the Atlantic sea lanes or in the jungles of Malaya. To the degree that "net" assessment gets the forthcoming conflict right as a whole, that may not matter too much; but to the extent that victory in war is the sum of various campaign victories, it is a point of some relevance that the nation's armed forces do not lose too many battles in detail. And this is where the *departmental* aspect of net assessment becomes very important indeed.

The naval component of British net assessment in the 1930s is reasonably easy to trace, since it did not involve much in the way of new structures or methodology on the Admiralty's part. Information about foreign navies was gathered from a variety of sources, from official publications and announcements to personal observations by the British naval attachés and visiting officers. Given the obsessive secrecy and censorship of the Fascist regimes, it was increasingly difficult for the attachés to get information upon newer warship types; and yet, as the post–Washington/London treaty naval arms race resumed after 1936, that was precisely what the Admiralty's own planners and designers wanted: How fast was the *Bismarck?* What was the displacement of the latest Japanese heavy cruisers?

Perhaps the most candid acknowledgement of this ignorance came as late as 13 June 1939 during a discussion of the Cabinet Committee on Foreign Policy, when the Prime Minister referred to a *Daily Telegraph* article concerning evidence that German heavy cruisers were far more powerful than their British counterparts. Not only did the Admiralty know nothing of the evidence, but the First Lord doubted whether they would ever know early enough if Germany were building new and more dangerous types of warships for Admiralty planners to respond to. To this admission the Minister for the Coordination of Defence (Admiral Chatfield, previously the First Sea Lord) added: "At the present time, we had no information as to what new types of Naval vessels Japan might be building. For all we knew she might be constructing battleships of 40,000 tons with 20-inch guns."[11] As World War II showed, both German and Japanese large warships (heavy cruisers and up) possessed a larger displacement, heavier armament, and better defensive capabilities than British vessels—a benefit of having been built in secret, and often in breach of treaty limitations.

Lacking good details about the *quality* of potential enemies' warships, the Admiralty was generally reduced to "bean counting." Yet even this was fraught with problems, especially if the planners attempted to project the naval balances in, say, one or two years' time—and this in a period (the late 1930s) when a large number of the world's major warships were being modernized and when the post-1936 "naval race" was bringing many new vessels into service. The Admiralty's response to this difficulty was to play cautious. During the Tientsin crisis with Japan in June 1939, when the Cabinet Committee on Foreign Policy contemplated a Chiefs of Staff report that (in Sir Samuel Hoare's words) "painted the picture from our point of view as dark and gloomy as it could well be painted," the Foreign Secretary

Lord Halifax felt bound to add that "the Chiefs of Staff calculations were based on the assumption that while all our ships would not be available, all the Japanese Capital ships would be available." To this Chatfield could only admit that the Admiralty had "practically no information on the subject."[12]

The second and more difficult element in assessment concerned how, and how well, the enemies' navies might fight. While the Royal Navy had learned a great deal about Italian naval doctrine and operations in Mediterranean waters, it knew much less about the German navy. Here, secrecy prevented much in the way of direct observation, with the consequence that the Admiralty fell back upon traditional preconceptions. The chief early hindrance to a proper assessment of the German navy was the assumption that Raeder's new warships were being built with a view to dominating the Baltic and that Germany had quite given up that Tirpitzian ambition to challenge the Royal Navy's command of the sea.[13] Even when it finally dawned upon the Admiralty that the German navy might expand *westward,* the Royal Navy's chief focus of attention was on *battlefleet* actions. This is hardly surprising, since for much of the interwar years the navy was mentally engaged in refighting the Battle of Jutland—and this time getting it right! The annual Naval Staff publication *Progress in Tactics* would therefore contain much more coverage under the rubric "Night Fighting" than under either "Convoy" or "Combined Operations."[14]

Such a concern was not without beneficial consequences, at least in the Mediterranean, where the Royal Navy was well trained to "have a go" at the Italian battlefleet, night or day. But this surface battle obsession made it difficult for the Admiralty to react to a German naval challenge that would be expressed partly by individual raiding cruises to disrupt the Atlantic sea routes, and chiefly by a renewal of the U-boat attack upon merchant ships, a danger that the Admiralty greatly underestimated. By extension, therefore, the Royal Navy had prepared itself well for a conflict against the Japanese fleet, since it too was structured for large surface actions. But it accompanied its desire to fight a new "Jutland" in the South China Sea with a distinct arrogance toward the Japanese navy, consistently rating it as having only 80 percent effectiveness of equivalent British forces and thereafter subtracting from that.[15] Above all, it never got a full measure of the striking power and efficiency of the Japanese naval air arm, perhaps because the Admiralty's own conception of the use of aircraft carriers, and the sorry history of the interwar Fleet Air Arm, was so different.[16]

The Admiralty's greatest difficulty was the assessment of which navies it would be fighting against, and which (if any) would be allied with the Royal Navy—a calculation that had to be done, but was itself conditioned by the kaleidoscopic nature of Great Power relations as the 1930s unfolded. For much of the 1930s the Admiralty's gaze was fixed upon the Japanese naval threat in the Far East, and it continued to be cast in that direction even when the other two services, the Foreign Office, and the Prime Minister, became increasingly worried about the German menace and wondered about either compromising diplomatically with Japan or simply scrapping the "Main Fleet to Singapore" strategy.

The Admiralty's fixation with a Far Eastern war not only made it an "appeaser" in Europe, with Chatfield especially arguing that Hitler ought to be diverted eastward, but also dislocated its assessments; it rarely cooperated with the Industrial Intelligence Centre (IIC), for example, and its belief that the German fleet was intended for Baltic operations only meant that it was late in the day before the Naval Staff gave serious thought to the allocation of battleships as between home waters, the Mediterranean, and the Far East. By the time it did so, Italy had become a potential enemy and the Admiralty faced an endless series of contingency plans, most of which tended to cast doubt upon the possibility of getting a large fleet out to Singapore while other dangers threatened closer to home. Even before the outbreak of war in Europe, priority had been given to the Mediterranean over the Far East (the security of the British Isles always being the top priority), and the greater part of the Admiralty's strategic assumptions had been rendered void.[17] At the time of the Chiefs of Staff *European Appreciation* of early 1939, that alteration had not yet been made, but the document itself reflected a strong "European" orientation with which the Admiralty was only reluctantly coming to agree.

If the Royal Navy was fixated upon Japan, the Royal Air Force's overwhelming concern was Germany. The advent of the Third Reich made Europe after 1933 a much more dangerous and unpredictable place, and yet one in which the RAF's concept of possessing a powerful aerial striking force to "deter" aggression would become ever more pertinent—or, if deterrence failed, one in which the Nazi war effort might be crippled by more effective means than those employed in a maritime blockade. Moreover, as the Luftwaffe grew in size and in perceived destructive power, so the RAF's need to provide aerial defense for the United Kingdom also increased in importance. By the mid-1930s, indeed, the German air threat so exercised the British public and politicians that these domestic pressures were, if anything, insisting that *more* resources be given to the RAF. Finally, Germany was the most technologically and scientifically advanced of the "revisionist" Powers and the one with the largest aircraft-building potential. It followed, therefore, that if Britain could match Germany in the air, it could certainly deal with Italy and, most probably, with Japan.*

But if the RAF was right to concentrate upon Germany, its actual assessments of the Luftwaffe's size and role, and of its own ability to attack German industry and communications, were considerably off the mark. Little will be said here about the latter problem, since the story is well known and was generic to all "strategic bombing" assumptions in the interwar years: that is, the belief that "the bomber will always get through." As it transpired, it was only in 1944 that long-range strategic bombing assumed the role that Trenchard, Mitchell, Douhet, and other advocates of air power had forecast two decades earlier.

The real importance of the Air Staff's focus upon strategic bombing was that it influenced its perception of the Luftwaffe's role when that service emerged as a serious threat. If the true function of the RAF were to cripple Germany's war effort, it followed that the true function of the German air force was to cripple Britain, and by a "knockout blow." Intelligence revelations that the Luftwaffe was much larger than the RAF produced an enormous crisis for the Air Staff. On the one hand, it grew increasingly dubious of its own ability to inflict much damage upon Germany, so that by late 1937 it was openly admitting that the "Metropolitan Air Force in general, and the Bomber Command in particular, are at present almost totally unfitted for war."[18] On the other, it led to political pressures for defensive as opposed to offensive aerial warfare and to a concentration of minds upon ever more ambitious expansion "schemes" between 1936 and 1938 rather than upon what the Luftwaffe could do. The anxious efforts of the air intelligence directorate to get accurate figures of German production totals—an effort joined by the Foreign Office, the Secret Intelligence Service (SIS), and the IIC, not to mention Churchill and his private informants—turned much of the Air Staff's assessment into "bean counting," which included preposterous and arcane calculations about the average tonnage of bombs that could be dropped on Britain daily.[19]

---

*That it actually could not deal with the Japanese aerial onslaught in 1941–42 had much more to do with the RAF's relative backwardness in the Far East Region than with any general backwardness.

Although during the Munich crisis many of the Air Staff properly pointed out that a German strike against Britain was "highly improbable while war was in progress against Czechoslovakia and France,"[20] the general sense of pessimism that Britain had *lost* the air race and should avoid a conflict with Germany clearly affected the political atmosphere in the Chamberlain Cabinet's discussions.

In drafting its part of the *European Appreciation* in January–February 1939, the Air Staff found itself in the midst of a transition of views. The assessment still had to deal with the possibility that Germany might, at the outset of a European war, launch a surprise aerial blow against Britain; and it still showed a strong tendency to count numbers rather than ask questions about the *range* of German bombers, or their *capacity* to find targets in cloudy conditions. Nonetheless, the document radiates a more confident tone about Britain's own aerial defenses and an increasing feeling that Britain could withstand early German offensives, a judgment confirmed by the events of 1940. On the other hand, perhaps precisely because of this overwhelming concern about the power of air forces to damage an enemy's *homeland*, the RAF gave little consideration to the possibility that such forces might also support the battlefield. Only a few months earlier, the Air Staff had felt that "the German Army Command believes in the potency of air power in land operations,"[21] yet the Chiefs of Staff's February 1939 report discussed the military balance in Western Europe merely in terms of numbers of French, British, and German army divisions.

Of all three services, the difficulties facing the War Office during the interwar years were the most profound, and significantly affected its contribution to British net assessment. To begin with, the army, even more than the navy, was structured to deal with Britain's imperial, extra-European liabilities; as in Cardwell's time, its chief problem was in finding the resources to maintain its large garrison in India, in addition to the extensive military establishment in Egypt, the festering sore of Palestine, and smaller contingents ranging from Hong Kong and Singapore to Gibralter and Bermuda.[22] In early 1938, 64 of the army's battalions were in the British Isles, but 74 were deployed in India and the colonies—a disproportion that none of the other Great Powers approached. This in turn meant that a considerable amount of army personnel and intelligence was devoted to assessing the possible Russian "threat" to Persia and India, or the politico-military problems of the Near East, which made the service somewhat complacent toward the growth of the German army, at least until 1936.[23]

The second element that deeply influenced army assessments was its awareness of how unpopular it was in the eyes of public opinion and politicians, still nursing gloomy memories of the Great War and determined to avoid commitment of a military force to the Continent. Although such sentiments contradicted the traditional British concern with the European balance of power, not to mention the specific guarantees of the Locarno Treaty, the army could do little against the prevailing doctrine of "limited liability" espoused by the Prime Minister and the Treasury, by influential outside critics such as *The Times*'s military correspondent Liddell Hart, and at least tacitly by the navy (which looked to the Far East) and the RAF (which held that it could deter aggression).[24] Thus, after the 1934 report of the Defence Requirements Sub-Committee proposed a scheme for modest but balanced expansion of all three services, the army's portion was cut to the bone. In the War Office's eyes, the contrast between the neglect of provisions for its own "Field Force" and the vast resources the Nazi regime was apparently allocating to the Wehrmacht could not be more marked. When it became clear (after 1936) that the German army had exceeded its 36-division limit and that it was expanding to well over double that number, the War Office's assessments of the European situation became progressively gloomier—climaxing in that array of private and official communications to the Cabinet during the 1938 crisis which suggested that nothing could be done to assist the Czechs and that there was an urgent need to buy time.[25]

As many historians have pointed out, British defense planners—led, if anything, by the War Office—failed to provide a proper "net assessment" at Munich. The vast French numerical superiority in army divisions along Germany's western border was discounted, as was the defensive strength of the Czech army. The Wehrmacht's problems with a too-rapid expansion were ignored. The only consideration of whether it might be better to fight immediately or later—at the cost of losing Czechoslovakia—was couched (by General Ismay) overwhelmingly in terms of *air* strength.[26] Given that Germany's relative advantage vis-à-vis the West actually increased between 1938 and 1939, it was particularly ironic that the War Office was in the forefront of the curious surge of optimism that occurred about three months after the Munich settlement. By that stage the army had stopped focusing upon numbers of divisions, where its intelligence estimates were very accurate, and was concentrating instead upon the Wehrmacht's "overstrain" from a too-rapid growth. In late February 1939, in fact, the War Office informed the Foreign Office that the 100-division German army was "an imposing façade of armaments behind which there are very little spares and reserves."[27]

This change of mood could be seen in the War Office's input to the *European Appreciation* of that same month, one much more confident in its assessments of a Franco-German land conflict than that of five months earlier. This in turn leaves one major puzzle in the army's portrayal, that is, the total lack of *qualitative* assessments about mobility, firepower, and overall efficiency. During the preceding three years, the Military Intelligence department had steadily accumulated a good sense of the various components of the Blitzkrieg strategy— speed, concentrated armor forces, and close air support—and also sensed that the French army had fallen a long way behind in those areas.[28] But such distinctions were not included in the February 1939 net assessment.

While the three services made the chief contributions to British strategical surveys, the other departments also played roles, some major, some minor. The Colonial Office and Dominions Office can be placed in the latter category. It is true that the delicate relationship between Britain and the Dominions, which had legally acquired a *separate* foreign policy status by 1931, meant that Whitehall worried about a "breakup" of the Empire if the country were again committed to a European war of which Canada, South Africa, and Eire disapproved; and it is also true that many imperial problems increased the British desire to remain uninvolved in Europe. But such external pressures toward "appeasement" merely reinforced Neville Chamberlain's own intentions, and in any case they had reached their peak in the Munich crisis. Thereafter, one has the sense that the British government mentally "took note" of Dominions' isolationism but had concluded that it must make its decisions concerning peace or war regardless of sentiments in Ottawa and Pretoria.[29]

By contrast, the Foreign Office's contribution remained most significant. As is well known, the Office was by no means united in its response to the various crises of the 1930s, with the Permanent Under Secretary Vansittart becoming so critical of Nazi Germany that he was shunted aside into the honorific position of "Chief Diplomatic Advisor," and with contradictory advice being received from its diplomatic representatives abroad (e.g. Berlin vs. Warsaw; Tokyo vs. Peking– Nanking). In particular, the strongly pro-appeasement advice of Nevile Henderson from Berlin caused enormous discontent within the Office, which also played a role in "stiffening" Halifax to push for a stronger line toward Germany.[30] But in its contribution of the *European Appreciation* of February 1939, with its built-in assumption that Britain and France *would be* at war against Germany and Italy, the Foreign Office was much more impressive and balanced, commenting accurately upon the likely attitude of the other powers, large and small.[31] It was well aware of just how restricted by American public opinion Roosevelt felt himself to be; and it was also aware of the uncertainties that attended, and would probably deter, any drastic Japanese move in the Far East during 1939. The reader may be struck by the importance the Foreign Office gave to the position of Spain and Turkey, and perhaps even more by its deep concern about the precariousness of Britain's position in the Middle East (chiefly caused by Arab reaction to the Palestine issue). By contrast, another region of great importance in the Foreign Office's judgment—Eastern Europe and Russia—receives little attention in the *Appreciation,* presumably because of the terms of reference employed. Had the report been drafted two months later, the emphasis would have been significantly different.

What was clearly not a useful source in the formulation of British "net assessment" in the late 1930s was the *Secret Service.* This was partly because of the incredibly confused and shadowy "war of the foxes" going on at that time, as well as the failure of the intelligence community to coordinate (the Joint Intelligence Committee was only set up in July 1939 following a whole series of fiascos). With Vansittart running his own private intelligence agency, with the Abwehr and various anti-Nazi circles in Germany feeding a host of false rumors to shock the British into standing firm against Hitler, and with the three armed services relying on their own rather limited intelligence departments, the overall contribution of these bodies was to *add* to the confusion in Whitehall. For every report from a secret source that proved accurate, there were three or four totally misleading or mischievous ones.[32] Yet even if this sort of intelligence had been better organized and more accurate, it probably would not have contributed much to the overall picture presented in a "net assessment" document, simply because the Secret Service was not really focusing upon those elements which contributed to the longer-term global strategical balances, but was endeavouring instead to discover what Hitler's "next move" would be.

One organization, however, that deliberately concentrated upon those elements was the Industrial Intelligence Centre, set up in 1931 and headed by Desmond Morton.[33] Its brief, of assessing foreign countries' economic strengths and weaknesses, their armaments capacity and vulnerability, was one of the few genuinely innovative parts of the British intelligence process.[34] Although Morton's staff was minuscule and its sources of information sporadic (visiting businessmen, oil industry newsletters, and the likes), it swiftly occupied an important position in the British assessment system—partly because of the island-state's interest in "economic blockade," and partly because the IIC filled a vacuum, and thus endeared itself to the Air Ministry and the Foreign Office. As Professor Wark and others have pointed out, however, Morton's conception of an efficient, centralized Nazi "command economy" not only missed certain of the weaknesses and incoherences in the German system but also contributed to the 1936–38 feelings in Whitehall that a liberal, democratic Britain had no real chance of matching the Third Reich in the armaments race.[35] When those ultra-pessimistic views were replaced in early 1939 by a plethora of reports and references concerning an "overheating" of the German economy, the IIC remained more cautious, pointing out both the strengths and the probable weaknesses (in raw materials) of the dictator countries.

Although the information provided by the IIC on the state of the German economy was valuable and often accurate, there was no way in which it could assist the British Cabinet as it wrestled with the international crises of the late 1930s. For example, did the evidence of Germany's shortage of foreign currency mean that Hitler would be *more,* or *less,* inclined to risk hostilities? It was impossible to say. On the other hand, if a general war *were* assumed, then the IIC's information was vital for British planning.

The importance ascribed to the Centre by Whitehall can be seen in the large share of the *European Appreciation,* and in the separate Appendix II, which is devoted to the economic aspects of the coming war.[36] In sum, it provided the intellectual underpinnings to the British "long war" strategy and remained in place even after Hitler's moves against Prague and Poland, and the signing of the Nazi–Soviet Pact.

One further department played an absolutely central role in British net assessment for much of the 1930s: the Treasury. In 1934 and again in 1937, for example, its conception of strategic challenges and priorities prevailed, to the disgust of the armed forces and the anti-appeasers.[37] By early 1939 its influence had been much reduced, with interesting consequences for the net assessment process.

PERCEPTIONS OF FOES AND FRIENDS

Perhaps the greatest difference between British net assessment in the 1930s and American net assessment in (say) the 1960s was the extraordinary fluidity and multipolarity of the international scene in the earlier period. At the beginning of the 1930s, the British widely regarded the Soviet Union as the greatest land enemy of the Empire, while in naval terms the chief rivals were the United States and Japan; they saw Mussolini's Italy as temperamental, France as unduly assertive and difficult (but not hostile), and Germany as still prostrate. Five to eight years later, Japan appeared as a distinct challenge to British interests in the Far East, Germany had fallen under Nazi rule and was assessed as the "greatest long-term danger," and Italy's policies appeared aggressive and hostile, whereas the United States was more unpredictable and isolationist than ever, Russia had become somewhat less of a direct strategic threat (but remained an ideological foe), and France's weaknesses were more manifest than its strengths.

Indeed, even in the space of less than two years, the strategic landscape could be profoundly altered. In April 1938 the Foreign Office, discussing the "revised terms of reference" for the Joint Planning Sub-Committee, listed the "principal new developments" since the previous assessment, in the autumn of 1936, as "(1) the consolidation of the Rome–Berlin–Tokyo axis; (2) the existence of a state of war between China and Japan; (3) the development of the Spanish Civil War; (4) the temporary weakness of the Soviet army as the result of the recent (and still continuing) "purge"; (5) the annexation of Austria by Germany; (6) the dangerous state of Anglo-Italian relations and the attempt now being made to improve them; (7) the progressive deterioration of our position in the Middle East as a result of events in Palestine, with consequent risk to our oil supplies and communications with the East." Although the Foreign Office optimistically went on to claim that "the general effect of these events and developments has been to clarify to some extent the possible causes of war in the near future and the probable alignment of the Powers,"[38] most readers would probably share the gloomier reaction of the Chiefs of Staff: that in such a kaleidoscopic international order, it was an extremely difficult task to fit all the permutations and possibilities into a coherent strategic plan.

As war-games today will confirm, the greatest problem in strategical assessment lies in identifying the political-diplomatic dimensions of the conflict in question. At the end of the day, the British planners of the time had to go for what seemed to them the most plausible assumptions, but with no guarantee that all of those conditions would be fulfilled. As one planner, Major Hollis, put it when referring to the "terms of reference" of the Joint Planning Sub-Committee in January 1938:

> A foundation of Great Britain and France *versus* Germany, regardless of the attitude of other powers, seems so unrealistic a picture that, far from providing a sound basis, it might prove a dangerous one. On the other hand, it is impossible to range everyone up on one side or the other in a general world conflagration and, in addition, to spot the neutrals. Perhaps somewhere halfway between the unilateral war and the world war would provide the best setting, i.e., Great Britain, France and Czechoslovakia *versus* Germany and Italy; Turkey benevolently and Spain, from expediency, neutral. It is for consideration how we should cast the U.S.A., the U.S.S.R. and Japan.[39]

Yet, however plausible a proposal as a whole, its nicely understated final sentence indicates what a host of uncertainties remained.

A further implication of all this complexity is that net assessment is to be seen not only as an amalgam of departmental (and other) *inputs,* but also as an amalgam of eventually agreed-upon *perceptions* about the various Powers in the international system and how they related to each other. It is not usual for historians to offer graphic representations, but in this case the figure shown below may serve to convey the idea that net assessment involves both individual *contributions* to the process and agreed-upon *perceptions* and policy forecasts as a result of the process. Thus, in "deconstructing" a net assessment document such as the February 1939 *European Appreciation,* one can detect by archival analysis just how a variety of departmental *inputs* had been brought together in such a form. But the same document can also be viewed (and is usually read) as a summary statement of official British

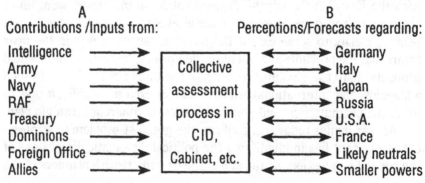

A Contributions /Inputs from:		B Perceptions/Forecasts regarding:
Intelligence →		← → Germany
Army →	Collective	← → Italy
Navy →	assessment	← → Japan
RAF →		← → Russia
Treasury →	process in	← → U.S.A.
Dominions →	CID,	← → France
Foreign Office →	Cabinet, etc.	← → Likely neutrals
Allies →		← → Smaller powers

perceptions of the position and potential of the various large and small Powers as war approached, and as a set of operating principles for the early conduct of that war. Yet while A and B are distinct, they are also intimately connected; the prescriptions as to how to fight Germany (B) represent conclusions drawn from the opinions about the quality of the Wehrmacht's divisions, the changing balance of advantage in the air, the fragile state of the German economy, and so forth, that had been submitted earlier by a number of agencies (A). In sum, net assessment has to be understood as being perceptions, process, and product.

British perceptions of Japan did not change much between 1935–36 and the outbreak of World War II in the Far East. The key change had occurred earlier, in the reassessments that occurred following Japan's occupation of Manchuria in 1931. At that time many pro-Japanese voices could still be heard in the British foreign-policy decision-making system, and sympathy with Japan's frustrations in dealing with the Chinese nationalists combined, after 1933, with the feeling (held by Chamberlain and the Treasury) that the worsening European scene made it desirable to maintain reasonable relations with Tokyo. Nevertheless, by 1934 the Committee of Imperial Defence had accepted its Defence Requirements Sub-Committee recommendation that Japan be regarded as an enemy—the "more immediate" danger, with Germany the greater but longer-term one—and that the threat of further Japanese aggressions in the Far East be seriously planned for.[40] The Anti-Comintern Pact of 1936, the Japanese invasion of China proper in 1937, a whole series of unfriendly actions against British interests, and Japan's southward moves in 1940–41 simply confirmed that judgment.

The greatest British difficulty, as always, was that it did not enjoy the luxury of being able to plan for war against Japan alone. Its assessments of an Anglo-Japanese armed conflict were therefore nearly always accompanied by reference to third parties: What would the attitude of Germany and Italy be if war broke out in the Far East while unsolved problems remained in Europe? What could be done if Japan attacked *after* a European war had broken out? If hostilities occurred in the Far East, would the British be fighting alongside the French and the Dutch? Above all, what would the position of the United States be? Assessments of the American role clearly influenced assessments of the expected course of the conflict, the more especially since it was likely to be chiefly a *maritime* campaign, in which the U.S. Pacific Fleet would be a critical factor. Obviously, a war between Japan and "the West," with Germany and Italy neutral, gave much more cause for optimism than one in which Japan attacked while a European war was already raging and the United States remained on the sidelines. Given the variables involved, the broad political and strategical component of British assessments of a war against Japan could only be a moving picture, to be frequently amended as new developments occurred. After 1939 the issues became simpler: Would Japan take advantage of the European conflict to attack and, if so, when? Would the Americans be drawn in? The news from Pearl Harbor on 7 December 1941, therefore, immensely simplified things by providing affirmative answers to both questions.

The fighting capacity of the Japanese armed forces proved equally difficult to assess. Despite very strict Japanese controls, much information reached the British from intelligence-gathering organizations, photographs, and private reports. Although individual observers caught glimpses of Japan's fighting efficiency, such insights were never brought together, and racial prejudice all too frequently played a role in suggesting that the Japanese military institutions were not as effective as those of the West. (A variation of this was the common remark that the Japanese were on a par with the Italian armed forces.) If Japanese personnel were disciplined and brave, they were also "fanatical," unable to react to unforeseen events, and unimaginative. Their ship designs were curious; their technological and economic base underdeveloped; their generals and admirals somewhat inferior.[41] Against this general set of cultural and racial stereotypes, the British easily downgraded specific reports about the excellent coordination of the Japanese naval air force.

As for the British army, it was so convulsed by the European crisis and its own expansion in the late 1930s—and then by the actual war—that it had little time to study Japan's forces thoroughly. Laconic British minutes of "very interesting," which were made upon secretly acquired Japanese army documents concerning forest and jungle warfare, river-estuary operations, and landings (with an emphasis upon flank attacks), suggest an intelligence and assessment organization focused much more on the Belgian plains than on the Malay peninsula.[42] When the Far Eastern war finally broke out, there was no real British surprise at either its timing or its location since their own intelligence had made that fairly clear; there was also no equivalent of Pearl Harbor or Clark Field. What was *not* accounted for in the British net assessment was how successfully the Japanese forces could wage war, whether in the Malayan jungle or in the dive bomber attacks on Force Z.

The same pattern is observable in British assessments of Nazi *Germany*, albeit with one or two interesting variations. Since the literature upon this topic is now so vast, one can only attempt a brief synthesis here.[43] Given the experience of World War I, there was considerable British respect for the German's organizational, technical, and fighting qualities. But it was difficult for British officials not to adopt a "mirror-imaging" attitude in assessing Germany's immediate problems of rearmament in the early 1930s; if the British armed services were finding it difficult to secure adequate resources, to develop newer weapons types, to evolve new methods of command and control, to maintain a sufficient infrastructure and trained personnel, then surely Germany, more badly affected by the Depression, would be in an even worse condition? That certainly was the view of the Air Staff and, to some degree, of the War Office, whereas the Royal Navy's concentration upon the Japanese danger meant that, for quite another reason, it viewed German rearmament with equanimity.

All this early departmental confidence was shattered (except for that of the navy, which steamed ahead regardless) from 1936 onward, in a flurry of reassessments. The Luftwaffe was admitted to be superior in size, and drawing farther ahead. The German army had announced that it was already past the 36-division size. And the Industrial Intelligence Centre's vision of a centralized, totalitarian economy, efficiently preparing an entire economy and people for war, suggested a degree of Nazi preparedness well ahead of anything that laissez-faire Britain could hope to muster.[44] All this provided the backdrop for that well-known, excessively pessimistic "input" by the Chiefs of Staff at the time of Munich. Germany's striking power was unassailable. The Czechs had no chance of defending themselves. The French deficiencies were plainly outlined. The Royal Navy could do little to hurt Germany. The army was incapable of helping Czechoslovakia. The Royal Air Force, far from being able to "deter" German aggression in Central Europe, was judged unlikely to be capable of defending the British homeland from the 945 tons of bombs estimated to be rained upon it each day.

That the Chiefs of Staff offered a "worst-case scenario" is now generally admitted.[45] The Czech army was considerably downgraded, whereas the size and efficiency of the German army was greatly emphasized. The availability and size of the German and Italian heavy warships was exaggerated. The Luftwaffe's capacity to deliver a "knockout" blow to Britain if Germany were heavily involved in a war with Czechoslovakia and France was not seriously challenged, nor was there any debate about the limitations of range, although that was certainly a factor restricting the RAF's ability to bomb much of

Germany.[46] What is only now recognized is the extent to which that excessive pessimism of September 1938 had been transformed into optimism by early 1939, the time of the *European Appreciation* memo itself. Indeed, the change of mood went too far, and if the 1939 assessments gained a better understanding of Germany's weaknesses, they ignored many of the strengths of their deadliest and most formidable enemy.

By contrast, the evidence suggests that the British consistently overestimated Italy's power. This may have been caused in part by the shock of Italy's 1935 defection from the pro-Allied nations over the Abyssinian crisis, an event that not only threw the Chiefs of Staff into confusion at the time[47] but immensely complicated all later plans for force deployments. It was also influenced, at least to some extent, by the tendency toward "bean counting," so that, for example, in paragraph 20 of the *European Appreciation* the Italian air force might be supposed to be the equivalent in striking power to the Royal Air Force,* and its "active infantry divisions" (paragraph 12) the equivalent in efficiency of the Wehrmacht's. On the whole, however, the British military and naval experts who had observed the Italian armed forces were almost unanimous in thinking that they would not be difficult to beat, and these sentiments were reinforced by the increasing awareness of Italy's dreadful economic weaknesses and its acute dependence upon imported raw materials. In consequence, there were many Britons early in 1939 who advocated giving the Italians a "crushing blow" just as soon as war broke out.[48]

That such arguments would be eventually rejected by the Chiefs of Staff in the early summer of 1939 was chiefly due to fears of larger threats elsewhere. Mussolini's attack upon Albania, the Allied guarantees to Greece and Turkey, the reinforcement of the Italian garrisons in Libya, and British worries about their entire position in the Middle East suggested a "showdown" with Mussolini in order to eradicate these various Mediterranean uncertainties. But that in turn assumed that the Royal Navy's "main fleet to Singapore" strategy would be even further amended, and made ever more conditional, which in turn was dependent upon whether the United States Navy would be able to take care of Japan in the Far East. By June, British hopes of such American naval assistance had been dashed; the government found itself in the midst of

---

*Paragraph 23 does suggest that the Italian pilots' morale would be inferior, but there is no attempt at comparison between, say, a Spitfire and the Fiat CR42.

the Tientsin crisis with Japan and agonizing over whether it should after all send a battlefleet to Chinese waters—and what the implications of *that* would be for Britain's ability to handle the German and Italian navies closer to home. Professor Pratt observes: "In both instances the crises in the Far East and Mediterranean interacted to paralyse policy and to rule out coercive solutions, such as the Mediterranean offensive or a naval demonstration against Japan."[49] The result was that preference for an Italian neutrality which weakened the prospects of putting economic pressure upon Germany.[50]

In turning to assess their potential allies, the British found their global dilemmas only intensified. By far the most important factor was the United States. Its fleet was regarded as the key element in the strategic balance in the Far East, an assessment that became even stronger following the outbreak of the war in Europe. By 1940–41, British ministers were clear that "the real deterrent to Japanese aggression in the Far East can only be found in the willing cooperation of the United States."[51] More generally, there was a widespread appreciation of the enormous industrial-productive capacities of the United States and of its great financial staying power. But all this was overshadowed by the British feelings of frustration, despair, and even anger at the political unpredictability of the Americans, their willingness to preach firmness but not to offer any concrete support, and the ways (especially the Neutrality legislation) in which American decisions were hurting Anglo-French chances of improving their own military strength by borrowing abroad.

Chamberlain himself was often extremely suspicious of Roosevelt, holding his policies to be hypocritical and "all words"; Churchill and many anti-appeasers were strongly pro-American and urged understanding. The Foreign Office itself was more pragmatic: It recognized the great importance of maintaining good relations with the United States, but it also was realistic enough to see that it could not count upon active American aid unless further changes occurred in both international affairs and domestic American opinion.[52] So far as one can tell, the Foreign Office did not share Chamberlain's apprehension that, if Britain became involved in another great war, the net result would be that it would lose its economic independence to a United States which would then make demands for the ending of the sterling block, imperial preference, British rule in India and Southeast Asia, and the like (items that would indeed form a major part of Anglo-American relationships after 1941);[53] or, if the Office did feel such unease, the danger seemed less pressing and more hypothetical than those posed by the Third Reich. As Gladwyn Jebb grimly put it, it was preferable that Britain become the next American state than another German *Gau!*

This point brings us to an element in British net assessment that is not often detectable in the official documents but nonetheless was part of the traditional thinking of the "Official Mind"—namely, that it was important to plan not just to avoid defeat (Chamberlain) or secure victory (Churchill) in the next war, but to ensure that the postwar order would be one satisfactory to Britain's long-term interests. During World War I, for example, some British ministers and officials had felt uncomfortable at the idea that a total defeat of Germany would leave the British Empire alone to face its two old imperial rivals, France and Russia.[54] In British eyes, what was ideally sought was a certain *equilibrium* among the other Powers, allowing London to concentrate chiefly upon domestic and colonial affairs and ultimately, if forced to choose, an option to move toward one Power or another. Choices had had to be made, before and during World War I, but each of those choices (e.g. the Entente and then the alliance with France) had inevitably involved obligations, constraints, restrictions—all of which the British hoped to be free of after 1919.

This mentality probably conditioned British assessments of France and Russia during the interwar years to a far greater degree than did strictly military considerations. Despite a cultural Francophilia, there was widespread resentment of French policies and politics: France's hard-line attitude over reparations, the 1923 occupation of the Ruhr, and its financial pressures during the *Kreditanstalt* crisis, had all, in British eyes, stoked the fires of German nationalism. The corruption and fecklessness of French domestic politics in the 1930s did nothing to improve this negative image. Behind everything, one suspects, there was a subconscious resentment at France because of the fact that it tied Britain to the Continent of Europe, whether or not there was a formal treaty of assistance. At the end of the day, the British knew that they could not let France fall; geography and strategy determined that. But this constraint did not foster warm feelings toward the French, the more especially when France's own obligations and treaties bound it (and by extension Britain) to the fate of such countries as Czechoslovakia and Poland. Much of the British energies expended during the 1938 crisis were devoted to detaching France (which had to be defended) from Eastern Europe (which was negotiable).

Ultimately, this sort of separation was meaningless. A Hitler bent upon the domination of Europe was a threat to both east *and* west. But at the time the *European Appreciation* was being composed, the British government itself was only halfway through that remarkable metamorphosis in its policies that occurred in the year following Munich. Faced with a series of reports in early 1939 about a possible French collapse and rumors of surprise German attacks upon the Netherlands or other small countries, the Cabinet had at last accepted the fact that France had to receive firm guarantees, including the promise of a British expeditionary force.[55] It was on the basis of that supposition that the *Appreciation* was composed. But it is remarkable that there is such little reference to Eastern Europe, the countries of which are presumed to remain, and to be allowed to stay, neutral while war rages in the West and in the Mediterranean. Within another month, ironically, the impossibility of assessing the fate of one "side" of Europe without much reference to the other "side" would be made clear.

On a strictly military level, the reader of the *European Appreciation* cannot help but be struck by its optimistic references to France's ability to withstand a German offensive. This was a reflection of the War Office's belief that the German military machine had overstrained itself and was "not ready to undertake more than an *attaque brusque* against a first-class power."[56] Other British military assessments of France, however, had drawn attention to its great weaknesses in the air, its failure to prepare the army for modern armored warfare, and its outmoded, defensively structured attitude to tactics and operations. Little of that qualitative assessment is visible here.

British governmental perceptions of the Soviet Union were, of course, even more influenced by political, cultural, and ideological judgments. Ever since 1920, the British had been trying to work out whether the Bolshevik state was a fundamental threat to the existing liberal-capitalist world order or simply a somewhat different sort of Great Power.[57] On the whole, Conservative administrations in London, and in particular Chamberlain, Halifax, Chatfield, Sinclair (the head of the Secret Service), and other "inner circle" policy-makers remained profoundly suspicious of the Soviet Union even when they were willing to admit that Nazi Germany had become a more immediate threat. At Munich, Chamberlain had been willing to accede to Hitler's insistence that Russia be excluded from the discussions; after the Prague coup of March 1939, that was no longer going to be possible.

Complicating the picture were the shifting British assessments of Russian military strength. The almost uniformly favorable judgments of the early to mid-1930s about the Red Army's capacity had been replaced by altogether more negative ones in the wake of Stalin's purges—and the belief that the Soviet Union had become militarily negligible seemed to be confirmed by the reports of the poor performance of its forces in the July–August 1938 border conflict (Changkufeng) with Japan.[58] In addition, the diplomatic and military dispatches from Warsaw and Bucharest made clear that the Poles and Rumanians would strongly oppose any anti-German security scheme that involved Soviet troops on their soil, a contradiction that the Anglo-French-Russian alliance negotiations of early summer 1939 completely failed to solve. Nevertheless, while these provided reasons for Chamberlain and his entourage to discount the Soviet Union as an important factor in the strategical balances, there were many in the Foreign Office and among the Chiefs of Staff who thought otherwise. While not claiming that Russia was a first-class military power, their argument was that it acted as a "bogey man," deterring both the Japanese and perhaps even the Germans from further aggression because of its unpredictable and menacing character.[59] The *European Appreciation* report diplomatically refers to Russia's ability to "exercise a restraining influence on Japan," but what is not expressed in the report—because of its focus upon a West European war—is any sense of the bureaucratic debate occurring early in 1939 about Russia's potential to be a "restraining influence" upon Berlin.[60] Also missing is any appreciation of the Soviet Union's economic importance in any future European conflict.

In sum, the British perceptions of likely enemies and likely friends among the Great Powers present us with a mixed bag. None of them was seen to be completely predictable. Each of them was viewed as possessing both strengths and weaknesses. All of them had to be taken into account by a British government that was being repeatedly urged by the Chiefs of Staff "to reduce the number of our potential enemies and to gain the support of potential allies."[61] But there was the rub. To reduce the number of potential enemies (e.g. by an agreement with Japan) would alarm and annoy potential allies (e.g. the United States). To stand firm against a potential enemy (e.g. by building up British naval strength against Italy in the Mediterranean, or against Japan in the Far East) meant a reduction of strength elsewhere (e.g. in Far Eastern waters or in the Mediterranean). To "gain the support of potential allies" when the United States remained isolationist and the Soviet Union inscrutable had been beyond the skills of British diplomacy. To gain France's support had always involved a military and political involvement in Europe that Britain and its Empire disliked. Those difficulties, those sentiments, had all been there at Munich. By early

1939 the British had at last recognized that France was the only ally they had, and that it was necessary to cooperate with it in the event of a war against "potential enemies." The *European Appreciation* was a reflection of that admission, but that alone did not solve the dilemmas of net assessment in a world where Britain's obligations outstripped its capacities. In Chatfield's words, "we were in a weak military position to meet a political situation which we could not avoid."[62] Net assessment, in other words, will all too often involve having to make a choice among evils.

THE UNFOLDING OF BRITISH NET ASSESSMENT, 1934–1941

The first substantive exercise in British net assessment began late in 1933, in the light of the "double crisis" occasioned by Japan's aggression in Manchuria and Hitler's withdrawal of Germany from the Geneva Disarmament Conference and the League of Nations. In October of that year, the Chiefs of Staff produced a gloomy Annual Review, which pointed out that, although the Ten Year Rule had been formally abandoned eighteen months earlier, the nation had done nothing (apart from a revival of the Singapore base scheme) to attend to the completely inadequate state of the defense forces; and yet Germany was beginning to rearm at a pace that would make it a formidable military power in a few years' time. If Germany did initiate aggressive actions that flouted the Versailles and Locarno accords, the Cabinet ought to be aware that "far from our having the means to intervene, we should be able to do little more than hold the frontiers and outposts of the Empire during the first few months of the war."[63] With the Geneva Conference in ruins, even the British Treasury agreed the circumstances were serious enough to warrant the creation of a special body, the Defence Requirements Sub-Committee (DRC) of the Committee of Imperial Defence, to report upon the worst deficiencies of the armed forces and a spending program to eliminate them.

The story of the DRC investigation is well known, and its outcome set a pattern in British defense priorities until after Munich. The subcommittee itself, which reported in February 1934, consisted of the three Chiefs of Staff (Montgomery-Massingberd, Chatfield, Ellington) and those powerful senior civil servants, Vansittart (Foreign Office), Fisher (Treasury), and Hankey (CID and Cabinet). Acting on the assumption that France, Italy, and the United States were friendly, the

Chiefs proposed a modest and balanced package of increases for all three services—a naval modernization program, creation of a small but mobile British Expeditionary Force, and an expansion of RAF squadrons—to meet both the Japanese and German dangers. The civilians pushed for altogether more drastic measures (such as reviving good relations with Japan and further strengthening Britain's air and land forces vis-à-vis Germany), but their ideas were overtaken when the DRC report was dissected by a committee of Cabinet ministers and then handed over for Treasury scrutiny. As a result of Neville Chamberlain's influence among his fellow ministers, the total cost of the DRC's five-year spending package was cut to two-thirds, from 97 to 59 million pounds, with the bulk of the increases going to enhance the Royal Air Force's "deterrent" role against Germany. By contrast, the army was virtually denied a Continental commitment function, while Chamberlain's radical scheme to scrap the "Singapore base" strategy was only just resisted by the rest of the Cabinet, but with the Royal Navy's hoped-for expansion much reduced.[64]

This exercise was a long way from being a full "net assessment" survey, and it would not be long before at least some of the policy imperfections and miscalculations of this first deficiency program became apparent. No real analysis had been done of the size and capacities of the armed forces of the two potential enemies, and even less attention was paid to the strengths and weaknesses of the presumed "friends." The economic and technological components of national power were missing. The diplomatic context was left aside. All that was being done was a partial "repair job" on a delapidated, overstretched structure of imperial defense. Perhaps its chief value was that it reminded senior ministers, battered by financial strains and such political setbacks as the East Fulham by-election (October 1933), that they had to confront external problems as well.

Within another two years, those ministers' minds were wonderfully concentrated upon external problems. The Japanese threat in the Far East remained and was, if anything, potentially greater following that nation's withdrawal from the London Naval Treaty discussions early in 1936.[65] Even more alarming was Italy's defection from the pro-Allied camp as a result of the Abyssinian crisis. This dramatic change of front, together with the large-scale Italian intervention in the Spanish Civil War, severely weakened France's overall diplomatic and strategical position in Europe; but from the British perspective its chief consequence was the specter of a new enemy, lying athwart the critical sea lines of communication to the East and threatening the entire British position in the Mediterranean and the Arab world. From this time onward, the Chiefs of Staff and their planners confronted a global strategic juggling act, especially in terms of naval forces, as they pondered how best to arrange their scarce resources to meet the awful possibility of having to confront three enemies at the same time.[66] Finally, and most threatening of all, there was the continued expansion of Nazi Germany. In March 1936 it had reoccupied the Rhineland, a flagrant breach of the Locarno Treaty, which neither France nor Britain felt able to contest. The Luftwaffe now proclaimed itself to be far larger than the Royal Air Force, news which not only shattered the Air Staff's earlier calculations but also increased ministerial and public pressures for aircraft building to be concentrated more upon fighters than bombers. The German army was expanding at breakneck speed, forcing the War Office to revise upward its calculations of German striking power. France, by contrast, looked much weaker than before, militarily, economically, and politically. From Palestine to India, local unrest was intensifying.[67]

One consequence of all this was that British defense spending projections moved smartly upward so that the services were now coming out of the "deficiencies repair" stage and at last entering the "enhancement" stage. But the size of these increases, with their threat of weakening British credit and exports, in turn was driving the Treasury to take an ever more active role in the ordering of defense priorities, with the RAF the chief beneficiary and the army the chief loser. Institutionally, the need to centralize this activity led to the creation of a Minister for the Coordination of Defence (Sir Thomas Inskip, appointed in March 1936), and to a strengthening of the role of a small committee of ministers (Defence Policy and Requirements Sub-Committee of the CID), both of which tended to place defense priority decisions and overall assessments in the hands of the politicians themselves, and in particular Neville Chamberlain. Moreover, while Britain's own increased spending worried ministers, it did not seem to be closing the "gap"; on the contrary, the Fascist states, whose ability to command national resources was admitted to be much greater than Britain's, appeared to be getting farther ahead. This in turn affected the British planners' assessments for the next two years, and their memoranda became gloomier and gloomier, especially with respect to the democracies' ability to halt German expansion in central Europe.[68]

All this formed the background to what has been termed the "blind" or ultra-pessimistic phase of British net assessments,[69] and fed into the government's handling of the Czech crisis in the autumn of

1938. Thanks to the accumulation of scholarly research, it is now possible to disentangle the various factors that contributed to London's conclusion that a peaceful settlement of the Sudetenland dispute chiefly on Hitler's terms—appeasement—was necessary. The first was the limitations of the British intelligence system concerning German power and intentions. Part of this was due to human weakness, as in the failure to probe the Luftwaffe's likely roles in a war begun by a German attack upon Czechoslovakia and the exaggerated respect for the "totalitarian" economy or for an army that had almost quadrupled in nominal size over the past five years. Part of it was caused by a genuine problem: Since the Third Reich was a closed society, information gleaned by (or fed to) the British was incidental and often anecdotal. And how could even a completely accurate breakdown of German aircraft production allow the Cabinet to know what Hitler planned to do?

The second factor was the excessively pessimistic nature of the Chiefs of Staff's advice to the political leadership, *without* however offering any assessment of the future European balance of power if Germany were allowed to swallow up Czechoslovakia.[70] The third was the way in which the Chiefs of Staff's advice could be used by Chamberlain to overwhelm doubters within the Cabinet, of whom there was a fair number (Stanley, Duff Cooper, Elliott, de la Warr, even Halifax). That is to say, it seems clear that the Prime Minister already had a large number of reasons for avoiding war:[71] He genuinely feared that it would inflict lasting damage upon the delicate British economy, undermining its international creditworthiness and making it dependent upon the United States; he also was concerned that another "total war" would alter the domestic-political balances, enhancing the position of the trade unions and the Labour Party and reducing that of *laissez-faire* Conservatism;[72] he disliked Russia, was dismissive of the central-European states, resented the French, and was concerned at Dominion isolationism—all of which were grounds for avoiding being drawn into a European conflict on behalf of a country "of which we know nothing";[73] above all, there was his sheer moral dislike for conflict, fighting, destruction, and bloodshed.

But none of the above reasons were as powerful, or as useful, as the arguments, readily supplied by the Chiefs of Staff, that Britain could do little to help Czechoslovakia, that the German army was a "terrific instrument" whereas its British equivalent was lacking in everything, and that the British Isles lay open to devastating aerial attacks from the Luftwaffe.[74] It was on *this* ground that Chamberlain, supported by a majority of the Cabinet, overwhelmed the Stanleys and the Duff

Coopers who wished to stand firm; and it was because of his position as Prime Minister, in control of the Cabinet and CID machinery, that he could head off the requests (e.g. by Stanley) for an assessment of how the overall strategical balances would look in a year's time *if* Germany swallowed Czechoslovakia.[75] In other words, this was not a "net assessment" at all in the proper sense of the term; it was, rather, Neville Chamberlain's *personal net assessment* of all the factors in the equation that he deemed important. And the subsequent historiographical debate as to whether Britain should have fought in 1938 instead of in 1939 is, in fact, chiefly a debate upon the Prime Minister's perception and misperception of international and national realities.[76]

On the other hand, within five months of Munich, the British government machine produced a far better-grounded, much more detailed, and much less biased "net assessment" in the form of the Chiefs of Staff's *European Appreciation, 1939-40* of February 1939. This is not to say that this strategic survey lacked faults but simply that it gives the historian the best opportunity to "deconstruct" British net assessment as perception, process, and product.[77]

Several reasons account for the much-improved nature of this *European Appreciation, 1939-40* document. The first is that it was brought together and composed over a period of time in which the crisis atmosphere of September 1938—or September 1939—was missing; the Chiefs of Staff were not asked to give a snapshot reply as to whether Britain should go to war immediately. Instead, the entire paper was written on the assumption that Britain and France were at war against Germany and Italy and with the purpose of advising how best to conduct that war. It was therefore a much more strictly military-strategic document, and generally free of the political concerns that had exercised Chamberlain and his fellow ministers during the Czech crisis. More to the point, it was not dominated by the Prime Minister, either in the perceptions expressed or in the process itself; it went instead through the full array of departmental and committee stages before ending up as a formal Committee of Imperial Defence document for senior ministers to scrutinize, but not as something requiring decisions and actions to be taken there and then. Finally, with a few amendments, this was to represent the general outlines of British grand strategy as it went into World War II and, indeed, until the fall of France in 1940.

The *European Appreciation* report was chiefly the work of the three service members of the Joint Planning Sub-Committee (JPC) of the CID, Group Captain Slessor, Brigadier Morris, and Captain Danckwerts, together with their staffs and the CID secretariat; but it also benefited by asking the advice of the Foreign Office on the international political situation, of the Industrial Intelligence Centre on the "Economic Situation in Germany, Italy and Japan," and of the Home Office on the state of air raid precautions. The individual service contributions, and those of the Foreign Office and the IIC, rested upon a variety of forms of intelligence, especially in regard to comparative force numbers and to the analysis of the Fascist Powers' economies; such intelligence was not itself the subject of analysis by the JPC, it was simply accepted as true. Once the JPC had woven the survey together, the Chiefs of Staff reviewed it at three meetings (7, 8, and 15 February) without offering any significant changes. That final version was accepted on 20 February and went to the CID on the same day.[78] Thereafter it was attended to by a special "Strategic Appreciation" subcommittee of the CID, which spent the following few months considering various aspects of the overall strategy such as Anglo-French military cooperation, bombing policy, and an offensive against Italy.[79]

The *European Appreciation* was composed at a time when British views of a conflict with Germany were becoming more resolute. This was perhaps chiefly due to a sea change in public opinion toward appeasement, which appears to have taken place as 1938 changed into 1939. Anger at *Kristallnacht,* a sense of guilt at having abandoned the Czechs, a feeling that Churchill and others were right in claiming that Hitler respected only force, and an appreciation that Britain needed to do more to help and reassure the French are all detectable in the private letters and publicly expressed feelings of this time.[80] In official circles a rising sense that the military and especially the economic balances were not so disproportionately tilted against the Allies as had been assumed a year earlier reinforced this mood. The army in particular had lost its awe of the German war machine and pointed instead to the Wehrmacht's problems in having expanded too far too fast. The Industrial Intelligence Centre and the Foreign Office focused attention upon Germany's raw materials shortages, its foreign exchange crisis, and its depressed public mood. The air force and other authorities felt that a German "knockout blow" was now much less likely to succeed against Britain's improved aerial defenses. While Chamberlain and his close entourage were still hoping to avoid a war, the Cabinet and government as a whole were much more ready to contemplate it. In February 1939, just as the *European Appreciation* was being drafted, decisions were being taken to expand the Field Force and begin staff conversations with the French.[81] After the Prague coup of the following month, London began offering guarantees to Poland, Greece, and Turkey. A renewal of the "Continental commitment" had replaced "limited liability."

It was in such an atmosphere that the joint planners put together the document. Read in their entirety, the 431 paragraphs of the *Appreciation* constitute an impressive strategical *tour d'horizon* of which there is simply no equivalent in the files of the other Great Powers of this period. Its summary, "Examination of Factors and the Broad Strategic Problem," is followed by a detailed consideration of operational aspects in theater after theater, and then by remarks and recommendations concerning the unfolding of the war and Britain's general strategical policy in it. The document concludes with a set of practical "Recommendations" with accompanying appendixes and maps. It is a superb and characteristic "product" of the Whitehall military-political-bureaucratic machine. It bears the stamp of authority and it did, indeed, contain the basic strategical principles upon which Britain sought to conduct strategy in the first few years of the war.

In the months that followed the appearance of the *European Appreciation*, the British armed forces and entire governmental system prepared for war. As a further sign of the flexibility of that system, the Cabinet established a "Committee on Defence Programmes and Their Acceleration" (a reaction to the German invasion of Prague and an indication of the newer sense of urgency that peremeated Whitehall); then, in July 1939, a "Committee on the Coordination of Defence Programmes" (to sort out the short-term, intermediate, and long-term demands upon British resources); and, finally, as war loomed, a "Defence Preparedness Committee" (set up on 22 August and dissolved at the outbreak of war).[82] In all cases, a small team of senior Ministers met several times a week to hammer out priorities and to "fine-tune" the preparations for conflict. If "readiness" and "preparedness"—rather than battlefield "effectiveness"—were the criteria by which this system were to be measured, it would have had no superiors and very few equals.

The swift unfolding of events between February and September 1939 did little to alter the basic strategical principles upon which the *European Appreciation* rested: If the British and French empires could withstand the early assaults of Germany (and, possibly, Italy), they would eventually be able to make their greater resources prevail; in the Far East, Japan was a major distraction but not a true first-class Power; the U.S.S.R. was unreliable; the United States, although not particularly helpful, was to be cultivated; and other neutrals were to be handled with tact. The Allies were superior at sea, could probably hold their own on the ground, and were reducing their inferiority in the air.

It is, indeed, worth arguing that most of these principles survived into the war itself, certainly through the "Phony War" of 1939–40 and in many respects even until the total transformation of the conflict in the second half of 1941. Churchill's accession to the premiership may have brought a more activist and more centralized form of administration to the making of British strategy, and the actual experience of fighting may have answered many of the questions the British had about their enemies' operational and tactical behavior. But a great part of the prewar "net assessment" prevailed during the first two years of the war.

That being the case, it is important to return to the *European Appreciation* itself and to note just how much was missing from this analysis, despite its thorough and impressive pedigree. This is not to imply that the report was completely wrong. Its assessment of the overall political and diplomatic context, ranging from the probable neutrality of Spain and Turkey to the wait-and-see attitude of Japan and the Soviet Union, was entirely correct. Its recognition of the economic weaknesses of the Fascist Powers was also accurate and has been confirmed by many later studies.[83] Finally, it was right to conclude that, with the Allies superior only at sea but significantly inferior in the air and on land, the Anglo-French strategy would necessarily be much more of a defensive than an offensive one, at least until the resources of Britain were fully mobilized. Both Whitehall officials and outside critics like Churchill were willing to concede that the dictator-states had about a two-year lead in armaments over the democracies, although it was held that such an advantage "has probably been achieved largely at the expense of latent strength,"[84] implying that if the West could hold on for a year or so, the balances would steadily swing in its favor.

Nevertheless, the Chiefs of Staff report turned out to have two major areas of weakness, one at the strategic level and the other at the operational or war-fighting level. The strategic errors all to some extent involved a misreading of the economic element in the proposed Allied grand strategy. The first example was the contradictoriness of the assessments of Italy. On the whole the tendency in London was to overestimate the power of the Italian armed forces, especially its navy and air force, and this viewpoint, which was even more firmly held by the French, suggested that the Allies should try to persuade Italy to stay out of any war instigated by Germany. On the other hand, as

Williamson Murray has pointed out, Italy's economic weaknesses were so great that it would be a drag upon Germany if it became a belligerent (which is why German strategic advisers preferred to have Mussolini stay neutral), and its chronic problems, exacerbated by war, might well have diverted German resources from other fronts.[85] As it was, the British felt unable to reduce their Mediterranean Fleet even when Italy remained on the sidelines in September 1939; indeed, such was Whitehall's concern about the security of the Eastern Mediterranean that, several months before the outbreak of war, it reversed its traditional order of naval priorities and put those waters *ahead* of the "main fleet to Singapore" pledge.[86] For the first nine months of the conflict, therefore, Italy's neutrality both weakened the Allied plans for an economic blockade against Germany and pinned down substantial Allied forces in the Mediterranean theater.

An even greater gap in the British scheme to exploit Germany's economic shortcomings lay in Eastern Europe. Indeed, given the unfolding of events after February 1939, it is amazing how little attention is given in the Chiefs of Staff's report either to Germany's eastern and southeastern flanks or to the Russian factor. No doubt this was primarily due to the fact that the terms of reference for the *European Appreciation* assumed a German-Italian war against Britain and France within a short while (April 1939), so that the geographical focus was upon Western Europe, the North Sea, and the Mediterranean. Nevertheless, it is difficult to see how the British planners could place so much weight upon economic pressures if Germany's important trade with Eastern Europe, most of Scandinavia, and the Balkans were unimpaired. In fact, by the late 1930s, much more than in 1914, the structure of German imports and exports made it much less dependent upon extra-European commerce.

Furthermore, within six weeks of the acceptance of the Chiefs of Staff's proposals, the whole situation in Eastern Europe had been changed by the German invasion of Czechoslovakia and then by the British guarantees to Poland. Although that in turn implied that Germany might have to fight on both fronts, it also meant the diversion of scarce Anglo-French credit, arms, and economic support to the Balkans and Eastern Europe. More important still, it offered Hitler the chance to turn eastward first, while London and Paris stayed on their strategic defensive, and thus permitted the expansion of the German sphere of control. The only serious obstacle to this *Drang nach Osten,* as Chamberlain's critics pointed out after March 1939, was the Soviet Union. But the desultory Western dealings with Stalin and the latter's decision to offer his own version of "appeasing" Hitler by means of their August pact, completely undermined the Anglo-French position. Yet even at the outset of World War II, indeed even after the overrunning of Poland, British memoranda were still claiming that it was economic pressure "upon which we mainly rely for the ultimate defeat of Germany."[87] As the so-called Phony War drifted into 1940, Chamberlain could be found writing: "What we ought to do is just to throw back the peace offer and continue the blockade. I do not believe that holocausts are required."[88]

The third and perhaps most egregious error was the almost complete failure to consider Britain's own economic and financial difficulties in the event of another great European war. On the contrary, the Chiefs of Staff report was sprinkled with cheering references to the Allies' "staying power" and "latent strength." One reason for this was that the information provided by the IIC concentrated upon "The Economic Situation in Germany, Italy and Japan on April 1st, 1939," and therefore did *not* subject the British and French economies to a similar scrutiny of their foreign exchange reserves, availability of skilled labor, "surge capacity" of their industries, and general ability to sustain an expensive all-out war. In sum, this was not a properly comparative net assessment of each side's economic strengths and weaknesses.[89]

The one department that might have injected realism in this sphere was the Treasury. But here was the greatest irony of all. For twenty years the Treasury had exerted its claim to be the most important department in the central government structure. Warning of the severe consequences of heavy defense spending upon the economy, it had repeatedly cut down the Chiefs of Staff's bids for fresh funds, and, even when rearmament had begun, it had imposed its own priorities upon service requests. It occupied a central strand in the whole story of British appeasement policy—until early 1939, when both the public and the government came to believe that military security was more pressing than economic stability. As a consequence, the Treasury's power to influence events was fading fast, and even the Prime Minister was distancing himself from its stance. Defense spending was spiraling up at a remarkable rate, and under the pressure of the international crisis all three services were now being allocated sums that a year earlier would have seemed beyond the dreams of avarice. In these totally changed circumstances, therefore, the Treasury does not appear to have been consulted in the deliberations that attended the composing of the *European Appreciation*.

Even if the Treasury had been a part of the process, it might not have dented the rosy optimism of the strategists that Britain, while a slow starter in the race, possessed the greater endurance. But at least a debate might have ensued about the Chiefs of Staff's economic assumptions. Because there was no such debate, the greatest contradiction of all in Britain's 1939 net assessment was virtually ignored. While the military planners were refining their scheme for the implementation of a long war (since they openly admitted that they could not win a short one), the Treasury was doing some deeply disturbing calculations about the explosion in defense spending, the widening of the merchandise trade gap, and the fearful reduction in Britain's gold and dollar earnings. In March 1939 one alarmed Under Secretary noted:

> Defence expenditure is now at a level which must seriously call into question the country's ability to meet it, and a continuance at this level may well result in a situation in which the completion of our material preparations against attack is frustrated by a weakening of our economic stability, which renders us incapable of standing the strain of war or even of maintaining those material defences in peace.[90]

And a month later, in April 1939, the Treasury coldly pointed out: "If we were under the impression that we were as well able as in 1914 to conduct a long war, we were burying our heads in the sand."[91] This particular communication was not hidden from the strategists; it was, in fact, the Treasury Under Secretary's statement to the Strategic Appreciation Sub-Committee which was charged with the task of following up on the *European Appreciation* report. And three months later, as Britain was bracing itself during the German-Polish quarrel over Danzig, the Cabinet was warned that Britain's gold reserves were running out, even in peacetime "let alone at a war rate."[92] But this did not alter the new British strategy.

The crux of the matter was that the Chiefs of Staff were perfectly right to urge the need for further armaments, and the Treasury was perfectly right in its warnings about financial bankruptcy—a condition only narrowly avoided by Lend-Lease in March 1941 (when Britain's gold and dollar reserves totaled a mere $12 million). Each were critical parts of an effective long-term grand strategy, and both ought to have been included in the net assessment process. If the influence of economic factors upon British external policy had been excessive in the years up until 1939, it was hardly wise to ignore them altogether when the country was contemplating entering a great and lengthy conflict.

One is bound to wonder what all this would have meant had France

been able to withstand the German offensive of May 1940. In many
respects the strategical situation might not have been dissimilar to that
of early 1915, with German forces in occupation of parts of Belgium and
northern France, and the BEF being built up to take a larger section of
the "western" front. Professor Murray has pointed to Germany's
economic weaknesses, which, he suggests, the defensive-minded Allies
failed to exploit.[93] But it is also possible to hypothesize that a Great
Britain involved in a 1914–18-style continental military commitment
might have run out of gold and dollars at a faster pace than it actually
did, especially since (unlike the earlier war) it now could not raise funds
in the United States. As matters turned out, such a hypothetical
scenario—involving the economic exhaustion of both Germany and the
Allies—was rendered impossible by another factor: the efficiency of the
German war machine at the operational level, which led to the swift
defeat of France and a transformation of the entire strategic landscape
in the summer of 1940.

This brings us to the second area of weakness in the British net
assessment of the immediate prewar period: the inability to know how
its own forces, and those of the perceived enemies, would perform in
actual fighting. Perhaps this is an impossible demand to make of such
broad-sweep surveys. If a country's naval advisers state that a rival's
fleet contains one hundred effective submarines, or if its air force insists
that it has better-quality planes and pilots than those possessed by
another power, how can that be checked on or countered at the
ministerial level? If there was no challenge to the Foreign Office's
observations upon the position of Turkey, why should one expect the
War Office's observations about the French army's ability to hold its
own to be questioned? As noted earlier, such information, supplied by
the individual departments, simply became one of the "givens" or
"building blocks" in the Joint Planning Committee's weaving together
of the various submissions. This is, clearly, a much more general
problem. Indeed, it could be argued that such a structural weakness in
the assessment system is, to a large extent, understandable and that it
can probably be corrected only by *structural* means, such as building a
"devil's advocate" system into each department, or even by having a
parallel intelligence-assessing organization.

Nevertheless, however natural this weakness, the pre-1939 British
assessments misjudged the actual war fighting in an alarmingly large
number of areas, and involving all three services. Perhaps the Admiralty was the worst offender here. It seems to have had an exaggerated
opinion of the Italian fleet and Italian air power, whereas successive

British C-in-Cs of the Mediterranean Fleet had a robust confidence that they could give the Italian navy a drubbing. On the other hand, the Admiralty planners underestimated the dangers from Germany in two critical areas. The first was the threat posed to surface warships from the air, something British naval planners had certainly considered during the interwar period but had felt could be handled by placing more anti-aircraft guns on board their ships.[94] In the 1940 Norwegian campaign, for example, there was no hesitation in sending "a squadron into Trondheim with no reconnaissance, and with the certainty that they would be bombed."[95] As it happened, the Luftwaffe cramped the Royal Navy's operations during the battle for Norway and inflicted even heavier damage off Crete. Second, the Admiralty was unduly confident about its ability to deal with the U-boat menace, believing that ASDIC (SONAR) had solved the problem of detecting submarines under water. Doenitz's tactic of encouraging U-boat attacks on the surface and at night consequently upset British calculations and turned the Battle of the Atlantic into one of the most serious and uncertain struggles of the entire war. Far from the Allied blockade bringing the German economy to its knees, the Nazi counterblockade of U-boats and long-range bombers threatened to starve the British into surrender.[96]

But the Royal Air Force itself was hardly free of miscalculation. Although it had repeatedly warned the politicians about the danger of a German "knockout blow" from the air, and still made reference to that possibility in the *European Appreciation,* it was beginning to feel more confident about checking aerial attacks upon the British homeland; the coming of radar, the increase in the number of modern fighter squadrons, and a whole variety of air-raid precautions gave reasons for such hope, and the successful conclusion of the Battle of Britain confirmed it. Nonetheless, this appears to have caused no serious rethinking of Bomber Command's own assumption that its planes would succeed in the strategic bombing campaign against the Third Reich even if German aerial attacks upon the U.K. failed. Finally, because of the RAF's interwar obsession about an "independent" strategic bombing mission, it had given little thought to tactical air power and to providing the British army with the type of support that the Luftwaffe could render to German troops. Only as the army began its rushed preparations to send a Field Force to France in 1939 was this deficiency debated between the services and the CID—the chief result being that all sides recognized the problem but had no real solution to it.[97]

Yet even as the War Office was calling attention to the German advantages in tactical air power, it itself had failed to grasp the overall nature of the Blitzkrieg style of warfare, which was being developed in the late 1930s. Certain observers—for example, Wynne in his study *If Germany Attacks* (published in 1940)—appreciated the importance of the German stormtrooper assaults in the closing campaigns of World War I, and others suspected that the Wehrmacht would use its armor and its air support in a more concentrated way.[98] Moreover, this was reinforced by copies of *German* after-action reports of the successes of their close air support of the army in the Polish campaign.[99] But none of this seems to have shaken the British army's presumption (as is clear in the *European Appreciation*) that the Germans could be held in the west by the French, the Belgians, and the BEF. This meant in turn that the British were not at all prepared for the swift collapse of France in May–June 1940; nor, incidentally, were British Empire forces prepared to handle the explosive, mobile power of Rommel's *Afrika Korps* when it was sent to aid the Italians in recovering Cyrenaica. Even as late as the 1944 Normandy and Italian campaigns, the British (and other Allies) had difficulty coping with the Germans, unit for unit[100]—which casts in doubt the entire process of measuring military strength merely by totaling numbers of divisions and brigades on each side.

In the Far Eastern fighting of 1941–42, one also has the distinct sense that the British assessments of Japanese fighting power were flawed. After all, the overall *strategic* shape of the Pacific War was extremely favorable from Britain's perspective. Japan had to leave considerable armed forces in Manchuria, it had about 1 million troops bogged down in China, and it had gone to war not just against the British Empire and the Dutch, but also against the United States. Yet that level of assessment was of little consolation to the crews of the *Prince of Wales* and *Republic* as they discovered the brutal efficiency of the Japanese naval air arm; to the British Empire units in Malaya and Burma as they struggled in vain against a Japanese army much better trained for jungle warfare; or to Admiral Doormann's ABDA navies in the Battle of the Java Sea when they first encountered Japanese "long lance" torpedoes.[101]

By early 1942, of course, the whole basis upon which the Chiefs of Staff's *European Appreciation* rested was quite transformed. The entry into the conflict of the Soviet Union, Japan, and the United States—all presumed neutral in the February 1939 report—really did change things from the "last European war" into a "world war."[102] Moreover, despite the early brilliant offensives of both Germany and Japan, the underlying economic and technological balances were heavily tilted in favor of the Grand Alliance, making the concept of a long-war strategy altogether more plausible than that inherent in an Anglo-French versus German-Italian struggle. After the news of Pearl Harbor, Churchill was right to conclude that "we had won after all!"[103] But that happy state of victory was not to be secured along the lines of Britain's prewar net assessment.

3

Net Assessment
in Nazi Germany
in the 1930s

Williamson Murray

To a GREAT EXTENT, the Germans determined the history of the first half of this century. Positioned, in terms of their diligence, industrial power, and educational system, to become the other great superpower along with the United States in the twentieth century, they instead caused two catastrophic wars, which together came close to destroying European civilization. How and why these events came to pass is a subject for psychology as well as for history. This essay, however, will aim to elucidate the problem of how the Germans came to launch the second great world war, one which they came close to winning but in the end lost, largely because of their incapacity to assess their own power and its relation to that of their potential opponents.

The weaknesses within the German system of net assessment rested as much on a flawed national understanding of strategy and of the Reich's real position in the world as on the failings of the bureaucratic system. Unfortunately, Adolf Hitler's ideological construct, while obviously an extreme expression, fell within a national tradition that reflected the values and direction of German society of the early twentieth century. This tradition "nurtured [an] idealistic rejection of modern society and . . . resentment against the imperfections of western ideals and institutions."[1] Above all the Germans possessed an almost mystic belief that human will could substitute for much of the material factors upon which national power rests.

World War I reinforced the peculiarities of Germany's national view of itself and its role in history. Defeat in 1918 did not cause any fundamental reappraisal within German society, its intellectual elite, or the ruling military and civilian bureaucracies. The "stab in the back" legend—that Jews and communists at home had stabbed the German military in the back in summer 1918, thus turning victory into defeat—appeared even before the collapse of September–November 1918. By 1919 Ludendorff, Hindenburg, Tirpitz, as well as other more sinister figures on the fringes of national politics, were using the *Dolchstoss* legend to divert attention away from the real causes of the national catastrophe. Even the Social Democratic first President of the new Republic, Friedrich Ebert, greeted returning troops as "unconquered in the field."[2]

A rewriting of the foreign policy and strategic record of Wilhelmine Germany soon followed this distortion of the causes of the September–November collapse. This disinformation campaign began within the foreign ministry. Its willful and clever authors were not only the German bureaucracy but the academic community as well. The product sought to confuse and disorient the German body politic as well as substantial numbers of foreigners.[3] In the resulting fog the Germans proved incapable of profitably learning from their recent disaster.

To be sure, some avoided self-deception. Wilhelm Groener, chief of the general staff at the end of the war, admitted shortly after the conflict that Germany had failed because it had aimed at both Continental hegemony and world power with the "High Sea Fleet." Even during the war the historian Hans Delbrück displayed a keen sense of the failure of German policy-makers to connect strategic goals to operational means. Delbrück's criticism after the war was even more pointed. The German high command had failed in 1918, he argued, because of its complete disregard of Clausewitz's principle that "no strategical idea can be considered completely without considering the political goal."[4]

Unfortunately, the views of most Germans, particularly of "informed" opinion, remained closer to the violently anti-Semitic simplifications offered up not only by the Nazis but by German nationalists. Heavily influenced by the Foreign Ministry's disinformation campaign, they believed that internal enemies had stabbed the army in the back in 1918 and that the hostility of the Reich's European enemies had fully justified German policy both before and during the war.

Germany's problems on the strategic level went beyond institutionalized efforts at self-deception. Germans had traditionally abdicated responsibility for strategic policy and thought to the military. Admittedly Bismarck had maintained control over national strategic policy in the wars of national unification. But the glow of the 1866 and 1870 victories conferred on Prussia's *Generalität* a reputation for strategic wisdom and expertise that it did not deserve. When Bismarck departed, no civilian minister held the prestige or authority to contest strategic policy with the generals. Moltke the elder had lost nearly all the strategic arguments to Bismarck; his successors in the Wilhelmine Reich won their arguments.

As a result of the constitution and civilian deference, the German military controlled strategic policy-making throughout World War I—a role for which by education and inclination it was thoroughly unprepared. In the early twentieth century the education of general staff officers, the intellectual elite of the army, no longer provided for the study of Clausewitz or any other significant political or strategic thinker.[5] The postwar educational system represented no improvement.[6]

Nevertheless, the German military had dominated strategic policy-making in Germany from the onset of World War I.[7] They attempted to solve the complex issues raised by that conflict as a series of six-month operational problems and disregarded or missed the strategic-political problems.[8] The peculiar fashion in which the German military addressed submarine warfare is a case in point. Entirely on the basis of operational analysis, the navy persuaded the army that unrestricted submarine warfare would win the war; the leadership of both services either refused to address America's long-range potential or dismissed it as unimportant.[9]

The confusion between strategy and operations reached its low point under General Erich Ludendorff. The Quartermaster-General of the OHL (the army high command) and de facto dictator of Germany defined his strategic conception for the March 1918 "Michael" offensive thus: "I object to the word 'operation.' We will punch a hole into [their line]. For the rest, we shall see. We also did it this way in Russia!"[10] The result was disastrous; tactical and operational excellence on the battlefield were no substitutes for strategic or political wisdom. Ironically the battlefield performances of the German army played an important role in prolonging both world wars and in raising the strategic and political price that Germany had to pay for its defeats.[11]

Those brought up within the German political culture and those who were products of the military system had considerable difficulty judging and understanding strategy. Consequently, the ability of German leaders to weigh such strategic issues as the relationship between means and ends remained clouded. More often than not, where means and ends failed to match, Germans fell back upon Nietzschean will. This is not to suggest that Germany's strategic choices could be easily discerned, or that national strategy was a simple, easy matter. But the overall distortions suggested above went beyond the norms for other nations and may help to explain why the Germans lost *two* world wars.

If the Germans had difficulties in analyzing the world of strategy and policy, the arrival of the Nazis in power in January 1933 only served to reinforce national idiosyncrasies. Hitler's ideology provided a revolutionary dynamism to the foreign and strategic policies of the Reich.[12] For Hitler, race was the primary determinant of civilization and human values, as opposed to the Marxist-Leninist definition that class formed the primary basis of human affairs. The Aryan race, loosely defined as the German nation, had, according to Hitler, provided the essential motive force behind the advance of European civilization. To the east, in the great spaces of the Eurasian land mass, the Slavs, incapable of creating an advanced civilization, blocked the Germans from the spaces needed to realize their full national potential. The populated regions to the west offered lesser possibilities. Therefore, while Hitler planned to deal with Germany's enemies in the west, particularly the French, he looked primarily to the east. Yet the greatest enemy in his racial framework was an internal one: the Jew. According to him the Jews had undermined the viability of racially strong regimes from the days of Rome. "No nation can dislodge the fist of the implacable world Jew from its throat except by the sword. Only the united, concentrated forces of a mighty insurgent nationalistic passion can defy the international enslavement of the nations. But such a development is and remains a bloody one."[13]

Intimately intertwined within this drive to achieve racial superiority was Hitler's desire to achieve *Lebensraum,* an expansion of Germany's territory by conquest up to the Urals. He told the Reich's senior foreign policy and military leaders in November 1937:

> The aim of German policy was to make secure and to preserve the racial community and to enlarge it. It was therefore a question of space. Germany's future was wholly conditional upon the need for space, and such a solution could be sought, of course, only for a foreseeable period of about one to three generations.[14]

These three sentences encompassed the crucial factors in Hitler's *Weltanschauung:* racial purity, living space, and the shortness of time. Not surprisingly, Hitler viewed himself as unique and essential to achieving these ideological goals. Again, he told his generals immediately before the outbreak of the war:

> Essentially all depends on me, on my existence, because of my political talents. Furthermore, the fact that probably no one will ever again have the confidence of the whole of the German people as I have. There will probably never again in the future be a man with more authority than I have. My existence is therefore a factor of great value.[15]

Within this ideological framework, Hitler possessed clear conceptions of how he would reach his goals. Unlike most Germans, he was willing to strike a deal with the Italians and believed that the British, despite their behavior in the 1914–18 war, would stand aside from the next conflict, provided that Germany did not threaten their strategic position. Above all he understood that achievement of his ideological goals required a war to destroy the European status quo established over the previous thousand years. As he warned his military leaders within a week of his gaining power, if France possessed statesmen and military leaders of any fiber, Germany would face war in the immediate future.[16] From that moment, German foreign policy ran risks that neither its military nor its diplomatic experts imagined possible. The level of those risks and Hitler's drive become understandable only when one recognizes his long-term ideological goals.

But war was not only for external conquest. Hitler aimed to utilize foreign conquest for the legitimation and prestige that it conferred on the Nazi regime and above all on himself to complete his internal revolution. In particular, Continental victory would allow the Nazis to settle accounts with the churches, the remnants of the aristocracy, and the industrial barons and bankers. The underlying principles on which the regime rested were revolutionary; foreign policy represented a significant part of the revolution. MacGregor Knox has pointed out:

I have throughout [this article] endeavored to use the term *revolution* in as neutral a fashion as possible, without assuming that revolutions (violent attempts to achieve rapid, fundamental changes in dominant values and myths, political institutions, social structures, leadership, and governmental policies) are of necessity "progressive." I have also applied the term to relationships between states, to mean an attempt to achieve violent, fundamental change in power relationships and the distribution of territory. The widespread assumption that only the Left makes revolutions contains a hidden but indefinable teleology, and when applied to the twentieth century falls afoul of the obvious confusion between political extremes: was Stalin "Right" or "Left"?[17]

Hitler's revolutionary drive represented the crucial factor in the international balance in the late 1930s. There were many within both the Reich's military and the civilian bureaucracies who recognized the possible consequences of Hitler's risk-taking, but they consistently found themselves driven in headlong flight as the Führer drove German policy toward World War II. As every successive position against Hitler's risk-taking collapsed in the face of the Führer's palpable successes, those who quarreled with the regime's course found themselves in retirement or accepting the dictator's *Weltanschauung*.

Magnifying the impact of Nazi dynamism was the fact that the other major European statesmen proved generally unable and unwilling to recognize its revolutionary drive. To British governments it seemed inconceivable that Germany would deliberately court another major war.[18] In an early September 1938 Cabinet meeting, Lord Halifax, the Foreign Secretary, admitted that the Führer might be quite mad and that "this view . . . was supported by a good deal of information from responsible quarters" in Germany.[19] Obviously in Halifax's eyes an individual who would court war after the experiences of World War I must obviously be insane; until 1 September 1939 he and Chamberlain clung to the hope that Hitler would not prove "mad," at least according to their definition. Such attitudes only increased the magnitude of Hitler's successes and further inflamed the dictator's willingness to take risks.

But it was the Soviet Union that paid the highest price for its refusal to recognize the revolutionary nature of Hitler's regime. Stalin explained the Nazi phenomenon as monopoly capitalism in the last stages of decay. Such an interpretation resulted in a number of disastrous mistakes. In the final days of the Weimar republic, Stalin ordered German Communists to support the Nazis in attacking the Republic and singled out the Social Democratic Party for their most direct attacks.

Stalin believed that the political triumph of Nazi "monopoly capitalism" would ultimately lead to the collapse of capitalism in Germany and victory for the German Communists.

The failure of German capitalism to disintegrate after Hitler's triumph did not change Stalin's estimation. The great German victory of May 1940 with its resulting seizure of the highly industrialized region of Western Europe only served to confirm his belief that Nazi monopoly capitalism had now achieved its goals. Therefore, he deemed it unlikely that the Germans would attack in the east. After all, the industrial acquisitions of May 1940 should fully satiate any regime dominated by capitalists. However, the Nazis were hardly the representatives of monopoly capitalism. Everything they had achieved through 1941 only represented a starting point for the racial-agricultural conquest of Russian *Lebensraum*.[20]

Any understanding of the processes of net assessment in Nazi Germany, then, must understand the strategic culture within which the Germans attempted to assess the balance. That process was largely determined by an ideological framework among the avid Nazis and by flawed strategic understanding among the wider circle of decision-makers. Consequently, even before one examines the institutional difficulties of net assessment, the cultural and strategic idiosyncrasies of the German *Weltanschauung* contributed mightily to the coming catastrophe.

THE ORGANIZATION OF GOVERNMENTAL ASSESSMENT

The traditional picture of Germany depicts a well-organized and disciplined people, ruled by a state with clearly drawn lines of authority. In reality, however, the Germans lived in an environment of bureaucratic ambiguity from the founding of Bismarck's Second Reich. In order to ensure the Prussian king's prerogatives and to avoid interference from the Reichstag, the constitution of the new German Empire placed its army and the navy outside of direct parliamentary control. To compound matters, Kaiser Wilhelm II magnified the constitutional vagaries in terms of strategic policy and military organization; at one time no fewer than forty army officers and eight naval officers possessed the right of direct access to the Kaiser.[21] The result was a general incoherence in strategic policy and an incapacity to assess Germany's position within the European balance.

The framers of the Weimar constitution attempted to provide the new Republic with a more coherent bureaucratic structure. The President of the Republic would provide stability; the Chancellor and Cabinet would make policy and handle day-to-day matters. The new constitution reflected Continental processes with its establishment of a civilian Defense Minister to control the army and navy (because of the restrictions of the Treaty of Versailles Germany did not possess an air force). Unfortunately, the early ministers of defense, particularly Otto Gessler, were hardly more than rubber stamps for the military.[22] This allowed the army to establish an independent position; the first head of the secret general staff (the so-called Truppenamt, with a disguised title since the Treaty of Versailles forbade a general staff) and father of the postwar army, General Hans von Seeckt, accurately described the Reichswehr as "a state within a state."

Despite the constitutional changes, the Reichswehr assumed responsibility for strategic planning. In late 1922 it designed a joint war game for 1923 with the German navy (now reduced to a pre-dreadnought force) to thwart a Franco-Danish invasion of North Germany. The French soon underlined the lack of relevance of such a game to Germany's real strategic situation when they invaded and occupied the Ruhr industrial districts. A German failure to make the reparation payments demanded by the Treaty of Versailles had given the French the excuse; the Reichswehr had made no preparations to meet such a contingency. Within the Truppenamt Joachim von Stülpnägel urged that the Reichswehr undertake an improvised popular war of liberation; Seeckt rejected such an approach out of hand.[23]

As with the Empire, the Weimar Republic did not possess a coherent means for analyzing the strategic and diplomatic issues confronting it. One can contrast this situation with that of Britain after World War I, where a system of strategic assessment and coordination was rapidly beginning to develop.[24] Indeed, even before the war the British had created the Committee of Imperial Defense to provide guidance on Britain's strategic policies.

Only under Wilhelm Groener, Defense Minster from 1927 to 1931, was an attempt made to bring some coherence into the assessment of Germany's position. In April 1930 Groener issued a directive, "The Tasks of the Wehrmacht," in which he argued for "the paramount importance of political viewpoints in defining the tasks of the armed forces."[25] Above all, he attempted to introduce an air of realism into Reichswehr preparations to defend German territory. A study tour in late 1928 designed by the Truppenamt suggests how difficult a task that was. General Walther von Blomberg designed the political portion of a war game involving Germany and Poland to have the League of Nations intervene and impose an armistice at precisely the moment when the Reichswehr ran out of ammunition. According to the scenario, the Soviet Union would then offer an alliance, join the conflict, and enable the Reichswehr to go over to a massive offensive to crush the Poles.[26] Blomberg's exile to East Prussia followed hard on the heels of this bizarre scenario.

The Process of Net Assessment
in Nazi Germany

If anything, the structure of the Nazi regime only exacerbated these administrative weaknesses. Hitler divided authority among competing bureaucracies. In addition to the Republic's existing structure, the Nazis created an independent bureaucracy of the Nazi Party that competed, with increasing success, for authority. Hitler's management style rejected coherence and consistency; his style placed considerable emphasis on *ad hoc* groups and access to his entourage. At the top of the Nazi pyramid stood the Führer, who after Hindenburg's death in 1934 combined the offices of Chancellor and President of the Weimar Republic with the power of undisputed chieftain of the Nazi Party. By 1935 the process of *Gleichschaltung* had incorporated or destroyed all other political organizations in Germany. The Nazi party remained a crucial player in Hitler's government, providing alternative means not only of analysis but of interpretation. For example, Joachim von Ribbentrop, self-styled Nazi foreign policy expert, consistently provided estimates through early 1938 that stood in direct contradiction to those of the Foreign Office. In February 1938 this anomaly ended when Hitler displaced Foreign Minister Constantin von Neurath and named Ribbentrop to the post. While the result may have provided more coherence between party and diplomacy, it hardly brought more effective assessment to government.

Under the Weimar constitution, the Cabinet was to play the crucial role in policy-making and government. However, it rarely met in Hitler's Germany and was certainly not in use as a deliberative, policy-making institution. Hitler, of course, had no intention of allowing the Cabinet to participate in any decision-making process. As he told his senior advisers in the infamous meeting recorded by his army aide, *Oberst* Friedrich Hossbach, "the subject of the present conference was of such importance that its discussion would, in other countries, certainly be a matter for a full Cabinet Meeting, but he had rejected the idea of making it a subject of discussion before this wider circle of the Reich Cabinet just because of *the importance of the matter.'*[27] Part of the explanation for Hitler's action undoubtedly had to do with security. But even more important was his desire to exclude as many and as much as possible from strategic evaluation. The Hossbach meeting represented an exclusion of the Cabinet from the process; moreover, the strongly worded objections of several of the attendees made this meeting the last of its kind in the Third Reich. Nevertheless, in the summer of 1938 Hitler held meetings with the chiefs of staff of the most important army and Luftwaffe formations. Here too, he ran into substantial arguments and debate over his assumptions. As the future Field Marshal Erich von Manstein testified at Nuremburg in recounting an August 1938 meeting between Hitler and the more junior generals, that occasion was the last of *its* kind at which the Führer allowed substantial discussions from the floor.[28]

Hitler's War Minister, Blomberg, with his chief military assistant, General Walther von Reichenau, attempted to center German strategic planning and control within the War Ministry. In retrospect it is doubtful that Hitler would have allowed such a concentration of power; however, he did not have to intervene. Hermann Göring, the Luftwaffe's new head, used his political position as Hitler's chief assistant to thwart the War Ministry efforts to bring the Luftwaffe within its sphere of control. Not surprisingly, the army was no more willing to serve under a "joint" higher command. The navy simply sailed in the lee. General Walter Warlimont noted in his memoirs on the workings of the German system: "In fact the advice of the British Chiefs of Staff and the US Joint Chiefs was a deciding factor in Allied strategy. At the comparable level in Germany there was nothing but a disastrous vacuum."[29]

With Blomberg's fall in January 1938, Hitler assumed command of the German armed forces. The War Ministry staff became the Oberkommando der Wehrmacht (OKW, Armed Forces High Command) under the future Field Marshal Wilhelm Keitel; but in fact under the new arrangements the OKW only served as Hitler's personal staff. It had no independent status, and through 1941 the three services dealt directly with Hitler. Consequently, one cannot talk about joint strategic assessments within the German high command. That, of course, reflected the peculiarities and traditions of the German military. It also fell in with Hitler's conceptions of how best to control the defense establishment and the evolution of German strategy. As he announced on one occasion, the business of the generals was to prepare forces for war and then to fight. They were to leave strategy to their Führer.

In the late 1920s Groener had concentrated intelligence gathering services of the army and navy within the Defense Ministry in an organization called the Abwehr.[30] Groener hoped that the Defense Ministry staff would serve to coordinate and control strategic and political analyses, while allowing the services to maintain control over operational and tactical intelligence. The Abwehr, under the leadership of Admiral Wilhelm Canaris, attempted to strengthen its position within Blomberg's War Ministry. However, even under Groener the Abwehr had run into resistance from military and civilian agencies in its claim that it should be the focal point for strategic and political assessment.[31] Blomberg's failure to control defense policy resulted in the collapse of Abwehr pretensions that it was the center for collation and assessment of strategic and political intelligence. Instead, under Canaris's leadership, it turned more and more to espionage, counterespionage, sabotage, and eventually plotting against the regime itself.[32]

In the peculiar circumstances of Hitler's regime there was a proliferation of intelligence organizations, including the SS, nearly every department of government, and the military services. Virtually every agency of government involved itself in the business of intelligence, since without information the services, bureaucratic organizations, and political leaders in Nazi Germany were quite literally at sea. The fragmentation of intelligence and assessment capabilities continued even within the services themselves. Within the army, the staffs of Foreign Armies East and Foreign Armies West maintained independent and uncoordinated organizations that by 1943–44 had the former working for the OKH (Oberkommando des Heeres, Army High Command), while the latter worked for the OKW. None of these intelligence organizations displayed much interest in strategic assessment; rather, particularly in the case of military intelligence, the focus remained on operational matters.

In the final analysis, within the hazy ideological conception of the Nazi state, responsibility for strategic analysis lay entirely within Hitler's sphere. The regime combined overcentralization with fragmentation of bureaucratic authority to allow Hitler considerable latitude in determining his course. Moreover, the Führer deliberately sought to avoid consultative mechanisms such as those that allowed the British government to examine strategic questions from such wide perspectives. He did so for several reasons: A bureaucratic approach was anathema to his style, but it also represented a substantial impediment to his flexibility and freedom of action.

There were indeed extraordinary differences between the German and the British systems. Under the British system there was a smooth flow of questions from the Cabinet down through the bureaucracy, and thorough analyses by the bureaucracy in response, often involving a number of agencies.[33] German assessments of the strategic situation, on the other hand, rested almost entirely on individual rather than bureaucratic efforts. Strategic net assessments during the summer 1938 crisis were the product of individuals, admittedly highly placed, who opposed the risks involved in Hitler's foreign policy regarding Czechoslovakia. The foremost examples were those studies written by General Ludwig Beck, the chief of the army's general staff.[34] But a number of other figures, military as well as civilian, produced net assessments of the strategic situation that echoed Beck's analyses. The most notable examples were studies worked up by Captain Hellmuth Heye and Admiral Günther Guse of the Seekriegsleitung (naval high command) and the State Secretary of the Foreign Ministry, Ernst von Weizsäcker.[35]

Hitler had little interest in such thorough assessments of the international situation, which is not to suggest that he refused to weigh the strategic balance confronting Germany. On a number of occasions he made clear *his* evaluation of the balance. In August 1938, obviously in response to criticisms raised by Beck and others, he commented that if Germany waited until it had prepared all of its military forces, then everyone else would be prepared as well. The crucial issue to Hitler was not how well the German military was prepared for conflict, but rather how well prepared the Reich was in relation to other powers.

It would be useful at this point to follow the course and nature of Hitler's assessments of the strategic situation as well as the response of those who disagreed with the Führer's strategic *Weltanschauung* and the extraordinary risks that he was running. The changes in Hitler's views along with the collapse of an alternative view within civilian and military bureaucracies explains both the extraordinary successes that Hitler was able to achieve in the late 1930s and early 1940s and the catastrophic final results of the German smashup.

In the Hossbach meeting of November 1937 Hitler began by underlining the importance of achieving *Lebensraum* for the expansion of the German people; he then admitted that history suggested that one could achieve such goals only "by breaking down resistance and by taking risks; setbacks were inevitable." Britain and France, according to Hitler, represented substantial stumbling blocks; moreover, while the short-term strategic prospects for the Reich were good, in the long term "our relative strength [will] decrease in relation to the rearmament which would by then have been carried out by the rest of the world." As a result Nazi Germany should move soon, particularly if external events created favorable strategic situations. In particular Hitler suggested that such occasions might involve either civil strife in France or a war in the Mediterranean embroiling the French and the Italians. The immediate object of his interest was, significantly, Czechoslovakia (not Austria), and he suggested that "Britain, and probably France as well, had already tacitly written off the Czechs." The Führer found it unlikely that the French would intervene, while a French offensive in the West "without British support, and with the prospect of the offensive being brought to a standstill on our western fortifications, was hardly probable." The danger lay in waiting—"in this connection it had to be remembered that the defensive measures of the Czechs were growing in strength from year to year, and that the actual worth of the Austrian army was also increasing in the course of time." Finally, the speed and swiftness with which the Wehrmacht moved would be decisive in keeping the Poles and Russians out of a Central European confrontation.[36]

A. J. P. Taylor singled out the so-called Hossbach memorandum in his argument that few of the events of 1937–40 resembled Hitler's picture of the strategic situation and his future intentions.[37] Nevertheless, what was essential in these discussions was Hitler's enthusiastic willingness to assume great risks and his assessment of his potential opponents. Hitler told an assemblage of generals in August 1939:

> It was clear to me that a conflict with Poland had to come sooner or later. I had already made this decision in the spring, but I thought I would first turn against the West in a few years, and only after that against the East. But the sequence of these things cannot be fixed. Nor should one close one's eyes to threatening situations. I wanted first of all to establish a tolerable relationship with Poland in order to fight first against the West. But this plan, which appealed to me, could not be executed, as fundamental points had changed.[38]

To Hitler's dismay, several of his military listeners voiced serious doubts about his assessment of the strategic situation. Field Marshal Blomberg, War Minister, and the army's commander-in-chief, Colonel General Werner von Fritsch, "repeatedly emphasized that Britain and France must not appear in the role of our enemies." Moreover, they warned that even should the French become embroiled in war with the Italians, they would have more than enough troops to invade the Rhineland. The two generals argued "that the state of French preparations must be taken into particular account and it must be remembered apart from the insignificant value of our own present fortifications—on which Field Marshal von Blomberg laid special emphasis—that the four motorized divisions intended for the West were still more or less incapable of movement."[39] Considering Hitler's lack of appreciation for those voicing independent opinions, it is not surprising that within two months he had seized upon Blomberg's *mésalliance* to purge the War Minister, Fritsch, the Foreign Minister, and a number of other senior advisers. That in turn resulted in the most serious confrontation between Hitler and his officer corps in the Third Reich's history. The crisis appears to have played a crucial role in driving Hitler to pressure Austria and in the eventual *Anschluss* of March 1938.[40]

Because of Hitler's speed in striking, as well as the mistakes of the Austrians and the internal turmoil within the German military, no significant assessments of the strategic environment occurred in March 1938. Hitler concluded from his success with Austria that Western opposition to further moves, particularly against Czechoslovakia, was most unlikely.[41] Before the month was out Hitler was hard at work conspiring with Sudeten German leaders to cripple the Czech Republic. His military had already delineated the framework within which they felt a confrontation with the Czechs could occur. An OKW directive supplementing *Fall Grün* (deployment plan for eastern contingencies) noted:

> When Germany has achieved complete preparedness for war in all fields, then the military conditions will have been created for carrying out an offensive war against Czechoslovakia, so that the solution of the German problem of living space can be carried to a victory and even if one or other of the Great Powers intervene against us. . . . But even so, the government *[Staatsführung]* will do what is politically possible to avoid the risks for Germany of a war on two fronts and will try to avoid any situation with which, as far as can be judged, Germany could not cope militarily or economically.

The memorandum then suggested that should "the political situation not develop, or only develop slowly, in our favor, then the execution of operation 'Green' from our side will have to be postponed for years." However, if Britain refused to concern itself with the affairs of Central Europe or if war were to break out in the Mediterranean between

France and Italy, then Germany could risk eliminating Czechoslovakia, even if the Soviet Union involved itself, "before the completion of Germany's full preparedness for war."[42] This directive encompassed the strategic arguments over summer 1938 between Hitler on one side and Beck on the other. The former argued that Germany must move while the West was displaying such weakness; Beck posited that the Western Powers would eventually recognize that they must stand by Czechoslovakia. The great mass of the officer corps floundered some where in between these two views.

May 1938 was the crucial moment in German decision-making over the Czech problem. In mid-month Hitler journeyed to Italy to visit Mussolini; as the preparatory protocols underline, Hitler felt that Italian ambitions were essential to support his aggressive policy toward Czechoslovakia. If Mussolini were interested in "imperium Africa" then Hitler could "return with Czechoslovakia in the bag . . . Czech question only to be solved in face of Fr[ance] and Br[itain] if closely allied with Italy."[43] Even with Italian cooperation considerable caution remained in Hitler's attitude toward a military strike against the Czechs. On 20 May Keitel passed on to Hitler a new draft for "Green"; the preamble (for Hitler's signature) stated that "it is not my intention to smash Czechoslovakia by military action in the immediate future without provocation unless an unavoidable development of the political conditions *within* Czechoslovakia forces the issue, or political events in Europe create a particularly favorable opportunity which perhaps may never recur."[44]

However, the May crisis at the end of the month during which the Czechs mobilized to deter the threat of a German invasion radically altered Hitler's strategic conceptions. A reworking of the "Green" directive ten days later now began: "It is my unalterable decision to smash Czechoslovakia by military action in the near future."[45] But Hitler had already mulled over how best to remove the Czech Republic. On 22 April he had posited three possibilities to a military aide. The first, a bolt from the blue, he rejected as too dangerous until Germany had eliminated all its enemies but one on the Continent. The second, "action after a period of diplomatic discussions which gradually lead to a crisis and to war," was unsatisfactory for military reasons; the final possibility, a mixture of the first two, might involve a precipitatory event "(for example the murder of the German Minister in the course of an anti-German demonstration)" followed by a great political crisis and a "lightning German invasion."[46]

Hitler now fixed on a swift destruction of Czechoslovakia to provide the Reich with victory within the first days of an invasion. "Thus it is essential to create a situation within the first two or three days which demonstrates to enemy states which wish to intervene the hopelessness of the Czech military position, and also provides an incentive to those states which have territorial claims upon Czechoslovakia to join in immediately against her."[47] Hitler's strategic and foreign policy from this point followed a direct, simple logic of isolating Czechoslovakia over the summer by diplomatic means, concentrating the Wehrmacht's military power around the Republic's frontiers, and destroying the Czech state in the fall before anyone could intervene. Hitler's assumptions were enormous and risky; they depended on operational perfection, a dubious prospect given the still incomplete rearmament, and on the incalculable actions of numerous statesmen and national polities.[48]

In this atmosphere of growing crisis significant opposition to Hitler's strategic assessments appeared for virtually the only time in the Third Reich's history; the chief of the general staff, General Ludwig Beck, posed a direct and serious challenge. In early May he underlined three disturbing aspects of the international situation: the international balance, the military strength of the Western Powers, and Germany's military potential.[49] Unlike his counterparts in Great Britain, Beck recognized the advantages of Britain's position as a world power. He doubted whether Japan and Italy would act in concert with Germany in a world war, while the Sino-Japanese War and its resulting drain on Japanese resources had removed the latent Japanese threat to the British position in the Far East. Britain and France, as they had done in the Great War, would act in concert in any military confrontation. The Reich would face the Soviet Union as an enemy in any conflict, while Rumania, Yugoslavia, and Poland were all doubtful quantities from the German point of view.

Turning to the Western Powers, Beck suggested that the Sino-Japanese War and the lessening of tensions in the Mediterranean now made it easier for the British to devote their full attention to European affairs. The British, Beck argued, understood that Germany's rearmament was not complete and that its economy was in serious trouble. Admittedly France did not desire war, but there were limits beyond which even the French would not allow the Reich to go. Moreover, Beck believed, the French army was still the best in Europe. Czechoslovakia would represent a point of honor for France and should France come to its defense the British would follow suit.

As for Allied strategy, the chief of staff believed that Britain and France would pursue a limited conflict, at least on the ground.

Admittedly such an approach would not immediately help the Czechs, but as with Serbia in World War I, Beck argued, the course of a future war, not its first moves, would determine the Czech Republic's fate. He had no doubts as to who would win a conflict starting in 1938. Germany's strategic position was definitely inferior to what it had been in 1914. The Reich possessed neither the economic nor the military base to fight even a Central European war, much less a world war, while the economic base was in worse shape than it had been in 1917–18. The Czech problem could find no solution without the agreement of the Western Powers, and it seemed unlikely that they would give Germany a free hand. Should Nazi Germany nevertheless attempt to force a solution, it would face a coalition of overwhelming strength.

Barely three weeks later, immediately following Hitler's "unalterable decision" to smash Czechoslovakia by the fall, Beck completed another assessment.[50] He began by making clear that his argument was not with Hitler's goals but rather with the risks that the dictator was running:

1. It is correct, that Germany needs greater living space. Such space can only be captured through a war.
2. It is correct, that Czechoslovakia is unbearable for Germany in its form imposed by the Versailles Diktat and that a way must be found, even if necessary by war, to eliminate it as a danger [to] Germany. . . .
3. It is correct that France stands in the way of every extension of Germany's power and that it in this respect will be a certain enemy of Germany's.
4. It is correct that there are a number of grounds to justify an immediate solution employing force to solve the Czech question:
   a. The increasing strength of the Czech fortifications
   b. The advancing rearmament of France and England[51]

Beck, however, contradicted Hitler's assumption that Nazi Germany could get away with a limited war against Czechoslovakia. He stressed that Germany could not yet wage a war on Britain and France; the Czech army was a serious military factor; and it was doubtful whether the Wehrmacht could overrun Bohemia and Moravia so quickly as to preempt intervention by the Western Powers. As opposed to Hitler's hopeful call for a two- to three-day campaign, Beck expected that the Czechs could put up significant resistance, lasting three, and perhaps more, weeks. Should Britain and France intervene, the outcome of the war would not depend on the first clash of arms but rather on a whole series of factors over which Germany had little control.

Besides Beck, the state secretary in the Foreign Ministry, Ernst von Weizsäcker, also warned of the enormous risks that Hitler was running. In an 8 June memorandum written for the Foreign Minister, Weizsäcker argued that, although France was Germany's most implacable enemy, England was her "most dangerous foe."[52] In a major war Germany would find the Soviet Union and the United States associated with Britain and France. Such a situation, Weizsäcker argued, demanded that Germany avoid conflict with the West. Even in Eastern Europe the Reich could achieve its goals only with the sufferance of those powers. Blocking the West (through construction of the Westwall) and conquest of Czechoslovakia would not decide the issue. To win, Germany must dictate peace in London and Paris, and the Reich lacked the military means to do that. Weizsäcker did believe that Britain and France had little interest in Czechoslovakia, but that Germany must proceed with care: The situation was definitely not ripe for a surprise attack. Any such action would only bring Western intervention. Germany could only hope that through diplomatic pressure and claims of self-determination it could gain the Sudetenland and dissolve the Czech state. Any such course would have to represent a gradual, long-term project.

Assessments of the strategic situation have little importance, except to scholars, unless they are available at the highest levels of bureaucracy. Beck's memoranda did not enjoy wide circulation, but rather remained within the OKH (including the general staff). This was a considerable contrast to Britain, where COS assessments enjoyed wide dissemination within the Cabinet, the Committee of Imperial Defence, and the foreign policy community. In mid-July the enormous differences in assessment pictures between Hitler and the army chief of staff broke into the open, when Brauchitsch, with some editing help from Keitel, passed along to the Führer Beck's 5 May 1938 memorandum. Hitler exploded in fury and reserved special contempt for Beck's estimate that the French possessed superiority in ground forces. He characterized such calculations as *"kindische Kräfteberechnungen"* (childish calculations) and stormed that he would make his own assessments, including SS, SA, and police formations, and then "hold it in front of the noses of the gentleman" responsible for such estimates.[53] By August Hitler was well aware that his drive toward a military confrontation had aroused widespread opposition within the German military. Brauchitsch screwed up enough courage to show the Führer a further memorandum of Beck's (written on 15 July) and to inform Hitler that it had been read at a senior assemblage of generals.[54]

Again Hitler was furious. He exclaimed to his entourage: "What do I have for generals, when I as chief of state must drive them to war? . . . I demand not that my generals understand my orders, but that they obey them."[55] On 10 August Hitler met with a group of important junior generals (the chiefs of staff of immediate and mobilized commands) at Berchtesgaden. Hitler held forth for his usual extended oration; among his main points were the desperate plight of the German minority in Czechoslovakia, the fact that Britain had hardly begun its rearmament while the French were in domestic turmoil, and the general lack of enthusiasm in the West for war. Finally, he argued, in the east Poland and Hungary were eager to participate in the butchering of Czechoslovakia, while the Red Army was in no position to fight because of the purges. To Hitler's annoyance, he again ran into considerable opposition. The chief of staff of the western army group doubted whether the Reich's western fortifications could hold against a determined French counterattack for more than three weeks. This drew the rejoinder from Hitler that the line could be held for three years.[56]

Five days later, on 15 August, Hitler confronted his critics among the generals at Jüterborg. He told his listeners that it had been his fundamental drive since he had embarked on a political career to make Germany the most powerful nation in Europe. His greatest fear was that he might be removed before he had completed his mission. After treating his audience to a discussions of the crucial role of *Lebensraum* in Germany's future, Hitler turned to the current strategic situation:

> Czechoslovakia—the "Soviet Russian aircraft carrier"—must be eliminated. Armies were never strong enough to suit their leaders, and success depended on rightly gauging the politico-military balance. So far he had always been right in his assessments. The other powers would not intervene: "Gentlemen, with that possibility you need not concern yourselves." English threats were bluff, as [their] efforts at compromise showed, and [they] would keep out as long as Germany showed no sign of weakening. . . . "Fortune must be seized when she strikes, for she will not come again! . . . I predict that by the end of the year we will be looking back at a great success."[57]

By now, in late summer, the general officer corps had fractured into three distinct groups. Some remained firmly convinced that an invasion of Czechoslovakia would unleash a general European war that Germany would not only lose but lose quickly. At the other pole, particularly among the younger generals, there was a general acceptance of the

Führer's assessment. In response to the 10 August blowup, Jodl disconsolately noted in his diary that the senior officers were bound up in the traditions of the old army and "lacked the strength of heart, because in the final analysis they did not believe in the genius of the Führer."[58] The soon-to-be chief of staff of the Luftwaffe, Hans Jeschonneck, sputtered after the concluding remarks by Beck to a spring 1938 war game over a hypothetical attack on Czechoslovakia that "the blind will see as soon as Beck will! Thirty days for those ridiculous Hussites! As if there wasn't any Luftwaffe! Schlieffen set back military technique by 20 years, and on the Marne we paid the price. For Beck, our squadrons are only a troublesome appendix. But all of you will soon see the most stupendous things!"[59]

The great bulk of the generals fell between these two views, but one must note a steady migration toward Hitler's point of view. There was no chance of presenting the Führer with a united front of opposition. A gathering of senior officers on 4 August foundered on the inability of those present to agree on even a symbolic gesture against Hitler's policy. Moreover, as the summer unwound, evidence from abroad (through the Foreign Ministry as well as military attachés) seemingly lent greater credence to Hitler's assessments. It was apparent that there was considerable unwillingness in the West to engage the Third Reich in a war. Even more important was the fact that intelligence evaluations were now casting doubt on how quickly the French army could launch an attack on Germany's western frontier.[60]

By late summer Beck was clearly in an untenable situation. The army's commander-in-chief would not stand up to Hitler, the officer corps was riddled with Hitler devotees, and most who maintained any distance from the Nazi Regime and its leader were on the fence. In late July, Manstein wrote his former mentor, Beck, a long letter urging that the chief of staff remain at his post. Manstein based his plea not on the dangerous strategic situation but largely on the argument that only Beck's presence could prevent the OKW from seizing control over German strategy from the OKH. On the great issue as to whether the Western Powers would intervene in the case of a war with Czechoslovakia, Manstein had no opinion, for, as he said, the final responsibility was Hitler's. The military should attempt to deter such an eventuality and make sure that Hitler understood the risks. But, added Manstein, "Hitler has thus far always estimated the political situation correctly."[61] In view of this strategic framework within which one of his closest collaborators and one of the brightest German generals worked, it is not surprising that Beck soon resigned.

Hitler continued to confront a less than willing general officer corps. Nevertheless, a major conference between the Führer and the military commanders in the west made clear how the grounds for the argument had shifted:

> The Führer spoke first and in a long speech gave his views on France, in effect as follows: France possesses a peace-time army of 470,000 men and can raise a wartime army of at most 1,700,000–1,800,000 men. The capacity of French industry is limited, no essential changes have taken place in French armaments since the end of the war. . . . Today France is not in a position to despatch her entire Field Army to the Northeast frontier for she must maintain strong forces against Italy. England, at present, can intervene with five divisions and one armored brigade. The motorization of these five divisions is not yet completed. . . . The tank arm has passed its peak. . . . On the Western Front we have 2,000 anti-tank guns and we possess an excellent means of defense in the tank mine.[62]

By now the mood among the generals had shifted to a wary acceptance of Hitler's strategic vision. A few—Halder, Witzleben, and Hoepner, among others—dabbled with thoughts of removing Hitler, but with only scanty documentary materials on the 1938 conspiracy it is difficult to judge the potential of the "plot." Hitler drove relentlessly throughout September toward a military solution of the Czech problem. Here he became involved in a fierce confrontation with Brauchitsch and Halder over operational matters; but Hitler's concern with the strategic and political balance manifested itself in his demand that the OKH's operational plans aim at achieving such a sudden decisive success against the Czechs that the Western Powers would be deterred from intervention.[63]

In the end Hitler backed off from war; the fact that the Western Powers were willing to serve the Czechs up to him undoubtedly helped pull him back from the abyss. But it was not decisive. Most probably it was a combination of factors: the doubts of many among his senior generals, the military preparations of Britain and France, questions about the Poles, and the considerable economic difficulties the Third Reich was experiencing combined to make Munich possible. Hitler almost immediately regretted that he had agreed to a peaceful solution. His success, however, had a crucial impact on German assessments of the balance. It served to convince Hitler that his views were infallible. On the other hand, it undermined the opposition to Hitler's assessments. There would be no memoranda the following summer on the dangerous risks that German policy was running as Hitler and Goebbels stoked the fires of the Polish crisis.

Hitler's assessment of the 1939 crisis ran on lines of thinking similar to those of 1938. He aimed to isolate the Polish Republic, create the basis for a sudden and brutal descent that would deter intervention from the West, and intimidate and undermine the willingness of the West to intervene. In effect the Nazi–Soviet Non-Aggression Pact made Hitler's policy even more successful. Moreover, Hitler's contempt for Western leadership reinforced his belief that he could get away with a short war over Poland. As he told his entourage, he had seen his enemies at Munich and they were worms. In a long, detailed speech to his generals and admirals on 22 August 1939 Hitler laid out the assessment on which he was launching the Third Reich into World War II:

> It was clear to me that a conflict with Poland had to come sooner or later. I had already made this decision in the spring, but I thought that I would first turn against the West in a few years, and only after that against the East. But the sequence of these things cannot be fixed. . . . I wanted first of all to establish a tolerable relationship with Poland in order to fight first against the West.[64]

Hitler underlined his assessment of the factors that favored the Reich at the present moment. Not surprisingly, the personalities of the two leaders of the Axis states was first:

> Essentially all depends on me, on my existence, because of my political talents. Furthermore, the fact that probably no one will ever again have the confidence of the whole German people as I have.

Hitler then moved to the economic and strategic factors that buttressed his decision to take the risks associated with an invasion of Poland and the possibility of another World War:

> It is easy for us to make decisions. We have nothing to lose; we have everything to gain. Because of our restrictions our economic situation is such that we can only hold out for a few more years. . . . We have no other choice, we must act. Our opponents will be risking a great deal and can gain only a little. . . . Our enemies have leaders who are below average. No personalities. No masters, no men of action. England and France have undertaken obligations which neither is in a position to

fulfill. There is no real rearmament in England, but only propaganda. A great deal of harm was done by many Germans, who were not in agreement with me, saying and writing to English people after the solution of the Czech question: The Führer succeeded because you lost your nerve, because you capitulated too soon. This explains the present propaganda war. The English speak of a war of nerves. One factor in this war of nerves is to boost the increase of armaments. But what are the real facts about British rearmament? The naval construction program for 1938 has not yet been completed. . . . Little has been done on land. . . . A little has been done for the Air Force, but it is only a beginning. . . . The West has only two possibilities for fighting against us:

1. Blockade: It will not be effective because of our autarky and because we have sources of supply in Eastern Europe.
2. Attack in the West from the Maginot Line: I consider this impossible.[65]

In comparison with Hitler's statements in the Hossbach protocol, one is struck by the continuity in themes. But by late summer 1939 Hitler had reached a point where he entirely dominated the business of net assessment. No longer were his advisers encouraged or even allowed to speak their minds. In fact, by this point senior military and policy makers either fully accepted Hitler's strategic assumptions or kept their mouths shut. One suspects that the great majority of his listeners on 22 August 1939 fully subscribed to Manstein's comments of the previous year: "Hitler has thus far always estimated the political situation correctly." It is also worth noting that in many cases this acceptance would involve a wholehearted embracing of the Führer principal, that Adolf Hitler could do no wrong. As we shall see in the next section, the stunning successes of the first two years of the war would further debilitate and destroy the independence of judgment that is so necessary to any intelligent and sophisticated attempt to calculate the balance. The disastrous course of "Operation Barbarossa" largely reflected that collapse of independent judgment.

One comes away from the business of analyzing the process of net assessment in Nazi Germany with a sense of watching a train rapidly heading toward an abyss with the engineer opening up the throttle rather than applying the brakes, while berating its crew for cowardice and insisting that if they can get up enough speed, the train will leap the yawning chasm. And bit by bit the crew becomes persuaded and goes about its task of oiling the machinery with more and more enthusiasm. The process of net assessment in any realistic, carefully nuanced sense quite simply disappears in Nazi Germany in the last years of the 1930s. Rather, Hitler's very successes robbed his advisers of their judgment. Of course, the German intellectual and cultural climate already predisposed them to follow the Führer. While his views were an extreme expression of their *Weltanschauung*, his was nevertheless a world view with which they had considerable sympathy, and as he enjoyed more and more success, they were predisposed to accept his vision in its totality. By 1941 the Führer and his advisers were in complete agreement on the strategic and political levels of German policy-making.

THE FACTORS IN THE MAKING OF GERMAN
NET ASSESSMENT

Where then did Hitler get the information on which he based his views on the overall strategic situation, if not from the bureaucracy? His general framework remained his racial *Weltanschauung*. Some reports, such as those of the German military attaché in Washington, consistently reinforced and played up to his beliefs. Those who conformed to Hitler's racial *Weltanschauung* found an attentive audience in their Führer. Those, however, who contradicted his conceptions received short shrift. The OKW, particularly its chief, Wilhelm Keitel, proved particularly adept at providing Hitler with support that echoed his opinions. In fact, Hitler probably selected Keitel for the top slot in the OKW on the basis of his servility. Those who dominated the upper levels of German bureaucracy in the late 1930s and early 1940s increasingly reinforced Hitler's preconceptions. That was precisely in accordance with his wishes; those who maintained independent judgment quickly found themselves in retirement.

One of the clear trends in the Third Reich is the erosion of independent judgments and of the capacity to assess the strategic situation in realistic terms. In 1933 there was little doubt within the leadership, including Hitler, about Germany's weakness within the European balance of power. Hitler's carefully calculated moves from 1933 to 1936 reflected his realistic sense of what was acceptable to the Powers—in other words, what risks one could take without becoming involved in a conflict. Significantly, when the Austrian Nazis assassinated the Chancellor of Austria, Engelbert Dollfuss, Hitler disowned his followers when the Italians appeared to take a stand.

By 1938 Hitler's view of the European political balance was

becoming more optimistic; successful occupation of Austria reinforced his sense that his international opponents were lacking in will.[66] Certainly Britain's weak response to the *Anschluss* and the collapse of the French government seemed to justify his view. Hitler's policies over the summers of 1938 and 1939 reflected a judgment about both the political and the military weaknesses of his Western opponents. The Wehrmacht's enormous success in spring 1940 turned confidence into megalomaniacal overconfidence, not only in Hitler's mind but among many of his advisers. Consequently, the German leadership failed to catch the significant change in British leadership that came with Winston Churchill's arrival in power—something that the Italian Foreign Minister, Galeazzo Ciano, sensed as early as August 1940.[67]

The German misestimate of the political strength and will of Stalin and his Soviet regime needs special emphasis. By 1941 Hitler and his entourage had become so infatuated with the myth of the Führer as "the greatest field commander of all time" that few were capable of making reasonable judgments about the impact of operational realities on the political and strategic situation. By education and inclination the German military was already on the road to a mindless acceptance of Hitler's "genius" in 1938, as Manstein's letter to Beck underlines.

On operational and tactical intelligence (the "bean counting" aspect of net assessment), German intelligence performed more creditably. This was a sphere of technical competence that the military felt was their preserve. Within this narrow area the Germans accurately assessed the probable strength of their putative opponents. Nevertheless, there were problems. German assessments of opponent strength were most accurate within the Central European arena. In other words, they were very good at estimating the military strength of opponents like Czechoslovakia, Poland, and France. The Manstein plan that led to the overwhelming German victory in spring 1940 rested in large measure on a thorough understanding of French doctrine and the probable French responses to German moves.

However, the Battle of Britain suggests that once the Germans moved beyond the Central European arena, they had increasing difficulty estimating the balance accurately. In retrospect, the Luftwaffe faced insurmountable problems in coming to grips with Fighter Command. Nevertheless, intelligence reports, particularly the July 1940 intelligence summary produced by the Luftwaffe's chief of intelligence, Beppo Schmid, suggest an overconfidence that is breathtaking. Schmid's summary missed the British radar network entirely, rated the Bf 110 as superior not only to the Hurricane but to the Spitfire as well, and ended with the judgment that "the Luftwaffe, unlike the RAF, will be in a position in every respect to achieve a decisive effect this year."[68]

The following year's preparations to invade the Soviet Union suggest a more egregious incapacity to calculate even the numerical balance. A diary entry of the chief of the general staff, *Generaloberst* Franz Halder, in early August 1941 catches the extent of the German miscalculation in estimating Soviet potential military strength:

> [The] whole situation shows more and more clearly that we have underestimated the colossus of Russia—a Russia that had consciously prepared for the coming war with the whole unrestrained power of which a totalitarian state is capable. This conclusion is shown both on the organization as well as the economic levels, in the transportation, and above all, clearly in infantry divisions. We have already identified 360. These divisions are admittedly not armed and equipped in our sense, and tactically they are badly led. But they are there, and when we destroy a dozen, the Russians simply establish another dozen.[69]

Perhaps the strongest point in the German assessment processes lay in the Wehrmacht's ability to estimate its own strengths and weaknesses and then to use those estimates to improve its capabilities. From the *Anschluss,* German armed forces vigorously evaluated performance of front line units in peacetime maneuvers and in combat. Those evaluations began with after-action reports at regimental level and reached all the way to army level. These reports generally represented honest, realistic, and thorough examination of what had gone right or wrong in the exercise or combat environment. The army then utilized these reports to create realistic, demanding training programs to correct deficiencies that appeared. These reports tended to become more critical the higher the level of command reviewing troop performance.[70] The Polish campaign in September 1939 suggests the degree to which this ruthless self-evaluation process reached:

> The preparation of the German army in the phony war indicates several important points. First and perhaps foremost, is the fact that the German high command, within the limited sphere of its military competence, possessed the organizational integrity to recognize that the operational success in Poland had revealed major flaws and weaknesses. Moreover, it was willing to learn from experience. Having evaluated the Polish campaign in the harsh light of its high standards, the German general staff then instituted a vast training program to correct deficiencies by closely tying its training to its "lessons learned" analysis of events in Poland. Of critical importance to this process was the fact that there

existed an implicit trust between the different levels of command. Commanders were not afraid to give accurate critical reports on the status and performance of their troops. In addition, the high command expected commanders to give negative evaluations of their units, if there were weaknesses. This is not to say that a unit commander would not do all in his power to correct such deficiencies. There were simply no Potemkin villages.[71]

The process of self-evaluation after the Polish campaign helps explain the blowup between the army's senior leadership and Hitler in fall 1939. The former argued that the deficiencies that had appeared in the Polish campaign must be corrected before the Wehrmacht met the French in the west. From the army's perspective the argument did not involve the operational design for the proposed fall campaign, much less the Führer's strategic vision. Rather, the senior army leadership cast its evaluation entirely on the tactical, battlefield level.

As war approached, the German capability to assess the strategic balance substantially decreased. This reflected increasing Nazification in the upper levels of bureaucracy. Part of this process was direct, with replacement of individuals like Neurath and Fritsch with Ribbentrop and Brauchitsch. But equally important was an increasing acceptance of the Nazi *Weltanschauung,* as Hitler's successes in diplomacy and war continued unabated. Hitler's success at Munich in September 1938 was a crucial moment in undermining the arguments of those who believed the risks he was running were too great. The result was twofold. On one hand, many senior officials and generals became out-and-out Nazis. On the other hand, particularly among the Generalität, senior leaders who were in a position to raise strategic issues confined themselves to narrow technical issues within their field of expertise. Thus, in fall 1939 the generals did not question Hitler's argument on the Reich's strategic position. Rather their interest centered on the tactical and operational problems raised by the war. By 1941 the convergence of these trends was even more pronounced.

The arguments by his senior generals against the fall 1939 offensive outraged Hitler. It only served to confirm his increasing contempt for generals who from his point of view did not want to fight and who had consistently argued against his foreign policy initiatives since the mid-1930s. Brauchitsch made the mistake of suggesting that in Poland German soldiers had not performed as well as they had in 1914. Brauchitsch believed that inconsistent levels of preparation, resulting from massive military expansion, were at fault. Hitler, however, took the army commander-in-chief's comments as suggesting that the Third Reich had not prepared its soldiers adequately; he was even more furious when Brauchitsch went on to suggest that the morale of the troops was analogous to what it had been in 1918. In the ensuing explosion, the Führer demanded to know, if this were the case, how many death sentences the army had handed out and accused the army of "not want[ing] to fight."[72]

This concentration on the narrow technical aspects of military professionalism existed in all three services. The navy had had a long tradition of confusing operations with strategy; it is only in this light that one can understand why the Seekriegsleitung pushed throughout summer and fall 1941 for a declaration of war on the United States.[73] For the navy all that mattered were the operational possibilities that a declaration of war would open up for German U-boats off the east coast of North America.[74] In judging the overall strategic situation in December 1941, when word of the Japanese success in Hawaii came in, none of Hitler's advisers, including naval aides, knew the location of Pearl Harbor in the Pacific.[75] Not surprisingly, both the army and Luftwaffe concentrated on similar narrow technical aspects of assessment.

For the Germans, then, evaluation of the strategic balance increasingly rested on a framework reflecting military and operational consensus. In 1938 those, like Beck, opposed to Hitler's Czech policy cast surveys that assessed the larger framework beyond a Czech–German confrontation. Hitler's Munich success cut the ground from underneath such attempts to deal with strategic realities. From that point on, the senior leadership within the Wehrmacht and the foreign policy establishment largely executed Hitler's will. For Ribbentrop this meant slavishly following the Führer's genius with absolute faith. The military no longer produced strategic analyses, but confined itself to gaming the narrow operational possibilities of whatever the next conflict might bring.

The two methods by which the Germans assessed the military environment consisted of war-gaming and static force comparisons. In both areas the OKH generally captured an accurate picture of the operational balance and possibilities in a future conflict. In summer 1938, the war-gaming of a Czech–German conflict—conducted as the Hitler–Beck argument reached its height—indicated that Czechoslovakia did not present the Wehrmacht with insurmountable problems. A general staff map experience in late June suggested that war with Czechoslovakia would be a relatively quick affair and that by the twelfth day German forces would break the back of Czech resistance. Within seven days, it concluded, the Wehrmacht could begin transferring units from Czechoslovakia to the west.[76] While this did not directly contradict Beck's assessments, especially in regard to the strategic framework of the crisis, it served to undermine his credibility among generals like Manstein, who regarded Hitler's political wisdom as sufficient.

Kriegsspiele (war games) were particularly useful in elucidating operational possibilities. The March 1940 game played a crucial role in convincing senior German commanders that a major armored push through the Ardennes offered substantial operational advantages over earlier conceptions.[77] But there were limits to what war games could tell. The gaming of Barbarossa is particularly instructive in this regard. The 1940–41 operational games carried clear implications about what the Germans would encounter in force-to-space ratios, especially after the Wehrmacht had advanced deep into the Soviet Union.[78] There is little evidence, however, to suggest that Germans planners allowed such warnings to affect the overoptimistic calculations on which so much of Barbarossa rested.

Besides *Kriegsspiele* the Germans also used numerical comparisons to quantify the strength of possible opponents. Within the Western and Central European context these were quite good. Moreover, the Germans exhibited circumspection in estimating the qualitative strengths of opponents. Throughout the French campaign, the Germans retained a high regard for the battlefield capabilities of the French. That undoubtedly explains the nervousness that the leadership exhibited after the Ardennes breakthrough on the Meuse and why the German army halted on the coast before Dunkirk was in its hands. Not only Hitler but most senior generals (including Guderian) feared that the French might repeat the "Miracle of the Marne" with a counterthrust, especially against the vulnerable southern flank along the Somme.

Even so, by 1940 the Germans were beginning to minimize the qualitative capabilities of potential enemies. The Battle of Britain underlines this growing overconfidence. The Germans entirely missed the fact that Fighter Command enjoyed a substantial technological superiority in its development and deployment of a radar system. But in the Russian campaign German miscalculations reached an even greater magnitude. The discovery of the T-34 medium tank, captured early in the campaign, demonstrated that the Soviets possessed an armored fighting vehicle far superior to *anything* in the German inventory, or even on their drawing boards. Similarly, the Germans expressed consistent amazement in the first months of Barbarossa at the tenacity and fighting power of Soviet infantry formations. When one realizes that qualitative misjudgments went hand in hand with quantitative misestimates, the seriousness of German miscalculations becomes clear. The Germans did improve their order of battle picture of Soviet forces as the war continued. Nevertheless, as recent historical work has indicated, from Stalingrad on German intelligence was consistently caught flatfooted by Soviet deployments before each of the great offensives that battered the Wehrmacht back into Central Europe.[79]

The Germans were not much interested in long-term trend analysis. Hitler himself did display considerable interest in trends, but only in terms of his own idiosyncratic interpretation. His ideology rested on a belief that he was swimming against the tide of history. According to him, the forces that had shaped the nineteenth- and early-twentieth-century world were gradually but steadily eroding the racial basis on which German civilization rested. Only his "unique" political genius could reverse this process; and if he did not grasp the opportunity, he might die and history would not turn onto new paths. Consequently, Hitler was driven by the restless conviction that he must reach his goals in *his own lifetime;* and, as he suggested, he could be assassinated at any moment.[80]

This drive reinforced Hitler's own reading of the strategic balance in the late 1930s. Germany had begun rearmament in 1933 and therefore possessed a considerable lead over its opponents by the late 1930s. That lead, however, represented a wasting asset. The British and French were both mounting impressive rearmament efforts, at least on paper, by 1938. Moreover, the seizure of Prague in March 1939 led the British to abandon the severe limitations they had placed on their rearmament; particularly of the ground forces.[81] By summer 1939 the British had thrown themselves wholeheartedly into rearmament. They ticketed enormous increases for the RAF, and with the help of conscription the British army was creating a field force for commitment on the continent of more than 30 divisions.[82] That British effort with its attendant propaganda warned Hitler that whatever advantages Germany possessed in 1939 were ones that *in the long term* it could not maintain.

This was particularly due to economic problems that had emerged as early as 1936. In that year shortages of raw materials and foreign exchange retarded the German rearmament so much that Hitler created a special economic authority under Göring, "The Four Year Plan," to find alternatives to the Reich's heavy dependency on imports of raw materials. "The Four Year Plan" hoped to give the German war economy sufficient strength to resist a blockade while the Wehrmacht conquered the larger economic and raw material base required to fight a true "world war."[83] By 1937 and 1938 German economic difficulties had severely impacted on rearmament. From September 1937 through February 1938 German industry met only 58.6 percent of its scheduled and contracted orders because of raw material and foreign exchange shortages as well as the lack of industrial capacity.[84] A report of the War Ministry's economic section warned as early as 1935: "We are becoming poorer from day to day because of our clear internal preoccupations and . . . without exports we will create no foreign exchange and . . . without foreign exchange no rearmament is possible."[85]

Even with the *Anschluss* and seizure of the Sudetenland, economic trends hardly improved over the winter of 1938–39. Signs of economic collapse appeared immediately after the success over the Western Powers; the economy seemed to have reached a breaking point. In October the Reich Defense Committee reported that "in consequence of Wehrmacht demands (the occupation of the Sudetenland) and unlimited construction on the Westwall so tense a situation in the economic sector occurred (coal, supplies for industries, harvest of potatoes and turnips, food supplies) that continuation of the tension past 10 October [1938] would have made an [economic] catastrophe inevitable."[86] At a sitting of the same committee the next month, Göring admitted that the economic strain had reached a point where no more workers were available, factories were at full capacity, foreign exchange was completely exhausted, and Germany's economic situation was desperate.[87] These economic difficulties finally forced Hitler to reduce Wehrmacht steel allocations 30 percent, copper 20 percent, aluminum 47 percent, rubber 14 percent, and cement 25 to 45 percent.[88]

The crucial point here is that Hitler was well aware of these economic trends that were making it impossible to fulfill his grandiose rearmament plans. That is the underlying message of the Hossbach discussions of November 1937; in 1938 the *Anschluss* and in 1939 the occupation of the remainder of Czechoslovakia tided the Germans over temporarily. Such success, however, did not solve the problem that no peaceful expansion of the economy could possibly support the rearmament programs that Hitler and his military advisers were pushing. But then it had never been Hitler's intention to confine himself to peaceful expansion; the attack on Poland (and if not on Poland, then on someone else) was implicit from his accession to power.

However, the Germans and their Führer failed to understand that the victories of spring 1940 (over Norway, Denmark, the Netherlands,

Belgium, and France) hardly changed the unfavorable economic balances and trends that had marked the period from 1936 to 1939. While German economic difficulties eased with inclusion of Western Europe within the Reich's sphere of influence, German success did not change the fact that Britain and the United States controlled the oceanic world economy and that the Soviet Union controlled the raw material and economic potential of European and Asiatic Russia. The Germans dawdled from summer 1940 through to the defeat of Moscow in the idle belief that their easy victories in 1940 had solved their economic and strategic problems. They had not, since the British and the Americans were mobilizing their economic resources for the long haul. This would show particularly in the great air battles of 1943 and 1944, where Anglo-American quantitative superiority swamped the Luftwaffe.[89]

CONCLUSIONS: THE RESULTS OF GERMAN
NET ASSESSMENT

In the dust and rubble of Germany in 1945, it was convenient to blame the crash on Hitler. Indisputably, without him much of the disaster would never have happened. As Fritsch commented, Hitler was Germany's fate for ill or for good. But the community of interest as well as the abdication of strategic responsibility within the senior leadership is suggested by a letter Fritsch wrote in December 1938:

> . . . It is really peculiar that so many people should look to the future with increasing fears, in spite of the führer's indisputable successes during the past years. Herr von Weigand's letter interested me very much . . . Unfortunately, I am afraid he is right when he speaks of the profound hate which is directed to us by a large part of the world. Soon after the war [World War I] I came to the conclusion that we should have to be victorious in three battles, if Germany were to become powerful again:
>
> 1. The battle against the working class—Hitler has won this
> 2. Against the Catholic Church, perhaps better expressed against Ultramontanism, and
> 3. Against the Jews.
>
> We are in the midst of these battles and the one against the Jews is the most difficult. I hope everyone realizes the intricacies of this campaign.[90]

The framework within which German net assessment occurred is very much wrapped up in the growth of the Hitler legend. That legend resulted in a steady erosion of the position and credibility of those who urged a more cautious approach. But the course of German history over the past hundred years had undermined the position of those who served as a brake on the regime's revolutionary impetus. From the 1860s and 1870s the officer corps had achieved a unique position of intellectual and cultural respect within German society that allowed it to dominate military matters. The professional officer corps, however, defined military affairs in such exceedingly narrow terms that strategy disappeared in favor of operational and tactical concerns. One should not, however, minimize the battlefield excellence that resulted from this operational and tactical expertise.

But this concern with the tactical and operational led the Germans to minimize the strategic and the political. Geyer von Schweppenberg's casual dismissal of Clausewitz as a person to be read only by professors suggests the incapacity of the officer corps to deal with larger questions of war. Thus, it is not surprising that the Mansteins and Guderians abdicated their political and strategic responsibility to Hitler and concerned themselves almost entirely with operational and tactical matters. The extent to which they ignored strategic and political questions is suggested by the fact that Manstein used his family fortune to buy an estate *in East Prussia* in the fall of 1944.[91] The officer corps' disdain for strategic and political matters only reflected societal and educational values. The widespread belief that the German army had not lost World War I but had been stabbed in the back enjoyed enormous popular support throughout German society by the early 1920s. Admittedly, the disinformation campaign of the Foreign Office further muddied the water. This national consensus consequently made it difficult to provide a coherent, conservative basis on which those opposed to Hitler's risky course might take a stand.

The individual strategic surveys undertaken by those like Beck suggest what might have been possible had a more coherent, systematic approach existed within the old bureaucracy. Groener had attempted to create such analytic capabilities within the Defense Ministry in the late 1920s; nevertheless, even Groener's efforts would not have led to the creation of an equivalent of the Committee of Imperial Defence, where a wide variety of viewpoints, political as well as military, were present. However accurate a survey of the international strategic environment Beck's studies and memoranda may have represented,[92] Hitler was correct in the final analysis in his judgment that the British and French were unwilling to fight for the Czech Republic. He almost precipitated a European war through his belief that he could get away with a small war, but at the last moment he settled for diplomatic success, which rendered Czechoslovakia indefensible and began the rout of Anglo-French interests in Eastern Europe.

Consequently, it is Hitler with whom we must deal in addressing German net assessment in the 1930s. In every sense, the Führer's ideology and goals made Nazi Germany a rogue state. Hitler recognized the brutal alternatives on which his foreign policy rested— *Weltmacht oder Niedergang* (world power or defeat)—in a fashion the Wilhelmine Germans did not. Moreover, he understood that the European Powers possessed the strength to crush the Nazi state in its early years before it reached full military potential. But the desperate rearmament effort, first to catch up and then to provide the Wehrmacht with a margin, came close to bankrupting the state and had a direct impact on the rearmament rate. Only the most desperate of measures coupled with external acquisitions (Austria, the Sudetenland, and Czechoslovakia) kept the economy and rearmament on track.

Hitler, at least in 1937, would have preferred avoiding a major European war until 1943. Admittedly he indicated in his memorandum in 1936 establishing the Four Year Plan that the army must be combat ready and the economy prepared to meet the demands of war within four years.[93] The push to war in the late 1930s resulted from Hitler's sense of Germany's economic woes and his belief that the strategic moment of greatest Allied weakness had come. His judgment of the Allied leaders, confirmed by meetings with them in September 1938, reinforced his instinct to strike at weakness. A British observer writing on Britain's initial rearmament efforts in 1936 commented: "Here is of course the salient difference between us and Germany that they know what army they will use and, broadly, how they will use it and can thus, prepare . . . in peace for such an event. . . . In contrast we here do not even know yet what size of army we are to contemplate for purposes of supply preparation between now and April 1939."[94]

It was Hitler's diplomatic skill and intuitive judgment that destroyed the existing balance in the 1933–40 period. Knowing that war was inevitable and possessing military organizations of considerable operational and tactical competence, the Germans prepared with a ruthlessness of which their opponents were simply incapable. But luck also played a role; Germany's substantial weaknesses, even though Allied strategists recognized them, did not result in any significant strategic or operational impairments. Consequently, the invasion of France and the Low Countries projected maximum German military power into the greatest weakness of the Allied Front—the crucial joint in the

Ardennes. That offensive, however, represented an enormous gamble; for example, German stocks of petroleum had sunk by one-third over the period of the "Phony War" from 2,400,000 tons to 1,600,000 tons.[95] If the victory over France represented a strategic success that substantially altered Germany's position, it did so only in the sense that it allowed the Reich to escape from its economic difficulties and to utilize the economic strength of Western Europe to the advantage of its war economy.

It was in summer 1940, however, that the Germans lost the war.[96] Two factors were at work, and both deserve attention in understanding why the Germans failed at net assessment in 1940–41. On the one hand the Germans, from Hitler on down, caught the "victory disease." Jodl noted in a strategic survey on 30 June 1940, "the final victory of Germany over England is only a question of time."[97] Hitler, of course, wholeheartedly agreed with the assumption that he was "the greatest military leader of all time" and that the British would soon recognize the hopelessness of their position. If not, then the Wehrmacht, led by the Luftwaffe, would batter Britain into submission.

On the other hand lay the German evaluation of Germany's present and putative opponents in the post–May 1940 assessments. In Nazi eyes the British, degenerate inheritors of a world empire they could no longer protect, had decayed through the influences of liberalism and Jews. The United States represented a mongrelized society in which waves of Jewish and Slavic immigrants from Eastern Europe had diluted the good racial stock. Reports from Washington only reinforced Hitler's contempt for the United States. While such estimates did suggest American economic potential, neither the reporters on the American scene nor the recipients of their information took the American threat seriously. With great glee, Goebbels recorded every Anglo-American disaster in 1942, while dismissing as idle boasting the American production programs.[98] Göring casually dismissed warnings on America's industrial potential with the comment that Americans "could only produce cars and refrigerators."[99]

But it was for the Slavic nations that the Germans registered the most contempt. The Poles were first to feel the full weight of the Nazi racial attitudes.[100] It was in its estimates of Soviet military potential and of the strength of Russian national character that the Germans so severely underestimated their opponents. From the first, Hitler's ideology had emphasized that the Russian revolution of 1917 had destroyed the ruling Germanic elements and had turned the government over to the Jews and Slavic *Untermenschen* (subhumans).[101] Not surprisingly, Hitler believed that an invasion of the Soviet Union would lead to a quick and sudden collapse of Stalin's regime. As he commented to his entourage, once Germany kicked in the door, the whole rotten Soviet regime would collapse like a house of cards.[102] Hitler's views found a considerable response in the officer corps. Günther Blumentritt, a general staff officer, commented shortly before the invasion that "Russian military history shows that the Russian combat soldier, illiterate and half-Asiatic, thinks and feels differently" from the German.[103] The great majority of those responsible for the planning of Barbarossa fully accepted such a *Weltanschauung*. Consequently their ideological orientation led them to underestimate Soviet potential; on the other hand acceptance of Hitler's racial goals and ideology with the concomitant atrocities against the Soviet civilian population ensured that the Germans would not be able to undermine Stalin's regime. Rather, the German approach rallied the Russian people behind a popular war for which Stalin and his henchmen had hardly prepared.

Consequently, by 1941 virtually no strategic judgment remained in Germany. Conservative critics had lost all credibility within even their own class. The great majority of the generals and bureaucracy were technocrats who had abdicated strategic responsibility to the regime. Even more disastrously, most of the technocrats were now enthusiastic supporters of the regime. Like Alfred Jodl and Erich von Manstein, they sang the praises of the Führer. They could no longer judge the potential of their opponents except in terms of Hitler's ideological preconceptions, and those preconceptions contributed directly to strengthening their opponents' potential, particularly in the Soviet case. The reaction of the senior officers and the bureaucracy to the attempt on Hitler's life underlines how much, even at the end of the war, those who should have provided independent judgment were incapable of doing so.

Hitler had provided the malevolent genius and drive on which the German success of the 1930s had rested. With victory over France, he seems to have substituted the flattery of his advisers for his ability to judge the ambiguities and weaknesses in his opponents. But this process had already begun in the late 1930s. Hitler became more and more determined to drive events in accordance with his beliefs. In the end he substituted will for judgment, and his strategic and political misconceptions resulted in a national catastrophe that no operational or tactical expertise could salvage.

The lessons that the Nazi German regime present to current policy-makers are not simple, nor are they direct. They suggest that some states in the international system are not open to assimilation and may be so hostile in their orientation as to remove "rational" calculations from the equation. British and French statesmen (and American as well) assumed in the 1920s and 1930s that international conflict represented such an unmitigated horror that no state would deliberately set out to cause such a catastrophe. Yet in fact that was precisely what Hitler intended to do. The Nazi aims were so vast in compass and so uncompromising that they left no alternative to Allied statesmen except war or surrender. In the final analysis the latter was unacceptable, but by the time the Powers recognized the choice, they had almost given the game away.

For Hitler the crucial issue was to choose that moment when the balance between Germany and its opponents gave him the best chance to destroy his enemies. Almost entirely, he rested the choosing of that moment on his intuition. He came within hours of starting World War II in 1938; had he done so Nazi Germany would probably have failed to break out from its immediate economic and strategic weaknesses. The following year, Hitler's policy was even more successful in isolating the intended victim. But his intuition on how the British and French would act was flawed, not because he misjudged the leadership but because he failed to understand how the shifting national moods had handicapped those leaderships.

Throughout those crucial years, Hitler rejected efforts to provide a more coherent and organized effort to assess the international environment. He fully understood that such bureaucratic assessments would limit his room for maneuver and his ability to make *the* decision for peace and war. His system of government from the moment of his appointment as Chancellor aimed to destroy the ability of the bureaucratic system to provide independent judgment on the strategic environment. Ironically, the intellectual perceptions and training of most of those in the diplomatic, the intelligence, and the military bureaucracies were all too close to Hitler's preconceptions. Their attitude made possible, in a direct sense, the triumphs of Hitler's early years and the catastrophes of the later years.

4

The Impatient Cat
Assessments of Military Power in Fascist Italy, 1936–1940

Brian R. Sullivan

Have you ever watched a cat while it studies its prey and then, with a leap, is upon it? Watch one. I intend to act in the same way.

—Mussolini speaking to Fascist labor leaders, 21 April 1940.[1]

AS THE OUTBREAK of World War II approached, the leadership of Fascist Italy paid careful attention to the balance of force in Europe. Despite incessant Fascist boasts of Italian might. Mussolini's lieutenants recognized the dubious nature of their claims. They did share the Duce's conviction that his genius and the new warrior spirit introduced by Fascism could raise Italy to mastery over the Mediterranean and vast regions to the south and east. Yet the Fascist *gerarchi* (leaders) appreciated the slender resources at Italian disposal. As the power of Germany and Japan surged, the determination of France and Britain wavered, and signals of the intentions of the United States and the Soviet Union flickered uncertainly, tempting possibilities arose for Italian aggrandizement. A serious misstep, however, one that would bring Italy into conflict with superior strength, could shatter Italy's fragile power base.

The turbulent events through which Italians had lived in the seventy-five years preceding the Fascist dictatorship left vivid lessons for Mussolini and his *gerarchi* to ponder. The Europe of the 1930s seemed to offer close parallels to the unstable conditions under which Cavour had expanded his little subalpine state into the Kingdom of Italy. The Austro-Hungarian and Ottoman empires had disintegrated. The Soviet Union had been driven to the fringes of Europe. And although victorious in the Great War, both Britain and France had suffered a marked decline from their prewar power. It seemed that neither Italy's former enemies nor its allies any longer stood irremovably blocking Italian expansion across the Balkans, the Mediterranean, and beyond. Both the long years of frustration that had followed the Risorgimento and the humiliating settlement imposed at Versailles appeared at an end, now that Italy enjoyed the leadership of another genius of vision and determination.

Many Italians believed that their country's destiny lay in an emulation of Roman imperialism. Not just Fascist propaganda but a century of Italian patriotic rhetoric had proclaimed this fate. The twin prophets of the Risorgimento, the monarchist priest Vincenzo Gioberti and the radical republican Giuseppe Mazzini—polar opposites otherwise—had both insisted that Rome would rule the Mediterranean world again. The question was when and how.

POWER, DISCUSSION, AND DECISION-MAKING IN THE FASCIST REGIME

Despite the creation of the Fascist regime, the 1848 constitution officially remained in force. The King was still head of state and commander of the armed forces. Many other pre-Fascist constitutional arrangements had ceased to function, but the close relationship between the King and the officer corps continued. What respect Mussolini showed for Vittorio Emanuele III came largely from the fact that the army remained an independent power center at the King's potential disposal. Unlike the heads of other royal houses, Vittorio

Emanuele III and Crown Prince Umberto wore no other uniform than that of the army. Even in the supposedly totalitarian Fascist regime, the army remained royal—the *Regio Esercito*.[2]

Second only to the King in military prestige stood Marshal Pietro Badoglio, Chief of the Supreme General Staff since 1925. He had helped guide the nation to victory as Army Deputy Chief of Staff in 1917–18, had broken the Arab revolt in Libya in 1928–31, and had conquered Ethiopia in 1936. Despite his impressive title, Badoglio had no Supreme General Staff over which to preside. Mussolini had rejected the creation of such a staff as a possible locus of opposition to his power, allowing Badoglio instead to loosely coordinate the activities of the chiefs of staff in times of crisis. Badoglio also served as Mussolini's chief military adviser, and the dictator usually deferred to the marshal's judgment in professional matters. While no Fascist, Badoglio's greed for riches and titles made him subservient to Mussolini. But ultimately, Badoglio served only himself.[3]

In the late 1930s, however, Mussolini enjoyed the security that flows from power. He had transformed the office of prime minister (more properly, President of the Council of Ministers) into that of permanent *Capo del Governo* (Head of Government). He buttressed this office by his position as *Duce del Fascismo* (Leader of Fascism) in a system in which the Fascist Party had become the only legal party. In addition, through a chief of staff, Mussolini commanded the Fascist Militia, the militarized internal security force commonly known as the Black Shirts.

Mussolini, in contrast to Stalin, had deliberately based his position on government, rather than party, institutions. In 1933 Mussolini had permanently assumed the offices of War, Navy, and Air Force minister. Since 1926 he had held the position of Minister of the Interior, granting him direct control of the police and internal surveillance organizations. Mussolini stepped down as Foreign Minister in June 1936, but he gave that post to his most trusted subordinate, his son-in-law Galeazzo Ciano. Thus, Mussolini stood at the apex of twin party and governmental structures but exercised power principally through the latter.[4]

Complicating matters, however, particularly in the spheres of intelligence gathering and analysis, was considerable overlap between the party and government institutions. After mid-1933, virtually all civil servants had to be members of the party. Membership in the Fascist Party spread rapidly within the army officer corps after

Mussolini's appointment of the ardently Fascist general Federico Baistrocchi as War Under Secretary in July 1933. A few months later, Mussolini's selection of Admiral Domenico Cavagnari as Navy Under Secretary placed another enthusiastic Fascist in administrative control of the *Regia Marina*. Fascist sentiment had permeated the air force since its inception in 1923. Nonetheless, the King remained the official head of both these services, as their titles indicated: *Regia Marina* and *Regia Aeronautica*.

Given the adulation of Mussolini within the party after 1935 and his growing megalomania and detachment from reality, the increasing Fascist influence within military and government organizations meant decreasing objectivity and willingness to report honestly.[5] In addition, the Duce increasingly surrounded himself with sycophants. Thus, fears of dismissal and hopes of reward for obsequiousness and flattery inhibited Mussolini's access to objective analysis and stifled free debate among his advisers.

This problem assumed acute form in the two possible forums for Mussolini and his lieutenants to assess Italy's strength relative to its possible opponents. Potentially the more useful in this regard was the Supreme Defense Commission, although it sat but once a year. The Fascist Grand Council, while it considered a wider range of topics than just military-strategic questions, did offer the advantage of meeting two or three times a year in the 1936–39 period, in clusters of sessions spread over one to three weeks.[6]

The Supreme Defense Commission, as defined by law in May 1940, was "an interministerial organization for coordinating the studies and decisions on all questions pertaining to national safety and defense, organization and mobilization of the nation for war, and development and better utilization of all resources, as well as all state activities involving defense."[7] Since its establishment in March 1923, the Commission had gradually increased its power, at the partial expense of the independence of the individual services, and had played something of the role formally legislated in 1940 since the period of the Ethiopian War.

The Commission consisted of twenty to twenty-five members, including the major Cabinet ministers or under secretaries, the armed forces chiefs of staff, the Secretary of the Fascist Party, the Militia Chief of Staff, and Lieutenant General Alfredo Dallolio, who headed the *Commissariato generale per le fabbricazioni di guerra* (COGEFAG: the General Commissariat for War Production)—all under the presidency of Mussolini. Other officials would attend when topics relating to their competency were discussed. A permanent secretariat of four military officers dealt with the Commission's administration.

The Commission discussed economic, educational, legislative, social, financial, and industrial issues that influenced Italy's ability to wage war effectively. Perhaps its most practical role was to keep the two most powerful members of the regime, Mussolini and Ciano, informed of Italian war-making potential and to educate various members of the regime about their counterparts' attitudes and problems. Members of the Commission did make candid statements about Italy's industrial and economic weaknesses. Frequently, healthy discussions took place among the participants. However, Mussolini tended to downplay material factors. He insisted that Fascist spirit could overcome the most imposing obstacles. Rarely did Mussolini's subordinates summon the courage to dispute such dogma. Often, they believed it themselves.[8]

By 1936 the Fascist Grand Council had assumed the role of the supreme political assembly of the state. Originally the governing body of the Fascist Party, the Grand Council had evolved into a combination of cabinet and legislature as the constitutional system had withered. The Council varied from some thirty to forty members in the decade before World War II, including the major nonmilitary members of the Council of Ministers, the Presidents of the Senate and the Chamber of Deputies, the Secretary and Vice Secretary of the Fascist Party, the Chief of Staff of the Militia, the heads of the major Fascist syndicalist organizations, the President of the Special Tribunal for the Defense of the State, and a few other leading members of the party. The Council had no military members, as such. But Air Marshal Italo Balbo (Governor of Libya since January 1934), Marshal Emilio De Bono, and Admiral Costanzo Ciano (father of Galeazzo) held seats by virtue of their party credentials. Each represented the views of their military services. Many members of the Council also sat on the Supreme Defense Commission, adding to the ability of the Council to consider matters from an informed strategic and military viewpoint. However, the Council did not discuss strictly military affairs, and by 1936 rubber-stamp approval of proposed decrees had become the norm. The Grand Council held no meeting between 7 December 1939 and the fateful session of 24–25 July 1943, which provoked the downfall of the regime. As a result, in the December 1939–June 1940 period, the meetings of the Council of Ministers took on greater importance.

Throughout the years of Mussolini's rule, military matters were a frequent subject at Cabinet meetings. However, after 1933, when Mussolini held the portfolios of the three armed services, he himself represented the armed forces ministries at Council of Ministers sessions. The military under secretaries, always generals or admirals who did the actual work of running their ministries, were not invited. Under these circumstances, meaningful discussion rarely took place. Instead, Mussolini simply lectured his ministers on military matters. But in the months from December 1939 to June 1940, these pronouncements provided the ministers with the opportunity to ascertain Mussolini's plans for war, generating considerable discussion among themselves beyond the Duce's hearing.[9]

Since Mussolini and most *gerarchi* sat on two or three of these bodies, they could acquire a clear picture of Italy's military posture. At the same time, hardening psychological and ideological attitudes on Mussolini's part restricted the influence of this information upon him and thwarted the attempts of Mussolini's subordinates to persuade him to act prudently. After the conquest of Ethiopia in May 1936, Mussolini considerably decreased his previously frequent conversations with foreign and domestic visitors and withdrew into ever greater isolation. The death of his brother Arnaldo and the end of his twenty-year love affair with Margherita Sarfatti had already deprived him of his two closest human relationships. Claretta Petacci, with whom he commenced a love affair in late 1936, offered Mussolini diversion but no real companionship. As a result, he sank deeper into bitter loneliness and emotional deprivation, leading to increasing distrust and suspicion of his ministers.[10]

The partial exception was Galeazzo Ciano, who had married Edda Mussolini, the only one of the Duce's children to inherit something of their father's intelligence. Until August 1939, Ciano offered blind obedience and genuine hero worship to his father-in-law. In return, in the summer of 1936 Mussolini had handed over the day-to-day running of the entire government to his thirty-three-year-old Foreign Minister. Galeazzo and Edda Ciano shared an admiration of Nazi Germany, a loathing for France, and a deep suspicion of Britain and the United States. They were also determined to succeed the Duce and set about undermining his faith in his other ministers' opinions, including any contrary ideas about foreign policy. Since daily meetings with Ciano provided Mussolini with his main source of information on foreign affairs, his son-in-law's views shaped considerably the Duce's picture of the world.

In his solitude, Mussolini pondered history as he saw it. He became convinced that European civilization stood on the brink of an upheaval that could propel Italy to a position of world power. Mussolini came to believe that he alone possessed the understanding and ability to lead Italy through the coming crisis to triumph. No risk would be too great, because such an opportunity would not recur for centuries, nor would an Italian leader like him appear again. This view gave Mussolini the confidence to ally Italy with Nazi Germany. Despite all evidence to the contrary, Mussolini retained the conviction that he could dominate Hitler with his intellect and could yoke German power to the Italian chariot. Ciano encouraged him in this illusion until the spring of 1939. But even after his son-in-law came to recognize the errors of this foreign policy, Mussolini remained convinced that his genius would outweigh the material weakness of Italy vis-à-vis Germany.

When Mussolini fell under the influence of these meditations, the warnings of his advisers about Italy's lack of resources or military might struck him as childish. In fact, he gradually came to the conclusion that he could rule better without ministers at all, relying solely upon technicians and bureaucrats.[11] However, such periods of perceived infallibility afflicted Mussolini only intermittently. At other times, he judged matters with keen lucidity, guided by his high intelligence, his prodigious memory for facts and statistics, and his lengthy experience as a statesman and political leader. In times of crisis, such as during the February 1940 meeting of the Supreme Defense Commission, Mussolini displayed a clear understanding of the problems afflicting the Italian forces and the limits these placed on his actions.[12]

On these occasions, however, Mussolini still had difficulty appreciating the military potential of Italy and of other states. After World War II, General Mario Roatta, who had come to know Mussolini well, observed:

> While being, in general, a man who saw things in a wide perspective, [in military matters] he would seize upon a detail and attribute to it a decisive importance, while in that given moment or circumstance, it had only a secondary value. . . . The substance, the true essence of military questions, escaped him completely.[13]

For Mussolini's subordinates, deprived of the Duce's access to information, the problem was far greater. Not only did Mussolini restrict the flow of intelligence, but grave flaws afflicted the Italian acquisition and analysis system.

Intelligence Agencies and Personalities

Mussolini enjoyed a wealth of information on the military potential and strategic intentions of the nations surrounding Italy. His principal sources of intelligence were the three military intelligence services, the Foreign Ministry, the various police agencies under the Ministry of the Interior, the Ministry of Press and Propaganda (renamed the Ministry of Popular Culture in May 1937), the Fascist Militia, the Ministry of Colonies (renamed the Ministry of Italian Africa in April 1937), the Finance Ministry, the Bank of Italy and other financial institutions, executive agents and personal emissaries, and letters from, and conversations with, a wide range of foreign and domestic personalities, including heads of government, ministers, ambassadors, attachés and assorted notables.

Following the Ethiopian War, Mussolini's main source of information on the military and strategic posture of foreign states came through reports and publications. His most important suppliers were the military intelligence services: *Servizio Informazioni Militari* (SIM) for the army, *Servizio Informazioni Segreto* (SIS) for the navy, and *Servizio Informazioni Aeronautiche* (SIA) for the air force. Of these, SIM was the largest and most important and SIA the least significant, having only been created in 1935–36.[14]

SIM had acquired real vitality only in January 1934 with the appointment of Colonel Mario Roatta as its head. Roatta formed a close working relationship with Ciano, wedding the service more closely to Mussolini (and his son-in-law) than to the army leadership. However, Mussolini's reorganization of the armed forces high command on the eve of the Ethiopian War greatly strengthened the cooperation between the intelligence organizations and their chiefs of staff. Mussolini's assumption of the three armed forces ministerships in 1933 had given him too many responsibilities, and he turned over the majority of his ministerial duties to the under secretaries. In 1933–34, Mussolini appointed each of the under secretaries to be the chief of staff of his service, as well. This created the appearance of unity of administration and command. In reality, each of the deputy chiefs of staff assumed the duties of chief of staff, leaving two men at the top of each service struggling to carry out the obligations of three. Furthermore, since each of these men functioned at one step above their official assignment only through Mussolini's delegation of powers, each became particularly dependent on the dictator. Mussolini further cemented his control over the armed services by appointing true Fascists to the combined posts of under secretary and chief of staff: Federico Baistrocchi for the army, Giuseppe Valle for the air force, and Domenico Cavagnari for the navy. Mussolini made another ardent Fascist, Alberto Pariani, Deputy Chief of Staff of the Army in October 1934. In the case of the army, therefore, Roatta served under two military superiors as wedded to the regime as he was, and this relationship between the heads of SIM and the army high command continued until November 1939.[15]

Mussolini dismissed Baistrocchi in October 1936. Baistrocchi had pointed out that arms transfers to the Spanish Nationalists, coming on the heels of the Ethiopian War, thwarted the *Regio Esercito*'s preparations for a general European war. Mussolini replied to this honesty by replacing Baistrocchi with Pariani. After this, Pariani always demonstrated absolute loyalty, as well as fervent Fascism. One way the new Army Chief of Staff did this was by placing SIM entirely at the disposal of Ciano, recently appointed Foreign Minister. Thus, SIM became even more deeply involved in covert action, further diluting its effectiveness as an intelligence organization.[16]

As deputy chief of staff, Pariani had directed SIM's activities for more than two years. Roatta had enthusiastically cooperated by employing SIM in a wide range of clandestine political activities. However, Pariani and Roatta had understood the pressing need to expand SIM's intelligence activities and had the foresight to target both Britain and Germany as special new subjects of intense interest for Army Intelligence. They also had increased the number of SIM agents abroad, enlarged the radio intercept capacity of the service, and penetrated most of the embassies in Rome. Soon a considerable increase in the flow of intercepted and purloined diplomatic documents crossed Mussolini's and Ciano's desks and thickened the contents of SIM's daily intelligence summaries and monthly reports.

Nonetheless, SIM had great difficulty in supplying detailed reports on the strength and disposition of foreign armies and accurate appreciations of how the military strength of other states influenced their foreign policies. Still, Pariani did receive a remarkably accurate picture of British, French, and German strategic war plans, which he passed on to Mussolini and Ciano.[17] But what Mussolini primarily needed to know was *if* foreign governments were prepared to go to war, rather than their planning for such eventualities.

Unfortunately for SIM, Mussolini had come to expect such information. During the international crisis provoked by the Ethiopian War,

SIM had given him a precise picture of British naval and military dispositions in the Mediterranean, the Middle East, and northeast Africa. By revealing the inadequacy of British deployments, SIM's intelligence greatly assisted Mussolini to conclude that Britain would not go to war with Italy, unless provoked. At the same time, Dino Grandi, then Mussolini's Ambassador in London, had sent him an accurate description of the nonbelligerent attitude of the British Cabinet and of most of the ruling class. With these two sets of information, Mussolini had been able to act with just the right balance of daring and prudence.[18]

Thereafter, SIM exercised a far greater influence on Italian foreign policy. However, this success and Mussolini's consequent increase in self-confidence had resulted in such demands on SIM that it could no longer perform its primary functions in an adequate manner. The size and resources of the service, adequate for Italy as a regional power, were not sufficient after Mussolini decided to cast his nation in the role of a Continental, and even world, power. Furthermore, on a day-to-day basis, SIM acted on directives from the army leadership. Apart from Pariani, Mussolini's generals showed little interest in the world beyond the Mediterranean and the Balkans, while their continued distrust of SIM led to their refusal to inform the intelligence service of its own general staff's war plans. Consequently, SIM had little idea what investigations should receive priority in the allocation of its slender resources.

The other Italian foreign intelligence services could not compensate for SIM's deficiencies. SIA was too small, inexperienced, and narrowly focused on internal security and military police work. SIS did have a wider geographical range of interests than SIM and a worldwide agent network. But it still was a small, underfinanced organization with a purely naval orientation. Furthermore, even within its maritime sphere, SIS served a high command single-mindedly intent on war with France and utterly unwilling to prepare for war against the dreaded Royal Navy.

Mussolini's nonmilitary intelligence services provided him with information but no systematic analysis. The Ministry of Popular Culture, for example, supplied both Mussolini and Ciano with a wide range of foreign publications. Such sources offered useful details about events and thinking abroad, but they provided no context within which to interpret them. Thus, Mussolini could rely on the sensational *New York Daily News* to study American public opinion. When a well-informed individual did offer him an unwelcome but accurate net assessment, Mussolini could dismiss it as only one man's opinion.[19]

MEASUREMENTS OF MILITARY CAPABILITIES

No other nation's military experienced operations of the range or duration of those carried out by the *forze armate* in 1935–40. These included the two-front campaign against Ethiopia, the pacification operations that continued in East Africa up to Italian entry into World War II, Italian participation in the Spanish Civil War, and the invasion of Albania. In addition, the Italian armed forces underwent two general mobilizations, in the summers of 1935 and 1939, and limited alerts during the "Pirate Submarine" crisis of August 1937, the crisis preceding the Munich Conference, the confrontation with France from November 1938 to February 1939, and the tension during Mussolini's seizure of Albania that spring.

To these rich sources of experience were added major military maneuvers in Italy, the Mediterranean, and Libya during those same years. Paradoxically, actual Italian military operations in East Africa, Spain, Albania, and the Mediterranean proved less useful in shaping accurate net assessment than maneuvers, especially those of the army. From his victories, Mussolini received only the impression that his forces were generally effective.

In August 1937 Pariani held maneuvers both in western Sicily to test the army's new armored brigade and in the Veneto to demonstrate the effectiveness of a proposed new infantry division containing only two infantry regiments. The following spring, Pariani attended exercises in Libya to determine the feasibility of defense against invasion from Tunisia, while simultaneously mounting an attack on the Nile Delta that he and Balbo planned. After maneuvers east of Rome in August 1938, Pariani received Mussolini's permission to transform all the infantry divisions of the army to the two-regiment model, to create full armored divisions, and to join them with motorized divisions in a mechanized army based in the Po Valley. With such units Pariani believed that he could protect industrialized northern Italy from a French invasion, defend the western frontiers of Libya, and conquer Egypt as well. The final test of these concepts would take place at the August 1939 exercises.[20]

Despite these shows, the weaknesses of their forces in battle had

shocked many Italian officers since their engagements with the Ethiopi-
ans in late 1935. Reinforcing these concerns were problems encountered in combat over the next four and a half years. Reports on these
shortcomings had worked their way up the chain of command and had
been brought to Mussolini's attention. But he had either dismissed
them or assumed they were being corrected. Nonetheless such complaints had injected certain worries in the Duce's mind, although he
held them in check.

Even more difficult for Mussolini was an accurate appraisal of the
military effectiveness of his likely opponents (France, Britain, Yugoslavia, and Greece), possible opponents (the Soviet Union and Rumania),
and allies (Germany, Hungary, Nationalist Spain, and, perhaps, Bulgaria). None, save the Spanish Nationalists, engaged in major hostilities in
the 1935–39 period. Still, the Spanish Civil War did offer hints about
French capabilities and real lessons about those of the Germans. That
Mussolini and his lieutenants failed to appreciate these indications
points out one weakness in their net assessment system. It took the
events of August 1939 to May 1940 to make matters clearer. By then,
however, the previous failures of Italian judgment about the military
balance had placed the Fascist regime in a hopeless position.

As early as 1936, however, the Italian military leadership viewed
the condition of their individual services with varying degrees of
discontent. Even before the Ethiopian War, the army high command had
recognized the need for the total renovation of its artillery. Operations
in East Africa revealed other shortcomings in weapons and equipment,
and combat in Spain reinforced this awareness. But Mussolini made it
clear to Pariani that the needs of the navy and air force meant that the
army could not expect funds to begin to remedy its needs until
mid-1938.

However, Mussolini and Pariani did discuss the material shortcomings of the army frequently in the 1936–39 period. Furthermore,
starting in September 1938, at the time of the Czech crisis, Pariani
began regular meetings with Dallolio, the head of COGEFAG, and with
the Ministers of Finance and Exchange, the Governor of the Bank of
Italy, and major industrialists to coordinate and expand arms production
for the army. These interchanges made the serious weaknesses
afflicting the *Regio Esercito* clear to them all.[21]

But within the army a peculiar process of dishonesty prevented
forthright assessment of its problems. The example of the army's
appreciation of its tank forces is illustrative. Italian tank units in
Ethiopia had discovered the inadequacy of their poorly armed and

poorly armored fighting vehicles and the ineptness of their organization. In Spain, the Italians observed the superior armored equipment, doctrine, and organization of the Germans and Soviets. Italian tank commanders reported such matters to their superiors. The response, however, was either to dispute that such defects mattered or to issue false promises of hasty rectification. Until the fall of 1939, such attitudes extended to every other shortcoming in the *Regio Esercito*, with obvious impact upon its ability to judge itself or its likely opponents.[22]

Pariani therefore expressed a high degree of unwarranted optimism about the effectiveness of the army. Partly, this resulted from wishful thinking and from a self-serving desire to please Mussolini. The Army Chief of Staff also placed great hopes in the use of poison gas. Italian employment of chemical weapons in Ethiopia had greatly impressed Pariani. He had given some thought to using poison gas against the Spanish Republicans but had decided against it, apparently to keep Italian chemical warfare developments secret. But Pariani had every intention of using chemical weapons in a general European war. Convinced about Italian ability to employ gas offensively and to defend against it, Pariani faced the possibility of a general war with aplomb. He seemed to believe that the use of chemical weapons could alone redress the balance of force in Italy's favor.[23]

Similar attitudes made it even more difficult for the air force leadership to evaluate the weaknesses of their service. *Regia Aeronautica* involvement in Spain disrupted plans to expand from 115 to 170 squadrons by spring 1938. Scarce funds and hundreds of aircraft were diverted to support operations. New questions about the direction of air force development arose from lessons learned from combat in the Spanish skies and from contact with the Luftwaffe. Many air force commanders became disillusioned with Douhet's grandiose ideas and were attracted to building a bomber force for ground attack missions. Seeing the new German fighter aircraft in action and growing awareness of the capabilities of the British Hurricanes and Spitfires convinced many Italian fighter commanders that the air force had to abandon its attachment to biplanes. Meanwhile, operations in Spain steadily chipped away at air force strength. In late December 1937, the *Regia Aeronautica* counted 1,670 aircraft; by late December 1938, the number had fallen to 1,147, of which only 930 were combat-ready. Hopes for air force expansion in the near future collapsed.[24]

Nonetheless, Valle resisted a radical change of direction. To renounce Douhet's theories meant to reject the paramount role for the

Regia Aeronautica in a future general war. The Air Force Chief of Staff hesitated to abandon the biplane, which had proved so effective in Spain. After all, by the end of the war the Italians had lost only 73 biplanes in aerial combat while downing at least 450 enemy aircraft. Furthermore, building large numbers of all-metal, mono-wing fighters would prove fabulously expensive.[25] Valle also knew that the concentration of Italian industry in the Po Valley, especially aircraft factories, left it highly vulnerable to bombing attacks. To shift aircraft assembly to new and more easily defended plants in the south and to order large numbers of new fighters would both disrupt aircraft construction and shift resources away from bomber production.[26]

By refusing to change course, Valle ignored the deficiencies plaguing the *Regia Aeronautica*. Whatever the validity of Douhet's theories, air force problems made implementation impossible. Bomber pilots were generally poor and unable to place their ordnance on target; all aircrew training suffered from orders to save scarce and costly fuel; engines supplied by Italian industry were woefully underpowered; and the air force certainly lacked anything like the numbers or kinds of bombers called for by Douhet's concepts. In reality, the air force leadership knew that it had no effective doctrine whatsoever.

In early 1938, Valle did award the first contracts for experimental modern fighters. Simultaneously, he ordered the development of another biplane. Only in mid-1939 did he abandon biplane development and settle on metal monoplanes. But Valle chose the inferior designs of those available. He appears to have been bribed.[27]

For the naval leadership, awareness of the weaknesses of the *Regia Marina* revolved around one problem. The Italian navy had always prepared for a conflict with the French. From 1935 onward, however, Cavagnari and his admirals had to plan for a contest with Britain, for which they had no stomach. To make matters worse, Italian warships had been specifically designed for combat with French vessels. Given the extended building times for Italian ships owing to shortages of raw materials and of skilled workers, this included all major warships that would enter service through 1943.

Cavagnari worsened the problem by wishful thinking and passive acceptance of Mussolini's authority. During the Ethiopian War, the *Regia Marina* had made significant progress on the development of new surface and underwater assault weapons, which offered great hopes for success against the Royal Navy. The 1935–36 crisis had also underscored the efficacy of extensive mine warfare to counter the British. But once the immediate danger of war passed, Cavagnari withdrew support for these programs, concentrating his scarce resources on submarines and battleships.[28]

The admiral believed Mussolini's assurances that he would avoid a general war until Italy and its navy were prepared. Furthermore, as a proponent of the battleship, Cavagnari fully accepted Mussolini's directives to prepare the *Regia Marina* to strike offensively with its battlefleet once the conflict began. Nor did he contest Mussolini's exaggerated expectations of what Italian submarines might accomplish in the Mediterranean. Yet Cavagnari recognized that his fleet could not carry out such offensive operations against both the British and the French. He knew it would be difficult simply to protect the convoy routes to Libya.[29]

While the chiefs of staff knew the deficiencies of their own services, they did not readily reveal them to each other or to Badoglio. The lack of a combined general staff hindered the dissemination of such information by other channels. When Mussolini authorized Badoglio to convene conferences of the chiefs of staff, some problems of a particular service might be revealed to all, but generally the service chiefs planned in isolation and in ignorance of their counterparts' capabilities and disabilities.

When they discussed strategic planning during their rare joint meetings, each chief revealed the insularity of his thinking. In the meeting of 2 December 1937, for example, Pariani asked for support for an offensive from Cyrenaica to seize the Suez Canal, in case of war with Britain. But Cavagnari and Valle demanded freedom to conduct independent sea and air wars. Valle rejected the admiral's demands for air support, while Cavagnari rejected employing the fleet to supply Pariani's proposed operations in North Africa. Badoglio thought that Pariani's plans were unrealistic and that there should be close air force–navy cooperation. Yet the marshal lacked authority to impose his views.[30]

Mussolini, the King, and Badoglio had a clearer picture of the overall situation, but Mussolini alone seems to have had access to all available relevant information on the state of his armed forces. Furthermore, he knew the details of the Italian setbacks in Ethiopia and Spain, and of the bungled invasion of Albania.[31] Save for the period of the Czech Crisis in September 1938, what mitigated his anxiety was Mussolini's conviction that he could avoid a major war until 1943. Mussolini also convinced himself he could engage France in an isolated conflict. He would fight Britain only after victory over France and in alliance with a powerful Germany. This final conflict would take place sometime in the mid- or late 1940s. By then, Italy would have rebuilt its forces. Mussolini's disclosure of this scenario did much to lessen his subordinates' worries. Furthermore, despite the repeated war scares since 1935, the Duce not only avoided a major war but had achieved his territorial and political objectives. These successes offered the chiefs of staff even more reassurance that their forces would not be put to any major test until fully prepared.[32]

THE PACT OF STEEL AND THE
OUTBREAK OF WAR

Following the Munich Conference, Mussolini remained seriously confused about the European balance of power. His greatest error was to believe that Italy possessed the means to maintain the Munich settlement until it suited him to upset it. The limited mobilization of September 1938 had revealed the disarray of the *forze armate.* Mussolini knew that the modernization of his forces was years from completion. Yet he acted as if this counted for little. Instead, he seems to have believed that his political genius and willpower could overcome any obstacle.[33]

In late 1938 Mussolini assumed that he could secure Italian influence in the Balkans by seizing Albania and erecting a barrier to German expansion consisting of an Italian-led coalition of Poland, Hungary, and Yugoslavia (or an independent Croatia). Furthermore, Mussolini believed that he could deflect Hitler's interest from Europe temporarily by synchronizing Italian claims on French territory with German demands for the old German colonies. Finally, Mussolini considered the British to be so cowed by the Axis that they would abandon France in favor of an understanding with Italy. Then Italy could attack France and gain Nice, Corsica, Tunisia, and Jibuti.

Mussolini revealed his thinking to the Fascist Grand Council on 4 February 1939. He described Italy as a "prisoner in the Mediterranean." The nation would have to break out or be strangled. The time was fast approaching, however, when Italy would take action to gain access to the oceans. Mussolini proposed a war with France first and envisioned primarily an aero-naval contest. Just how such a war would lead to conquest of the territories Mussolini sought, he did not say. Nor did he expect to be ready before 1942, but suggested that the French might simply surrender in the face of Italian might.[34] News of these fantasies reached not only the King, whom Mussolini did not want

informed, but also French intelligence. The French began pressuring
the British to resist the Italians.[35] Already Chamberlain had rejected
Mussolini's offer of a special relationship and Hitler had refused to
support Mussolini's attempted intimidation of France. Then Mussolini's
schemes unraveled.

The French rebuffed Italian efforts to bully them. Prince Paul of
Yugoslavia dismissed his pro-Italian prime minister. Hitler seized the
remnants of Czechoslovakia without any warning. Yet the Duce continued to insist that Italy could wage a war with France and persuade the
British to remain neutral. True, some developments had favored Italy.
By acquiring Ruthenia in March 1939, Hungary gained a common
border with Poland. Later that month, the Nationalists achieved
complete victory in Spain. In April the Italians seized Albania as some
compensation for Hitler's destruction of the Munich settlement. But
the balance of power in Europe had now tipped in German favor.
Furthermore, these acts of Axis aggression were followed by the
announcement of Franco-British guarantees to Greece and Rumania;
then came separate British and French security treaties with Turkey in
May and June. Both the British and the French accelerated rearmament
and began serious war preparations. In April the British took the
unprecedented step of introducing peacetime conscription.

In May 1939 Mussolini responded to the Franco-British security
arrangements, as well as in hopes of restraining Hitler, by agreeing to
the offensive-defensive military alliance with Germany known as the
Pact of Steel. But soon after, Mussolini informed Hitler that Italy could
not be ready for war until the beginning of 1943 at the earliest.
Negotiations with the Spanish in June and July, aimed at offsetting the
recent Franco-British security agreements, indicated the need for an
even longer period of peace. Franco told Ciano that the Spanish were
too exhausted to join the Italians in another conflict until at least 1944.
In view of plans for Spanish construction of a large fleet, including four
battleships modeled on the Italian *Littorio* class, the date could be even
later.[36]

Even before the signing of the alliance with Germany, Mussolini
had authorized Pariani to meet with General Wilhelm Keitel in early
April for military discussions. These were followed by similar talks
between Valle and General Erhard Milch in late May, and between
Cavagnari and Admiral Erich Raeder a month later. In late June Valle
held additional talks with Göring. Both parties agreed that their forces
would not be ready for a clash with the West until 1942–43. Neither
gave the other a very precise idea of his planning. No plans were made

to create joint staffs. Underneath the boasting both engaged in, the Germans sensed Italian insecurity, while the Italians were impressed with growing German might.[37]

While accomplishing little else, these talks reinforced Mussolini's belated recognition of Italian military and economic weakness. In late July he decided to seek a meeting with Hitler. Since early May he had known the Germans were seeking a comprehensive agreement with the Soviets, and he feared the consequences. Mussolini hoped to gain a firm commitment to avoid war until Italy was ready. Furthermore, he sought agreement for a conference with Chamberlain and Daladier. Such a meeting, Mussolini believed, could allow the Axis to extract fresh concessions from the craven Western powers. Instead, the unexpected events of August 1939 showed Mussolini that he had already lost much of his ability to influence developments. The maneuvers of the newly created Sixth Army in the western Po Valley offered the first proof.[38]

In the Sixth Army, Pariani had concentrated his new armored and motorized divisions, supposedly the pride of his forces. But the August 1939 maneuvers, even the military review that capped the exercise, provided a disastrous display of army unpreparedness. Chaos on the roads and railways, confusion in the assembly areas, and lack of minimal coordination during the maneuvers all revealed an army incapable of conducting mechanized warfare. The single company of medium tanks Pariani had managed to acquire were driven by the manufacturer's technical representatives disguised as soldiers. Pariani's new divisions lacked modern equipment altogether, and what vehicles they possessed were pitifully outmoded.

While the King and the *gerarchi* looked on in outraged embarrassment and the foreign military observers struggled to conceal their amusement, furious Italian generals rushed about screaming orders to set things right. During the final parade, the disgusted look on the face of the King and the ironic smiles of the assembled attachés summed up Pariani's accomplishments as they watched the best units in the Italian army pass by in a pathetic display of their wretched equipment. Two weeks later, when the King described the maneuvers to Ciano, he still could not contain his rage. Despite the efforts of the regime's propaganda organs, the state of the Italian army soon became public knowledge.[39]

After a hasty trip to Germany, Ciano reported to Mussolini on 13 August that Hitler was determined to invade Poland and expected Italy to plunge into war alongside Germany. Later that day Ciano brought along Pariani, Valle, and Cavagnari to buttress the Foreign Minister's

case that Italy was perilously unprepared. On 16 August, in a meeting
with Badoglio, Mussolini said that he intended to remain neutral. In
turn, Badoglio stressed the weaknesses of the *forze armate*. Before and
after an inspection of the frontier defenses, Marshal De Bono warned
Mussolini that the army was in no condition for war. Each time,
Mussolini agreed.

Nonetheless, Mussolini repeatedly changed his mind and surrendered to his burning desire to lead Italy into war. If he could not attack
France, he believed he might take advantage of the crisis to invade
Yugoslavia or Greece. News of the Nazi–Soviet Pact raised his hopes
that it might deter Franco-British action. Behind Ciano's back, Pariani
argued in favor of Italian intervention in the impending conflict. At the
same time, both Mussolini and Pariani were aware of the glaring
deficiencies of the army yet simultaneously denied the truth to each
other. Valle engaged in the same game with Mussolini in regard to the
air force. Italian net assessment had ceased to involve rational calculation and had come under the sway of wishful thinking—at least as far as
Mussolini was concerned.

Only on 26 August, after a further meeting encouraged by the King
and arranged by Ciano—with the chiefs of staff in tow—did Mussolini
finally admit that Italy must avoid conflict with the West, at least for the
time being. In a letter to Hitler, Mussolini explained he could not go to
war unless Italy received essential raw materials, 88mm anti-aircraft
guns, and machine tools for artillery production. Mussolini deliberately
listed requirements that he knew Hitler could not possibly supply. At
any rate, Italy did face real supply problems. For example, the Germans
had not delivered all the coal promised to the Italians in 1939. As a
result, the Italians held only one to two weeks' supply, a crippling
restraint on their arms industry. For these reasons, Mussolini and
Pariani continued to plan an attack on Yugoslavia. This seemed one
sure way to seize the raw materials the Italians needed.[40]

Meanwhile, as a precautionary measure, the armed forces mobilized. The disorder produced by the call-up of the army's reserves
showed that Pariani had failed utterly to improve matters since the
Czech crisis. Mussolini already knew of the army's lack of artillery and
the weaknesses of the armaments industry. The maneuvers of early
August had revealed the pitiful state of mechanization. By early
September, however, mobilization revealed an army almost literally
naked and roofless. Severe shortages of uniforms and equipment,
compounded by administrative incompetence, produced chaos. Tens of
thousands of reservists camped in the streets near their mobilization

centers in the single set of civilian clothes they had arrived wearing. When the army could provide food, it was inedible. But even if clothing and food had been abundant, the army would still have been an empty shell. Weapons and ammunition were virtually unavailable for the reserves.

These deficiencies had a devastating influence upon morale. But even before the reservists had reported, they had demonstrated a disturbing lack of discipline and martial spirit. At one point on the Alpine frontier, troops fraternized with the French. These incidents thoroughly alarmed Pariani. The army of 1939 did not even measure up to that of 1915, let alone his grandiose visions of armored Fascist legions ardent for combat and conquest.[41] Yet, as recent events indicated, such facts had come to play a secondary role in the Italian net assessment process. The divisions within the Italian leadership reflected disagreements not so much over the shortcomings of the *forze armate*—even Mussolini now admitted them—as over the best course of action for Italy. The key factor involved calculating German power.

No Italian leader, not even Ciano or the King, was pro-Western. But attitudes toward Germany among the *gerarchi* ranged from admiration to hatred. Some, perhaps Mussolini most of all, entertained both feelings. But where did Italian interests lie? The question was how to take advantage of the situation created by the war. Should Italy remain neutral, enter the conflict on the German side, or join the West against the Third Reich? This last option, of course, represented the antithesis of Mussolini's foreign policy since 1936. It implied, if not his overthrow, at least a reduction of his power.

NONBELLIGERENCE

Mussolini had avoided declaring Italy officially neutral, as his adoption of the formula "nonbelligerence" on 1 September 1939 to describe Italy's diplomatic situation indicated. But he writhed under his awareness that, after his bellicose posturing, he had nonetheless chosen neutrality. He took solace in the fact that the war had broken out at a most inconvenient moment for Italy. But if the war continued, he intended to join Germany in the conflict at the appropriate moment, after Italy was ready. He refused to consider joining the West under any circumstances. These attitudes were encouraged by the most extreme Fascist leaders, as well as by Pariani. Like Mussolini, they feared that a break with Germany ultimately would mean the end of their power.[42]

Others, particularly Ciano, preferred indefinite neutrality, to profit from trade with both sides. Mussolini had brought the economy to the verge of collapse by his wars in East Africa and Spain, added to his ruinous armaments program. The war had delivered an unexpected opportunity to restore the health of Italian state finances. Ciano expected the conflict to last for years. Eventually, the Foreign Minister believed, a major shift in the European balance of power would dictate Italian intervention on the winning side. Furthermore, Ciano foresaw the possibility of active participation by the Soviet Union in the struggle on the German side. In that case, he advocated immediate Italian intervention on the Western side to prevent the spread of Bolshevism.[43]

When it became clear that the French would respect Italian "nonbelligerence," Mussolini ordered a partial demobilization. Planning for an invasion of Yugoslavia continued. But Pariani informed his commanders that such operations would occur no earlier than April 1940. Meanwhile, on orders from the Duce, Pariani had begun preparing the army as well as he could for a general war.

After he gained a clear picture of the situation, the Army Chief of Staff set a goal of acquiring enough small arms, uniforms, and supplies to equip an army of some 2.5 million men and 64 divisions by 1 May 1940. As more equipment became available, Pariani planned to expand the army to 126 divisions. As a result of his conversion of the army to two-infantry-regiment divisions, manpower for so many new units would be no problem. But Pariani realized that he could not expect even minimally sufficient numbers of modern tanks or artillery until 1942. Lack of anti-aircraft guns to protect Italian cities presented a particularly serious problem and greatly worried Mussolini. Yet, despite his professed enthusiasm for war in August, Pariani had known of these shortcomings in detail since at least May and probably earlier.[44]

As knowledge of their incompetence and dishonesty spread, Mussolini came to the painful conclusion that he must dismiss Pariani and Valle. Still, while the two generals had lied to him about the efficiency of their services, Mussolini had always known the truth, at least in its general outlines. Furthermore, Pariani and Valle had been loyal Fascists and had shown enthusiasm for war with the West. These were rare qualities among Mussolini's military leadership. But Mussolini needed scapegoats to explain the mess into which the army and air force had fallen. As both War and Air Force Minister, these were Mussolini's responsibilities. But it was politically necessary for Pariani and Valle to take the blame.

Finally, on 31 October 1939, Mussolini dismissed Pariani and Valle, while retaining the more competent Cavagnari as head of the navy. In place of Valle, Mussolini appointed General Francesco Pricolo. Mussolini divided Pariani's old posts between General Ubaldo Soddu, who became War Under Secretary, and Marshal Rodolfo Graziani, who became Army Chief of Staff. To assist Graziani, who lacked general staff experience, Mussolini brought back Roatta from Berlin, where he had been serving as military attaché. The former head of SIM became Army Deputy Chief of Staff.[45]

Unhappy with SIM's recent performance, Mussolini gave it a new head, General Giacomo Carboni. But Carboni faced serious difficulties since the new arrangement for control of the army placed him under Roatta for intelligence functions but under Soddu for administration. Worse, Carboni and Soddu were bitter rivals.[46] Under Badoglio's direction the new military leadership gave priority to determining the true state of the *forze armate,* particularly the army and air force. Despite recent revelations, Pariani had left office insisting that the army was able to field 38 combat-ready divisions. Upon his departure, Valle claimed the air force had 8,500 aircraft. In fact, the figures presented to Badoglio on 1 November revealed the army possessed only 10 effective divisions and the air force some 1,800 combat-ready aircraft. But, as Pricolo determined, modern planes actually airworthy numbered only 850. Furthermore, each of the services suffered from crippling shortages of fuel and ammunition, and could offer virtually no anti-aircraft protection either to themselves or to Italian cities.[47]

When the chiefs of staff, their deputies, and Soddu met with him on 18 November, Badoglio reiterated the policy he had insisted upon since September. Given the circumstances, the armed forces must concentrate on ensuring the defense of the borders, creating adequate anti-aircraft defenses, and assembling stockpiles. Any plans for offensive land operations must be abandoned for the foreseeable future. Badoglio deliberately refrained from discussing war plans. The marshal estimated that, with hard work, the military might be ready for war in twenty-four to thirty months but not in 1940.[48]

Three weeks later, Mussolini received an even more sobering appreciation from General Carlo Favagrossa, who had succeeded Dallolio as head of COGEFAG in August. Based on guesswork and optimistic projections, Favagrossa calculated that if Italian industry received all the raw materials required, it would still take at least until 1944 to produce most of the weapons and equipment needed to make the army combat efficient. The artillery program could not be completed until the end of 1949. The navy and air force faced a less serious situation. Most air force needs could be met by mid-1941, and most of the navy's by late 1943. The next day, during a meeting with the chiefs of staff, Mussolini agreed to drop Pariani's plans and to aim at a target of 73 divisions, of which 60 were to be ready by August 1940.[49]

Throughout the fall of 1939, the *forze armate* leadership struggled to understand the nature of the unfolding war. Reports of officers, including Roatta, who had been able to visit Poland and the study of the Polish campaign compiled by SIM created considerable grounds for worry. The Italian observers ascribed the Germans' victory to their superior numbers, the devastating power of the Luftwaffe, and Polish errors. The destruction inflicted on both the Polish forces and Warsaw greatly impressed the Italians. But the Italians gained only limited appreciation of German combined arms mechanized warfare, describing it as audacious but perhaps effective only against an inferior opponent. Employed against the French, such methods might fail, Roatta thought.[50]

Still, such reports emphasized Italy's unpreparedness by stressing the importance of the modern aircraft, tanks, artillery, anti-aircraft guns, and radios it lacked. When these reports reached the Sixth Army, they produced consternation. Better acquainted than others with the rudiments of mechanized operations, the division commanders of the Sixth Army were forced to recognize the hopeless inferiority of their forces to both the Germans and the French.[51]

Yet the weakness of his armed forces did not impress Mussolini as they did his new military leadership. Throughout the fall of 1939 and into early 1940, he noted other factors. Refusal to react to Soviet aggression against both Poland and Finland impressed Mussolini as a sign of British and French cowardice. Such inaction indicated that he might be able to attack Yugoslavia or Greece with impunity. French diplomatic feelers in early September, offering to consider Italian colonial demands, indicated fear and weakness. Fascist spirit might matter more than the superior numbers of Western arms, he thought. SIM reports from Finland showed how courage could defeat overwhelming strength. Other SIM reports reinforced Mussolini's perception of the rotten morale of both the French army and the French people, yet also described the German internal front as fragile.[52]

As a result, until March 1940 Mussolini saw possibilities for a peace settlement. Such a solution would create a respite during which Italy could prepare for a future Axis conflict with the West. But all the while, Mussolini pressed military preparations. Barring a settlement, he expected that events would await the moment of Italian readiness. Even before the war began, Mussolini had believed that the Maginot and Siegfried lines made major land offensives in the west impossible. The inactivity from September 1939 to May 1940 reinforced that opinion. He thought that the war could continue for years, possibly longer than World War I.

However, Mussolini judged the Germans to be in a far stronger position than in World War I. Eventually, he foresaw that the balance would tip in their favor. At that point, Italy would enter the struggle to wage a parallel war against the West. This would probably provoke American intervention to save Britain from collapse, but the Axis would win before significant American help arrived.

Mussolini would rely primarily on his navy and air force to conduct war in the Mediterranean. To the Italian army would fall the easier task of defending the Alpine frontier and Libya, while conducting offensive operations in East Africa. Yugoslavia and Greece could not withstand the hammer blows of the Italian air force, leaving little resistance for the army to overcome in the Balkans. Meanwhile, Germany would overrun France. Of course, Germany would emerge very powerful from such a war. For that reason, Mussolini rushed the completion of the powerful line of fortifications along Italy's northern borders begun a year earlier. These would ensure the nation's security once all of Europe to the north fell under German domination.[53]

Yet for the first six months of World War II, the Italian government took on a decidedly anti-German cast. When Mussolini had dismissed Pariani and Valle, he also had replaced many of his ministers. The new Cabinet contained many political allies of Ciano, creating the impression that Mussolini had relinquished control of foreign policy to his son-in-law.

At the Fascist Grand Council meeting of 7 December, Ciano described the course of Italian–German relations over the previous four years, documenting every instance of German perfidy. When Mussolini spoke, he appeared defensive about the predicament in which he had placed Italy. But he stressed the danger of indefinite neutrality. If either side emerged clearly victorious, it would place the Italians beneath its yoke. Therefore, it would be best if the two sides tore each other to shreds. Nonetheless, he made it clear that he considered a British victory more dangerous than a German one and insisted on continued adherence to the Pact of Steel. He listed the armaments he expected the *forze armate* to acquire over the next eighteen months, leaving little doubt that he hoped to intervene during the second half of 1941.[54]

On 16 December, Ciano spoke to the Chamber of Deputies,

justifying Italian "nonbelligerence" by a none-too-subtle description of recent German behavior. Mussolini had approved Ciano's criticisms of the Germans to justify Italian neutrality, but when both Balbo and Grandi suggested that Italy denounce the Pact of Steel, the Duce expressed rage. Mussolini's loyalty to Hitler even survived credible reports of German designs on northern Italy. At first, Mussolini sought retaliation. When he received reports from the Italian military attaché in Berlin of an impending German attack on the Low Countries, he ordered Ciano to pass the information to the Dutch and Belgian ambassadors on 26 December. But Mussolini seems to have been motivated more by a desire to delay any decisive German offensive than by a wish for a German defeat. In any case, his anger at the Germans soon passed, and the events of December 1939 marked the nadir of Axis relations.[55]

Shortly after Christmas, Mussolini resumed his personal direction of foreign policy. In a letter delivered to Hitler on 5 January 1940, Mussolini urged him to consider ending the war with Britain and France, consolidating German gains in Poland, and then embarking on a war of conquest against the Soviet Union. The Western democracies were in the process of dissolution from their internal weaknesses, Mussolini argued, and it would be better to await their self-destruction. But, if Hitler was determined to continue the war with the West, Mussolini pledged to enter the conflict on the German side, when Italy was strong enough to be of significant assistance. In essence, Mussolini sought to defer Hitler's attack on the West, not to deter it.[56]

Hitler did not reply for two months. In the meantime, Ciano's belief that Italy could grow both rich and militarily powerful through prolonged neutrality proved illusory. Instead, Italy grew more reliant on German economic assistance. At the same time, hopes for major increases in the production of Italian arms faded. Even before the German victories of April–May 1940, Italian vulnerability and dependency already had made a break with Germany unlikely.

The Italians needed hard currency to pay for the imported coal and raw materials required for arms production. For years, the main source of such exchange had been Italian arms sales abroad, especially aircraft and warships. After September 1939 the Italians attempted to acquire as much foreign exchange as they could from weapons sales to neutral countries. Despite Cavagnari's desperate attempts to build up his navy, for example, Italian shipyards had accepted orders for two light cruisers for Siam in late 1939. Two destroyer escorts were sold to Sweden in 1940. But the high cost of imported raw materials left the Italians with slim profit margins in hard currency. Sales to neutrals simply did not provide enough foreign exchange. Thus, despite the obvious contradictions involved, Mussolini had approved arms sales to Britain and France in September 1939, and trainer aircraft and ammunition exports to France continued until late May 1940.

These sales hardly solved the Italians' problems in regard to foreign exchange and weapons production. Mussolini's decision to supply the Finns with arms and aircraft for their war with the Soviets, as well as the needs of the Hungarians for 500 million lire worth of Italian weaponry, placed additional burdens on the arms industry. By late December 1939 the Italians had become desperate enough to demand the return of artillery sold to the Spanish Nationalists during the civil war. Making matters worse, the Italians were competing with the Germans over arms sales to the Balkan states in return for raw materials. The Germans were selling arms to Greece and Yugoslavia, both Mussolini's potential victims. Most infuriating, the Italians discovered that the Germans had sold the Yugoslavs the very 88mm anti-aircraft guns the Italians had been begging for since August, while Göring had insisted that the Luftwaffe had none to spare. At the same time, in response to Soviet protests, the Germans blocked the transit of Italian arms to Finland. These matters were reported to Mussolini in detail.[57]

In mid-January 1940 the British offered the Italians a huge arms contract: 1.2 billion lire worth of hard currency for aircraft and antitank and anti-aircraft guns, and the equivalent of 500 million lire more for foodstuffs and raw materials. A few days later the British threw in an additional offer to purchase 380 million lire worth of Italian agricultural products, a grand total of nearly 2.1 billion lire in hard currency. Since the entire Italian military budget for 1939–40 stood at 28 billion lire, Mussolini could not sell so many weapons without crippling his rearmament plans. In addition, he considered such a deal dishonorable, however lucrative it might be and however treacherous the Germans had proved to be. The Duce not only ordered Ciano to reject the British offer, he canceled an existing contract for the sale of 400 light bombers, worth 680 million lire. To make up for the resultant lack of hard currency, he authorized the Bank of Italy to release 1 billion lire of its slender 2.3 billion lire gold reserves to pay for imports of British coal.

In retaliation for Mussolini's arms embargo, the British cut off the seaborne supplies of German coal they had previously allowed the Italians to receive through neutral ports, effective 1 March. This amounted to some 50 percent of Italian requirements and threatened to bring Italian industry to a halt. In the coldest winter in memory, this action would also threaten the Italian people with real misery. But with its reserves of hard currency nearly exhausted, and prevented by Mussolini's veto from selling enough arms to obtain more, the government could buy neither coal nor sufficient amounts of raw materials from abroad.[58]

Already, at the meeting of the Supreme Defense Commission in early February, the inability to supply the needs of the arms industry had become painfully obvious. The conflicts between available Italian resources and the weapons programs of the *forze armate* led to angry words. Raffaello Riccardi, the Minister of Exchange and Currency, pointed out that if the armed forces reached the weapons and manpower levels set by Mussolini, Italy would have to import 22 billion lire worth of raw materials in wartime. Riccardi proposed a far more modest weapons program, warning Mussolini that Italy faced imminent bankruptcy. Graziani replied with bombast, accusing Riccardi of impugning the patriotism of the army. Mussolini also defended the armed forces but offered no rebuttal to Riccardi. He simply stated that he would strip the country bare to supply the needs of the military.[59] Hitler came to Mussolini's rescue, promising to meet all Italian needs for coal, as well as for other raw material, under a barter agreement. The two countries reached agreement on 13 March, and thereafter Italy faced neither bankruptcy nor industrial vassalage to Britain.[60]

Ribbentrop arrived in Rome bearing Hitler's reply to Mussolini's January letter, and he conferred with the Duce on 10 and 11 March. Ribbentrop announced that Hitler intended to attack in the West during the summer of 1940. Greatly exaggerating the strength of the Wehrmacht, he stated that it would breach the Maginot Line with ease. At first Mussolini exhibited some doubts over Ribbentrop's optimism, but he agreed that Western morale was poor. Several overnight readings of Hitler's letter, which expressed determination to continue the war to complete victory and stressed the common interests of Italy and Germany, seemed to convince him. The next day, warming to the possibilities, Mussolini agreed that the Axis enjoyed the strength of superior numbers. His army alone would number 2 million men by May, half of them fully prepared for war. While Italy would face serious opposition on land and could not afford a long war, the Duce announced that Italy would enter the war at the appropriate moment. His navy would drive the British from the Mediterranean and free Italy from foreign tyranny in its own sea. Mussolini agreed to meet Hitler soon to discuss his momentous decision.

But soon Mussolini had second thoughts about the promises he had made. In particular, the idea of a German offensive in the West worried him. German success would leave an unprepared Italy trailing in the dust. A German defeat would place Italy at the mercy of Britain and France. When Ribbentrop telephoned to arrange a meeting with Hitler, Mussolini expressed irritation at the demand for an immediate conference. But, upon reflection, he decided he should meet Hitler soon, to dissuade him from attacking before Italy was ready. Nonetheless, as Ciano observed, Mussolini feared being excluded from great events even more than he worried about Italian unpreparedness.[61]

THE DECISION FOR WAR

Four days later Ciano accompanied Mussolini to the Brenner Pass. After they met, Hitler argued that a negotiated settlement to the war remained impossible. He exaggerated the strength of the German forces, insisting that he intended to attack and win the war by fall. But Germany might need help, and Hitler suggested that Mussolini send an army group to southern Germany to participate in the offensive. The Italians would advance parallel to the Swiss frontier, wheel leftward, and attack down the Rhône Valley, thus turning the French Alpine front from the rear. Perhaps Mussolini's limited grasp of German caused him to misunderstand Hitler's proposal, or else he may have understood but preferred to avoid a specific commitment. In any case, the Duce replied that his navy and air force would be ready in three to four months. It seems that Hitler ignored this broad hint that the Italian army could not undertake major offensive operations.

The dictators did agree that Germany would strike first, since Italy could not sustain a lengthy struggle. If operations developed favorably, Italy would intervene a few weeks later. If the German offensive stalled, Italy would remain out of the fighting until a decision appeared imminent. Afterward, Mussolini told Ciano that he expected Hitler to think carefully before launching any offensive.[62]

But over the next few weeks Mussolini wavered considerably in his opinion about what Hitler might do. After all, if the Germans were as powerful as Hitler had claimed, why had he asked for Italian assistance? Why were the Germans unable to deliver the anti-aircraft guns and machine tools that they had long promised the Italians? Mussolini also remained convinced that the Wehrmacht could not crack the Maginot Line.

But, as the days passed, he concluded that Hitler would attack in the west. Mussolini decided that he must enter the conflict, despite the condition of the army. But he would choose the time for his intervention carefully and limit Italian operations to a land campaign in East Africa and an aero-naval offensive in the Mediterranean.[63]

Mussolini had stressed the importance of his meeting with Hitler to the King, though he stated that he did not expect a German offensive soon. Vittorio Emanuele III decided that Mussolini was leading Italy to disaster. Royal representatives had already contacted Ciano about overthrowing the Duce. When he was approached by Prince Umberto in late March, however, Ciano declined to act. Meanwhile, Mussolini seems to have learned of the royal conspiracy and came close to dismissing Ciano. In the end, he did not. Ciano was simply the most prominent of those *gerarchi* who had doubted the wisdom of Mussolini's policy. Now many of his lieutenants had begun to accept Mussolini's analysis of the situation, leaving Ciano isolated.

Even Ciano approved of a war against the West if German victory seemed certain. The British blockade had driven home Mussolini's concept of Italy as a prisoner in the Mediterranean. Italy must gain free access to the oceans and secure the status of a true world power or suffocate. It could do so only through a war against the British and French. With most *gerarchi* now converted to these ideas, the King could only try to delay Italian entry into the war. He had the support of Badoglio, who believed that the Germans could not win and that Italy could not be ready until late 1942. But many generals, prominently Graziani, now supported Mussolini.

On 31 March the Duce committed his strategic ideas to paper. But he waited four days before sending his memorandum to the King and two more before distributing it to his lieutenants and the military leadership. In the meantime, in Cabinet meetings, he insisted on the necessity of war and the certainty of Axis victory. But, as Ciano, Grandi, and Giuseppe Bottai, the Minister of National Education, agreed, Mussolini was trying to convince himself more than his audience.[64]

In his memorandum, Mussolini reiterated many ideas he had been expressing in recent days. He had been heavily influenced by recent intelligence reports describing German morale as quite poor. But Mussolini also was convinced that internal rot afflicted the West. Therefore, Mussolini rejected the possibilities both of a negotiated peace and of a land offensive by either side. The West, he claimed, lacked the stomach for such an attack, while the Germans had already achieved what they wanted in Poland and would not "gamble everything on a single card." Instead, Germany would remain on the strategic defensive but would break the British blockade by expanded air and sea operations.

Italy had to enter the war. Neutrality would mean resignation to insignificance, reduction to "the level of a Switzerland multiplied by ten." To join the West, however, would mean immediate attack by Germany. But Britain and France would abandon Italy as they had Poland and Finland. Thus, Italy would have to enter the war on the German side, to gain supremacy over the Mediterranean and access to the open seas. Nonetheless, Mussolini felt constrained by two factors: Italy's limited resources and Allied strength in the Mediterranean and the Middle East.[65]

Italian weakness required a short war. Italy would intervene only at the right moment, to realize purely Italian objectives in the Mediterranean. But intelligence reports were discouraging. SIM considered French defenses in the Alps, Tunisia, and Syria formidable. Army intelligence also believed the British in Egypt, the Sudan, British Somaliland, Aden, and Kenya presented a serious obstacle to Italian attack and threatened Ethiopia. SIA thought French air units in southern France and North Africa equaled or surpassed anything the *Regia Aeronautica* could send against them. It described RAF units in the Mediterranean, the Middle East, and East Africa in similar terms. Furthermore, a recent report from Finland described the modern Italian fighters sent to help the Finns as markedly inferior to French, British, and American aircraft.

SIM and SIA calculations of Allied force levels were gross overestimates. At the same time, the distrust of SIM by the army leadership made intelligence-gathering difficult. Badoglio never invited Carboni to chiefs of staff meetings, nor did he inform him of general staff planning. Nonetheless, some SIM and SIA reports, such as those on the quality of Italian equipment, were quite accurate. And all intelligence, both good and bad, formed the bases of the decisions made by Mussolini and his chiefs of staff.

In contrast, the Allied navies struck Mussolini as less imposing. SIS knew nothing about the night fighting capabilities and little of the radar that would give the Royal Navy such advantages in the Mediterranean. Since the *Regia Marina* impressed Mussolini as the best-prepared of his services, he assigned it the major role in his war plans, supported by the air force. Only in the improbable case of a French debacle would Mussolini order the army to attack in the Alps. If the opportunity arose, offensives might be mounted against Yugoslavia and Greece. Mussolini left it to Badoglio to develop plans for these contingencies.[66]

Badoglio met with the chiefs of staff and Soddu on the morning of 9 April. They discussed Mussolini's vague strategic directives at length and concluded they could do nothing. Even Graziani abandoned his facile optimism. Three days earlier he had received a gloomy study from Roatta. The deputy chief of staff had emphasized that the army could not hope to undertake offensive operations anywhere, except against France if it collapsed. Even then, a successful campaign would require massive amounts of German equipment and large numbers of German armored and motorized units transferred beforehand. However, Mussolini's concept of an independent, parallel Italian war made such reinforcements politically unacceptable.

All agreed that the armed forces were simply unprepared for war. Mussolini had forbidden virtually every form of action. As for the navy, to which Mussolini had assigned an active role, Badoglio and Soddu suggested that it conduct only a submarine campaign. Even that seemed too much for Cavagnari. "One [British] fleet will station itself at Gibraltar and another at Suez, we will strangle inside the Mediterranean," he lamented. Badoglio ended the inconclusive meeting by advising study of the matter and later reports on the possibilities.

Apparently, Badoglio had carried out the King's orders. When Badoglio reported on the meeting to Mussolini, he stated that only an overwhelming victory by the Germans would allow Italy to enter the war. A few days later, after the German military attaché asked Graziani about Hitler's project for an Italian offensive from southern Germany, Badoglio reacted even more negatively. Not only did the *Regio Esercito* lack the forces for such a scheme, but such an expedient would be truly humiliating. Furthermore, Badoglio argued, given the uncertain situation, even to discuss the matter with the Germans would be extremely unwise. The project for the operation died.

In a separate report, Cavagnari had warned Mussolini that even if Italy emerged victorious from the war, the *Regia Marina* would be annihilated in a conflict with the West. "Italy could reach the peace talks not only without territorial gains but even without a fleet and perhaps without an air force," the admiral concluded. In every way they could, the chiefs sought to hold back Mussolini from action.[67]

In early April Balbo, who was Governor of Libya, and the Duke of Aosta, who was Viceroy of Ethiopia, visited Rome. Both colonial governors reinforced the pessimistic assessments of the military situation. After first conferring with Balbo in Bengasi, the Duke reported in separate meetings with Mussolini and with Soddu, Ciano, and Badoglio that his forces could not defend Ethiopia against the British and French. Offensive operations were almost totally out of the question. During the same period, Balbo confessed to Mussolini and Ciano that an offensive against Egypt was impossible, given the state of his forces. He urgently needed modern arms just to defend Libya.[68]

At the very time that the chiefs of staff were meeting on 9 April, the Germans showed just how mistaken Mussolini was in his strategic appreciation. That morning, the Wehrmacht invaded Denmark and Norway. In successive letters to Mussolini, however, Hitler stressed that he still would attack France in the immediate future. Mussolini reacted to the Scandinavian campaign with excitement, seemingly ignoring Hitler's warning about a decisive attack in the west. With the Germans, French, and British engaged in Scandinavia, Mussolini reasoned, he would be free to act in the Balkans. He began speaking of an invasion of Yugoslavia, convincing himself that the West neither could nor would react.

But a meeting on 11 April with the King left Mussolini frustrated and gloomy. The King judged his memorandum of 31 March "geometric" in its logic but refused to countenance any Italian military intervention until Allied defeat was certain. Two days later Mussolini received another restraining message, this time from Franco. On 8 April, Mussolini had informed the Caudillo that Italy would intervene on the side of Germany and that the moment was approaching. The invitation for Spain to join Italy was implicit. Franco replied sympathetically, promising to do what he could to help Italy. But the condition of the Spanish economy and armed forces made his participation in the war impossible.[69]

However, these hesitations failed to deter the Duce. Over the next few days, the irrational side of Mussolini's nature won out in his thinking. Thereafter he judged the situation primarily according to Fascist mysticism. When Bottai entered the Duce's office on 15 April, he found Mussolini reading a volume of Mazzini's collected works. Mussolini referred to the fulminations of the Risorgimento prophet against Cavour's furtive diplomacy. Once again, Mussolini insisted, Italy had to choose between the path of greatness and virtue and that of convenient disloyalty to its promises. Mussolini whipped out documents he had ordered from the archives detailing military conventions between Italy and Germany under the Triple Alliance. As late as March 1914 the Italians had agreed to send forces to Germany to help execute the Schlieffen Plan. How could Italy betray its ally for a second time?

When Bottai protested that it had been the Germans who had betrayed the Italians in 1914, Mussolini dismissed the facts. Bottai made no further attempt to argue.[70]

However, Mussolini still hesitated to move. As usual, Hitler was not informing him of German intentions. Furthermore, despite repeated promises, the Germans continued to delay deliveries of anti-aircraft guns and machine tools. From Berlin, the Italian military attaché reported on 16 April that a German general had told him that the OKW now believed the war might drag on for four more years. At the same time, intelligence reports to Mussolini continued to describe Allied forces in the Mediterranean as powerful. True, Mussolini had begun suspecting that these reports were doctored to dissuade him from action. He knew that Carboni was both anti-German and close to Ciano. Still, Mussolini did not dismiss SIM's pessimistic descriptions of the military situation out of hand.[71]

On 20 April, Mussolini spoke to Ciano about coming into the war in the late summer. But just two days later, after an angry conversation with the King, Mussolini was thinking in terms of intervention no earlier than spring 1941. While the Duce despised the King's caution, objectivity temporarily restrained Mussolini's emotions. He recognized the danger of plunging unprepared into the conflict, and as he assured an audience of labor leaders on 21 April that he would proceed with all the caution of a cat. Searching for alternatives, Mussolini sought to satisfy his hunger for war by an attack on Yugoslavia. When the German Ambassador informed him on 25 April that Hitler had no objection if Mussolini sought to improve Italy's strategic position in the Balkans, Mussolini decided to move ahead.[72]

By late April, independent reports of impending German action in the Balkans reached Mussolini from a variety of sources. So did information that the Allies would move into the Balkans to counter the Germans. For Mussolini, everything counseled an Italian attack on Yugoslavia. If the Germans, the Soviets, the French, and the British intervened in the Balkans, Mussolini needed to secure at least the eastern shore of the Adriatic. Hitler's apparent go-ahead on 25 April removed that obstacle. Furthermore, as the days went by, sources in Paris indicated that the French would not consider an Italian attack on Yugoslavia to be hostile, if taken to counter German and Soviet moves into the region. It appeared Mussolini might be able to make major territorial gains, while still keeping out of the war until a more favorable moment.

Even an Allied move into the Balkans offered Mussolini one

advantage. SIM calculated that French forces in North Africa numbered some 314,000; British forces in Egypt about 100,000; and the French army in Syria in the area of 200,000. Even after mobilization, the Italian garrison in Libya would come to only 220,000. But if the French Syrian army landed in Greece, an Italian attack on Egypt might be feasible.

On 6 May the chiefs of staff met to discuss reinforcing Libya. Badoglio argued that the Italians in North Africa could not even defend themselves without massive reinforcement, let alone undertake offensive operations. The chiefs concurred. Plans for an attack on Yugoslavia were mentioned in passing, but as Badoglio emphasized, Mussolini's directives to study such an invasion "does not mean that we will have to do it." Obviously, Mussolini's hopes for some form of action were not shared by his military leaders.

Nonetheless, by 9 May the *Regia Aeronautica* had received permission to use Hungarian bases to attack Yugoslavia. The Hungarians had even indicated willingness to allow the Italian army to launch offensive operations from their territory. But these understandings seemed to have been reached without consultation between Mussolini and his chiefs of staff. Nonetheless, Mussolini told Ciano that he had won Badoglio's agreement. German successes in Norway had impressed the marshal, but Ciano had come to recognize the pattern of the Duce's wishful thinking. None of the Italian military leaders had dropped their opposition to intervention. They shared the opinion that the industrialist Alberto Pirelli had expressed to Mussolini in mid-April: "The truth is, *Presidente,* that there is an imbalance between your aspirations and the real forces of the country."[73]

THE FALL OF FRANCE AND ITALIAN
INTERVENTION

After news arrived of the German attack on the Low Countries early on 10 May, Ciano had to struggle to persuade Mussolini not to take any immediate action. Even Edda Mussolini arrived at the Palazzo Venezia to urge an immediate declaration of war. After much argument, Mussolini decided to wait. But Ciano thought that the opportunity had come to move against Yugoslavia. Mussolini agreed and set the date for early June.

Later that day, however, meetings with Graziani and Soddu left Mussolini furious. Both warned Mussolini that Italy could not afford the risk of joining the war, at least until the situation clarified. Once his anger passed, Mussolini's war fever cooled as well for a few days. But, on 13 May, the German advance convinced Mussolini to abandon any caution. He told Ciano that he had dropped the Yugoslav operation as a "humiliating expedient." The Italians would launch an aero-naval offensive against the French and British within a month. Ciano realized that he could no longer do anything to deter the Duce. Only a German military setback could stop Mussolini from entering the war.[74]

It took another week or so to indicate that nothing would stop the Germans. By 15 May Guderian's panzer corps was across the Meuse. Five days later German tanks had reached the Channel. The scale of German success was too much even for Mussolini. He began hoping for a second Battle of the Marne to reduce the scope of the German victory and allow Italian intervention to tip the balance, preferably in the autumn. He simply needed more time to prepare, and continued French resistance, even if ultimately futile, might weaken the Germans and help preserve something of a European balance of power.[75]

As May 1940 passed, however, Mussolini came under increasing pressure to join Hitler in the war. By the end of May, it seemed clear that French collapse was imminent. Increasingly desperate offers from Paris to satisfy any Italian grievances convinced Mussolini that despair was overwhelming the French government. Somewhat less frightened suggestions from London sent the same message. Mussolini decided he must intervene immediately, before the Germans grabbed everything for themselves.[76]

Many in the army high command had expected French resistance to stop the Germans, as in 1914. But as the dimensions of the German victory became evident, their reluctance to enter the war declined. By late May many generals enthusiastically approved of intervention. Nonetheless, Graziani warned Mussolini that the army was in no state to undertake offensive operations, even against Yugoslavia. Mussolini agreed, although he apparently neglected to inform Pricolo. The air staff continued to prepare for an imminent attack on Yugoslavia.[77]

The *gerarchi* and the Italian public also embraced the idea of entering the war alongside the invincible Germans. Ciano swallowed many of his previous doubts and dreamed of huge territorial gains. Control of the Mediterranean and the Balkans could allow Italy to maintain its independence from *Grossdeutschland*. Ciano also convinced himself that Hitler's respect for Mussolini would protect Italy—so long as the two dictators lived. On his own authority, Ciano flew off on a brief trip to Albania to arrange a private offensive against Greece, which the army high command had considered but rejected.

Even Grandi began expressing enthusiasm for war. By 30 May the King too was convinced of German victory over France.[78]

The King had not changed his mind about the long-term consequences of intervention for both Italy and the monarchy. Despite the imminent fall of France, he believed Britain would hold out and the United States would eventually enter the conflict. He foresaw a long war and certain Axis defeat. But if he attempted to overthrow Mussolini, Vittorio Emanuele III expected a civil war and a German rescue of Mussolini. This seemed the worst possible alternative. If he refused to sign a declaration of war and went into exile, he believed his people would consider him a deserter and never accept his return. Instead, on 1 June the King acquiesced to war and to Mussolini's demand for operational command of the armed forces. Although Soddu argued otherwise, the King still did not think that this abdication of powers would allow him to escape blame for defeat. He had decided to share the fate of the Italians, even though he was certain the monarchy would not survive the catastrophe. Mussolini faced no further obstacles to war.[79]

On 29 May he had already ordered the chiefs of staff to be prepared to enter the conflict on 5 June. In a meeting with the chiefs and Ciano in his office, Mussolini described the French as beaten. Still, influenced by a recent report by the Italian military attaché in Berlin, he thought that they might resist for another month or six weeks. The danger had arisen, however, that if the Italians did not enter the war soon, the Germans might reject their claims for a share of the spoils. To avoid the appearance of jackals, and because operations in the Balkans would disrupt the flow of raw materials desperately needed by the arms industry, the Italians would concentrate their efforts on an aero-naval offensive against the British. Ciano abandoned his project to attack Greece.[80]

Meeting on 30 May, the chiefs of staff agreed to confine offensive operations to limited air strikes and submarine patrols. Only then did Pricolo realize that plans for an attack on Yugoslavia had been called off. But even the assumption of almost totally defensive dispositions left Badoglio uneasy. When Graziani expressed satisfaction with their arrangements, the marshal recalled the facile optimism of 1911. "We shouldn't believe that we're dealing with something so simple. Keep in mind that at the outbreak of the Libyan War they spoke of a military parade while, instead, it was a very different matter." Badoglio warned Mussolini the next day that he feared stubborn French resistance for two or three months longer. Even after the collapse of France, Britain would continue to fight. The marshal worried that the defenses of Libya were still so weak that the Allies might overrun the colony. He advised Mussolini to delay intervention until at least early July.

But powerful emotions had Mussolini in their grip. As Ciano had noted of Mussolini at the 29 May staff meeting: "Few times have I seen Mussolini so happy. He has achieved his real dream: that of becoming the military commander of the country in war." Furthermore, Mussolini already had informed Hitler that Italy would intervene on 5 June. After Hitler asked for a postponement—to avoid the dispersion of the French air force out of range of the Luftwaffe—Mussolini set the date for 10 June. On 2 June Hitler announced that 5 June would be fine, after all. But Badoglio's concerns had influenced Mussolini enough to cause him to order emergency reinforcements rushed to Libya. He kept the date of intervention set for 10 June, to allow their arrival in Bengasi. At the final meeting of the chiefs of staff before Mussolini's declaration of war, they devoted most of their attention to defensive arrangements: the last-minute reinforcement of Libya and precautions against possible French air raids on Rome from Corsica. Badoglio had already made it clear to the German military attaché that the condition of the army and air force made major offensive operations impossible. He expressed the wish that the Germans would bring the war to a swift conclusion.[81]

A curious sense of tranquility settled over most of the *gerarchi*. The miracle of 1935–36, when Mussolini had conquered Ethiopia against seemingly overwhelming odds, appeared to have been repeated. Once again, the doubts and fears of the leaders of the regime largely evaporated. Had not Mussolini foreseen the German triumph and maneuvered Italy onto the victorious side to receive the maximum gains at minimum risks?[82]

Dazzled by German success, Mussolini had made the classic error of basing a strategic decision on the outcome of a single operation. Yet his miscalculation was hardly unprecedented in history and should be placed in perspective. Many others believed that the fall of France had settled Europe's fate. Stalin saw the events of May–June 1940 almost exactly as Mussolini did.[83] Thanks to Italian geography, however, Mussolini was better situated than Stalin to take advantage of developments. Furthermore, the *forze armate* were much improved from August 1939. In June 1940 the army counted 1.6 million men, arranged in 75 divisions. Of these, 19 could be considered roughly up to strength and 34 incomplete but still efficient. Pricolo had managed to bring his force up to 2,500 aircraft, of which 1,600 were reasonably modern. The navy still counted only two modernized battleships actually ready for combat. But four more, including two modernized warships and two brand-new *Littorio*-class battleships would be ready in the next few months.[84]

The nation, the military, and the *gerarchi* returned to their accustomed obedience to the Duce. Given French collapse and expectations of the imminent British surrender, the *forze armate* seemed adequate for the short war that most people expected. However, Balbo and the Duke of Aosta felt far less optimistic. Both governors had returned to Africa resigned to defeat for their forces and death for themselves.[85]

As for Mussolini, he entered the war fully cognizant of the perilously weak state of his forces and of Italian war industries. In fact, gross overestimates by SIM of the strength of French and British forces in the Alps, North Africa, the Middle East, and surrounding Ethiopia made the Italian military situation seem even worse than it was. British counterespionage had arrested roughly 80 percent of SIM's agents in Egypt and Palestine. Most had agreed to become double agents and to transmit false reports to Rome, greatly exaggerating Allied order-of-battle in the Mediterranean area. Such disinformation blinded the Italians to the fleeting opportunities available to them in the summer of 1940.[86]

Yet such material factors seemed of relative unimportance to Mussolini. Clausewitz had stated that no one in his right mind starts a war without first being certain what he intends to gain thereby and how he intends to achieve his goals. But Mussolini rejected such Clausewitzian concepts as restraints on action. When he joined Germany in war with Britain and France on 10 June 1940, Mussolini knowingly entered a struggle of giants with only pygmy forces in an attempt to conquer a world empire for Italy. He did not envision war as force organized in pursuit of policy goals. He rejected the view of war as subordinate to, yet different from, politics. Such thinking would have forced him to recognize that he was wielding an instrument too weak to achieve his aims and, besides, one he had no skill in using. Instead, Mussolini envisioned war as no more than an act of politics.[87]

He had seized power in Italy by applying warlike violence to the usual variety of political actions. In June 1940 he was attempting the reverse, to make war by relying primarily on politics and diplomacy. These methods had brought him success in 1935–36 in Ethiopia and in 1936–39 in Spain. But those victories had obscured the fact that superior force on the battlefield had been as important in winning those wars as Mussolini's diplomatic maneuvers and threats to the British and

French. Instead, he seemed to believe that war was the continuation of politics with the very same means or, at least, that in war political means were superior to military means. Thus, his political genius could compensate for Italy's military forces, which Mussolini recognized as inferior to his enemies' and his ally's.[88]

Mussolini's megalomania and wishful thinking would be painfully revealed by the disasters into which he would lead Italy in the fall and winter of 1940–41. Once the Germans failed to defeat Britain in the second half of 1940, the original fears of Mussolini's military about Italian intervention in the war proved well-founded. Mussolini's attempts to conquer Greece and to overrun Egypt produced catastrophe. His political skills offered no adequate substitute for military power.

But even major Italian military success, such as the capture of Malta, seizure of the Suez Canal, or conquest of Greece, would not have brought Italy victory in its "parallel war." Italian weakness and geographical isolation prevented striking at the bases of British power. A crippling blow against the Royal Navy; against Britain's air defenses, maritime communications, or war industries; to the will of the British people—however the British centers of gravity in World War II are defined—lay beyond the means available to Mussolini.

As the Axis war expanded in 1941–42, Italian influence on its outcome, except negatively, virtually disappeared. Italy could match only a small percentage of Allied war production. Italian industry remained crippled by the inefficiencies and shortages presented to Mussolini before June 1940. What could Italy have done to help Germany win the Battle of the Atlantic or conquer the Soviet Union, even if free to concentrate all of its efforts on only one of those campaigns? Obviously little.

Despite its failings, the prewar net assessment process in Fascist Italy had produced a reasonably accurate picture of the military balance confronting Mussolini. But, entranced by dreams of glory and conquest, he chose to ignore reality. The result was the collapse of July–September 1943, the reduction of the Italian peninsula to a battlefield, and, for Mussolini, ignominious death in April 1945.

5

French Net Assessment

Steven Ross

AT THE HEIGHT of the Rhineland Crisis, a headline in a Parisian newspaper cried, *"Surtout pas de guerre,"* reflecting the attitude of the Republic's leaders and many—probably most—segments of French public opinion during the late 1930s.[1] The French did not fear defeat at the hands of a revanchist Germany as much as they dreaded the price of victory. "War, at no price," wrote an editorialist for a provincial paper in 1938. "The next war will be more murderous than the last."[2]

World War I had been a searing experience for the French nation—1.5 million dead, additional millions wounded, vast areas of the national patrimony devastated. No family remained untouched. Somber graveyards, the Verdun ossuary with the bones of more than 100,000 unknown soldiers, and the special bus and metro seats reserved for war invalids served as constant reminders of the tremendous sacrifices required to achieve the victory of 1918. No French statesman could ever again lightly commit the nation to a renewal of the slaughter of Guise, the Marne, or Verdun. To most French leaders war itself, not the possibility of defeat, became the worst possible prospect for the nation.

Traditionally suspicious of Germany, few Frenchmen had any

illusions concerning the nature and intentions of the Nazi regime. Some called for immediate and vigorous resistance to Nazi aggression. Others called for friendship with Berlin, while still others advocated policies ranging from pacifism to isolationism. The majority of the Republic's leaders and the public, however, recognized the threat posed by a rearmed, aggressive Reich. They regarded Hitler as sinister and dangerous but hoped against hope to establish a détente with Berlin. Somehow, French leaders felt, the Republic and the Reich had to resolve their differences without resort to war.[3]

The leaders of the 1930s, honest, intelligent, experienced men, were all haunted by the horror of another general war. All of the problems besetting the Republic—diplomatic isolation, economic recession, belief in Germany's superior war potential, and the doctrine of total war—served to strengthen the desire for peace. Léon Blum, for example, never changed his view expressed in April 1933: "The way to salvation is peace, the will to peace."[4] Edouard Daladier, the Bull of the Vaucluse, appeared much tougher, but he too rejected uncompromising nationalism and had a distaste for the old style of balance of power diplomacy and for the policy of refusing concessions to Germany. At the Riom Trial, he even asserted that had Hitler confined his demands in 1939 simply to Danzig, war could have been averted.[5] Daladier to the last moment sought to avoid another war. On 26 August 1939, he wrote personally to Hitler pleading with the Führer to prevent the outbreak of war. He assured Hitler that he wished only a sincere collaboration with Germany to establish a lasting peace in Europe. Daladier went on to point out that both he and the German leader were veterans of the last war and knew the horrors of combat at first hand. If war came, Daladier asserted, both France and Germany would fight in the confidence of victory, but the only victors would be the forces of destruction and barbarism.[6]

Daladier was not alone in his desperate search for a détente with Berlin. François-Poncet claimed that in the aftermath of Munich and despite his doubts, he tried to strengthen the accords and use them as a basis for a general European settlement.[7] On 1 September 1939, several hours after the German attack on Poland, Bonnet accepted an Italian proposal for a peace conference, insisting only that such a meeting deal not only with the Polish question but also provide the basis for the establishment of a general peace for Europe.[8] Most French leaders saw a Continental détente based on an agreement with the dictators as the only means of avoiding a new world war and worked assiduously for an understanding with Berlin. They did not delude themselves as to the nature and goals of the Nazi regime but hoped that a well-armed France willing to negotiate on a basis of equality with Germany could somehow tame Hitler's drive for hegemony.

The will to peace formed a filter through which virtually all French leaders viewed the strategic balance. Everything—the wavering, unstable diplomatic constellation, the foundering economy, a rejection in many quarters of traditional balance of power diplomacy, and deep rifts within the political spectrum—seemed to indicate that the risks of resorting to war to protect the nation's security were simply unacceptable. Germany was too strong, allies were too unreliable, and the public was too volatile for the nation's leaders to take the country into a total war where victory or defeat could have the same practical consequences: a decimated nation threatened by internal crisis, even civil strife.

THE FRENCH SECURITY STRUCTURE

In assessing the strategic balance French leaders implicitly understood that the Republic existed within a dynamic shifting power configuration. They realized too that a series of static measurements of foreign military and economic capabilities could provide at best a partial picture of reality. Decision-makers had to deal with a complex set of variables that required constant attention and analysis of both French and foreign intentions, strengths, and vulnerabilities. Although no single element in the bureaucracy had the specific mission of evaluating the state's overall strategic situation, the French system of net assessment was elaborate, well organized, and, on the whole, reasonably effective. Throughout the 1930s, decision-makers had generally reliable information on most issues relating to the strategic balance. What was lacking in both political and military circles was the will to draw the necessary conclusions from that information.

An experienced cadre of politicians was responsible for the country's security. Despite the accusation that the regime suffered from constant political turmoil, France in fact enjoyed adequate governmental stability. The numerous Cabinet changes in the early and mid-1930s were more a matter of redistributing portfolios than of fundamental political changes. During the late 1930s, only three men served as premier: Léon Blum, who served twice; Camille Chautemps, who was in office for less than a year; and Edouard Daladier, who had served in twelve previous Cabinets and had been premier twice before returning again to office in 1938. For much of his term, which lasted until March 1940, Daladier ruled by decree and also held the portfolio of Minister of National Defense and War. Governmental power was concentrated in the hands of relatively few individuals, and as Europe drifted toward war, an even more restricted group wielded authority.

Leading diplomatic and military posts were also held by a small group of experienced leaders. Only three men—Yvon Delbos, Joseph Paul-Boncour, and Georges Bonnet—served as Minister of Foreign Affairs between 1936 and 1939. One man, Alexis Léger, occupied the post of Secretary General, the highest permanent civil service position at the Quai d'Orsay. Military leadership was also stable. Maxime Weygand and Maurice Gamelin led the French army throughout the 1930s, and Gamelin as of January 1938 also served as Chief of Staff of National Defense with the authority to coordinate the wartime activities of all three services.

French political and military leaders had at their disposal a well-organized system for the gathering, analysis, and discussion of information concerning the country's security. The diplomatic corps and the military intelligence services were generally able to supply the government with both raw and finished intelligence concerning the intentions and capabilities of the nation's friends and enemies. Despite some glaring errors and omissions, reporting was of sufficient accuracy to enable French decision-makers to construct a comprehensive picture of the power balance and of the Republic's place within it.

The Foreign Ministry was a small organization. In addition to officials located in Paris, France maintained fourteen embassies, thirty-seven legations, and eight consulates. Ambassadors and others who chose a diplomatic career constituted a well-educated, well-trained elite. They were generally graduates of one of the *Grandes Ecoles*, where they had achieved outstanding grades in history, international law, and languages. Despite their background and the milieu in which they operated, individual diplomats made great efforts to report on more than the official position of the country to which they were assigned. Economic officers also made extensive and largely successful efforts to provide the Quay d'Orsay with detailed and accurate data.[9] Generally, the diplomatic service obtained a wide range of information and reported frankly and with a minimum of prejudice.

Military attachés played an essential role in the intelligence collection and assessment process. The Republic in 1935 had twenty-six army, eleven air, and ten naval attachés. Their mission was to obtain military information, which included everything from order-of-battle data to details of uniforms and equipment. They were forbidden to engage in covert activities, although some attachés did in fact develop their own networks of secret informants. In major foreign posts, attachés were at least lieutenant colonels with extensive experience, including service in the Great War, graduation from the École Supérieure de Guerre, and a tour on the general staff. Additionally, the attachés had frequently served on an interallied staff or as a liaison officer with a foreign army and were familiar with the language of the country to which they were assigned. The attaché in Japan in the 1920s actually served in a Japanese regiment, and the attachés in Berlin were usually bilingual. Attachés reported to their own services and frequently sent information copies to the Ministry of Foreign Affairs. While on post, they met often with the ambassador to discuss matters of mutual interest and concern.[10] The Service de Renseignements (SR) dealt with covert intelligence collection. With a headquarters consisting of twenty-five officers, twenty NCOs, and thirty civilians and a very limited budget, the Service nevertheless ran an extensive network of agents and handlers. The headquarters comprised four sections: administration; technical services, including cryptography and telephonic and microphonic listening devices; counterintelligence; and collection. The collection branch consisted of six subsections: Germany, the Mediterranean countries, the Soviet Union, Spain, war matériel, and air data.[11] The Service obtained most of its information from a series of posts located on both French and foreign territory. There were Service operatives in every European capital with the exception of London. By the late 1930s, the Service had some 1,500 agents in Germany. Most of them were low-ranking individuals, but a few were well placed within the German government, the military, or the Nazi Party.[12]

The Service de Renseignements maintained daily contact with the 2d Bureau, a section of the army general staff responsible for gathering and analyzing intelligence from all sources, both open and clandestine. The Bureau by 1938 contained six sections: missions, responsible for foreign attachés stationed in Paris; liaison, which dealt with foreign intelligence agencies; personnel; press, which monitored the German news media; collections, which was in turn subdivided into four geographical areas, one of which was Germany; and a study department that prepared reports based on intelligence received from all sources. The Bureau circulated the reports to the defense ministry, the War Council, divisional commands, and command posts of fortified regions. The 2d Bureau sponsored annual three-week courses for active and reserve intelligence officers from divisional to army group level and offered courses in intelligence methods and findings to the senior military schools.[13]

The head of the Bureau was kept fully informed by his subordinates. He received all of the studies as well as important attaché reports. The Bureau chief maintained daily contact with the Foreign Affairs Ministry and the head of the Service de Renseignements. The Bureau forwarded its studies to the personal staffs of the chief of staff of national defense, the chief of the army staff, and the commander of the Northeastern Theater of Operations. The Bureau chief also had frequent personal meetings with his superiors. Reports from the Bureau also went to the Minister of War's special military cabinet, which contained its own small study section. The head of the clandestine service or an assistant also met frequently with the minister's staff.[14] Other services also had their own intelligence collection and analysis elements, and their reports reached both service ministers and national decision-makers. Personal rivalries and the filter of ministerial staffs may have reduced the flow of intelligence, but Daladier never complained that he lacked essential information or that he was surprised by the actions of a foreign power.[15]

At the higher levels of government a series of interdepartmental committees brought together those officials responsible for evaluating the information supplied by diplomatic and military sources and framing appropriate responses. The Conseil Supérieur de la Défense Nationale (CSDN) included the President of the Republic, the premier, members of the Cabinet, high-ranking members of the armed services, and a Marshal of France. The Council's role was to furnish guidance on major issues concerning national defense, and it had a permanent secretariat to prepare agendas and perform necessary staff functions. After 1936 the secretariat was under the control of the defense minister.[16] The CSDN was a cumbersome body, but throughout the 1930s the French government steadily improved the efficiency of the national security decision-making machinery. In 1932 the Tardieu government created the post of Minister of National Defense in order to group the traditional independent ministries of war and navy, plus the new air ministry, under a single authority. The Herriot government suppressed the new position, but Daladier revived it during his short-lived regime in 1934. In June 1936 the Popular Front government of Léon Blum reestablished the ministry under the name Ministry of National Defense and War.

The Republic also created permanent institutions for interservice and interministerial coordination. The Haut Comité Militaire (HCM), established in 1932, included the premier, the defense minister, the civilian and military heads of the armed services, the service chiefs of staff, and the Inspector General of Air Defenses. The committee's role was to examine important defense issues, including the defense budget and the organization and employment of the armed forces. Meeting only rarely at first, the HCM began to hold monthly meetings in December 1934. The Popular Front government in June 1936 replaced the HCM with the Comité Permanent de la Défense Nationale (CPDN). The Minister of National Defense and War presided over the CPDN, which included the permanent secretaries of the Foreign Affairs and National Defense ministries and the permanent secretaries and chiefs of staff of the armed services. The CPDN met to discuss major security issues, although Daladier after 1938 tended to prefer direct meetings with the service chiefs or their chiefs of staff.

The Conseil Supérieur de la Guerre (CSG) dealt with military strategy and the conduct of operations. The defense minister acted as president, and until 1938 the army chief of staff was the vice president. In wartime, the vice president of the CSG became the commander-in-chief of the principal operational theaters. In 1938 the government reorganized the command structure, creating the post of chief of staff of national defense to coordinate the conduct of operations of all the armed services.[17]

The national security decision-making system functioned effectively during the 1930s, but no system is better than the people who run it. Accurate information and proper analysis can influence the decision-making process, but leaders must still guard the state's interests by responding to information and by framing appropriate responses. The French dilemma in the late 1930s went far beyond the nature and structure of the national security apparatus. Beset by severe political and economic crises, bereft of effective alliances, and fearful of a repetition of the slaughter of World War I, France had to face a revanchist Germany determined to destroy the European balance.

FRENCH VIEWS OF THE STRATEGIC BALANCE

French political and military leaders viewed the Republic's geostrategic situation with a mixture of gloom and consternation. The French presumed that any new conflict with Germany would, like the last war, be global, total, and protracted. France would have to conduct an extended battle of attrition to wear down the enemy's resources before a counteroffensive administered the coup de grâce. War would also require the resources of coalition partners, including the United Kingdom, Continental allies, and perhaps the United States, because the Republic simply could not face Germany alone. Moreover, evidence concerning the Franco-German strategic balance, the state of the Republic's alliance structure, and perceptions of future warfare, served further to convince French leaders that even if France emerged victorious from another general war the nation would be bled white. Consequently, leaders tended to view gloomy assessments as reasons for inaction rather than as requirements for vigorous corrective measures.

THE DEMOGRAPHIC DIMENSION

The French were painfully aware that in the Franco-German strategic balance the demographic balance, already tilted against the Republic in 1914, continued to worsen after 1919. The German population in the 1920s outnumbered that of France by 20 million, and the trend continued unabated in the following decade. In 1937 France had 4.3 million males of military age, as against 8.3 million in Germany. German annexations and natural growth increased their numbers to 9.3 million by 1939. In 1940, according to French sources, Germany had 13 million mobilizable men while France had 6.7 million. Whatever the precise figures, it was clear that the Republic suffered a growing population imbalance in comparison with its major rival.[18]

THE ECONOMIC DIMENSION

German industrial production was approximately twice that of France. Moreover, much of French industry, including a number of critical defense-related sectors, was antiquated. The Swiss in the 1930s employed more men in the machine tool industry than France, and the French aircraft industry in 1938 employed only 47,000 workers.[19] The Depression further hampered the development of French industry. In 1933–34, while other nations were beginning recovery, the Republic was still in the midst of an economic decline. A deflationary fiscal policy designed to protect the gold value of the franc only exacerbated downward economic trends. Growing fear of the political consequences of the economic crisis led to capital flight or hoarding, and even the Popular Front was unwilling to check the free flow of money. Additionally, the Blum government's reforms led to higher wages, shorter hours, reduced profits, and consequently, slower recovery. Daladier, by his willingness to break with his predecessor's reforms and by in effect floating the franc, restored business confidence, but by the start of World War II, despite vastly increased defense spending, the economy had not fully recovered. Industrial production was only 86 percent of 1929 levels.[20]

In terms of defense expenditure France also fell well behind Germany. Whereas in 1932 French defense spending amounted to 5.2 percent of gross national product contrasted to 1.9 percent in Germany, by 1938 the figure had grown to 8.6 percent in France but had rocketed to 17.2 percent in Germany. The following year saw a substantial increase in defense outlay to 23 percent of GNP in France, but Germany maintained its lead, directing 30 percent of its GNP toward defense in 1939.[21] France never caught up with the Reich, and German defense spending had begun from a larger industrial base.

Numerous problems beset the German defense effort, including a shortage of critical natural resources and a lack of sufficient hard currency to import them, inefficient allocation of industrial tasks, and the inability of the military industries to meet the demands of the armed forces. The French were generally aware of the Reich's problems, but the knowledge provided scant comfort. France had to import many of its own critical raw materials and feared that in wartime the national merchant fleet could not carry sufficient tonnage to sustain the defense effort, nor could the French navy alone provide adequate protection to civilian shipping.[22] French defense spending also followed an unfortunate trend, for just as the Nazi regime came to power and introduced a policy of rapid armament, the Republic reduced defense spending as part of its deflationary fiscal response to the Depression. Paris cut defense spending by more than a billion francs in 1934, and after 1935 growth was slowed because of fiscal and political constraints.

THE DIPLOMATIC DIMENSION

Alliances were the answer to German numerical and economic superiority. They had proved their worth during World War I, but the French were equally aware of the fact that their postwar security structure was far less reliable than the pre-1914 system.

Having destroyed the German High Seas Fleet and reduced the threat of Prussian militarism, Great Britain sought to return to a policy of limited Continental liability. Imperial rather than European security became the arena of primary concern to British statesmen. London's adherence to the Lorcarno System, the French noticed, was a commitment to the postwar status quo in the West and was not an automatic guarantee of French security. In theory, England might find it necessary to side with Germany if France ever decided to mount a preemptive attack. Overt hostility to Poincaré's occupation of the Ruhr found voice in continued British suspicions that the Republic was seeking to entangle Britain in Great Power confrontations that served only France's interest. British antiwar sentiment also gave rise to the widespread belief that international disputes could be resolved either through the League of Nations or by direct negotiations between the contending parties.

Belgium, the Republic's other major ally in the West, drew steadily away from the French orbit. In the 1920s the Franco-Belgian agreement, according to French interpretation, permitted France to send forces into Belgium upon warning of planned German aggression. The deployment would shield northern France from invasion and provide a shorter defense line. But growing resistance on the part of the Flemish population to close ties with France ultimately forced the Belgian government to revise its foreign policy. In March 1936, at almost the same moment that German troops moved into the Rhineland, Brussels informed Paris that Belgium would return to its traditional policy of neutrality and provide for its own defense. If Germany attacked, Brussels would, of course, welcome French assistance, but French troops could no longer expect to enter Belgium prior to an act of overt aggression.

After 1936 Belgian authorities continued to hold secret staff talks and intelligence exchanges with the French, but the Belgian policy shift seriously weakened the French strategic position. In a new war, the French could no longer count upon meeting the initial German offensive well forward of the northern departments, nor could the High Command mount coordinated operations with the Belgian armed forces.[23] Rather, the French faced the bleak prospects of awaiting the enemy offensive in northern France or risking an encounter in a hasty effort to establish a front in central Belgium.

In theory France's East European allies could field more than 100 divisions and constitute a major second front against Germany. In reality, however, the web of Eastern alliances was more a sieve than a rampart. The allies were divided among themselves and regarded their participation in the French security system primarily in terms of narrowly defined particular interests rather than as a common effort to cope with common threats.

Because of its geographic situation, Poland required French support against both Germany and the Soviet Union. In 1936 the head of Polish military intelligence told his French counterpart that the German danger was Poland's second preoccupation, and that in case of war with the Reich, Poland, even if threatened with defeat, would refuse to call upon the Soviets for assistance.[24] Poland demonstrated its worth as an ally by signing a nonaggression pact with Germany in 1934, by refusing to grant transit rights to Soviet forces during the Munich crisis, and by joining Germany in the partition of Czechoslovakia.

All of the Eastern alliances were predicated on the assumption that, as in 1914, Germany would attack France first, and the allies would force Germany to divert troops to the East. If Germany chose to strike first in the East, the basic rationale for the alliances disappeared, and they became a strategic liability.

Far from strengthening the Republic's Eastern system, the pact with the U.S.S.R. created both foreign and domestic complications. The initial impetus for the pact came from Louis Barthou, the rightist Foreign Minister in the early 1930s. Barthou was under no illusions about the nature or intentions of Hitler's regime, and his thoughts turned instinctively to a Russian counter to German strength. Ideological differences did not matter to him; after all, in the nineteenth century Republican France had concluded an alliance with Tsarist Russia, and a Communist Russia could be just as useful in the twentieth. The French right initially tended to agree with Barthou's approach, especially because the threat posed by domestic Communism seemed minimal.

After Barthou's murder, his successors continued to work for a pact, but with a significant change in emphasis. The growth of the Communist vote in France convinced most conservatives that an alliance with the Soviets would strengthen the domestic left. Paris, therefore, signed a diplomatic pact with Moscow in May 1935 but avoided concluding a military convention. The army also wished to avoid a military link. In April 1935 the 2d Bureau noted that it was in French interests to prevent a German victory over Russia, but it was not necessary to commit the Republic in advance to a conflict that did not concern the nation directly.[25] In 1935 the army attaché reported favorably on Soviet military capabilities, but the following year a different attaché, more in tune with the attitudes of the High Command, asserted that the U.S.S.R. could not successfully conduct a war with a first-rate European power.[26] The army was satisfied with an arrangement that denied Russian raw materials to Germany but remained opposed to direct military ties to the Soviets.

In May 1937 the army staff produced a study of the consequences of a military convention with the U.S.S.R. emphasizing the serious diplomatic problems that would ensue. The diplomatic agreement already alarmed the Eastern allies and Great Britain, and in wartime British aid would far outweigh any assistance that the Soviets could offer. Consequently, before concluding any military agreement with Moscow, London's assent was essential. Another requirement was the prior consent of the Eastern allies and an understanding between them and the U.S.S.R.[27] The staff doubtless realized that such agreements were not feasible. The Republic thus found itself with a treaty that alarmed both the state's allies and the domestic right. As the Communist vote increased and the number of Communist deputies grew, the right began to replace its traditional suspicion of Germany with the fear that a Franco-German confrontation would benefit only Moscow.

On the other side of the political spectrum French relations with Fascist Italy produced additional problems. Pierre Laval avidly pursued an alliance with Mussolini. France and Italy had been allies during the Great War, and Paris assumed that Rome had a continuing interest in preserving Austrian independence and resisting the growth of German influence in the Danube basin. Moreover, an alliance with Italy would relieve the French armed forces from the tasks of securing the Alpine frontier and the colonial possessions bordering on Italian African territories. An alliance would also free troops for service on the crucial Northeastern Front and secure the line of communications between the Métropole and North Africa.

To French strategic planners, Italy represented a vital linchpin in the creation of a continuous southeastern front, but Mussolini's invasion of Ethiopia presented the Republic with a cruel dilemma. The British public was outraged and virtually forced the government to oppose the invasion and impose economic sanctions on Italy. Many in France would have preferred to treat the invasion as the latest in a long series of colonial wars but also realized that the Republic could not afford to alienate Great Britain. Paris, therefore, reluctantly joined London in the imposition of League-mandated sanctions. The advent of the Popular Front government in France, and Italian military intervention in a popular front government in Spain, ended for all practical purposes efforts to secure a rapprochement and an alliance with Italy.

The diplomatic scene thus offered the Republic scant comfort. England was at best a reluctant ally, Belgium was no longer reliable, ties with the Soviet Union were tenuous and divisive both at home and abroad, and relations with Italy grew steadily worse. Nor did the East European allies offer a viable substitute for a Great Power coalition. In the face of German aggression, French leaders were acutely aware that they would stand virtually alone. The lack of an effective alliance structure also provided French decision-makers with a rationale for inaction in the face of German initiatives. Since France would have to face Germany alone in the opening phases of a conflict, it was better to wait until the security structure was stronger.

The domestic political situation placed additional constraints upon French policy-makers. The rise of right-wing leagues, the explosive growth of the Communist vote tally, and a growing belief in intellectual circles that the Republic was outdated and doomed frightened moderates and contributed to their reluctance to undertake bold foreign policy initiatives. Left-wing pacifism, right-wing defeatism, and the not insubstantial support for Wilsonianism, as manifested by the earlier popularity of Briand, further complicated the calculations of the country's leaders. Behind the fear of foreign war lurked the specter of domestic chaos.

THE MILITARY DIMENSION

Despite their desperate search for détente, the French did not neglect their military strength, and after 1935 the pace of defense spending increased steadily until 1939, growing from 12.797 billion francs in the former year to 93.687 in the latter.[28] The army received the lion's share of the defense budget: 52.6 percent in 1936, climbing to 60.7 percent in 1939.[29] The 1936 four-year defense plan called for the production of 6,600 antitank guns, more than 60 battalions of tanks, and 50 groups of 105mm field guns. By the spring of 1940 the army had 25 battalions of light infantry support tanks and fielded 582 tanks in three light mechanized divisions and 624 tanks in three armored divisions. French tanks were at least the equal of the German machines they faced. German tanks were on the whole faster and had better radios, while the French armored vehicles contained heavier guns and had thicker armor.[30]

The air force also received a substantial share of the defense budget: 18 percent in 1936 and 27 percent by 1939.[31] With the creation of an independent air force, the Air Ministry contemplated a shift in mission from ground support to strategic bombardment. The realization that the Luftwaffe had surpassed the French air force in numbers of bombers raised serious doubts about the feasibility of launching strategic bombardment missions against an opponent whose ability to retaliate was so great. Consequently, in 1937 the Air Ministry began to concentrate on the production of air defense fighters. Plan V of 1938 called for the purchase of 6,858 fighters by 1941. In the same year, France ordered almost 1,000 aircraft, mostly fighters and reconnaissance planes, from the United States.[32] By spring 1940 the air force had a front-line strength of 3,289 modern planes, of which 2,122 were fighters.[33] Despite significant progress in 1939 and 1940, the French air force remained inferior to the Luftwaffe in numbers and mission capabilities. Shifts in mission priorities, inadequate funding, and the problems associated with introducing new aircraft types into operational squadrons delayed major improvements of the air force.

French naval spending was also substantial: 23.6 percent of the budget in 1936; 24.1 percent in 1938; and 11.2 percent in 1939.[34] The basic goal of French naval planning was to ensure superiority over the combined German and Italian fleets, and by 1937 France possessed the world's fourth largest fleet. In the late 1930s the Naval Staff came to regard the Italian fleet as the main threat, but the French believed that their navy was effective enough to check the Italians and control the lines of communication and supply between the Métropole and the Empire.

The goal of French rearmament, however, was not war fighting but deterrence. Only a strong France could negotiate with Germany from a position of strength, and reasonable statesmen sustained by adequate forces might, the French hoped, convince Berlin that a resort to war was not a viable option. Deterred from war by the prospect of having to deal with a strong, well-armed France, German leaders would find it in their best interests to seek a peaceful resolution of outstanding differences.

French military organization and doctrine presented the government with a limited range of options. The military system, essentially, admitted only general war as the alternative to peace. With the introduction of one-year military service in 1928, the army became a cadre and covering force dependent on full mobilization to attain full combat readiness. Forces in Metropolitan France consisted of recruits undergoing training and 20 active divisions. Upon mobilization the active divisions absorbed reservists and supplied cadres for A and B class reserve formations. The A divisions had a higher percentage of active troops than the B units. The system relied upon the active divisions breaking up and forming the fully mobilized army.[35] For all practical purposes, the active forces functioned as a school for soldiers and as a mobilization base.

The army did devise methods for partial mobilization to provide covering forces for the exposed frontier regions, but in every case of partial mobilization the active forces had to absorb reserves and supply cadres for activated units. Consequently, the army could not wage a limited war without placing at risk its mobilization base and its ability to fight a total war. The system suited most Frenchmen. Fiscal conservatives approved of the reduced expenditures involved, republicans believed that the system embodied the Revolutionary ideal of the citizen-soldier, and the professional soldiers accepted the system because it preserved their status and reflected their views concerning the lessons of World War I and the shape of wars to come. The reintroduction of two-year service, designed as it was to compensate for the empty years, led to no fundamental changes in military organization or doctrine.

During the war the French learned that major advantages accrued to the defense. Entrenchments, wire, machine guns, and massive artillery fire had made the task of assaulting prepared positions both difficult and costly. Frontal assaults were suicidal unless supported and sustained by enormous superiority in manpower and material. Any future conflict, the French concluded, would also be a gigantic war of matériel attrition. Given Germany's superiority in resources coupled with the efficacy of defensive firepower, the French army rejected as disastrous any attempt to mount an *offensive à outrance*.[36] French military doctrine after 1918 called for protecting the national territory from a surprise attack that might disrupt mobilization and deprive the Republic of vital industrial regions. The army and its supporting air arm would then seek to blunt the initial enemy assault while the nation methodically organized its human and economic resources for total war.

The army high command also understood that armor would play a vital role in any future conflict. Tank battalions would accompany and support infantry attacks, and additional battalions would provide a commander with a mass of maneuver. Within corps and divisions no specific commander of tanks was designated since the tanks would operate under the control of the higher unit commander. The 1937 Provisional Instructions for the Employment of Tanks called for the use of armor by surprise and in great numbers along large fronts. Tanks could not, however, occupy terrain, and they were to advance by successive bounds protected by the concentrated fire of artillery and by infantry in close support.[37] Tanks, the army reasoned, could increase the rhythm of the attack, but their presence on the field of battle did not eliminate the requirement for movement by carefully delineated successive bounds. Centralized control of offensive operations was still essential. The 1939 Regulation on Combat Tanks reemphasized the requirement for close liaison with the artillery. Tanks could impart a more rapid pace to operations, but only within the context of the methodical battle.[38]

General J. B. Estienne, the father of French armor, after his retirement in 1927 served as a civilian in the tank technical section of the Department of Infantry and continued to advocate the creation of an independent armored branch of service. He criticized the army's emphasis on the production of light infantry support tanks as well as heavy tanks designed for breakthrough operations. He called instead for the production of a single all-purpose medium tank. In 1934 the CSG rejected his views and called for the production of both heavy and light support tanks. In 1936 the general staff decided that three-quarters of the army's tanks should be light vehicles, and the remainder heavy. Large concentrations of the tanks were accepted as an essential element of warfare but only as part of the methodical battle.[39] Given the high command's view on the nature of battle, the formation of armored divisions was not a high priority. General Estienne and a few others, including Lieutenant Colonel Charles de Gaulle, continued to advocate the creation of autonomous armored divisions, but as with armor advocates in many other countries, their view remained minority opinions.

The high command saw no compelling reason to create armored formations, especially since the production of the heavy B1 and B1b tanks remained painfully slow because of both costs and technical problems with the tank's complex steering system. Consequently, not until late in 1936 did the high command, prodded by Daladier, begin to study the possibility of employing large armored units. In February 1938 Daladier ordered the creation of another special study group. The group issued a report advocating the establishment of a large armored unit, but the army continued to resist the formation of armored divisions. After Munich, the CSG called for the establishment of three armored divisions, but by the time the war began, the army had yet to create its first tank division. Only in January 1940 did the army activate the first two armored divisions.[40] The divisions were not to operate as autonomous units but were to function as an integral part of the methodical battle. The French also had two and later three light armored divisions equipped with the excellent SOUMA S-35 tank. The divisions were combined arms formations, but their missions were essentially confined to the traditional cavalry roles of reconnaissance and security.[41]

French army doctrine was not purely defensive. Extensive debate within the officer corps convinced the high command and the civilian leadership that the official view concerning the lessons of World War I and the impact of technological advances since 1919 was properly understood. In a future conflict, the army, after a defensive phase, intended to mount offensive operations. The defensive phase would wear down enemy strength and permit France and its allies to mobilize their forces. Methodical attacks sustained by massive firepower would then overwhelm hostile positions.

The construction of the Maginot Line did not indicate the existence of a purely passive strategy. The Line was designed to defend the industrial areas of Lorraine against a surprise attack and to free additional troops from a static defensive role, thereby enabling the army to create an even larger mobile mass of maneuver. Nor did the army neglect motorization and mechanization; motorized and mechanized formations constituted a substantial portion of the mobile reserve force. The missions of the mobile reserve included meeting the initial German advance through the Low Countries either in Belgium or on the northern frontier of France and, when reinforced as the result of national mobilization, mounting a carefully controlled and modulated counteroffensive.[42] French doctrine had no place for a rapid war of maneuver or for limited operations designed to bring immediate pressure upon an enemy.

During the 1930s a number of military and civilian commentators publicly criticized the army for refusing to create a force capable of rapid offensive operations that was not dependent upon full national mobilization. De Gaulle called for the creation of a rapid reaction force, and in the Chamber of Deputies Paul Reynaud echoed de Gaulle's views. As early as the 1920s Reynaud had insisted that France required a highly mobile army in order to enforce the Versailles Treaty and support the allies in Eastern Europe. Reynaud later noted:

It is an axiom that a country's army is one of the instruments of its policy. A country must, therefore, have an army suitable for its policy. On the morrow of Versailles two policies were conceivable:

1. That of the Wall of China: to build a Maginot Line stretching from the North Sea to Switzerland and to place behind it a defensive army. . . .
2. That of a European Balance of Power: to find allies capable of balancing German power in the east and at the same time to create an offensive army fit to attack Germany if she attacked our allies.[43]

Although neither critic claimed that the current system would not work, they believed that an additional capability was required, for without a mobile strike force a fundamental contradiction would exist between the Republic's foreign policy and its military strategy.

On 21 July 1936 the head of the War Minister's Military Cabinet submitted a paper in response to calls for a special intervention force. A professionalized strike force, according to the high command, would be expensive, would drain the army of vital professional cadres, and would create an army within the army with potentially dangerous consequences for civil–military relations. Moreover, a mechanized intervention force would not be militarily effective. Successful attacks required both careful preparation and an immense superiority in men and material. The army did not believe in passive defense. Rather it believed in initial defense to protect the integrity of the national territory while the country mobilized and prepared for a counteroffensive. As far as rendering aid to allies was concerned, those countries with a common frontier could count upon the prompt arrival of French forces. Allies geographically distant from France would receive indirect assistance: French air and naval forces would render immediate help, and the army's mobilization would require the Germans to retain substantial forces on the Western Front. Ultimately the Republic would send an expeditionary corps to operate with the Eastern allies.[44]

The army, the report concluded, was indeed the army of the nation's policy. France did not seek war and would never start one. The nation's military policy was, therefore, fully in accord with the state's policy and interests.[45] The army thus admitted that it had neither the capability nor the intention of supporting efforts to maintain the status quo by offensive operations against Germany. The conviction that superior German human and economic resources would lead only to a lengthy total war was reflected in the army's post-1918 war plans.

Even during the 1920s, when France enjoyed its greatest relative military advantages over Germany, war plans were tinged with pessimism. Plan P, drawn up in 1920 and in effect until 1923, assumed that an 80-division French army required the support of the Belgian and Czech armies to disrupt German mobilization by advancing into the Ruhr and the Main River Valley in order to cut Germany in half. Having severed Germany, the plan called for the establishment of light field fortifications to resist counterattacks while diplomatic intervention brought the war to a successful conclusion. Plan A, in force from 1924 to 1928, required more than 80 French and Belgian divisions to advance across the North German Plain to rescue Poland from a German offensive.[46]

After the introduction of one-year conscript service, plans became even more pessimistic in their assumptions. Plan B, in effect from 1929 to 1931, sought to resist German and Italian attacks on the nation's territory, and there was no further discussion of operations east of the Rhine. French forces in the Rhineland were to withdraw through a series of fortified lines while other units guarded the Alpine frontier and Tunisia. Only after full mobilization would the army undertake offensive operations. Plan C, written after the end of military occupation of the Rhineland but while the region was still demilitarized, was in effect from 1931 to 1933. The plan sought to counter surprise attacks against Belgium, Alsace, Lorraine, or Switzerland. Mobile forces were to counter the initial assaults and secure the national territory while the country mobilized.[47] The last prewar plan, Plan D, remained in force to 1939. Its goals were to secure the frontier with less than full mobilization, to parry surprise attacks, and to provide mobile forces to assist Belgium and Luxembourg if Germany attacked either country. Reservists could be recalled to reinforce the covering or the mobile forces, and the army could cover the nation's borders and screen a general mobilization.[48]

On 15 April 1939 the army staff produced a paper discussing the nation's strategy in the likely event of war in the near future. Germany, according to the report, possessed 54 active, 35 to 40 reserve, 32 to 36 Landwehr, and 17 frontier divisions. With second echelon formations mobilized, the Reich would be able to place 200 divisions in the field. Italy had 75 divisions in Europe and 10 in Africa. To face the Axis powers, France had 67 field divisions, 17 fortress divisions, 7 divisions in North Africa destined for the Western Front, and 7 for local defense. Great Britain could eventually deploy 19 divisions on the Continent. Poland had 50 divisions, Rumania 35, and Yugoslavia 35. Greece and Turkey together possessed 50 divisions. The Axis powers could not sustain a long war because of serious economic problems, especially a shortage of petroleum products. The Germans and Italians would seek a rapid victory. The formation of a coalition would be a slow process, and only England could supply direct support to France. Therefore, the army staff concluded, France and England would have to endure until the moment when they could undertake offensive operations. In the initial phases of a war, they would seek to establish a solid Western Front, force the Germans to fight on two fronts, blockade the Reich, protect the Mediterranean lines of communication, and, when fully mobilized and sustained by the Eastern allies, attack Italy and finally Germany.[49]

Most French political leaders agreed with the high command's projections concerning the nature of a future conflict and, like the military, rejected the concept of limited offensive operations as a prescription for disaster. Consequently, even before Hitler began to rearm the Reich, the French had abandoned any idea of initial offensive operations against Germany. French generals and politicians believed that they could, if fully mobilized and fully backed by coalition partners, win a second war against Germany, but they were unwilling to pay the price of victory.

RESPONSE TO CRISES

In every crisis preceding World War II, the French response was similar. Because of resource imbalances, the Republic could not face Germany alone. Allies were unreliable or unwilling to resort to arms to halt Nazi aggression, and if war came, victory would bleed France white. Consequently, French civilian and military leaders tried to avoid war even at the price of strategically vital concessions, to increase the pace of military spending in order to convince Hitler that he could not defeat France in a direct clash of arms, and to negotiate a general détente with Berlin and Rome. Intelligence assessments sustained the government's gloomy picture of the nation's strategic position by indicating that France, in the absence of reliable allies, faced an immensely strong Germany and would have to bear the initial phase of a conflict alone.

Aware of the increased pace of German rearmament after 1933, French intelligence concluded that in 1934 Germany possessed an army of 300,000 active troops supported by 100,000 paramilitary police, 300,000 reservists, 400,000 recruits undergoing military instruction, and 2.8 million SA Troopers.[50] A 2d Bureau assessment of 28 January 1935 placed the German strength at 300,000 regular troops, a number that would climb to 400,000 by spring and would be supported by 300,000 trained reserves and more than 1.8 million paramilitary troops. The air force contained 1,300 combat aircraft, 400 trainers, and 1,500 civil aircraft of military utility. There were 6,000 trained pilots in the German air arm. In war the 2d Bureau estimated that Germany could mobilize 90 to 100 divisions, of which 40 were capable of offensive operations. By the end of the year estimates of German strength rose even higher. Estimates for 1937 indicated that the Reich would have about 1 million men under arms.[51] Given the perceived force balance, it was not surprising that when Hitler in 1935 reintroduced conscription in direct violation of the Versailles Treaty the French response avoided threats of force. France sought closer ties with Italy, but the idea that Germany had created a *casus belli* never, according to François-Poncet, entered anyone's head.[52] Nobody seriously contemplated reducing Germany to obedience by force of arms.

The Rhineland crisis witnessed a similar response. As early as October 1934, the army informed the Foreign Minister that Germany intended to occupy the Rhineland no later than fall 1936.[53] In May 1935 the consul in Cologne noted that the Germans were preparing to move into the Rhineland the following spring.[54] By January 1936 the French knew from multiple sources—the attaché in Berlin, consuls in Cologne and Dusseldorf, and information supplied by the Swiss general staff—that reoccupation was imminent.[55] The army high command informed the government that because of German strength France could do nothing short of general war to stop the German move. It recommended increased defense allocations but made no proposals for a direct response to German initiatives.[56]

On 17 February 1936 the Defense Minister informed the Minister of Foreign Affairs that in case of a German move into the Rhineland, France should undertake a number of countermeasures: reinforcement of the fortress troops, placing all fortress troops on full alert, and recalling certain reservist classes to strengthen the frontier defenses. There was no suggestion of a direct riposte against Germany. Nor did the government ask for such an option.[57] Two days later, in a conference of the service chiefs of staff, General Gamelin stated that France could not act against the Reich without allied support. He repeated the statement on 8 March, on the same day the 3d Bureau reported that only full mobilization and total war would force the Germans to relinquish the Rhineland.[58] All the French could do was reinforce the frontier garrisons against the contingency of a sudden German advance from the Rhineland into Lorraine.[59]

Although Léger at the Foreign Affairs Ministry told the Premier that strong French action would force London and Brussels to support Paris, Gamelin, aware of the reluctance of the government to undertake a strong response, continued to emphasize the dangers of unilateral action.[60] On 11 March and again on 28 March, he told government officials that the Germans had 295,000 troops in the Rhineland and that the Republic's military system did not give the nation the option of organizing an expeditionary corps to counter the German initiative. To act decisively, France would have to establish a million-man covering force and proceed to undertake general mobilization. Even then an invasion of the Rhineland would quickly produce a strategic deadlock.[61] The Republic could not in fact achieve victory outside the ranks of a major coalition. However, instead of attempting to improve the nation's diplomatic and strategic situation by forceful action, leaders used the problems as an excuse for inaction.

The French were aware that Austria was next on Hitler's agenda. As early as April 1936, the Austrian Foreign Minister expressed fears of German aggression to the French chargé in Vienna, and in late 1937 the 2d Bureau predicted that Berlin's next move would be the seizure of Austria.[62] Once again, fear of German strength and alliance disunity provided French leaders with reasons for inactivity. In June 1936 French intelligence placed German strength at 34 active, 50 frontier, and 17 reserve divisions.[63] In January 1937 the air attaché in Berlin reported that Luftwaffe strength had grown to 2,055 combat aircraft, of which 1,233 were modern first-line planes.[64] In June the army staff noted that the Red Army was seriously weakened by purges and that Poland remained hostile to closer ties between Paris and Moscow.[65] Growing tensions with Italy, British reluctance to become involved in Central European affairs, and the absence of treaty obligations to defend Austrian sovereignty combined to persuade the French to remain passive in face of the *Anschluss.*

After the occupation of Austria, the French realized that Czechoslovakia, the only reliable French ally in Eastern Europe, would be the next German target and quickly concluded that because of the *Anschluss* the Czech state was strategically exposed and indefensible.[66] The day after the German march to Vienna, Gamelin noted that Czechoslovakia was encircled and that a French attack in support of the Czechs would quickly grind to a halt against the German Westwall. The *Anschluss* had added ten Austrian divisions to the German order-of-battle, bringing the total to 120 divisions—a number that would soon grow to 200. If war came, France could do no more than defend the Métropole and the Empire.[67]

During the following months, French military and diplomatic officials continued to emphasize the dangers inherent in seeking to sustain Czech independence. In a memo of 14 March 1938 dealing with the consequences of the *Anschluss,* Daladier, as Defense Minister, noted that the Czechs were encircled, and in case of war France could not easily or rapidly break through the German defenses in the west.[68] Gamelin agreed with his civilian superior and on 15 March 1938 issued a memo dealing with the general conduct of a war with Germany. French strategy called for halting the initial enemy offensive, mobilizing, and launching a counterblow. An immediate attack to assist an Eastern ally was not feasible, because the best route through the Low Countries and into the Ruhr was foreclosed by Belgian and Dutch neutrality. Terrain in other parts of the Rhineland was too difficult and too well fortified to promise an avenue for offensive operations.[69]

On the same day the CPDN met to discuss possible French initiatives. Again the high command insisted that the Republic could not directly assist the Czechs. In case of war, France could only mobilize and thus force the Germans to station substantial numbers of troops in the west. No other power could supply direct assistance to Czechoslovakia. An army staff study of 13 September noted that in case of war France should assure its territorial security, seek allies, and establish a blockade of Germany. The staff did not even mention offensive operations in the opening phases of a conflict.[70]

Bleak assessments continued throughout the crises. On 4 April the Secretariat of the CPDN reported that the only way to assist the Czechs was to create an eastern front, but the Eastern allies were not willing to cooperate, and the British were far from ready for a major war.[71] The next day the Minister of Foreign Affairs informed the Cabinet that neither Poland nor the Rumanians would support the Czechs in case of a German attack. The French ambassador to the Court of St. James's reported on 7 April that England was not prepared for a major war, and a month later the attaché in Bucharest noted that the Little Entente would not support the Czechs in a conflict with Germany.[72] On 21 September the 2d Bureau estimated that it was futile to fight to preserve Czech independence and territorial integrity and that Prague had no realistic choice but to accept territorial sacrifices in the hope of retaining national sovereignty.[73] The same day Gamelin informed Daladier that the Czechs could not resist a German assault for more than a few days.[74] Five days later the air force chief of staff told the Air Minister that in a war against the Reich the French air force would lose 64 percent of its strength within the first two months.[75] Although he did not predict German losses or specify the operational conditions under which the French would suffer such heavy casualties, his report was passed to the Cabinet, which used it as further evidence of the futility and danger of resorting to war.

The French government had substantial evidence concerning Germany's difficulties in sustaining its armaments expansion. Paris also had information indicating that in a war the Czechs would give a good account of themselves and were not, in fact, completely cut off from outside assistance. The government nevertheless remained undissuaded from its desire to avoid a conflict.

Reporting from Germany had for several years indicated that the economy was in difficult straits. In December 1936 the ambassador in Berlin reported that the Reich was experiencing severe shortages of raw materials and lacked the hard currency to purchase them.[76] On 13 September 1938 he telephoned Paris to report that the Reich was undergoing a severe inflationary spiral and needed to import 2 million tons of grain annually.[77] The 2d Bureau, meanwhile, had noted that in addition to severe economic problems, Germany was experiencing severe problems in the realm of military expansion. The army had a shortage of more than 20,000 commissioned officers, and the Luftwaffe was receiving aircraft faster than it could train pilots and ground crew personnel. The French also knew that the Westwall was far from complete and that the concrete in many of the works had not yet hardened.[78]

In June 1937 the French ambassador in London reported to Paris the British belief that the Czechs could resist a German offensive for three months without outside assistance.[79] In June 1938 the 2d Bureau reported that the Czech army mobilization of the previous May indicated that the Czechs could respond rapidly and effectively to a crisis.[80] Other reports indicated that the Czech army had good equipment, well-trained officers and staffs, and high morale.[81] Gamelin told Daladier on 9 September that the Czechs, when mobilized, were able to place 34 divisions in the field, and on 26 September, despite his gloomy predictions of the 21st, he informed the British Committee of Imperial Defence that the Czechs were capable of offering significant resistance in Bohemia and if overwhelmed would retreat to Moravia and continue the war.[82] He met with Chamberlain on 27 September 1938 and told him that the Czechs would fight on after the loss of Bohemia and that Germany, because of the lack of trained military cadres and a serious shortage of primary materials, especially oil, would be unable to sustain a long war.[83] Gamelin appears to have been playing a double game, assuring the British that a Franco-British coalition could emerge victorious from a conflict with Germany while sustaining the belief of French political leaders that a war would not save the Czechs and would be a costly conflict of attrition. Meanwhile, 2d Bureau and attaché reporting from Prague continued to indicate that the Czechs would offer substantial resistance to any German attack.[84]

Estimates of Soviet strength and of Moscow's ability to assist Czechoslovakia were also reasonably optimistic. The military attaché in Moscow on 22 March 1938 reported to Daladier that the Soviets were rapidly developing their heavy industry and that the media defined Germany as the main enemy.[85] A Czech report passed to the French asserted that the purges had not seriously reduced the Red Army's capabilities,[86] and on 8 April the French military attaché reported that the Soviet armed forces could defend their country and launch limited offensive operations in the West.[87] Ten days later the ambassador informed Bonnet that the Soviets could supply aircraft to the Czechs and in fact had already delivered twenty to Czech airfields.[88] Paris realized that neither Poland nor Rumania would permit the passage of Soviet ground units, but the Rumanians told the French that they would not hinder the passage of Soviet aircraft across their territory on their way to Czech aerodromes.[89]

Despite information describing German problems, Czech strength, and Soviet willingness to aid the Prague government, the French continued to take a pessimistic view of the overall strategic situation. Instead of striving to persuade London, Warsaw, and other powers to take a firm stand against German demands, Paris chose to emphasize problems rather than opportunities. On 19 September, Daladier told the Cabinet that the British refused to become involved in a war in Central Europe. He went on to assert that the Luftwaffe outnumbered the French air force by three to one and that the army could not breach the Westwall without tremendous losses and in any case would not be able to breach the German defenses in time to render assistance to the Czechs.[90] To the government, war itself—not defeat—was the greatest possible disaster, and throughout the crisis Daladier was content to allow the British government to take the lead in appeasing Germany. The French position was that the Republic would resist an armed attack on Czechoslovakia but would accept the diplomatic dismemberment of the Czech state even to the point of placing substantial pressure on

Prague to relinquish to Hitler all that he demanded. France thus poised itself to prevent Germany's taking by force what would be given to it by negotiation.

After Munich, France continued to seek closer ties to Britain, to provide for the defense of the Empire, and to search for an understanding with Berlin and Rome as a prelude to a Europe-wide détente. While not deluding themselves as to the nature of German intentions, French leaders continued to hope for a peaceful reintegration of Germany into the European system. Continued German aggression coupled with a sharp turn in public opinion against further concessions finally convinced the leaders of the Republic that they had to toughen their stance. The government increased the pace of rearmament in the hope that deterrence could replace appeasement as the basis of French policy.

In the aftermath of Munich, the French realized that the dismemberment of Czechoslovakia opened all of Eastern Europe to German expansion. Gamelin noted that the French position in Central Europe had received a serious blow, and the nation therefore had to strengthen its ties with Britain, prepare to fight a long war in order to wear down the enemy economy, and seek new allies.[91] During the last months of 1938, the 2d Bureau and the ambassador in Berlin predicted further German efforts to expand to the east. Gamelin informed Daladier on 19 December that Germany's next target was Poland, which was a step on the road to the conquest of the Ukraine.[92]

Paris, meanwhile, tried and failed to obtain international guarantees for the independence of the post-Munich Czech state and soon came to the realization that Hitler's next move would be not a drive to the east but the final liquidation of Czechoslovakia. Reports that in case of hostilities the Germans would place up to 250 divisions in the field led Paris to react with a combination of outrage and inactivity to the destruction of what remained of Czech independence.[93] The day after the German occupation of Prague the 2d Bureau noted that Germany had neutralized up to 40 Czech divisions in 1938 and had now acquired arms and equipment for 34 infantry and four armored divisions. On 20 March 1939 the military attaché in Prague informed Daladier that without firing a shot Germany had acquired 1.5 million rifles, 20,000 machine guns, 600 tanks, 750 military aircraft, and control of the large and efficient Czech munitions industry.[94]

After the occupation of Prague, French attention again focused on Eastern Europe as reports of German plans to move east resumed. French intelligence ultimately came to the realization that Hitler's next target was Poland. The attaché in Berlin in January 1939 noted that

Germany would not be ready for war in the current year but was carrying out covert mobilization. On 23 March he reported that it would be a mistake for Germany to attack Poland, which had a good army and could receive assistance from both the Western Powers and the U.S.S.R. If Germany struck at Poland, an attack would come only after Berlin attained bases in Rumania and Lithuania, and the next German move would be directed at Rumania and Yugoslavia.[95] On 5 April, however, the 2d Bureau noted that the occupation of Bohemia and Moravia was only the first step of even larger operations that directly threatened French interests, and a month later the Bureau reported that Hitler had abrogated the 1934 nonaggression pact with Poland, indicating that Poland was in fact his next target.[96] The 2d Bureau also reported that Berlin's ultimate objective was to push to the Black Sea in order to gain control of raw materials needed for a long war. In such a conflict, the Italians would assist the Germans by attacking French lines of communication in the Mediterranean, would attempt to open a second front along the Pyrenees, and would launch air attacks against French positions in Chad.[97]

Italian activities continued to alarm the government during the winter and spring of 1938 and 1939. In February Paris learned that by the beginning of March the Italians would have 800,000 men under arms.[98] A report on forces available to defend the Empire indicated that France had 441,000 men and could handle almost any Italian threat in the region, but continued reports of Rome's plans to hold major maneuvers on the Italian mainland in August, when viewed in conjunction with the German mobilization, presented an ominous picture.[99]

As the German buildup in the east continued, Paris and London sought military talks with Moscow. Reporting from the U.S.S.R. suddenly became more optimistic concerning Soviet military capabilities. On 13 June the attaché noted that the Soviet army contained 110 active divisions and 5,000 tanks. The weapons were modern, and the troops were well trained and well motivated. Because of the purges, the officers were young and lacked experience, but the attaché asserted that this problem was only temporary.[100] Closer ties with the U.S.S.R. would either deter Hitler or, in case of war, deprive him of vital resources and perhaps create a major threat in the east.

The negotiations, however, proceeded very slowly, primarily because of Anglo-French reluctance to deal with Moscow. French officials in Moscow began to warn Paris of growing Soviet impatience. On 13 July the military attaché warned Bonnet that unless the government acted quickly the Soviet Union would adopt a neutral stance in the

Polish crisis and might even turn to Berlin and arrange a fourth partition of Poland.[101] From Berlin, the French air attaché warned of a major shift in Soviet foreign policy, and upon his return to Paris, he insisted upon a meeting with the Foreign Minister and repeated his warning.[102]

Intelligence reports indicating a change of direction in Soviet foreign policy failed to persuade London and Paris to speed their efforts to conclude a security pact with the U.S.S.R. The Hitler–Stalin Pact destroyed all chances of creating a united front that might have deterred Hitler from striking at Poland or forced him to undertake hostilities under unfavorable circumstances.

On the evening of 23 August 1939, the CPDN met to assess the strategic impact of the Nazi–Soviet Pact and to discuss the future of French strategic responses to German aggression. Daladier asked whether in the light of the drastically changed international circumstances France should continue to honor its commitment to Poland or reconsider the policy and profit from the time gained to strengthen the nation's defenses. The response to the question was essentially a function of the strategic balance. Gamelin told the CPDN that Poland could resist a German attack long enough to prevent the Germans from attacking in the west before the spring of 1940. Consequently, the Committee concluded that France had no choice but to hold to its previous commitments to Poland. General Gamelin and Admiral Darlan asserted that the army and navy were ready. The Air Minister stated that the air balance was much better than in 1938. French and British fighter strength was roughly equal to the combined strength of the German and Italian air arms. Modern French bombers would not be available until the beginning of 1940, but British bombardment aircraft could strike at targets in northern Germany. Gamelin and Darlan indicated that at the start of a conflict France could do little directly against Germany but could act vigorously against Italy if Rome sided with Berlin. The Committee, therefore, concluded that France should begin to put the covering forces in place and begin general mobilization.[103]

The French had also achieved one of their major goals—a security agreement with Great Britain. Staff talks in late March and early April had produced a basic agreement on Anglo-French strategy. The two powers' war aims were to maintain the territorial security of their empires, to check any German invasion of the Low Countries, and to seek the defeat of Italy before attacking Germany. The French also believed that Germany lacked the manpower, money, and raw materials for a long war, and with the help of the Royal Navy planned to mount a sustained blockade of Germany.[104] Thus, despite last-minute efforts to avoid hostilities, France entered World War II in a reasonably optimistic frame of mind.

FRENCH ASSESSMENTS

In each crisis between 1936 and 1939, the French government received timely, detailed information concerning German intentions. Information flowed from the field to the decision-makers in a precise, orderly manner, and the quantity of operational and tactical data increased as the Germans prepared to strike. For example, the number of consular, 2d Bureau, and SR reports concerning preparations for the reoccupation of the Rhineland increased dramatically in the spring of 1936. In 1938 the government was fully informed about German preparations to move into Austria, and during the Munich crisis Paris received detailed reports of German troop movements down to regimental levels.[105] In 1939 German mobilization and troop concentrations along the Polish frontier were known in Paris by early summer. The system functioned as it was supposed to, and in no case was the government surprised by German political and military initiatives.

The French were also fully and acutely aware of Hitler's short-term and long-term goals. As early as August 1936 the 2d Bureau noted that Hitler intended to incorporate all German-speaking people in the Reich, defeat France in a quick war, isolate England, and conquer living space in the east.[106] The French were able to predict with substantial lead time the timing to within a matter of days of each German move, and they quickly understood the strategic consequences of Hitler's initiatives.

The government recognized well before 1936 that German reoccupation of the Rhineland would have near catastrophic consequences for the Republic's Eastern alliance system. Paris also grasped that the *Anschluss* would simultaneously strengthen Germany and endanger Czechoslovakia. Daladier was bleakly aware that Munich not only marked the betrayal of an ally but also represented a major strategic defeat for France. The leaders of the Republic quickly understood that the occupation of Prague allowed Germany significant military benefits at no cost and destroyed hopes of transforming the Munich agreements into a general détente.

There were points of confusion and debates over precise details. For example, after the occupation of Prague, French intelligence was undecided about the direction of future German expansion for several weeks, but French leaders were generally aware of the goals of the Third Reich and of the timing of German moves. Such knowledge, however, made relatively little difference, given the overwhelming French desire to avoid another world war. Appeasement, deterrence, and even defeatism proved to be stronger motives than a willingness to preserve the *status quo* by force of arms.

Since Germany was the Republic's traditional enemy and most significant security threat, the government devoted a major portion of its intelligence assets to the collection and analysis of information on all aspects of the German state and society. Thus, in addition to seeking to uncover German political intentions, French intelligence also provided the government with assessments dealing with the state of the German economy and public morale. Paris was well aware that the Reich labored under severe economic constraints, which created numerous problems in the rearmament effort and would make it difficult for Berlin to face the challenge of a total protracted war. Long-term economic problems would not be as relevant in a short-war scenario. French analysts realized that the Germans sought rapid wars precisely to avoid their economic problems, but believed that any conflict involving France would have to be protracted.

Reporting from Germany also enabled the French government to learn that the German public was fearful of a new war. During the Munich and Polish crises, Paris was fully informed of the problems besetting the German home front. French intelligence produced accurate assessments of both the German economy and the state of public opinion.[107] Given the inevitable limitations of French resources and the difficulty inherent in collecting information in a totalitarian state, information was of necessity episodic, but it was sufficient to provide the government with a clear and generally accurate picture of German society.

The French did occasionally misinterpret the internal politics of the Nazi hierarchy. Diplomatic reporting often presumed that moderate and radical Nazi cliques and other interest groups exercised genuine influence over Hitler's decisions, a logical mistake since most regimes, including the Third Republic, contained influential factions and interest groups. The French did not comprehend that Hitler encouraged chaos in his inner circle because it made him the final arbiter on all major issues and enhanced his personal authority. On the other hand, in the absence of highly placed reliable informants, it is almost impossible to obtain precise information on the inner workings of any government, and the French belief in the existence of factions did not seriously distort their understanding of the Nazi regime.

Although Germany was their primary concern, the French realized that the strategic balance was not static. The reactions of other powers were a critical factor in understanding the Republic's overall positions, and Paris understood that German moves would have repercussions throughout Europe. Reporting from other capitals kept the government regularly informed of the reactions of other powers to developments in the Franco-German balance.

French leaders always believed that an alliance with Great Britain was a sine qua non of the Republic's policy and strategy, and Paris constantly sought closer ties with London. In the late 1930s the French assumed that at the start of hostilities only the Royal Navy and the RAF would play a significant role, while land forces would reach the Continent only after a substantial period of preparation.[108] In the aftermath of every crisis, France sought to use German success as leverage to obtain a more effective relationship with Britain. The French also found England's reluctance to become involved in Continental affairs a convenient excuse for their own unwillingness to take a strong stand against German expansion. Paris was in fact quite willing to let London take the lead in appeasing Germany.

By the late 1930s Paris presumed that Italy was hostile and that Mussolini would probably side with Hitler in a general war. The French were not particularly afraid of the Italians and regarded the Italian armed forces as well trained and well motivated but ill equipped for modern war. French intelligence also believed that Italy lacked the natural and industrial resources to sustain a protracted conflict.[109] France also found Italy to be a useful interlocutor with Germany. As it became more obvious that a clash with Germany was unavoidable, remaining French fears about Italian participation on the side of Germany gave way to optimistic appraisals of the ability of the Franco-British forces to achieve early victories at Italy's expense.

The French wished to use the U.S.S.R. as a counterweight to Germany but were reluctant to establish precise and detailed ties with Moscow. French authorities were satisfied with an arrangement that denied Soviet resources to Germany while at the same time providing Moscow with minimum leverage over French policy. Reluctance to strengthen ties with the Soviets, coupled with the knowledge that the British were now committed to French security, offers a partial explanation of the absence of alarm in Paris when the government received reports of the forthcoming shift of Stalin's policy. Domestic political considerations combined with anti-Soviet positions held by Britain and a number of Eastern allies restrained France from doing more than holding the U.S.S.R. at arms' length. Reporting from the Soviet Union was constantly shifting in its appraisals of Russian strength and military capabilities and often seemed to be designed to follow the views of the high command and the government.

French analysis of Czech capabilities was constantly flawed by adherence to worst-case assumptions and a prior commitment not to go to war to protect Czech sovereignty. The high command understood that the government needed to see a weak, helpless Czechoslovakia in order to justify its policy of appeasement. Thus during the Munich crisis Gamelin told two stories, assuring the British that the Czechs could offer extended resistance and telling the CPDN that Czechoslovakia would collapse quickly under a German onslaught. He was apparently attempting to establish closer ties with the British and simultaneously to support his own government's policy of war avoidance. His gambit was successful, as the French government in 1938 was in fact not concerned with determining the possibilities of resisting German expansion but was seeking a way out of having to fight, even at the price of significant strategic concessions.

The military intelligence agencies were, naturally, concerned with providing estimates of the German order-of-battle and overall military capabilities. Both the SR and the 2d Bureau made substantial errors in order-of-battle data in the middle and late 1930s, although their estimates became more accurate as war approached. Of course, obtaining accurate information concerning another country's forces is a difficult task. Even a friendly power is not always forthcoming with information describing its armed forces, and a hostile totalitarian state will make collection as difficult as possible, attempting not only to conceal information but also to engage in efforts at disinformation. In the summer of 1938, for example, the commander of the French air force paid a visit to the Luftwaffe and returned to inform the Cabinet that in case of war the French air force would be virtually destroyed within the first two months. In fact, however, the Luftwaffe was by no means ready for full-scale combat and had presented him with a giant hoax, declaring prototype aircraft to be in full production and producing strength figures that had no relation to reality.[110] Unless collectors can blanket a target country with a vast network of open and covert sources, there will inevitably be gaps in order-of-battle data. Constructing an order-of-battle—bean counting—is in fact a daunting task, a reversal of the notion that it is easier to count beans than to divine intentions.

French intelligence in the 1930s faced these standard problems, and its views were influenced by a great respect for German power derived from previous wars, governmental pessimism concerning the military balance, and general fear of a new war. The French remembered that during World War I the German army had expanded from 87 to 252 divisions. The French also recalled that from the outset of hostilities the Germans had employed reservists in a front-line role. The French also used territorial formations effectively, and the postwar reliance of the French army on mobilized reservists to attain full combat strength further convinced French observers that Germany would also make effective use of reserve units.

Reluctance to engage in a new war was prevalent in both military and civilian circles. Gamelin, a loyal republican, was determined to avoid a clash with his civilian superiors and supported their views on the dangers and costs of renewed conflict. His insistence on civil–military concord coupled with the army's strong hierarchical structure placed a damper on analysts who held views of German strength different from those accepted by the generals and politicians. Consequently, French intelligence tended to overestimate the Reich's military strength by focusing primarily on the numerical balance and giving limited attention to the quality of the German armed forces.

French intelligence did predict accurately the number of German active divisions but consistently overestimated the number and capabilities of reserve units. On one occasion, the SR simply divided the total number of reservists by 25,000 to arrive at the number of reserve divisions available to the Germany army.[111] The French paid little attention to reserve equipment and training. The World War was primarily an infantry and artillery conflict, and tactics were relatively simple. Presuming that the German army of the 1930s was still primarily an infantry army, the French doubtless concluded that, despite severe officer and NCO shortages, reserve forces could be brought to a state of combat readiness with relative ease. Moreover, the vision of a large and proficient German army conformed with the views of the civilian leadership: Strong German forces meant that a war would be very costly, thus increasing the necessity of avoiding such a conflict. The existence of a powerful enemy also justified greater defense spending to deter the threat. Thus, the military's appraisals of the strength of the German army coincided with civilian perceptions and provided the government with a rationale to justify a policy of war avoidance.

French estimates of German air power fluctuated widely, for in addition to the usual problems involved in establishing an air order-of-battle, the French tended to employ worst-case assumptions to justify their reluctance to engage in a major war. Thus air intelligence placed the front-line strength of the Luftwaffe at 124 squadrons and 1,800 front-line aircraft in 1937 and 9,000 planes in 1938. The estimates declined in 1939, and the 2d Bureau in a summary covering the first months of the year placed Luftwaffe strength at 253 squadrons with 3,800 first-line aircraft.[112] In their examinations, the French paid relatively little attention to qualitative issues, including logistics, ready rates, pilot training, and ground crew availability. The French knew that their pilots had more experience than German airmen and that German factories were producing airframes faster than the Luftwaffe could absorb them, but they did not rate qualitative issues as a critical factor in judging the air balance.

French predictions of air losses in 1938 were based on general assumptions about air warfare rather than upon an analysis of sortie rates and specific missions. The French also expressed fear that the Luftwaffe could devastate the nation's cities, disrupt mobilization, and wreak havoc upon the civilian population. Such fears dissipated as war approached. Increased production and promised help from the RAF reduced the perception of German air attacks from a critical problem to one of manageable proportions.

French assessments of German operational doctrine were, on the whole, quite accurate. As early as 1923, French intelligence reported that although forbidden by the Versailles Treaty to possess tanks, the Germans nevertheless studied armored warfare, and infantry units conducted exercises using tractors as a substitute for tanks. In 1934 the 2d Bureau reported that the Germans were creating tank battalions and discussing the creation of even larger armored formations designed to strike rapidly and deeply into enemy rear echelon positions. On 5 April 1936, the 2d Bureau translated an article by Guderian on armored warfare noting that the basis of Guderian's doctrine called for armored divisions to attack by surprise, penetrate deeply into the enemy's territory, strike at strategic objectives, and work in close cooperation with air power. The 2d Bureau produced additional translations of Guderian's writings, including a 1938 study of *Achtung Panzer.*[113]

Reports on the 1937 German army maneuvers, which involved experiments with division-size armored units, made it clear to the

French high command that Guderian and other advocates of armored warfare had attained a sympathetic audience from the highest levels of the German leadership.[114] French intelligence also supplied numerous studies of German tank and antitank weapons and examined small-unit tactics.[115] By 1938 French political and military leaders understood that Germany would begin a war with a savage full-scale armored assault in a bid for a rapid and decisive victory.

Although the French understood the basic elements of the German doctrine of the continuous battle, they remained convinced of the superiority of their own concept of the methodical battle, which was the result of a great deal of study, debate, and analysis. The German system, the French believed, would work against lesser powers lacking natural or man-made defenses and adequate antitank weaponry but would fail when it encountered modern, well-equipped French forces. German tanks might rupture a portion of the French front at a terrible cost, but French armored and mobile divisions would counterattack and quickly seal off any penetration. With 14,000 antitank guns and more than 2,000 tanks coupled with the defensive power of the Maginot Line and other prepared positions, the French army was confident that it could halt any German offensive. The 2d Bureau in 1939 noted on a number of occasions that even the German army was not fully convinced of the efficacy of its armor doctrine and that German armor could not attain more than local successes against well-organized modern forces.[116]

Reports from China and from Spain seemed to confirm French views. French analysts attributed successes against armor to the inherent superiority of defensive firepower and presumed that tank breakthroughs were the result of inadequate defensive preparations. A French observer of the Sino-Japanese war noted that badly prepared attacks insufficiently supported by heavy artillery fire were bound to fail.[117] Reports from Spanish battlefields indicated that German tanks were mechanically defective and too lightly armored. They could not break through seriously prepared positions. Armor had to operate *en masse* in close conjunction with artillery and aviation. Armored forces also had to work in coordination with infantry units. The effectiveness of the tank attack was, according to French observers, a function of close liaison with other arms.[118]

General Dufieux, the Inspector General of Infantry, writing in the *Revue d'infanterie* of November 1938, concluded: "The Spanish experience has confirmed the lessons of the Great War on two important points: (1) Tanks should be employed in mass and on a front as extended as possible. . . . (2) They are not able to fight without the support of the artillery and the support of the infantry which is alone capable of clearing and occupying terrain."[119] The general concluded that the army's doctrine was essentially sound and required no drastic alterations. In his 1939 book *Une Invasion, est-elle encore possible?* General Narcisse Chauvineau derided mechanized forces and armored columns, asserting that they were easily halted by fixed and field fortifications and were subject to devastating counterattacks. A laudatory introduction by Marshal Pétain assured the public that French doctrine could defeat any new German operational techniques.[120] The German shift from light to medium tanks beginning in 1938 seemed to provide added confirmation for the army's view that lightning warfare might work in Eastern Europe but was ill suited to prevailing conditions in the West.[121]

Convinced that they had drawn the proper lessons of World War I and had responded effectively to postwar advances in technology, the French army viewed their own operational doctrine as superior to the new, untested German approach to modern war. Given the facts that only a small percentage of the German army consisted of armored and motorized divisions and that Guderian's doctrine was not battle-tested, the French assumption of superiority was not unreasonable. Moreover, challenging the conventional wisdom, especially when such wisdom was sustained by victory in the field and by meticulous postwar analysis, was not a task lightly undertaken. That the French did not fully understand the potential of armor and mechanization was not provable a priori. Honest, patriotic men could find that the army's operational doctrine was sound without being accused of intellectual rigidity or dishonesty.

French intelligence also failed fully to grasp the impact of air power and underestimated its tactical importance while overstating its strategic significance. In April 1937 the 2d Bureau reported that in Spain Soviet aircraft had attacked two Italian divisions and inflicted heavy losses upon them. The report also noted that the Italian formations had been surprised while still in marching columns and were poorly protected by anti-aircraft weapons.[122] In the following year the 2d Bureau reported that air power in Spain was generally employed in support of ground troops rather than against civilian targets and that tactical aviation was effective primarily against positions that lacked effective air defense assets.[123] Moreover, prior to the Polish campaign there were no clear cases in which tactical air power played a critical battlefield role, and even the Germans were not fully satisfied with air–ground cooperation during the war against Poland.

Strategic air power advocates throughout the 1920s and 1930s claimed that air power would be decisive in the next war and that strategic air power could provide victory without the necessity of extensive and costly ground combat. Such theories were, however, untested before World War II. The Spanish experience provided no guidance concerning the impact and effectiveness of strategic air bombardment. Nevertheless, the French took the strategic air threat very seriously, and fears for the safety of the civilian population and the belief that air attacks could disrupt mobilization and hamper war production contributed to the reluctance of the Republic's leaders to risk another war. When discussing Allied strategy in the late spring of 1939, the French decided to refrain from attacking German civilian targets because of fear of retaliation.

French military intelligence provided the government and the high command with detailed analyses of the Polish campaign both during and after hostilities. The 2d Bureau noted that the Polish army numbered 300,000 men in peacetime and upon mobilization could expand to about 2 million. The troops were hardy and well trained, but Polish artillery was limited in numbers and capabilities, and the army was weak in armor and motorization.[124] On 8 September 1939 General Faury, head of the French military mission, noted that German air power was assisting the advance of the armored divisions by breaking up Polish counterattacks, immobilizing reserves by attacking crucial road and rail centers, and destroying essential communications links. The panzer divisions, working in close cooperation with the Luftwaffe, never gave the Poles a chance to regroup and launch counterattacks. On 22 September the 2d Bureau noted that the panzer divisions not only pierced the Polish front but also struck boldly at Polish artillery positions and command posts.[125]

On 23 September General Faury submitted a long report to Gamelin. He noted that German armored divisions, acting in close liaison with aviation, played a preponderant role in the recent campaign. Because of the weakness of Polish anti-aircraft defenses, the Luftwaffe was able to fly its missions at low altitude during daylight with very light losses. After a breakthrough, the armored formations moved well ahead of other units and prevented the Poles from establishing new defensive lines. When the Poles sought to regroup in new positions, they would immediately encounter German tanks, and the German infantry had only to deal with positions and units already severely disrupted by the panzer divisions. The Luftwaffe successfully disorganized efforts to mount counterattacks. German armor attacked *en masse* with as many as 400 tanks at the main point of assault and after breaking through the

Polish front immediately assailed artillery positions and communications facilities in a successful effort to disrupt Polish command and control capabilities. The Germans, Faury warned, would use similar methods in the west. The most dangerous type of German attack would be a violent assault to rupture the French front, followed by immediate attacks on the rear of forces already immobilized by frontal attacks launched by infantry divisions.[126]

Despite timely and accurate reporting from Poland, the high command saw no reason to reexamine the fundamentals of its doctrinal approach to war. The army accepted the fact it would have to meet assaults of exceptional violence but continued to believe that German armor could not do more than achieve local successes. German doctrine was, according to the high command, simply not applicable in the west. The French army was far better trained and armed than the Polish forces, and the terrain in northern France and Belgium was far better suited to defensive warfare and the methodical battle than the open plains of Poland.

The Polish campaign failed to shake French confidence in their assessment of the nature of modern war. The French were convinced that they were entering upon a protracted conflict that in the long run promised victory. Unfortunately for the Republic, wars are also fought in the short term, and a nation must be able to respond effectively to episodes as well as to tendencies.

The unacceptability of war, however, overshadowed all other considerations. Unfavorable shifts in the strategic balance were less important to French leaders than the overriding need to avoid a new round of hostilities. Political leaders were in tune with popular sentiment when they chose the path of appeasement and accommodation rather than resistance, and popular opinion until the spring of 1939 supported rather than constrained French leaders in their resolve to avoid conflict with Germany. The post-Munich change in public opinion did not force the government's hand since the Republic's leaders were themselves reluctantly concluding that a change in policy toward German expansion was necessary. The argument that governments must lead and educate the public and not simply reflect popular moods may well be correct, but it goes well beyond the issue of net assessments and their influence on national policy. That a government has all the necessary information upon which to base decisions does not constitute a guarantee that the government will make the correct choice.

Ironically, the French belief that the next war would be a protracted conflict of attrition requiring massive mobilization by all the belligerents and years of struggle before the Allies attained victory was quite correct. The French were also correct in their assumption that the defeat of Germany would require the united efforts of a Great Power coalition. Finally, the French were right in assuming that a new world war would destroy forever the European power balance. Unfortunately, French long-term wisdom did not help the Third Republic in dealing with the immediate threat.

6

Soviet Net Assessment in the 1930s

Earl F. Ziemke

THE PIVOTAL YEAR in the interval between the two world wars began on 1 January 1930. The symbolic height of the postwar search for permanent peace had been reached in 1929, when the Kellogg–Briand Pact, which purportedly outlawed war, went into effect. But change was in the air. Five years of prosperity had ended, and a worldwide economic Depression was bringing governments under threat from the right and left. The search for permanent peace through collective security agreements continued during the year in a political and economic climate that was becoming perceptibly less propitious. In June 1930, when Britain and France terminated the occupation of the German Rhineland five years earlier than the Versailles Treaty required, the German government instantly raised complaints about other treaty impositions. German paramilitary groups were soon demonstrating in the restored territory, and France began building the Maginot Line along its northeast frontier.[1]

In July the signatories to the five-power Washington naval limitation treaty of 1922 convened a meeting in London to consider limiting other categories of naval vessels in addition to capital ships. Japan, angered by the continued restrictions placed on its battleship fleet, expanded its airfield building program in the mandated Pacific islands to convert them into surrogate aircraft carriers. France and Italy refused to attend the conference, and Germany, at the very least loosely interpreting the limits imposed on its naval building under the Versailles Treaty, was pushing to completion *Panzerschiff "A"* (later *Deutschland*), the first of a programmed series of three pocket battleships.[2]

The Soviet Communist Party held its Sixteenth Party Congress in June. Since the five-year plan for industrialization and the progress of agricultural collectivization were already in full swing, other considerations also figured significantly in the proceedings. The disastrous decline in the capitalist economies and the concurrent Soviet economic upswing proved the correctness of the Soviet course, yet the world economic crisis engendered a grave threat to the Soviet Union and justified an across-the-board speedup in development with "forcing" in heavy industry.

In addressing the latter concern, Stalin gave a snapshot survey of the international situation as seen through the lens of Marxist-Leninist and emergent Stalinist theory that would be employed in Soviet net assessment throughout the current decade—and beyond. Stalin posited a bipolar world in which the Soviet Union was "the citadel of revolution" and the United States "the principal capitalist country, the citadel of capitalism." The Soviet Union was, by its shining example, revolutionizing the working classes and colonial peoples everywhere. The United States, as the country in the most severe economic decline, would give a "colossal" impetus to the expansion and intensification of the economic crisis. Capitalism was in decay, and the result would be "an epoch of wars and revolutions."

There was another side, however, one that also would affect the net assessment process. The Communist Party could not deal exclusively in theory and the working out of the Marxian dialectic. It controlled the Soviet Union, which was a state no different from any others in most fundamental respects, and the state's interests imposed practical considerations. The Soviet state, Stalin told the Congress, was alone and "encircled" by capitalist states. While they were divided among themselves, they shared a common antagonism toward the Soviet Union and could be expected to consider "whether it would not be possible to solve this or that contradiction of capitalism . . . at the expense of the U.S.S.R." As deterrents to "adventurous attacks," Stalin maintained that the Soviet Union would rely on sympathy and support from the workers in capitalist countries, the growth of Soviet economic and political strength, increasing Soviet military power, and, most particularly, "undeviating pursuit" of the Soviet Government's peace policy. The Soviet Union, he asserted, adhered wholeheartedly to the "Kellogg Pact" and would continue "this policy of peace with all our might and with all the means at our disposal."[3]

Stalin's theoretical premises were not new. The ideas of inevitable armed confrontation with capitalism and capitalist encirclement were born in the 1917 revolution and matured in the Civil War. No nation existed under a more pervasive compulsion to assess its power against that of its enemies; and perhaps because the premises have not changed, no nation has made as continuous and deteremined an effort to conceal everything about such assessments. The attempt to investigate Soviet net assessment in the 1930s encounters at the outset the additional complication of the Soviet system having been in a state of flux that makes it difficult to discern even what the organization for net assessment might have been.

In the early 1930s the Soviet system completed its entry into the period to which Stalin's successors have applied the euphemism "cult of personality," but which actually constituted a conversion of the existing government and party organizations into a screen for an absolute autocracy. Stalin used the two inherently contradictory principles on which the Soviet system was based, collegiality and democratic centralism, to achieve what almost amounted to a second revolution. Collegiality had vested authority in an array of councils (soviets), collegiums, and committees. Democratic centralism had imposed a rigidly hierarchical structure that while retaining formal collegiality, greatly restricted its operation in the decision-making process. Stalin subordinated the entire structure to one authority, himself. That this circumstance must have profoundly affected the organization, the process, and the results of Soviet net assessment goes without saying.

ORGANIZATION

The Government

The highest executive body in the Soviet Government was the Council of People's Commissars, created in November 1917 and functionally comparable to the cabinet in other governments. Lenin had been the chairman from 1917 until his death in 1924. Vyacheslav M. Molotov became the chairman in 1930 and stayed in office until May 1941, when Stalin, who had not held any position in the government since 1922, assumed the chairmanship. The Council had early on become too large and diffuse a body to deal effectively with national security affairs, and the principle of democratic centralism had been applied in November 1918 (some months before it was officially adopted) to bring into being a war cabinet, the Council of Workers' and Peasants' Defense, under Lenin. During the Civil War the Defense Council had been the actual top executive organ in the government.

In late 1920, when the greater part of the Red Army's 5 million or so conscripts were being assigned to labor armies, the Defense Council had become the Council of Labor and Defense. The labor armies had been disbanded soon after, but the name remained. The Council was predominantly concerned in the early 1930s with determining the military share in the five-year plans. During 1935 and 1936 the emphasis shifted to the so-called technological reconstruction (*peres-troika*), the absorption into the armed forces of the weapons and equipment becoming available through the five-year plans. The Council of Labor and Defense was succeeded in April 1937 by the Defense Committee under the Council of People's Commissars, which was charged with "coordinating all measures pertaining to questions of defense related to the intensifying military threats against the U.S.S.R."[4]

Stalin's membership in the Defense Committee (although Molotov was its chairman) certainly confirmed it as the top governmental organization concerned with national security affairs, in fact, a war cabinet in reserve. That it became the State Defense Committee (with powers identical to those the Council of Workers' and Peasants' Defense had held during the Civil War) in June 1941, a week after the German invasion began, can be taken as additional confirmation. Strategic assessments would seem necessarily to have figured in the work of the defense councils and committees, but how they did their work or even that they did it has not been disclosed.

Direct governmental authority over the armed forces was vested in the people's commissars. People's commissariats for military and for naval affairs, established in early 1918, were merged into the People's Commissariat for Military and Naval Affairs in December 1922, which in March 1934 became the People's Commissariat of Defense. The navy acquired its own people's commisariat in December 1937 and thereafter came directly under the Defense Committee, but its people's commissar was not a member of the committee.

Kliment Y. Voroshilov was the People's Commissar for Military and Naval Affairs and of Defense from 1925 to 1940. Also a member of the Communist Party's Central Committee and its Politburo, within the commissariat he chaired its collegial body, which in the early 1930s was the Revolutionary Military Council (*Revvoyensovet*) of the U.S.S.R. He had been a leader in the so-called military opposition, party members who believed that they, not "military specialists" (ex-imperial officers), should command the Red Army and who opposed centralized command and formal discipline. The defense of Tsaritsyn (later Stalingrad) in 1918 during the Civil War had gained him a largely spurious military reputation and a close relationship with Stalin that contributed mightily to his subsequent rise in the party and the armed forces. In May 1940, in the aftermath of the badly bungled Winter War against Finland, Stalin made Marshal S. K. Timoshenko People's Commissar of Defense and moved Voroshilov to the deputy chairmanship of the Council of People's Commissars. In that capacity he served as chairman of the Defense Committee until Stalin took over in June 1941.[5] Of demonstrated military inability, Voroshilov nevertheless continued as a member of the State Defense Committee throughout the war.

The Military

The Workers' and Peasants' Red Army had been conceived in January 1918 as a volunteer, primarily workers' militia in which rank and class distinctions would not exist and leadership would be self-generated. Leon Trotsky, the People's Commissar for Military Affairs, had insisted, against stubborn opposition within the Party, that to meet threats of counterrevolution, renewed hostilities with Germany, and Allied intervention, the Red Army had to become a mass conscript army organized on conventional lines and trained and commanded by ex-imperial officers under the close surveillance of Party-appointed political commissars. He had also created a general headquarters of the armed forces with a supreme commander-in-chief, who was a military specialist, and a directing and planning organ, the Field Staff, that was manned by military specialists and was a general staff in everything but name.

To ensure political control over the general headquarters, Trotsky had formed the *Revvoyensovet*, in which he was the chairman, the commander-in-chief was a member ex officio, and the members (as many as fourteen) were senior Party men. Trotsky had also installed *revvoyensovety* in the field commands. Those consisted of the commander, the chief of staff, and their assigned political commissars, who were to confine themselves to political work and to warding off treachery. No military orders could be issued without the political officers' countersignature, however, and whenever the slightest doubt existed, the Party was likely to place more confidence in the commissar than in the commander.

In 1930 the *Revvoyensovet* received an assignment that appears clearly to have required net assessment in some form. The Central Committee ordered it to review the plan for armed forces development from two standpoints: (1) "numerical strength—in order not to be inferior to our probably enemies in the main theater of war"—and (2) "technology—to ensure that the decisive types of armament, aircraft, artillery, and armor, will be superior to those of the enemy." In the following year, the former was amended to specify "superiority over our probable enemies."[6] Since the plan was revised on an annual basis, the charge was very likely a continuing one.

An eighty-member, purely advisory body, the Military Council, replaced the *Revvoyensovet* in late 1934.[7] While the *Revvoyensovet*'s disappearance placed Stalin and Voroshilov in a position to assume total control over the defense commissariat, that was not its most immediate effect.[8] It and the simultaneous termination of the *revvoyensovety* in the field commands brought the military close to a long-sought goal, "unity of command," which meant freedom from direct political supervision. Consequently, the middle years of the 1930s were a bright period for the military leadership. In 1935 the Red Army Staff (formerly the Field Staff) became the Red Army General Staff, which appeared to give it stature equal to that of the general staffs in other European armies, and a command-service regulation terminated a prohibition on personal military ranks that had been in force since 1917. Thus V. K. Blyukher, S. M. Budenny, M. N. Tukhachevsky, Voroshilov, and A. I. Yegorov became marshals of the Soviet Union in 1935.[9] The appointments seemed to bring the military professionals to the fore vis-à-vis their chief, Voroshilov. In the next year, Tukhachevsky became first deputy people's commissar and war plans director, which all but confirmed him as commander-in-chief–designate.[10]

The military's heyday, such as it was, ended in May 1937. On the tenth of that month, the Council of People's Commissars passed a resolution reestablishing the commissar system throughout the armed forces and instituting "military councils" (*voyenny sovety*) composed of the commander, chief of staff, and a commissar in the field commands.

Tukhachevsky was relieved of all his posts and transferred to the out-of-the-way Volga Military District a day later.[11] A month later he would be executed. The purge was beginning.

In March 1938 the Central Committee created the Main Military Council (*Glavvoyensovet*) of the Army in the defense commissariat.[12] Voroshilov chaired the Main Military Council. The members were Marshal Blyukher, Marshal Budenny, Army Commander 1st Rank (full general) I. F. Fedko, Army Commander 1st Rank G. I. Kulik, Army Commissar 1st Rank L. Z. Mekhlis, Army Commander 1st Rank B. M. Shaposhnikov, Army Commissar 1st Rank Y. A. Shchadenko, and Stalin. Two more military members came into the council later, *General Armii* (full general) Kirill Meretskov, who replaced Shaposhnikov as chief of the general staff in August 1940, and *General Armii* Georgy Zhukov, Meretskov's successor in January 1941. Both were Civil War veterans, Party members, and career soldiers. Shaposhnikov and Meretskov stayed on the council as deputy people's commissars after being relieved as chiefs of the general staff.[13]

The Main Military Council was a general headquarters on standby modeled on the Civil War *Revvoyensovet*. (It became the *Stavka*, the World War II general headquarters, on 23 June 1941.)[14] The general staff was the planning and executive organ of the council, not of one or both commanders-in-chief. The other members, whether they held military appointments or not, represented the Party's interest and, more specifically, Stalin's interest. Who the commander-in-chief might actually be became uncertain early on and remained so until Stalin became supreme commander-in-chief in July 1941. Blyukher was executed in November 1938, Fedko in February 1939. Budenny became a deputy people's commissar in March 1939 and first deputy people's commissar in August 1940, which would seem to have singled him out as Fedko's successor; but Timoshenko was the people's commissar by then and, although he also was one of Stalin's Tsaritsyn group, was better qualified than Budenny to take over as commander-in-chief.[15]

Organizationally, the Main Military Council was a response to a narrowing focus on war. War had become more tangible and more imminent. The inevitable conflict with the capitalist world was coming down to specific balance-of-power concerns involving wars on one, two, or three fronts against Germany or Japan or both and possibly also Turkey. The threat from Germany in the West was the most dangerous, but in 1938 and 1939 that from Japan in the Far East was the most immediate.[16]

Stalin's membership in the Main Military Council fixed it solidly at the top of the military chain of command. Meretskov's memoirs give a guarded glimpse inside the council as it was in 1938, when he was its secretary in his capacity as deputy chief of the general staff. It met, he says, two or three times a week, usually to hear military district commanders' reports. Stalin attended frequently but was more than just a member of the council. "Virtually every military or military-economic issue," Meretskov states, "was settled with the direct participation of the General Secretary of the Central Committee of the CPSU [Stalin]." The council sent all of its decisions to Stalin and received the results of his action through Party and government channels in the form of directives.[17]

The navy, which had been the Bolsheviks' most reliable source of armed support until the Kronstadt mutiny of 1921, survived, but under a heavy political cloud and as an adjunct of the army. After 1924, the navy was the Directorate of Naval Forces in the *RKKA* (the Red Army), and its chief sat in the *Revvoyensovet* on the same footing as the army chiefs of infantry, artillery, and so forth. Although a naval staff existed, national plans and assessments involving naval matters were the Red Army Staff/general staff's responsibility. In effect, the navy was thereby shunted away from the strategic planning center, which was situated in the Main Military Council and the general staff. Andrei Zhdanov was Stalin's counterpart in the Main Navy Council. Zhdanov was the Leningrad Party secretary and as such nominally ranked next to Stalin in the Party and the Politburo, but all significant decisions still had to come from Stalin. Consequently, the navy had to work through Zhdanov and through the Defense Committee to get Stalin's attention and to rely on the not always cooperative chiefs of the general staff to keep abreast of current strategic developments.[18]

In 1918 Trotsky had created the Main Administration of the Workers' and Peasants' Red Air Fleet, which was charged with organizing air units and procuring supplies for them, and had established a section in the Field Staff to supervise the air units after they were assigned to support the troops at the fronts. It was an arrangement that continued throughout the pre–World War II period without much change other than in numbers of aircraft and personnel. The air units had 435 serviceable aircraft in 1918 and 228 in 1921. The Bolsheviks had developed a penchant for air power during the Civil War but did not have an aircraft industry. From 1924 to 1934, the chief of the then Directorate of the Air Force in the Red Army held a seat in the *Revvoyensovet,* and the Red Army Staff was responsible for air planning and operations. After the Main Military Council came into being, the deputy chief of staff for air in the general staff apparently was the air force's most direct source of access to the national assessment process.

The Communist Party

The ultimate authority in military affairs was vested in the Party's Central Committee, which in December 1918 had decreed that "the policy of the military department . . . is carried out on the precise basis of general directives issued by the Party in the name of its Central Committee and under its immediate control."[19] The Central Committee had from time to time exercised collegial control over military affairs during the Civil War and the early postwar years, but even then the principle of democratic centralism had acted to shift the exercise of its authority to the Politburo. By 1930 Stalin had eliminated all but a few traces of real collegiality in the Politburo and the Central Committee, and thereafter the Central Committee became the conduit through which he, in his capacity as Party General Secretary, had his decisions converted into directives to the Party and the government.

Stalin stood alone at the top of the Party and the organization for net assessment. Like the other leading Soviet figures of the time who were engaged in military and national security affairs, he derived his primary qualifications from the Civil War, and those, prima facie, were considerable. He had sat in on at least three of the four organizations that directed the Civil War, had been a plenipotentiary with unlimited powers at Tsaritsyn in 1918 and at Petrograd (Leningrad) in 1919, and had served as the chief commissar in several army groups. Important elements of what might be called Stalin's style in dealing with military matters also can be traced to the Civil War. He had displayed a towering confidence in his own ability. In the inner circle he had always deferred to Lenin, outside it to nobody; and he had not hesitated to lecture even Lenin in his dispatches from the field. He had been a master at putting himself in position to claim credit for correct decisions after the fact, and his military biography, first published in 1929 and updated at ten-year intervals thereafter, hailed him as an infallible strategist whose "masterly application of tactics [always] achieved the desired results."[20] During the Civil War he had formulated and vigorously applied a principle of war, "the stability of the rear," which required elimination of all actual, potential, or possible internal opposition to the Soviet regime.

Stalin had always ranked the military specialists foremost among the groups contributing to instability in the rear. He had shown an antipathy toward them that went a long way beyond the Party members' usual mistrust of former officers and involved a disdain for and suspicion of "specialists" in general and military professionals particularly. Nikita Khruschchev later described Stalin as a "specialist-eater" during the Civil War, who "remained a specialist-eater all his life."[21]

The Military Leadership

The technological reconstruction of the 1930s confronted Stalin with a tough problem: How to create a modern armed force that could stand up to presumed enemies without becoming a potential threat to his own authority. His initial approach was to give the military leadership a relatively free rein in the military-professional sphere and grant it a share in the national security policy-making process. As a result, until 1937 the Red Army's leaders appeared to be on the way to achieving a professionally autonomous position at least as close to the top as those their counterparts in other armies occupied.

The foremost figures in the army in those years were Tukhachevsky, Yegorov, Blyukher, Iona Yakir, and Iyeronim Uborevich. All five had been Party members since 1917 or 1918, had successfully commanded units as large as armies and army groups in the Civil War, were "legendary" war heroes, and had held high posts in the army throughout the 1920s. None owned his reputation or his advancement to Stalin. They were self-made men and prominent—and popular— public figures in their own right. All were elected to the Central Committee in 1934.[22]

The potent implications of Tukhachevsky's appointments as rearmament chief, war plans director, and first deputy people's commissar drew domestic and foreign attention to him in particular, attention he had worked at attracting throughout his Red Army career. The composer Dmitri Shostakovich, who knew him well in the late 1920s, remembered that he had then been called "the Red Napoleon."[23] His progressive advancement, published commentaries on military affairs, addresses to the Party congress in 1934 and the Party conference in 1936, and meetings with foreign leaders appeared to establish Tukhachevsky in a position of extraordinarily independent authority.

Stalin knew Tukhachevsky as an aristocratic former guards lieutenant turned Communist who had entered the Red Army in 1918 as a military specialist. While Stalin was an army group commissar, he had

twice resisted orders to assist army groups Tukhachevsky commanded.[24] Also, modernization plans Tukhachevsky had submitted while chief
of the army staff had so often encountered "unfriendly" receptions from
Stalin that he had asked for reassignment.[25] The biographer N. I.
Koritsky says Stalin had dismissed Tukhachevsky's proposals as "hare-
brained schemes."[26] When Stalin recalled Tukhachevsky to Moscow in
1931, he, for once, conceded a need for a "specialist." That he was also
prepared to tolerate a "Red Napoleon" is very doubtful, and after 1937
Stalin took care not to let another Tukhachevsky emerge.

Intelligence and Ancillary Organizations

The main organization with a capability for actually doing net assessment may have been situated outside the government and the military,
and may have been directly accessible only to Stalin. As General
Secretary of the Party, Stalin controlled the Central Committee's
rather large bureaucratic apparatus and within it had a secret personal
chancellery, which appeared in the organization tables as the Secret
Department before 1934 and as the Special Sector thereafter. Bypass-
ing all government and other Party offices, the secret chancellery was
the central clearinghouse for domestic and foreign intelligence and
coordinated and directed the intelligence agencies' work. It operated
behind a wall of secrecy that has yet to be breached.[27]

The secret chancellery had the security service, which went by the
initials OGPU until 1934 and NKVD thereafter, exclusively at its
disposal. The security service was not responsible to any government
agency. Its mission was to protect the Party by policing the population
at large, the government, and the armed forces. In the 1930s Stalin
extended its purview to include the Party, the Central Committee, and
the Politburo, thereby putting himself alone at the head of what John
Dziak has called a "counterintelligence state," a political system with
an "overarching concern with 'enemies,' internal and external."[28] The
perceived external threat from capitalism gave the OGPU/NKVD a
foreign as well as a domestic mission and added a dimension to Soviet
net assessment that would have required access to information available
only in the secret chancellery files.[29]

In the military command structure, the Red Army Staff/general
staff functioned as a joint staff. A 1937 regulation designated the
general staff as "the supreme organ of the High Command for resolving
all operational-strategic questions pertaining to forces employed on
land, at sea, and in the air."[30] General S. P. Ivanov's study of

the World War II initial period states that the general staff's pre-invasion plans were derived from "consideration of the military and political situation, the requirements of our military doctrine, and the real capabilities of the Soviet Union and its potential enemies."[31]

The Red Army Staff/General Staff's Intelligence Directorate, the RU, which became the GRU (Main Intelligence Directorate) in the late 1930s, ran extensive foreign military and technical intelligence operations. Strictly speaking, the RU/GRU was hardly any more the army's intelligence service than the OGPU/NKVD was the Party's. It also was closely tied to the secret chancellery, and it came under intensive OGPU/NKVD surveillance.

In matters affecting national security, Stalin was *the* intelligence analyst. Walter Laqueur has concluded that in the 1980s the Soviet leadership "seems to prefer information untinged by bureaucratic analysis and manipulation" and that the "style" is to use "data from the collectors, but estimates and 'net assessments' from the leadership itself."[32] Manifestly, Stalin would have been far less disposed than his successors are to accept net assessments from the bureaucracy.

The faculties of the Frunze Academy and the General Staff Academy (the latter opened in 1936) engaged in studying as well as teaching military art and science and were significant potential contributors to net assessment. Tukhachevsky drew heavily on them. The faculty members were military, many of them former military specialists with general staff and command experience acquired in the "old" (tsarist) army. The navy had (since 1923) an academy comparable to the Frunze Academy. Air force command personnel attended the Frunze Academy until 1940, when the Zhukovsky Air Engineering Academy expanded its offerings in command and navigation and became the Air Force Academy. An evaluation and assessment capability also existed outside the military in the national Academy of Science's Institute of World Economics and World Politics and probably some of its other institutes. But the military academies and the Academy of Science were no less subject to constraints than any other organizations, only somewhat lower in the heirarchy.

THE PROCESS

The Soviet net assessment process cannot be directly observed. Like a dark object in outer space, its probable nature can be discerned only from interactions with visible surroundings. Fortunately, its rigidly secret environment has been somewhat subject to such countervailing conditions. The Soviet Union was desperately concerned in the 1930s with establishing itself as a modern military power, and that could not be done inside the secret chancellery or the Defense Committee and the Main Military Council. Tukhachevsky and his associates conducted a relatively open discussion in print. Foreign developments were analyzed quite freely in the military press, then as now sometimes contrasting interestingly with the total silence on the same subjects as they pertained to the Soviet armed forces. Some restricted materials, for instance, field service regulations and the journal *Voyennaya Mysl (Military Thought)*, eventually found their way abroad.[33] The victory in the Great Patriotic War of 1941–45, which was—and is—the Soviet regime's absolute greatest achievement, necessitated a reexamination of the 1930s after Stalin's death to redistribute the credit for the victory, which Stalin had claimed virtually for himself alone, and to assess the responsibility for the early defeats. The resulting continuous stream of publications has yet to emit steady light, but it has intermittently given off illuminating flashes. Although those are closely regulated, they give some substantive information and more indirect guidance.

The Nature of War as a Problem

The most crucial concern of net assessments in the 1930s was not relative strengths but the nature of war itself. The contenders in World War I (except Russia, Austria-Hungary, the United States, and Italy) had been about equally well prepared, and the result had been a prolonged war of attrition in which the defensive proved so far superior to the offensive that movement became practically impossible. The war had ended with a victory that could be only loosely attributed to military art as it had been previously understood and left its future throughly beclouded. The question of what the next war was going to be like profoundly affected all assessments up to—and after—September 1939. Such theorists as B.H. Liddell Hart, J. F. C. Fuller, Giulio Douhet, or Hans von Seeckt contemplated radically new approaches. The leading circles in the military establishments, on the other hand, looked to empirical evidence derived from World War I, and it did not indicate any swift or cheap way of overcoming the superiority of the defensive. Barring radical and as yet unthought-of innovations, the last war was taken to have established the essential parameters of the next. Knowing the problems, however, by no means simplified them, and the projected solutions to them figured decisively in assessments.

The Soviet Union was a latecomer to the scene. The capitalist armies had worked out doctrine and attained what they took to be appropriate levels of proficiency in four years' fighting on the Western Front. Neither the Red Army nor the Imperial Russian Army had experienced that kind of war. Consequently, the Soviet assessment process was heavily dependent on a tenuous frame of reference derived from foreign sources.

Politics and the Civil War experience injected further complications into the assessment process in the form of what might be called articles of faith that, although they might not be objectively verifiable, could not safely be denied. At its inception in early 1918, the Red Army had been declared to be "an army of a new type" in which the troops fought for their own class interests and not, as they presumedly did in capitalist armies, for those of a hostile class, the bourgeoisie. That was taken to be a strength no capitalist army could possess. The Red Army, as its name implied, was also regarded as the army of the world revolution. Furthermore, as has already been indicated at some length, the political authority had the deciding word in all assessments. The star politico-military figure of the Civil War, M. V. Frunze, who was regarded as a theorist of war greater than Clausewitz, had called for a "unified military doctrine" that would depart from traditional doctrine and base itself on Marxist principles. He had identified certain qualities in which the Red Army was naturally superior, among them, offensive-minded-ness, decisiveness, and mobility.[34]

Frunze's unified doctrine had not been officially adopted, but the Civil War could be construed as having confirmed its existence in the Red Army even then. It had successfully mounted offensives on fronts larger in area than the whole Western Front and had regularly made advances hundreds of miles deep. It had retreated equally long distances but had almost always returned to the attack. Even with Allied support, the best White generals had gone down in defeat before it. A Party man with no previous military experience, Frunze, had won great battles. Lenin (and Stalin) had demonstrated genius at determining the correct point for the main effort. Why, then, should the Western Front be the model for the future? Why not the Civil War? The Frunze Academy's mission in the 1920s had been to study the experience and expound the lessons of "class war" (the Civil War). Soviet military science ranked class war above "imperialist war" (of which World War I had been the first) in all respects.[35] That distinction was bound to enter into assessments.

Assessing Contemporary War

The first phase of Soviet preparation for war, the technological reconstruction of the armed forces, began in June 1931 when Tukhachevsky took over as armaments chief and the Central Committee concurrently passed a resolution on command in the Red Army. The resolution gave the "main immediate requirements for raising the army's combat capabilities" as being "decisive improvement of military-technological competence in the command staffs and their mastery of advanced combat techniques and the intricacies of contemporary battle."[36] Tukhachevsky therewith received confirmation of an assessment he and some others had made several years earlier, namely, that the Soviet armed forces were far behind the leading foreign military powers in modern weapons and the ability to use them. Tukhachevsky had written the article on war in the first (1928) edition of the *Great Soviet Encyclopedia,* in which he had graphically shown the growing impact of artillery, automatic weapons, aircraft, and tanks in operations on the Western Front and had concluded that the example set there was much more likely than that of the Civil War to provide the model for future wars.[37] Vladimir Triandafilov, who had worked under Tukhachevsky as operations chief and deputy chief of the army staff, had (in 1929) submitted an extensive study, "Characteristics of Army Operations in Contemporary War," describing operations in which army groups composed of shock armies, each with four or five infantry corps and strong artillery, tank, and air elements, would oppose each other on broad, deeply echeloned fronts. (His work is also an early example of the everlasting Soviet preoccupation with quantifying effectiveness in terms of frontages, distances advanced, troops and weapons employed, and duration of operations.) In his general conclusions, Triandafilov came close to excluding ideological considerations from estimates of military effectiveness.[38]

Since the Soviet armed forces were far behind in most respects, the assessment process as it pertained to the technological reconstruction was concerned not with particular balances but with ascertaining the current state and trends of foreign technology. The treaty with Germany furthered that purpose. The German Reichswehr and the Red Army jointly operated aircraft, tank, and chemical warfare test and training facilities on Soviet territory, and the German Junkers company ran an aircraft plant near Moscow.[39] Catching up was not all that difficult. Western armies were not then intensively promoting new development, and designs they ignored could easily be had. In 1931 the Red Army took up an outstanding British Vickers light tank and put it into production, then bought two M1931 Christie tank chassis, into which the American designer J. Walter Christie had incorporated several revolutionary features.[40]

Technology was quantifiable; how the next war would be fought was not. World War I had demonstrated conclusively that more and better weapons would not by themselves spell victory. Conflicting theories and uncertainties about the effects new and improved technology would have, however, complicated the assessment process. In 1931, for instance, Soviet analysis accepted the French contention that the Maginot Line constituted a technological and strategic-operational breakthrough, and the Red Army began fortifying the western border (and the eastern a year later). The Central Committee, the purported source of definitive judgments, straddled the technological issue, instructing the military, on the one hand, not to overvalue the traditional service arms and, on the other, to exercise caution in regard to the bourgeois mechanization theories. In 1932 the Red Army activated two mechanized corps, each with 500 tanks and more than 200 other armored vehicles, apparently to keep abreast of Liddell Hart's and Fuller's entirely theoretical conceptions.[41] A year later it also established a corps-type organization for the TB-3s and other bombers that were coming into service.[42]

In mid-1933 Yegorov endorsed and sent forward an army staff study that undertook to assess the balance between the technological level the Red Army would reach in the next two years or so and its ability to respond effectively to the kind of war it would then have to fight. In the latter regard, the study concluded that the Red Army had correctly identified the requirements but was deficient in the tactical and operational competence needed to meet them. Defenses would be deep (60 to 70 miles), and combined arms shock armies and air power would be employed in appropriately deep offensive operations. The initial period of hostilities would be particularly, perhaps decisively, important. Both sides would strive at the outset to carry the war to the enemy's territory; and, if they had built permanent fortifications, would exploit those to carry out covert mobilization before war was declared. The Red Army would soon have the means to conduct such a war, but it lacked much else. Only the cavalry had relevant experience in deep operations (a compulsory obeisance to Stalin's old First Cavalry Army). The army as a whole had no applicable operational or tactical experience and had as yet not even worked out theoretical guidelines. That condition called for intensively organized research and acquisition of substitute experience through large-scale ground and air maneuvers.[43]

Earlier Soviet assessments had not focused on a specific enemy or hostile coalition, but the army staff's assessment came just at the time war clouds were visibly beginning to form on the international horizon in the east and the west. Stalin told delegates to the Seventeenth Party Congress in January 1934 that another "imperialist" war was in the making. "Military circles in Japan" and the "political leaders of certain nations in Europe" were hatching schemes for war against the Soviet Union as well. Those who tried "to poke their pig snouts into our Soviet garden" would receive "a crushing repulse," but the Soviet Union would pursue its peace policy resolutely and was prepared to conclude nonaggression treaties with all nations ready to do the same.[44]

Tukhachevsky, reporting on the armament program, told the congress that war would generate an enormous demand for weapons, equipment, and supplies of all kinds. The small Soviet industrial base would have to be built up and directed toward war production. It would be necessary to "deploy sufficiently gigantic technological resources to smash any country intruding on us."[45] Tukhachevsky was announcing the tremendous expansion of a massive armament buildup already under way, but the Soviet system's abiding faith in the inherent importance of numbers and a shortage of skilled labor impelled output toward easily mass-producible items. The armored vehicles turned out under the First Five Year Plan were almost all tankettes and light tanks, and the light tanks stayed in heavy production thereafter. The most numerous aircraft type was the U-2 (Po-2), a wood and fabric biplane trainer; and fighters and bombers developed (some with German assistance) in the 1920s continued in production into the middle 1930s. On the other hand, medium and heavy tanks began coming into the inventory in 1932 and in 1935 reached numbers not then matched anywhere else in the world. In 1932 a fruit of the collaboration with Germany, the TB-3, an all-metal, four-engine, cantilever monoplane heavy bomber went into production as the first of its kind anywhere. In 1934 the I-15, a biplane fighter, went into production; it was followed in the same year by the I-16, a cantilever monoplane fighter that was several years ahead of its time in speed and maneuverability.[46]

In the middle 1920s, early in R. A. Muklevich's term as chief of naval forces, when the prospect of some new building began to arise, the navy settled on a program for a "mosquito navy," one without battleships or cruisers that would confine itself to operations in coastal waters. In wartime, its elements would be subordinated to the adjacent land forces and would perform whatever offensive or defensive missions they required. The concept was well suited to the initial five year plans because it afforded a relatively quick way to achieve high unit output with limited technical expertise and without heavy preliminary investments in yards and docks. Plans and diesel engines secured from Germany had put submarine-building on a sound footing early in the First Five Year Plan, however, and in 1933 the Council of Labor and Defense authorized "a powerful underwater fleet."[47]

Air power complicated national assessments everywhere. The airplane was regarded as a potentially devastating, even decisive weapon, but pretense was heavily intermixed with reality in the claims made for it after World War I. Throughout the interwar period, the airplane figured in Soviet assessments as the quintessential symbol of technological advancement, but conservatism dominated the thinking on its employment. The air force remained what it had been during the Civil War, a technical service without a command function subordinated to the ground forces' field commands and the national air defense forces (a separate directorate within the army). Like the navy's submarines, the heavy bombers coming into the air force inventory in the early 1930s raised a prospect of missions extending beyond the ground forces' tactical purview. In 1936 the air force obtained authority to activate air armies in which TB-3s were the main components.[48]

The Tukhachevsky Era

Tukhachevsky's career was approaching it peak. On 7 November 1933 he had ridden on horseback out of the Kremlin through the Spassky Gate to take the salute at the army parade celebrating the October Revolution. Three months later he had addressed the Party Congress, and the Congress had elected him to candidate membership in the Central Committee.[49] In the arcane Soviet protocol these distinctions signified preeminence. What exactly they meant in terms of Tukhachevsky's influence in military affairs and particularly in decision-making at the highest governmental level is less than clear-cut. Although he could not have been given honors and advancement without Stalin's concurrence, those were at best doubtful evidences of his standing with Stalin, who rather obviously saw to it that he did not rise alone. Yegorov, Blyukher, and Budenny also became candidate members in the Central Committee at the 1934 Congress, and the pattern, of course, was repeated in their marshal's appointments.

The years 1934 through 1936 stand out in the Soviet post-Stalin literature as a golden age in which military genius and the party's innate wisdom combined to keep Soviet military science on a clear and steady course toward total theoretical and practical mastery of the art of war. The implication is that in those years the Soviet military leadership assessed the nature of future war more accurately and devised more effective responses than its foreign counterparts did. Since about 1960, the period has also been symbolically important to current Soviet military doctrine, initially in relation to the Soviet army's campaign against proposed conventional force reductions, more recently as support for the idea that the kind of war then envisioned can be fought in the nuclear era.[50] These considerations need to be kept in mind while examining the Soviet assessment process at that stage.

In the Soviet view, the fundamental strength of its military thought was—and, by implication, is—that it "kept clear of the capitalist states' characteristically onesided military theories" and consequently "surpassed them in the solution of many problems."[51] Marshal A. A. Grechko's 1975 work on the Soviet armed forces refers to the "then [pre-World War II] fashionable onesided concepts such as 'aerial warfare' and 'tank warfare,' which overestimated the role of individual types of weapons."[52] Ivanov credits "bourgeois" theorists with having "more or less accurately judged the role of tanks and aviation on the future battlefields" but charges them with have "propagated erroneous ideas on the possibility of achieving victory in a future war using small . . . professional armies."[53] The "onesided" theories, such as those of Fuller, Liddell Hart, Douhet, and von Seeckt, are implied to have dominated capitalist military thinking.

The "onesided" theories did enter into the assessment process in the mid-1930s, though not at the level of significance now attributed to them. The Politburo authorized a major change in the military system in May 1935, a shift from a militia to a cadre (standing) army. Since 1925, when the cadre army was limited to 562,000 men, most conscripts had done their service part-time in the militia.[54] Although the Politburo had made the decision, the changeover apparently still had to be justified, possibly—unlikely as it may seem—even to Stalin. Marxist doctrine rejected standing armies, and the military leadership outside Tukhachevsky's circle would have suspected a "onesided" emphasis on technological arms to the detriment of the traditional and more easily comprehended infantry and cavalry, which were what the militia primarily produced.

On 15 January 1936 Tukhachevsky delivered a strategic estimate to the Central Executive Committee, the Soviet legislature (now the Supreme Soviet), in which he greatly exaggerated the extent of the army's conversion to the cadre system. In a more sober vein, he told the delegates that the country was in growing danger of having to fight Germany and Japan simultaneously. He made a particular point of those potential enemies' ability to deploy very large forces on the Soviet frontiers in a short time.[55]

Also in early 1936, the Institute of World Economy and World Politics in the Academy of Science put out an assessment entitled *Armament of Capitalist States in the Year 1935*. Its thesis was that the year had conclusively proved theories about small professional armies to be "bankrupt," in fact to have been "political deceptions" all along. Citing the German return to conscription in March 1935, Ludendorff's design for total war, and General Douglas MacArthur's remarks on technology and maneuver in his final report (November 1935) as U. S. Army Chief of Staff, it concluded that the capitalist states had let their real views come into the open, and those had nothing to do with small armies fighting relatively humane little wars. Current bourgeois theory held that "offensive arms, such as tanks and aircraft, could achieve superiority over defensive means." Consequently, small armies were "out of fashion," and the trend was toward mass armies capable of exploiting the new technology to "deal blows right through the entire depth of the enemy's deployment."[56]

The Tukhachevsky report and the Academy of Science analysis, which the defense commissariat published and which Tukhachevsky or his associates may have had a hand in writing, sheds a modicum of light—however uncertain—on the Soviet assessment process at that time.[57] Tukhachevsky appears to have possessed a license to address in public a question of national policy (possible war with Germany and Japan) on which the party (Stalin) had not yet spoken. Both his speech and the Academy assessment were surprisingly free of the then obligatory credits to Stalin as the greatest authority on all subjects. The remarkable features of the two were their oblique and convoluted approaches. The decisive event in 1935, the one that profoundly altered the balance of military power, was the German reversion to a conscript army. It no doubt impelled the Soviet decision to convert to the cadre system. Yet Tukhachevsky did not mention it at all, and the Academy of Sciences analysts alluded to it only in passing. Perhaps it could be assumed to be well enough understood; but that leaves a question as to why, on the other hand, it should have been necessary to dwell at length on the various small armies theories, treating them at once as deceptions and as previously accepted doctrine. A plausible answer seems to be that the Soviet theory being applied in the technological reconstruction needed to be presented as both superior to and in conformity with that of the capitalist states. In any event, significant results may have been achieved. Between January 1936 and December 1937 the cadre army's strength increased to somewhat over 1.5 million men.[58] In April 1936 Tukhachevsky became war plans director and first deputy people's commissar in the defense commissariat.

Tukhachevsky and Deep Operations Doctrine

The *Soviet Military Encyclopedia* states that in 1930 the Red Army began conducting large-scale maneuvers "to raise the level of war-readiness" and to secure "practical verification for new propositions in military theory." In September 1935 the Kiev and Kharkov Military Districts conducted the "Great Kiev Maneuvers" with 65,000 troops, more than 1,000 tanks, 600 aircraft, 300 artillery pieces, and "other military technology." The Frunze Academy's operations faculty under Colonel G. S. Isserson developed the problem, which required the "blue" (enemy) force to execute a 150-mile-deep offensive from the vicinity of the western border to Kiev. First, the "blue" infantry with supporting tank battalions broke through a fortified defense line, and the "reds" counterattacked with a mechanized and a cavalry corps. Next, the "blues" resumed the attack and dropped a 1,200-man parachute regiment to seize a bridgehead on the Dnepr River east of Kiev, and two "red" regiments, one mechanized, the other cavalry, attacked the paratroops while the "red" mechanized corps staged a grand sweep around the "blue" right flank.[59] The late Marshal A. I. Yeremenko, who was an umpire at the maneuvers, wrote in his 1964 memoirs that "for the first time in the history of military art, the solutions to the problems of deep operational blows and the questions of deep battle were resolved in large-scale maneuvers."[60] Interestingly, it was apparently assumed, since the "blue" thrust did reach Kiev, that both sides would have found equally valid "solutions."

French, Italian, and Czech observers were present at the maneuvers in 1935, and British, French, and Czech at the Belorussian Military District maneuvers held in 1936. The parachute troops struck them as a sensational innovation, and the quantity and quality of the equipment, particularly the aircraft and tanks, impressed them.[61] But the French General Lucien Loizeau, who was there to evaluate the Soviet potential as an ally, reported strong doubts about the adequacy in tactics, training, and leadership.[62] Colonel Giffard Martel, who was a British tank specialist, saw the proceedings as "more like a tattoo than maneuvers." The maneuvers were staged in "ideal country for mechanized warfare"; the tactics were "nothing very new except for the parachute landing"; and in the action, the opposing sides "appeared just to bump into each other."[63]

In the winter, around the turn of the year, the Soviet High Command usually also sponsored war games in which some of the military district staffs participated. The first of those to involve a potentially actual rather than a hypothetical situation was apparently held in early 1936 at Tukhachevsky's suggestion and took a German–Polish attack north of the Pripyat Marshes toward Moscow as its premise. The general staff calculated that Germany could mobilize 100 divisions and would put 50 into the attack, while the Poles would put in 30. Tukhachevsky insisted that Germany could mobilize 200 divisions, and therefore would commit at least 80, and could conceal their deployment to achieve surprise. Tukhachevsky was overruled on both points, and the game was played through as a conventional frontier clash between approximately equal forces, "therewith losing all strategic interest," according to General Todorsky, the biographer of Isserson and Tukhachevsky.[64]

Voroshilov endorsed PU 36, the new field service regulations, on 30 December 1936, and they were published early in the new year. Since the late 1960s, PU 36 has been acclaimed in the Soviet literature as the high-water mark—for a time—in world military thought, the point at which successful assessment of the nature of the next war culminated in the Red Army's becoming the first to possess a doctrine of deep operations. Interestingly, Marshal M. V. Zakharov, in the 1965 volume of writings on strategy and operations he edited, only credited PU 36 with containing "some elements of deep operations." But in an article printed in 1970 he maintained it could be said with regard to the Soviet theory of deep battle and operations as it existed in the middle 1930s that "not a single army in the world had as profound and as thoroughly worked out a military theory as our armed forces did." On the other hand, he asserted in both places that the German army filched the idea of the deep operation from PU 36 and derived its Blitzkrieg operations from it.[65]

Despite much recent Soviet and some Western scholarship, the idea of the deep operation was not a Soviet discovery, and PU 36 did not advance it in any significant way beyond what was then elsewhere considered to be good doctrine.[66] A comparison of PU 36 with the German army's 1933 field service regulations, which had their antecedent in the 1918 "Attack in Positional Warfare" directive, shows only two notable differences between them: (1) a less dogmatic approach in the German regulations and (2) an assumption in PU 36 that cavalry would be capable of carrying out strategic operations in a future war.[67]

Looked at in the context of the time, PU 36 also does not appear to have constituted a clear-cut success for the Tukhachevsky group in the assessment process. In December 1934 Voroshilov rejected a move in the Military Council to declare deep battle (the tactical form of deep operations) to be a new form of war. Deep battle, he insisted, was a characteristic of all wars; battle in the future would not be different, only deeper. The question was not what to think about deep battle but how to conduct war in "all of its diversity."[68] In an article on PU 36 printed in the military newspaper *Red Star* on 6 May 1937, Tukhachevsky disclosed that he had encountered strong opposition from those who still believed that the Red Army had developed a unique "special mobility" of its own in the Civil War (particularly in the cavalry armies) and did not need to concern itself with maneuver in other forms.

Evaluating War Experience: Spain and the Far East

Civil War erupted in Spain on 17 July 1936 when the "Nationalists" under General Francisco Franco began a march on the "Loyalist" government stronghold, Madrid. Italian and German military assistance was on the way to the Nationalists before the month ended, and the Loyalists began receiving Soviet arms and advisers in October. As Isserson put it, the war in Spain was "the first trial of the new means of battle in Europe" and therefore "raised the curtain somewhat on the present-day battlefield."[69] The Red Army sent a number of promising junior general officers, particularly from the technical branches and the General Staff, to Spain as "volunteer" advisers.

The war generated an abundance of apparently unequivocal evidence for analysts in all countries. Tukhachevsky already gave attention to it in his May 1937 article on PU 36. "The war in Spain," he wrote, "demonstrates the importance and power of the defensive." He argued that tanks and artillery could nevertheless execute "completely successful" offensives if they were "employed in sufficient mass."[70] In its subsequent course, the war proved Tukhachevsky right with regard to the possibility of positional warfare's recurrence. A bloody stalemate persisted on the main front around Madrid from October 1936 to March 1939, when exhaustion and a power struggle between communist and noncommunist factions brought about a Loyalist collapse.

In 1939, the general staff academy issued a volume of "operational-tactical conclusions" on the experience in Spain for controlled circulation to command personnel. It expanded and brought into definitive form a two-part article that the author, Brigade Commandant S. Lyubarsky, had published a year earlier in the general staff's restricted journal, *Military Thought*.[71] Lyubarsky's fundamental conclusion was that "history repeats itself": The war in Spain had become a war of position after an even shorter period of maneuver than in World War I. There had been only isolated fragments of deep operations. Neither side, he conceded, had tanks, aircraft, and artillery in sufficient quantities, and the only form of offensive that could be effective was the deep operation. Nevertheless, the experience in Spain showed that "even if the forces have enormous strength and the most advanced technological means, operations will assume a prolonged character."[72]

In practical terms, according to Lyubarsky, history had also repeated itself, proving again the value of the mass army and the "decisive" role of the infantry. The war in Spain had demonstrated as well the "great importance" of fortifications. Tanks had confirmed the view that they were a powerful offensive weapon, but they had not proved to be a substitute for artillery. They had also been vulnerable to even light antitank guns, which indicated that infantry platoons and companies could probably be armed to defend themselves against tanks. Fighter aircraft had proved essential in the contest for air supremacy over the battlefield and as escorts for the bombers, which could not carry out missions without them.[73]

Also in 1939, the military publishing house printed a book, *The Air Army*, by Brigade Commandant A. N. Lapchinsky, who had been professor of air tactics in the Frunze Academy until his death in 1938. Lapchinsky's concern was to provide a doctrine for the air armies. The war in Spain, he concluded, had proved direct battlefield support to be by far the most important air mission. Only the destruction of the adversary's armed forces "secured victories." Bombing cities did not impair the "armed mass's will to fight." Interdiction and attacks on the enemy's rear area could be worthwhile, but only if they did not detract from direct battle support.[74]

The Red Army acquired battle experience in the Far East, where tension had been growing since the Japanese took over Manchuria in 1931. In the summer of 1938 Stalin was ready to assess the balance of power in the region by a controlled test of strength. Blyukher's reinforced Special Red Banner Far Eastern Army became the Red Banner Far Eastern Front on 1 July with 200,000 troops in two armies and an air army. From 3 to 11 August, G. M. Shtern, Blyukher's chief of staff, led a 32,000-man corps with 609 artillery pieces and 345 tanks in a frontal attack on a 2-mile-long ridge line west of Lake Khasan that the Soviet Union claimed as the Soviet-Manchurian boundary. Although Shtern only got about half of his ground force into action, he had a substantial superiority over the 9,000 Japanese troops with 37 artillery pieces. The incident ended in a truce at noon on 11 August with Soviet troops on the ridge and Stalin's curiosity satisfied.

Stalin ran a more extensive test in the summer of 1939 east of the Khalkhin-gol (Halha River) on the border between Outer Mongolia and Manchuria. In early June, on Timoshenko's recommendation, he sent Corps Commandant G. K. Zhukov to build an "army group" (more than a corps, less than an army) of 57,000 troops, 500 tanks, and more than 500 aircraft around a corps already stationed in the area. The Japanese Sixth Army apparently committed about 59,000 troops, 300 aircraft, and 180 tanks. Both sides strictly limited their operations to a 50-mile-wide, 10-mile-deep stretch of disputed territory between the Khalkhin-gol and the Mongolian settlement of Nomonhan. The Japanese held the initiative until 21 August, when Zhukov launched a very precise encirclement that in ten days trapped the Japanese force between Nomonhan and the river. Losses in the almost three months' battle were heavy on both sides, but Stalin again made his point, and Zhukov inflicted a severe prestige loss on the Japanese army.[75]

Although the Lake Khasan and Khalkhin-gol incidents provided the first tests since the Civil War of Soviet troops and technology in battle, they appear not to have generated general assessments like those derived from the war in Spain. The experience in Spain, because it was European, was assumed to be more valid from the technological standpoint; that in the Far East was taken to have limited applicability because the Japanese were presumed to be qualitatively inferior, and, of course, by the time the fighting on the Khalkhin-gol ended, a flood of new evidence for assessment was coming from Europe. In the final analysis, the Soviet forces in the Far East had not come off decidedly better than the Loyalists had in Spain. Lake Khasan was a victory but a somewhat disappointing performance. Effective infantry, artillery, tank, and air coordination had not been achieved, and the tanks had been vulnerable to antitank fire.[76] The Japanese performance had been sufficiently impressive to bring about a 350,000-man increase in the

Red Army, most of it for the Far East.[77] Zhukov's crushing finale at Khalkhin-gol had come after an expensive two and a half months on the defensive.

Zhukov's account of his report to Stalin on Khalkhin-gol offers a glimpse at Stalin's personal assessment process. On Zhukov's return to Moscow in May 1940, that is, eight months after the battle, Stalin called him to the Kremlin and, with Politburo members present, questioned him closely on the quality of Japanese troops and equipment and on the Soviet troops' performance. Stalin had earlier done the same with the advisers returning from Spain, apparently more intent upon judging the interviewees than securing information, which must already have been available to him from other sources.[78] Zhukov came off well and departed from Moscow with a promotion to the newly instituted rank of *general armii* (one step below Marshal).

While Stalin was engaged in the test of strength in the Far East, the balance of power in Europe, as he saw it, was threatening to shift dangerously against him. On 10 March 1939 Stalin told the Eighteenth Party Congress that Great Britain, France, and the United States were "egging on the Germans to march east," but the Soviet Union would frustrate their schemes by "strengthening business relations with all countries."[79] A month later, in the midst of a growing German-Polish crisis, he proposed a defensive alliance to Britain and France, but two weeks later he dismissed his long-time foreign minister, Maxim Litvinov, who was a Jew, and appointed Molotov to replace him. In Moscow on 23 August, Molotov and German Foreign Minister Joachim von Ribbentrop signed a nonaggression pact, which was to take effect immediately and specified that the other partner was to remain neutral if either went to war with a third party or parties.

During the 1938–39 drift toward war in Europe, the Soviet armed forces were engaged in the most comprehensive and urgent assessment effort since the start of the decade. Technology, organization, and doctrine were all affected. Stalin's willingness to align with the country's most dangerous potential enemy indicated the extent of the problems and how the balance stood in his personal net assessment.

Obsolescence had overtaken the products of the technological reconstruction during the war in Spain. The air force's I-15 was outclassed by a new generation of high-performance, all-metal fighters such as the German Bf 109. The 800 TB-3s were too slow and too lightly armed to be more than marginally effective any longer. The air force was having to rush new aircraft designs into production: the TB-7, an advanced four-engine bomber; two twin-engine bombers, the DB-3 and the Pe-2; and three high-performance fighters, the I-22, I-26, and MiG-1 (I-61). In Spain, light tanks had shown themselves vulnerable to small-caliber antitank fire, and a practice Tukhachevsky had promoted of designing tanks for specialized purposes had complicated organization and maintenance. In August 1939 the Central Committee held a military-industrial conference, which decided to concentrate production on two new tanks, the medium T-34 and the heavy KV-1, both of which used the same engine. When the war began in Europe, the Soviet Union was embarked on a second technological reconstruction to develop and produce a virtually entire new generation of weapons.

The navy entered into the second technological revolution in an unexpectedly big way. The naval limitation treaty had expired at the end of 1936 with practically no prospect of being renewed. Stalin could hardly not have perceived the possibility that a naval race was about to begin, and the intervention in Spain, moreover, had shown the lack of a surface fleet strong enough to project Soviet sea power beyond its own shores to be a distinct political and psychological handicap.[80] The emergence of the People's Commissariat of the Navy signaled a major shift in naval policy and, without the turmoil the purge induced, would probably have shown effects sooner than it did.

On 19 December 1938 the Main Naval Council held the final session of its year-end meeting in the Kremlin. Stalin discoursed on "combined forms of battle," which he maintained could be conducted by navies with battleships, cruisers, "and other powerful ships." The Soviet Navy, he concluded, was still weak and confined to coastal waters, but it could be made "strong at sea within eight or ten years."[81] Although designing and building large ships posed enormous problems for Soviet industry, Soviet shipyards had begun work in 1938 on two battleships in the 60,000-ton range. Two more were added in 1939 and 1940, along with two 35,000-ton battle cruisers. Destroyer and submarine programs continued at full tilt.[82]

Although the rapid progress in development during the last prewar years laid to rest all doubts concerning the airplane's tactical and operational effectiveness, the experience in Spain dimmed its future as a strategic weapon. Improved aircraft appeared to be bringing air supremacy into the realm of attainable strategic objectives, but that it could be pursued separately from the reliably established strategic objective, victory on the ground, was a knotty proposition, particularly where air power was as tightly integrated into the ground force structure as it was in the Soviet Union. In April 1938, as a result of what must have been a decision to keep the whole range of possibilities open without impairing the ground forces' entitlement to air support, the Main Military Council conferred the designation "armies for special purposes" on the air armies. Their missions would include independent strategic bombing, and their commanders would receive their orders directly from the defense commissariat.[83]

Suddenly, in late summer 1940, Soviet military periodicals directed a burst of attention to "assault aircraft" (*shturmovoi aviatsia*), whose only function would be low-level, tactical ground support. Designers, apparently looking for an answer to the German Ju 87, *Stuka*, which had attracted attention in Spain in 1938 and was a sensation in the Polish Campaign, had developed a somewhat less sophisticated alternative, the BSh-2 (later I1-2) armored *shturmovik*. Built around a very reliable engine designed for a single-engine passenger plane, 1,500 pounds of steel plate and powerful armament made it virtually a flying tank.[84]

The experience in the Spanish Civil War also brought the role of tanks into question. Although some officers favored the abolition of the Red Army's tank corps, a commission on tank forces organization in July 1939 concluded that Spain, where the fighting was mostly in and around cities, had not provided an adequate test. Two months later, in mid-September, two tank corps were committed in the march into Poland. Like almost everybody else, including some German generals, Stalin had not expected the Germans to advance as fast as they did; the hastily mounted Soviet offensive was a ramshackle affair in which the tank corps' performance was glaringly weak. On 21 November, without further discussion, the Main Military Council abolished the tank corps, assigned half of its tanks to four motorized divisions, and distributed the other half elsewhere.[85]

New field service regulations, PU 39, appeared in late 1939. Soviet accounts, particularly the more recent ones, pass over them lightly. The article on field service regulations in the *Military Encyclopedia* does not mention either them or PU 40, which came out the following year.[86] Nevertheless, PU 39 and PU 40 are two of the most significant documents pertaining to the Soviet assessment process. The first chapter in PU 39 consisted of several dozen aphorisms, among them the following:

> The Union of Soviet Socialist Republics will respond to any enemy attack with a crushing blow involving all the might of its armed forces.
>
> If an enemy unleashes a war on us, the Workers' and Peasants' Red Army will be the most offensive-minded of all the attacking armies that ever existed.

The Red Army's greatest asset is the new man of the Stalinist epoch. He will have the decisive role in battle.[87]

Those statements can be taken as sheer bombast or, as one Soviet history does, as "correct in principle" but bound to result in dangerous overemphasis on the offensive.[88] The bombast and overemphasis were no doubt responses to a deep concern about the army's offensive capability. In Spain, the Soviet advisers had military and political control over troops of about the same quality as those in the Red Army, and the war had been entirely defensive on the Loyalist side. In the Far East, an offensive capability had not been as positively demonstrated as the outcomes at Lake Khasan and on the Khalkhin-gol seemed to indicate.

In substantive doctrinal terms, PU 39 conformed to the published analyses. Infantry was designated as the chief arm, and all others served alongside it. Artillery possessed "the most powerful and farthest-reaching fire of all the ground arms." The tanks' "fundamental mission" was to support the infantry; in a mobile battle, they "could be utilized for deeper blows into the enemy's deployment." The air force's main mission was "to assist the ground troops in battle and operations."[89]

Evaluating War Experience: Finland and France

The Soviet Union declared war on Finland on 30 November 1939. What was initially designed as a warlike demonstration similar to one Hitler had staged against Czechoslovakia earlier in the year developed into two major operations. The first, in December and early January 1940, was an outright disaster. The second, begun on 1 February, eventually would have overwhelmed the small Finnish army, but Stalin agreed to an armistice on 12 March that gave him enough of a victory to disguise his loss of prestige at home. The campaign throughout was far from masterfully conducted. The Finnish commander-in-chief, Marshal Carl Mannerheim, described the performance in his memoirs. "The artillery," Mannerheim wrote, "kept up heavy fire, but it was badly directed and badly coordinated with the movements of infantry and armor. Tanks might advance, open fire, and return to their starting point before the infantry had even begun to move." He credited a distinct improvement in the second operation to more methodical preparation, but he observed that certain weaknesses had prevailed throughout: "a kind of inertia" in the higher commands that "displayed itself in the formalism and simplicity of the operational plan"; overreliance on the weight of matériel; "a striking absence of creative imagination where the fluctuations of the situation demanded quick decision"; and a frequent inability to exploit initial successes.[90]

The Central Committee met in a special plenary session from 26 to 28 March "to discuss the results and lessons of the armed conflict with Finland thoroughly." From 14 to 17 April, the Main Military Council did the same in a conference to which the operations personnel of the military districts and armies and the military academies' faculties were invited.[91] The meetings are frequently mentioned in Soviet accounts, but nothing specific has been disclosed about what went on in them. It is safe to assume, however, that conclusions similar to Mannerheim's were reached. The Central Committee "demanded a radical reformation of Red Army training to eliminate obsolete and inappropriate forms and methods in military instruction and political education of the troops." On 16 May Voroshilov's successor, Timoshenko, issued a training directive for the coming summer in which he insisted, "Teach the troops only what is necessary in war and only what pertains to war."[92]

A commission of the Main Military Council worked out "concrete recommendations" for improved leadership and training that were put into effect during the summer. The commission, having found that training had been too much oriented toward classroom instruction out of manuals, issued orders to all services and all commands to give their troops extensive practice at fighting in all kinds of terrain and "in all weather by day and by night." Commanders and staffs were to be familiarized with "the requirements of modern warfare" in field exercises and war games and educated "to exercise creative initiative" and "make correct decisions in difficult and fast-moving situations."[93] In August and September the military districts gave up the past practice of staging big, showpiece maneuvers and conducted field exercises at the divisional and lower levels. *Red Star* reported on 2 October that Timoshenko had met with the commanders in a wrap-up session at which he pronounced the exercises a success and said there was "no such thing as blitzkrieg."[94]

Initiative and a capacity for independent decision-making were manifestly not easy to instill in officers drawn from a society that ordinarily discouraged both and recently had inflicted the severest punishments on those suspected of having attempted to exercise them. The authorization in May 1940 of general officer ranks—prohibited since the Revolution as politically unacceptable—was a symbolic first step to enhance the commanders' authority. The second step did not come until 12 August, when a decree of the Presidium of the Supreme Soviet reintroduced unity of command. The decision must have been difficult to reach and no doubt would shed light on the assessment process if more were known about it. Unity of command was broader than it had been earlier in the decade, when lower-level commanders had still been mostly excluded, but, as before, the political control structure remained in place, as did also the NKVD special sections, which kept commanders and political workers alike under close surveillance.

The general staff engaged during the summer in war planning, which brought Stalin's supposed special talent for determining the location of the main effort into play. The two-front war problem had changed in two respects: Japan, chastened by the Lake Khasan and Khalkhin-gol encounters, could be expected to let Germany strike first, and Germany, following the collapse of France in June 1940, had become a more dangerous enemy than had previously been imagined. The thinking therefore centered on Germany. Stalin and the general staff agreed in substance that to get at the agricultural land and resources in the Ukraine and the oil in the Caucasus, the Germans would make their main drive south of the Pripyat Marshes. In September, however, new chief of the general staff Meretskov presented a plan to Stalin in which the general staff, following the doctrine that required a counterstrike to carry the war to the enemy's territory, placed the Soviet main effort north of the Pripyat Marshes on the most direct line to Germany. Stalin thereupon "expressed thoughts" on the enemy's main effort being in the south and ordered the general staff to place the Soviet main effort there as well.[95]

Stalin's assessment of the Red Army's war readiness and the balance of power between the Soviet Union and Germany can be deduced from a conversation he had with the British Ambassador, Sir Stafford Cripps. He admitted that a German victory over Britain would put the Soviet Union in a difficult and dangerous position, but he insisted that "it was impossible at the present time to invite the certainty of a German invasion of the Soviet Union by any alteration of Soviet policy." He preferred to risk having to fight Germany alone after a British defeat, because he believed a victory over Britain would "appreciably weaken" German military power, and it would then "be very difficult for the Nazi leadership to persuade the German people to embark on a new major military objective."[96]

Isserson, one of the few Tukhachevsky associates to have survived the purge, published a comparative assessment of the Spanish Civil and the German-Polish War in 1940 (with only a few allusions to the French campaign) and concluded that contemporary war could take at least three forms. In Spain, maneuver had terminated early and the "modern means" had not managed to prevent a war of attrition. Maneuver had prevailed from start to finish in Poland, and the result had been super-deep operations, but a question remained as to whether such deep battle could be conducted against "an opponent equal in strength and technology who has belts of border fortifications and large reserves in the rear." In Western Europe, a lengthy positional war terminated "with great force" in a war of maneuver that "disclosed a new path to a higher stage of development in military art applicable to major European wars."[97] In a 1965 memoir, Isserson said that those who had worked on mobile warfare theory before the purge—and like him survived—understood and analyzed the changes the Germans had introduced in France, but their conclusions did not get outside the offices "of some circles in the General Staff and the War Academy." Consequently, the "young, honest, and courageous" leaders who replaced those lost in the field commands during the purge were "not sufficiently oriented in the innovative aspects of deep operations."[98]

Nevertheless, the Soviet Command rather quickly, perhaps hastily, drew some conclusions from the war in Western Europe. In early June 1940, at the time of Dunkirk, the defense commissariat submitted a study to Stalin in which it apparently attributed the German armor's success to overwhelming mass. On 9 June Timoshenko approved a plan to organize nine mechanized corps, while German employment of parachute troops to attack Belgium revived interest in airborne operations.[99] Late in the year, the German air offensive against England stimulated some reassessment of strategic bombing.

PU 40 gave a doctrinal imprimatur to the hectic reassessment that had gone on during the year. Except for another reference to the Stalinist man, the high-flown aphorisms in PU 39 disappeared or were toned down, and others, more prosaic but remarkable in the context of the Soviet military system, replaced them:

> The commander organizes and directs the battle.
> The commander stands at the head of military formations.
> The commander bears complete responsibility for the condition and fighting efficiency of military formations, for operational direction of forces, and for their successful engagement in battle.

The former political commissars' functions were subsumed under the rubric "sections for political propaganda." Doctrine pertaining to the infantry, artillery, and tanks stayed as it was in PU 39. The air mission changed substantially. Ground support on the battlefield became "one of the main air missions." Long-range bombers were to "destroy war production centers, air and naval bases, and other important objects in the enemy's deep rear." Airborne forces, not mentioned in PU 39, were pronounced capable of executing a variety of tactical missions in the enemy rear area.[100]

The Final Assessment

The annual winter war games scheduled for the second week in January 1941 were unusual in that they were preceded by a weeklong conference, from 23 to 29 December, in which, besides the usual district commanders and chiefs of staff, branch chiefs and inspectors, army commanders, and some corps and division commanders participated, and Central Committee and Politburo members were in the audience. The memoirs of participants and the Soviet histories describe it as a very important event, and the official view is that its purpose and accomplishment were to give the higher leadership an opportunity to brush up on the niceties of current operational art. Timoshenko told the gathering that the German campaigns in Poland and France had "in no way been surprising in strategic respects."[101] A generous scattering of evidence, however, indicates that problems arose.

The conference followed a familiar format: A senior member presented a prepared report on an assigned subject and others delivered comments and raised questions. As chief of the general staff, Meretskov gave a detailed progress report on the past year's training program and concluded that training was not the success Timoshenko had announced. It was still not close enough to the actual requirements of battle, and revealed "shortcomings in operational and general military proficiency . . . in the upper command structure, the troop commands, army and front staffs, and especially in aviation."[102]

Zhukov spoke on the nature of the modern offensive operation. He attributed the German victories primarily to surprise and the shock of powerful blows delivered against weak and irresolute opponents and dismissed views that Russia, too, should create German-style panzer groups (armies). The problem as he saw it was not how to deal with a whole new style of warfare but to decide how to bring matériel and manpower to bear most effectively in a prolonged war of attrition.[103] Timoshenko said in his concluding remarks that because it would be necessary "to saturate a very long front with the modern means of war," general purpose field armies would be the rule.[104] Soviet military leaders and theoreticians, he added, "do not rely on lightning war." They believed that a major war "in the present epoch" would be "intense and protracted" and that individual operations would achieve "finite aims" resulting only in the long term in the attainment of strategic objectives.[105]

The general tenor of air force chief Rychagov's analysis was that a bid for air supremacy would require more centralized control than then prevailed in the Red Army and would have to encompass destruction of the enemy's production facilities as well as his aircraft and installations. Operational supremacy would require deep strikes against the enemy's airfields and bases, and control would have to be centered at the army group level. Other air force generals argued that commands lower than the army group could not effectively direct air operations, but Timoshenko ruled that the battle for air supremacy could be carried out within the purview of army group and army operations.[106]

On 11 and 12 January, the military district commanders and their chiefs of staff attended the war games. Two were played, but the Soviet accounts treat only the first as significant and barely mention the second. The problems were confined to single operations in the sense in which Timoshenko had described them at the conference. (Strategic war-gaming was apparently never undertaken in the prewar period.) The first game was situated north of the Pripyat Marshes and required the "red" commander, Pavlov, to respond to a "blue" attack in which Zhukov commanded. The "blue" force broke through on a 50-mile front and advanced almost 75 miles.[107] In the second game, sited south of the Pripyat Marshes, Pavlov commanded on the "blue" side and Zhukov launched a "red" offensive—with apparently at best indeterminate results.

Stalin, who had not attended the December conference, summoned the participants to a meeting in the Kremlin with the Main Military Council and Politburo members on 13 January. It got off to an unpleasant start when Meretskov gave what Stalin judged to be a superficial analysis of the war games.[108] The subsequent discussion turned acrimonious when General Y. N. Fedorenko, the army's tank chief, proposed diverting some artillery funds to tank production and Rychagov requested more money for new aircraft. Kulik, as chief of the Main Artillery Directorate, declared tanks to be "a sheer waste" because artillery would "make scrap" of them and insisted that increasing the infantry divisions to 18,000 men apiece with horse-drawn trains would eliminate the need for mechanization.[109] Stalin thereupon resolved the issue. Kulik, he said, was wrong; "contemporary war will be war of motors, on land, in the air, on water and under water."[110]

In his final remarks, Stalin reproached the Defense Commissariat and the general staff for not having given "the military districts problems they will have to solve in an actual war" and laid down specific requirements: to prepare for a two-front war, to expand and rearm the forces, to create reserves, to "learn how to conduct" a war of fast movement and maneuver, and to "work out the organizational questions" devolving from the other requirements. "War," he added, "is approaching fast. . . . We must gain a year and a half to two years' time to complete the armament plan."[111]

Stalin formulated what would be his final assessment in the Kremlin meeting but did not yet fully accept it himself. He told Meretskov, no longer chief of the general staff but still on the Main Military Council, on 18 January that a plan to activate more mechanized corps was "subject to further discussion," because the tanks could not be built until 1942.[112] The air force received authority in February to put the TB-7 back into production, and Stalin approved twenty additional mechanized corps for the army in March. At best, TB-7s could not have begun to come off the lines again until late in the year, and by Zhukov's estimate, the 16,000 KV-1 and T-34 tanks required to complete the mechanized corps would have taken more than a year to produce.[113] Preparations to resist aggression were therefore having to be accompanied by a necessity not to give Germany a direct excuse to unleash a war.[114]

During the winter and spring, the general staff simultaneously worked on and put into effect two plans: MP-41, a mobilization plan, and Plan 9, "a covering plan for the state frontier."[115] MP-41 was the latest in a series of annual plans based on an assumption, accepted since 1934, that in future wars mobilization would be carried out before, not after, war was declared. Mobilization, consequently, had already been going on for some years. Plan 9 embodied the general staff's final assessments of the nature of contemporary war and the balance of power in a German-Soviet war. Following the doctrine and theory developed over the previous ten years, the general staff assumed that in a war between two countries as large and powerful as the Soviet Union and Germany both sides' operations would have to be conducted in essentially the same way: The initial objective would be to carry the war to the enemy's territory; the forces would be deployed covertly before war was declared; surprise would not be possible; and after war was declared, there would be a two-to-three-week period of "creeping war" during which the parties would test each other and make adjustments before delivering their main blows.[116] When fighting began in earnest, "the war would inevitably become long and intense, and the achievement of victory would depend to a decisive degree on the ability of the rear to supply the front with human and material resources longer than the enemy could."[117]

In the spring Stalin received warnings that a German attack was impending. On 7 May, he became Chairman of the Council of People's Commissars, thereby giving a signal stronger than the one he had sent with Molotov's appointment to the foreign affairs commissariat a year earlier. That the signal was not directed at the Western powers was certain. British Ambassador Cripps said Stalin and Molotov were avoiding him and the United States Ambassador "like grim death."[118] In a Moscow railroad station on 13 April, where he was seeing off the Japanese Foreign Minister, who had just signed a Soviet-Japanese neutrality treaty, Stalin had singled out the German Ambassador among the dignitaries, thrown his arm around the Ambassador's shoulders, and declared, "We must remain friends, and you must now do everything to that end."[119] The Moscow morning newspapers on 14 June printed and the radio broadcast a TASS communiqué accusing the British Government of having spread false rumors about a crisis in German-Soviet relations. Instead, it stated, "Germany is unswervingly observing the provisions of the Soviet-German nonaggression treaty as is the Soviet Union."[120] A day later, in a radiogram from Tokyo, the Soviet master spy Richard Sorge predicted a German attack on 22 June "on a broad front."[121] Before dawn on 22 June, Operation Barbarossa achieved a devastating surprise.

THE RESULTS

Stalin's apparent failure to heed warnings about the German attack has often been cited as the greatest and most damaging error in prewar Soviet assessment. Churchill attributed it to "the purblind prejudice and fixed ideas which Stalin had raised between himself and the terrible truth."[122] Khruschchev, in his 1956 destalinization speech, spoke at length about the British warnings and others from the Soviet military attachés in Berlin and said that despite those, "the necessary steps were not taken to prepare the country properly for defense."[123] Churchill's charge, although it has become ineradicably embedded in

Western historiography, has at most no more than tangential validity. Khrushchev's does also, but it has had much less circulation either in or outside the Soviet Union. The interrelationship of the Soviet assessments and their results was too complex to be reduced to a single, simple judgment, which Churchill and Khrushchev both must have known when they pronounced theirs.

From northern Norway to the Pyrenees, the Germans, in early 1941, conducted Operation Harpoon, an elaborate deception designed to divert attention from the Barbarossa deployment by simulating one against England.[124] As far as British Military Intelligence could discern before 12 June, an invasion of England was as likely as an attack on the Soviet Union.[125] Stalin must have been getting the same intelligence picture. He, like Churchill, would have had to know that a deception was being played against one of them, but the prospect of another deal with the Germans could hardly have done other than suit him exactly. Stalin was mistaken but not purblind, and he shared his fixed ideas with MI and Churchill.

The 14 June TASS communiqué constitutes somewhat more viable evidence of gross misassessment on Stalin's part. Zhukov has said that on 13 and 14 June, Timoshenko and he requested permission to put the frontier military districts on alert and Stalin refused, saying, "That means war. Do you understand that or not?"[126] The *History of the Second World War* maintains that the communiqué was issued to probe for a German reaction, and the subsequent total German silence was quickly taken as a sign that war was about to break out. Therefore the Commissariat of Defense, between 14 and 19 June, ordered the frontier military districts to set up command posts from which they could exercise their appointed wartime functions as army group commands.[127] If Stalin believed a last-minute agreement with Germany was possible, he was not alone. The British Foreign Office, at the moment of the attack, had "no conclusive evidence that Germany intended to attack Russia and not merely to use diplomatic and military threats to intimidate her."[128]

The most durable charge brought against Stalin is that his attempt to escape an armed conflict crippled the Soviet deployment. Zhukov speaks of the "extreme caution Stalin displayed when it came to carrying out the basic measures contemplated in the operational mobilization plans regarding preparations for repulsing possible aggression."[129] The figures on mobilization, however, indicate that the General Staff's plan called for 170 divisions and 2 brigades to be deployed in the frontier military districts when hostilities began, and those were in position on 22 June 1941. None was at full war strength, but it was expected that the empty spaces could be filled in a few days during the anticipated hiatus with reservists drawn from the military districts.[130]

A question remains as to the balance of power existing at the front on 22 June. The standard Soviet contention is that the western military districts were outnumbered by 1.8:1 in troops, 1.5:1 in medium and heavy tanks, 3.2:1 in late-model aircraft, and 1.25:1 in artillery and heavy mortars.[131] The German records show the Barbarossa force to have consisted of 152 German, 15½ Finnish, and 15½ Rumanian divisions, totaling about 3.7 million men. Of those, about 2.5 million, all German, were engaged on 22 June. Soviet accounts give two figures, 2.7 and 2.9 million, on Soviet troop strengths in the western military districts, and neither include 100,000 NKVD border troops or four armies totaling 300,000 to 450,000 troops assembling along the Dnepr River.[132] The German force had 2,770 combat aircraft, 3,350 tanks, and 7,184 artillery pieces.[133] The western military districts had 34,695 artillery pieces and heavy mortars.[134] The Soviet accounts customarily give only three figures on aircraft and tanks, 1,540 late-model aircraft and 1,800 medium and heavy tanks, of which 1,475 were T-34s, and KV-1s; but from one recent Soviet history it appears that the total aircraft deployed in the districts would have exceeded 7,000, and the tanks would have been either about 10,000 or somewhat more than 8,000, depending on which number was used.[135] The greater part of the Soviet aircraft and tanks were obsolete or obsolescent, but then so were all of the German tanks from the moment they encounted the T-34 and KV-1; and the air force had 2,739 late-model aircraft, even though not all were deployed in the western districts.[136] All in all, neither side had a decisive numerical advantage, and the Soviet inferiority is a myth.

Nevertheless, the events of 22 June conclusively sustain the Ivanov statement that "the Soviet High Command had been unable to create the initial strategic grouping of the Red Army along the western borders in the form required by the developing situation." Ivanov takes Stalin's misassessment and a lopsided imbalance of forces to have been the decisive reasons why the high command was unable to create an effective strategic grouping; but if the first of those was a limited impediment and the second did not exist, there must have been others.[137]

Under the covering plan and MP-41, the strategic deployment was in three echelons: the first, 56 divisions and 2 brigades, was stationed within 30 miles of the border; the second, 52 divisions, was 30 to 60 miles farther back; and the third, 62 divisions, was in reserve at distances up to 180 miles from the border. The mission of the first two echelons was to "cover" the border with a tight, static defense.[138] (The 1930s theory of fortified lines made it seem advantageous to let the enemy attempt the first blow.) What was at work was a case of mirror-imaging similar to that which had afflicted the Allied commands in May 1940 when they expected the Germans either to wear themselves out under the guns of the Maginot Line or in a head-on collision on the Dyle River. The Soviet planners expected their German counterparts to think as they did, hence not to attempt a strategic surprise but to spend the two or three weeks after war was declared positioning themselves and thereafter to conduct operations at a relatively stately pace.

The *History of the Second World War* identifies another weakness in the planning, namely, that "as a practical matter, the military leadership left a strategic defensive out of consideration and assumed that all future Red Army . . . operations would be almost exclusively offensive."[139] The covering plan and MP-41 were offense-oriented. The covering echelons, after a short defensive period, were to have begun carrying the war to the enemy's territory. That was and probably still is, except for the more extravagant language in the field service regulations, good doctrine in any army.

On the other hand, the implications that a strategic defensive should have been considered and that one could not have been mounted because none had been contemplated point up the rigidity of the prewar assessment process. There is no evidence that Stalin took the room to retreat, which the German general staff regarded as his greatest strategic asset, into account in his prewar balance of power calculations. He also did not authorize a single timely withdrawal until July 1942.

Stalin, of course, also sited the main effort in the wrong place. His error, though, more than compensated in its unanticipated results for all his other misassessments. Although the German main effort was to the north of the marshes, Stalin had, if anything, underestimated Hitler's eagerness to get possession of the Ukraine and the Caucasus. More divisions on the north would, in all likelihood, only have enlarged the German success there, but the massive deployment in the south cut the tempo of the German advance sufficiently to arouse Hitler's impatience. The upshot was the great July debate between Hitler and his generals that culminated in the main effort being shifted to the south and, in the longer term, to the December disaster on the approaches to Moscow.

Had the state of the art in weaponry been at the 1935 level, the Soviet forces would have been splendidly armed when the war began.

As it was, the relative merits of artillery, armor, and aircraft had been debated too long, and the war's actual requirements were not fully appreciated until after it began. The Soviet Union had developed another shortcoming more distinctively its own: an overriding preoccupation with weapons. Motor vehicles had figured marginally in the technological reconstruction. Motorized divisions had less than half their authorized truck allotments, and the rest were to come from civilian sources. The system had worked very poorly in the Finnish war, but the blame had apparently been attributed to faulty organization. Significant motorization would not take place until 1943, when American Lend-Lease vehicles became available in large numbers.

On the other hand, the prewar assessments pertaining to arms production embodied a strain of prescience that is evident in its results but difficult to trace in the assessment process. That the Soviet Union rearmed during the war in plants evacuated from the German-occupied territory is mostly a myth. Although the output was then relatively small, the capacity to produce advanced weapons was in place in June 1941 and was situated where it proved to be out of the German reach. From the first, the five year plans had concentrated on developing three new industrial complexes: Moscow–Upper Volga, Urals, and Western Siberia (Kuznetsk Basin). Loss of the older Donets Basin complex in 1942 cut national coal and steel production by more than half, but it did not impair armament output, which increased during the year and continued to grow thereafter. Although the Soviet accounts prefer to credit economy in production, that achievement compellingly suggests that stockpiling strategic materials had also figured heavily in the prewar assessments.[140]

The consequences of faulty planning initially fell most heavily on the air force. The Soviet analysts had correctly concluded that the Luftwaffe would concentrate on ground support, but they had missed an essential point: The Luftwaffe operated alongside the ground forces, not under their control. It could therefore set its own objectives, and the first was to eliminate Soviet air power. A Soviet figure for the day's losses on 22 June is 1,200 planes, 738 of them at West Front, which lost 38 percent of its air strength. All told, the Luftwaffe, by its reckoning, destroyed over 6,800 Soviet aircraft before the battles on the frontier ended on 12 July. The air force's confidence was shattered. Until after the end of the year, bombers seldom ventured across the front, and fighters kept their appearances brief. The 1941 disaster terminated the debate on air doctrine. For the rest of the war, the air force confined itself to close ground support.[141]

Since the German navy was not heavily engaged in the east and the Germans early on had air superiority over the Baltic and Black seas, the surface ships of the Soviet navy figured only incidentally in the war, and the submarines hardly counted at all. All the navy had to show for the materials and labor invested in the 1938 building program were four light cruisers. With army help, the navy managed to hold the Kronstadt-Oranienbaum complex of forts while Leningrad was under siege and the Sevastopol fortress until July 1942. Those successes, together with a few of the "mosquito fleet" variety at sea and the fortuitous absence of outright disasters, brought the navy into some favor with Stalin. N. G. Kuznetsov, who had become navy chief in April 1939, stayed in command throughout the war and received the title Hero of the Soviet Union in September 1945.[142]

After ten years' intensive effort to assess the requirements of the next war, the Red Army was deficient in comprehension of the war it encountered on 22 June 1941 and in the technique and flexibility that would have been required to prevent the ensuing surprise from ballooning to strategic proportions. The Barbarossa Blitzkrieg was at a far remove from prewar Soviet deep operations theory and a radical departure even from the German operations in Poland and Western Europe. The double envelopment (better known in 1941 as the *Zangenangriff* or pincers movement) was its essential feature, not a chance outcome of deep penetrations as in Soviet theory or an exploitation of positional advantage as in the 1939 and 1940 campaigns. Strictly speaking, it should not be classed at all as a deep operation in the sense that applied before 1941 since its purpose was not to gain ground but to destroy the enemy's main forces as expeditiously as could possibly be done in terms of time and distance.

The Barbarossa-style Blitzkrieg was the closest approach to pure war of annihilation yet seen in the twentieth century, but it was born of necessity as well as art and therefore fragile. It could not be sustained beyond the summer of 1942. Thereafter, Soviet industrial production and the Red Army mass overwhelmed the German armies in an "extended war of attrition." At Stalingrad and on a few other occasions, the Red Army executed double envelopments, but it relied predominantly on the *rassekayushchy udar* (a splitting or splintering blow), a deep frontal attack (usually mounted in series on a broad front), which had first been used against Denikin in 1919 and in modernized form had been the central feature of Tukhachevsky's deep operations theory. In its major aspects, the 1930s assessment received its definitive validation in Berlin at midnight on 8 May 1945.

7

Franklin D. Roosevelt and the Craft of Strategic Assessment

Calvin L. Christman

FOR A STUDENT of the contemporary national security structure of the United States, the apparatus in the late 1930s must indeed seem inchoate, disorganized, and naïve.[1] There was no National Security Council, no Joint Chiefs of Staff, no Central Intelligence Agency, and certainly no Office of Net Assessment. When the Ecuadorian government in 1937 inquired whether the nephew of the President of Ecuador might attend one of the United States Army intelligence schools, President Franklin D. Roosevelt admitted that "unfortunately, we have no Army school for instruction in 'military intelligence.'"[2] Little wonder that when the British military staff first came in contact with the American defense structure at the January 1942 ARCADIA meeting, Sir John Dill observed incredulously that "the whole organisation belongs to the days of George Washington."[3]

This rudimentary apparatus, however, did not mean that the United

States—and more precisely President Roosevelt—lacked the means or intention to carry out strategic assessment in the increasingly hostile world of the late 1930s. When it came to assessment, all roads led to the Oval Office. Intelligence information regularly flowed to the President from the State Department and its personnel around the world, from the Military Intelligence Division (MID or G-2) of the army, and from the Office of Naval Intelligence (ONI). These agencies also exchanged information with each other on a regular basis. At the White House, military reports usually moved to the President through either his naval aide or his permanent military aide, General Edwin W. "Pa" Watson, although, depending on the information or source, communications often went directly to the President. By the fall of 1940, MAGIC added to this intelligence material by providing summaries of intercepted Japanese diplomatic messages. In addition, the Department of Justice and its Federal Bureau of Investigation (FBI), as well as the Departments of Interior, Commerce, and Treasury, periodically submitted various national security items.

Roosevelt, however, believed in the use of multiple channels for information and communication. With a personal inclination toward secrecy and intrigue, the President made extensive use of semiformal and informal sources to increase his feel for the texture of international players and events. He continually directed diplomats to write directly to him, and he often ended his own short replies with the closing, "Write again soon." Other business, governmental, newspaper, and academic contacts, acquaintances, agents, and friends also wrote the President. Some of these sources resided outside the country. Others, such as Vincent Astor and John Franklin Carter, provided the President with his own informal intelligence network from inside the country.[4]

Taken as a whole, Roosevelt's sources of information prior to World War II are certainly more impressive than the formal structure might suggest. Often the President would share this material with such officials as the Secretary of State, the Under Secretary of State, or the Chief of Naval Operations. Neither uneasy nor uncomfortable that he alone had all the sources of information, the President reveled in his position, for he had long had an interest in geopolitics and had complete confidence in his own knowledge and judgment of international affairs. After all, under the Constitution he was the Commander-in-Chief, and he never had any doubts that he would and could fill that role to its fullest.

Nor was FDR concerned about his own unsystematic, "impression-istic"[5] weighing and balancing of security information, for Roosevelt had normally practiced a personalized and "messy" (if not chaotic) management style. Lord Halifax, who came to Washington in 1941 as the British Ambassador, observed that Roosevelt's policy-making seemed "rather like a disorderly line of beaters out shooting; they do put the rabbits out of the bracken, but they don't come out where you expect."[6] Roosevelt often practiced bureaucratic disunity by allowing subordinate rivalries to undercut Cabinet leadership. The national security organization was not an exception, as the conflicts between Secretary of State Cordell Hull and Under Secretary of State Sumner Welles and between Secretary of War Harry Woodring and Under Secretary of War Louis Johnson attest. Bureaucratic tidiness was not a Roosevelt trait. Keeping all the threads in his hands was. Formal organizations could dissipate his power and lessen his control, a fact the President understood well. After World War II the United States Strategic Bombing Survey would conclude: "The structure of our prewar military organization provided no means, short of the President, for integrating our armed forces."[7] Roosevelt, it seems clear, would not have wanted it any other way.

Roosevelt shared his innermost thoughts with others only when he wanted to, and that was not often. "You won't talk frankly even with the people who are loyal to you," Secretary of the Interior Harold Ickes once complained. "You keep your cards close up against your belly. You never put them on the table." Ickes' words were echoed throughout Washington. When Roosevelt spoke there was a vague, amorphous quality in his words and demeanor, and his statements often seemed determined more by his audience than by his beliefs. Friends might accept this characteristic as the mark of an astute politician keeping his options open, but opponents often viewed it as outright mendacity. Roosevelt, as one critic asserted, was "a chameleon on plaid."[8]

Although Roosevelt was history-minded, he wanted no historians around the White House peering over his shoulder. Policy decisions were the public's business, but how policy decisions were made was not. He forcefully told members of the Senate Military Affairs Committee: "In arriving at the final determination of any question of government, the machinery is not of interest to anybody and it is not going to be."[9]

Taken together, these facts make it difficult to say with precision what Roosevelt was thinking at any given time or why he was thinking it. From a variety of formal and informal contacts the President received clearly argued, multipage reports on world affairs and leaders;

too often he replied with a short, banal paragraph, leaving a reader still to penetrate the haze and fog that regularly surrounded the actions and inactions of the President. Despite this problem, however, presidential documents leave the clear impression that Roosevelt quite early saw the Axis as a threat. Nor, once perceived, did he waver in that belief, even if he understood imperfectly the extent of the threat or what the United States should do about it. "The German-Italian-Japanese combination is being amazingly successful—bluff, power, accomplishment or whatever it may be," he wrote in the fall of 1937, and "we cannot stop the spread of Fascism unless world opinion realizes its ultimate dangers."[10] The President understood that those dangers would not go away. In the spring of 1938, he reflected: "Over here there is the same element that exists in London. . . . They would really like me to be a Neville Chamberlain. . . . But if that were done, we would only be breeding far more serious trouble four or eight years from now."[11] This negative assessment of the Axis, however, existed within the context of Roosevelt's essentially confident, optimistic temper, a characteristic that was basic to his personality, and one that he had amply demonstrated while fighting the Depression of the 1930s. He would continue to display this trait, especially toward the probability of Britain's survival in 1940 and the Soviet Union's survival in 1941.

Sometimes Roosevelt's optimism betrayed him. Relieved that the Munich settlement had averted war, he happily blurted, "I want you to know that I am not a bit upset over the final result."[12] But his euphoria disappeared almost instantly. Within a few days he turned his mind toward a war that now seemed nearer than before. Acting through a close English friend, Roosevelt privately pledged to Neville Chamberlain that if the British did find themselves in a war with Germany, Britain "would have the industrial resources of the American nation behind it."[13] In the eyes of the President, Hitler was a "pure unadulterated devil."[14]

Thus, when the Führer unleased war in September 1939, Roosevelt was not surprised. Nor, at the same time, did he harbor any doubts about his own ability to steer America through the oncoming storm and eventually bring it safely to port.

Roosevelt's introduction to strategic thinking came early in his life. For Christmas in 1897, his Uncle Fred and Aunt Annie Hitch gave him a copy of Alfred Thayer Mahan's *The Influence of Sea Power upon History*. Roosevelt was then fifteen years old. A month later for his birthday they followed with a copy of Mahan's *The Interest of America in Sea Power, Present and Future.* With the words of Mahan and the example of his hero and cousin Theodore Roosevelt, young Franklin quickly developed his lifelong love of the navy and interest in strategic affairs.

Roosevelt continued these interests as an adult. His experience as the Assistant Secretary of the Navy during World War I inevitably influenced his actions, thoughts, and perceptions as the world first staggered toward and then fell into a second world war. World War I greatly increased his knowledge of the day-to-day operations of the navy, and this knowledge in turn increased his confidence that he knew best the needs of his navy. Time and his other duties did not erode this confidence, for presidential records from the late 1930s show that along with being President, Roosevelt largely acted as his own navy secretary; he continually bombarded the Secretary of the Navy and the Chief of Naval Operations with questions and directives covering a plethora of large and little items ranging from officer promotions to the selection of names for future seaplane tenders.[15] In turn, these officials knew that the President expected to be consulted on almost all matters. In contrast, the President rarely demonstrated an equivalent interest in the army. This was a reflection of Roosevelt's knowledge of and interest in the navy, the relative importance of the navy as compared to the army at that time, and the very warm personal relationship the President had with his Chiefs of Naval Operations, William D. Leahy (1937–39) and Harold R. "Betty" Stark (1939–42), both of whom he had become acquainted with during World War I.

A knowledge of the navy and friendships with some of its officers were not all that FDR gained from World War I. Lessons were there to be learned. There was his (and the country's) conviction that America would never again be willing to send an army to Europe. There was the remembrance of Brest-Litovsk and the willingness of the new Soviet state to turn its back on its allies and seek a separate treaty with its enemy. There was the belief that, in the rush to gain the armistice in 1918, the chance had been lost to crush German militarism forever, for the armistice had furnished the German army the opportunity to avow that it had never been defeated on the battlefield. And lastly there was the view that if somehow events forced the United States to send an army overseas, American public opinion would demand its quick return once the hostilities concluded; any long-term American occupation role in Europe would be an impossibility.

Lessons from World War I were not all that confronted Roosevelt as he interpreted and balanced strategic perceptions during his second administration. Assessment occurs within a political environment, and the late 1930s were no different. Roosevelt had sought and gained reelection in 1936, but his second term brought on a presumed lame-duck status. His abortive effort at packing the Supreme Court in 1937, a sharp economic downturn the same year, increasing turmoil between management and labor, and the President's public failure to purge conservatives from within his own party all weakened his political influence further. The continuing economic depression and Roosevelt's New Deal hopes for recovery and reform demanded most of his attention. Additionally, America saw little threat to its security, for its two oceans gave it protection. Isolationist sentiment was deep, and its supporters vocal. When fiscal concerns demanded cuts in the budget, the already low level of defense spending seemed a logical target.

Roosevelt began to see the Axis as a serious threat to peace in 1936. As he later related to the Senate Military Affairs Committee in a confidential 1939 meeting held at the White House, "We got the pretty definite information that there was in the making a policy of world domination between Germany, Italy, and Japan."[16] The events of the following years hardened his perception. At the same time, however, the President would neither take nor be pushed toward precipitate action. Caution, indecision, and procrastination were not unknown elements of Roosevelt's leadership. He told Admiral Stark in 1940: "When I don't know how to move, I stay put."[17] In addition, any fledgling steps he might take to lend support to the European democracies or to block the Axis had to consider public opinion. He was loath to push that opinion too hard or to get in front of it too far.

Early in his career Roosevelt concluded that unity at home was a necessity if the United States was to have influence abroad. As Robert Dallek stresses in his study of FDR's foreign policy, the President had learned soon after World War I that "the first requirement of an effective role abroad was stable consensus at home."[18] Roosevelt held tightly to that lesson as first Europe and then the United States moved toward war.

Great Britain's movement from appeasement to resistance provided an example of the vital importance of public thinking. During the late 1930s and early 1940s, Roosevelt corresponded frequently with Arthur and Faith Murray in Scotland. He had first met them during World War I when Arthur Murray, a distant cousin, was the Assistant Military Attaché in Washington, D.C. Colonel Murray, C.M.G., D.S.O., had been a Member of Parliament before and after World War I, and he moved easily within top-level British governmental circles. His many letters chronicled the direction of British public opinion.[19] Roosevelt understood that it was only the ultimate realization that appeasement could not work with Hitler that finally united the British in their determination to fight. In short, without the failed policy of appeasement British unity would not exist.

The President realized that American public opinion would have to undergo the same process. Roosevelt's approach to public opinion, therefore, was cautious, gentle, and at times even fearful, much to the frustration of some of his own advisers. "I don't think we want to frighten the American people," Roosevelt declared. "We want them to gradually realize what is a potential danger."[20] He understood American determination not to send a future army to another European war, for FDR had the same reluctance. As Europe approached the Munich Crisis, Roosevelt reflected that if war did come he would not ask the people of the United States to practice a Woodrow Wilson–style neutrality of thought. Instead, he would "strongly encourage their natural sympathy [toward the Allies] while at the same time avoiding any thought of sending troops to Europe."[21]

Congress had its own opinion, and the legislators were determined that any natural sympathy for the Allies should not lead to an economic relationship that might suck the United States into a European war. This resolve narrowed the President's options and reduced in his own mind his ability to have a positive influence on the course of European events. Roosevelt's attempt to change neutrality legislation in the summer of 1939 presents an example of the President's problem.

Under the neutrality law at the time, the United States could not sell arms, ammunition, or war matériel to any belligerent. If war broke out in Europe, Britain and France would find themselves at a disadvantage, for they would be unable to obtain weapons from the United States. Having rearmed first, Germany did not need American weapons. In addition, Germany acquired impressive armament stockpiles and productive capacity in its seizure of Czechoslovakia. Thus, in the administration's mind, the so-called neutrality legislation actually would work in favor of the Third Reich and might well encourage a war.[22] Although a proposed "cash and carry" modification would offer some improvements (the British navy, expecting to control the Atlantic in any European war, would be able to carry back to Britain arms purchased with cash in the United States), Roosevelt did not consider it the solution. Such a modification would fall on the wrong side of the Sino-Japanese conflict. "The more I think the problem through," the President concluded, "the more I am convinced that the existing Neutrality Act should be repealed in toto without any substitute."[23]

Roosevelt failed to get his wish. In July 1939 Congress blocked either repeal or major revisions of the law. Roosevelt's defeat was made more bitter by the fact that many within his party opposed him. He chastised one New Deal Democrat who had broken ranks on this issue: "If war breaks out in Europe . . . an important part of the responsibility will rest on [Congress'] action . . . I honestly believe that the vote . . . was a stimulus to war."[24]

Throughout his second term, Roosevelt had to contend with his shrinking political power as a lame-duck president and with the constraints he believed this weakness placed on his maneuverability. The problems of the Axis would have to be faced by his successor— unless, of course, he decided to confront America's two-term tradition and seek an unprecedented third term himself. Roosevelt apparently had that possibility in mind when he wrote to the Republican leader Frank Knox in late December 1939, speculating that if a real crisis— such as a German victory—should develop in Europe, then "it would be necessary to put aside in large part strictly old fashioned party government, and the people would understand such a situation."[25] Yet Roosevelt's ultimate decision to seek reelection also limited his freedom, for much as he might wish to move the United States toward a position of military security and a *de facto* industrial alliance with Britain, he dared not move so far as to jeopardize his uncertain reelection.

By the spring of 1941, with his successful reelection followed by the passage of Lend-Lease, Roosevelt could reflect with some pride to the Murrays in Britain that "it has been possible, as you know, for me to carry the country along slowly, but I think surely."[26] One wonders if the Murrays, however, with their country standing alone against the combined German-Italian strength, might have thought ruefully that the critical word was "slowly" rather than "surely."

A primitive American military structure for carrying out national security assessment emerged as part of the military reforms established after the Spanish-American War. Although the Joint Chiefs of Staff was a World War II creation of Franklin D. Roosevelt, its forerunner went back to 1903, when an agreement between the

Secretary of War and the Secretary of the Navy created the Joint Army-Navy Board. Composed of four officers from the Army General Staff and four officers from the Navy General Board, the Joint Board considered military plans that demanded joint service deliberation. Its power, however, was restricted by the service secretaries' control of the issues to be considered and their freedom to ignore the Board's advice. Additionally, the lack of a separate staff limited the Board's ability to carry out necessary research.

During World War I, both President Woodrow Wilson and the State Department ignored the Joint Board completely. The Board's isolation demonstrated the problem that would haunt the agency during the 1920s and much of the 1930s: the lack of clear policy direction. If the President and State Department failed to express clearly and authoritatively the national policy of the United States, how was the Joint Board to consider and develop military plans to support that policy?

Following World War I, the Joint Board underwent important changes. Membership was trimmed to six officers: the Chief of Naval Operations, the Army Chief of Staff, their deputies, and the heads of the Navy and Army War Plans divisions. The Board could now consider issues on its own initiative rather than wait for the direction of the service Secretary. In addition, it received both a permanent civilian secretary and the necessary staff officers to carry out the detailed investigations necessary for the creation of joint war plans. This latter organization was the Joint Planning Committee, composed of eight officers, four each from the Army and Navy War Plans Divisions. It reported directly to the Joint Board, which in turn continued to require the approval of both Secretaries to translate its recommendations into action. With these improvements in place the Board achieved considerable success in dealing with joint service concerns during the interwar years.[27]

These changes, however, did not alleviate the absence of policy direction from above. Ironically, it was the young FDR, then Acting Secretary of the Navy, who tried to address that problem with a proposal in May 1919. Attempting to elicit a clear statement of United States policy in the Far East, he directed a letter to the Secretary of State that included an organizational blueprint to coordinate the planning efforts of the War, Navy, and State departments through a type of general staff. This link was necessary, Roosevelt asserted, because the military needed to know what foreign policy objectives it might have to uphold and because the State Department needed to understand the potential military costs required to uphold them.

Foreign policy, he declared, "depends for its acceptance by other nations upon the naval and military force that is behind it."[28]

Nothing came of the proposal. In fact, evidence shows that Roosevelt's carefully drawn blueprint not only was never discussed, it was not even opened.[29] The State Department was congenitally opposed to any reform that might seem to give the military a role in determining national policy.

The paucity of civilian collaboration with the military and the absence of clear policy direction would continue to plague national security affairs up to Pearl Harbor. A 1932 army study on the subject of joint war planning emphasized this point. An examination of war planning carried out by other countries demonstrated that in all other first class powers, "the civilian departments of the government share with the military in the responsibility for national defense, and this responsibility manifests itself in their war planning agencies." In the United States, even when direction or information did filter down from civilian agencies, it came only from informal contacts with lower-level officials whose statements were given "without the responsibility, and generally without the knowledge of the departmental heads."[30] Seven years later the Chief of the Army War Plans Division aired the same frustration to the Chief of Staff. In seeking national policy, he complained, the Planning Committee has been unable to gain "authoritative expressions of fact or opinion from representatives of other Executive Departments."[31]

The military services were not necessarily the only ones to be left unsure. After Roosevelt's reelection in 1940, the American Ambassador to Japan, Joseph C. Grew, wrote a letter to the President, attempting to draw out Roosevelt's thoughts. He began with the plea, "I would give a great deal to know your mind about Japan and all her works," and ended five pages later with the request, "If you are willing to give me even a cue to your thoughts . . . it will be of tremendous help."[32] Grew's hopes went for naught. Although the President's reply carried his signature, the words were not his. The letter instead was prepared by Stanley K. Hornbeck, the State Department's chief political expert on Far Eastern affairs.

Despite these problems, the Roosevelt administration had improved the links between the State Department and the military services. Events across the Atlantic and Pacific demanded it. In a statement reminiscent of young Roosevelt's dictum back in 1919, Secretary of State Cordell Hull observed the link between diplomatic leverage and military power. Concerning Axis diplomats, Hull had discovered that "they were looking over my shoulder at our Navy and our Army and that our diplomatic strength in dealing with [the Axis] governments . . . goes up or down with their estimate of what that amounts to."[33]

As a result, Hull increasingly sought advice from senior army and navy officers. This was especially true in matters dealing with the Far East and with Latin America. In 1935 Hull named Hornbeck to serve as a political adviser to the Joint Planning Committee and in 1938 he followed with a proposal for a Standing Liaison Committee. The President enthusiastically approved the idea.[34] Normally meeting once a month and composed of the Under Secretary of State, the Army Chief of Staff, and the Chief of Naval Operations, the Committee brought the State Department and the armed services together for the first time in a formal, operating organization that could consider the military and diplomatic elements of national policy.

Roosevelt had earlier used various *ad hoc* military–civilian committees to study specific problems. Some concerns had demanded cooperation of a number of departments, such as FDR's long-running vexation over possible Japanese espionage activities in Hawaii. During 1936 the President received reports that Japanese-American residents of Oahu often greeted arriving Japanese merchant ships and sometimes entertained crew members.[35] Without a casual aside to constitutional guarantees, Roosevelt responded:

> One obvious thought occurs to me—that every Japanese citizen or non-citizen on the Island of Oahu who meets these Japanese ships or has any connection with their officers or men should be secretly but definitely identified and his or her name placed on a special list of those who would be the first to be placed in a concentration camp in the event of trouble.[36]

The following May, FDR formed a special committee to investigate the activities of Japanese naval personnel and civilians in Hawaii. Chaired by Secretary of War Harry Woodring, it comprised the Attorney General and the Secretaries of State, Treasury, Labor, Navy, and War. Although not a member of the committee, the Secretary of Interior also participated in the discussions.[37] The President also expressed concern with possible Japanese activities in Mexico, especially in Lower California, and he directed that MID insert agents into the area to carry out personal observation.[38]

As war approached in Europe, Roosevelt took steps to increase his control as Commander-in-Chief. In an order of 5 July 1939, he removed the Joint Army-Navy Board, the Joint Aeronautical Board, and the Joint Army-Navy Munitions Board from the military departments and placed them within the Executive Office. With this order, the senior army and navy officers reported directly to the President, and the Joint Board now took an important step toward becoming the President's joint military staff. Appropriately, historians still argue as to whether that was what Roosevelt intended.[39] Whatever the case, by the time Roosevelt finished his second term as President and entered his third, collaboration between the armed services and civilian agencies had moved a long way from the near-separate paths that they had followed only two decades before. Yet, as Louis Morton reminds students of this period, "this collaboration was achieved very largely by informal and personal means through the agency of the President."[40]

Roosevelt's two most important military advisers came on board almost simultaneously with the onset of World War II. George C. Marshall became Army Chief of Staff on the same day German troops smashed across the Polish border; exactly one month earlier, Harold R. Stark had become Chief of Naval Operations. They joined the President's important civilian advisers, Under Secretary of State Sumner Welles and Secretary of the Treasury Henry Morgenthau. The following June FDR added two Republicans to the administration when he appointed Henry L. Stimson as Secretary of War and Frank Knox as Secretary of the Navy. Following his reelection, Roosevelt brought Harry Hopkins into the White House as a *de facto* national security adviser and troubleshooter. The President's pre–Pearl Harbor national security team was now complete. By spring 1941 FDR was meeting regularly with what became known as his "War Council": Knox, Stimson, Hopkins, Hull, Marshall, and Stark, with Morgenthau and other officials sometimes attending.[41] Of all these advisers, Stimson, Welles, and Hopkins were the most important to the President.

In comparison to the others, Harry Hopkins would seem to be woefully unprepared and totally out of place, yet he was the most vital. Although trained as a social worker, he became the nexus between Roosevelt and his other advisers. Totally loyal to the President and matching FDR's love of political intrigue, Hopkins had a brilliant mind, a superb ability to focus his attention on the crux of a problem (Churchill would dub him "Lord-Root-of-the-Matter"), an intuitive gift for knowing what Roosevelt was thinking, and a pragmatic approach to the problems at hand. At first military leaders looked at him with suspicion, but they soon came to value both his abilities as an individual and his access as a presidential alter ego. Marshall called him "invaluable," and Stimson, by March 1941, had concluded that "it is a godsend that he should be at the White House."[42]

With the events of September 1939, the sources of British information flowing to the President increased considerably. Roosevelt made the first move by writing to Winston Churchill, who had recently been appointed First Lord of the Admiralty. In a sentence that many of his own diplomats would recognize, the President made clear that "I shall at all times welcome it if you will keep me in touch personally with anything you want me to know about."[43] With this short letter began a flow of messages between the two leaders that would number almost two thousand by the time of Roosevelt's death in April 1945.

Before the war's outbreak, the flow of information between the two nations had been sporadic and tentative, depending upon the tension in specific areas of the world and the benefits the two countries expected to accrue to themselves through the exchange. Nor was the information necessarily valuable or accurate. In late February 1939 the British Ambassador to the United States passed along a secret political assessment concluding that British rearmament had now progressed to a point that it would deter any future German action.[44] Two weeks later, Germany absorbed Czechoslovakia. In turn, U.S. material was sometimes little better. In commenting on an American secret report passed along to the British, Desmond Morton, Churchill's intelligence aide, observed that "the Book of Revelations read backwards would be more helpful."[45] Notwithstanding such occasional shortcomings, Roosevelt expressed pleasure over the intelligence reports coming from both American and European sources. Writing to Arthur Murray during the latter part of the "phony war," the President praised the British and French governments for being "so frank with us," and he concluded confidently, "I imagine that I am getting better information from the world as a whole (except Russia) than anybody else."[46]

As soon as Churchill became Prime Minister, he ordered Lord Lothian, the British Ambassador in Washington, to forward British military intelligence summaries to the President. These reports covered a vast range of topics and sometimes came as often as twice a day. The British Embassy continued forwarding these reports directly to the President until America entered the war, at which time the reports moved to the President through the American section of the Secretariat of the Combined Chiefs of Staff.[47]

As the quasi-neutral United States moved from nonbelligerency in

1939 to a belligerent nonbelligerency in 1941, intelligence sharing naturally increased on all levels. Yet there were obstacles to be overcome. Mutual interests are not the same as mutual trust, and an anti-Axis stance was not automatically tantamount to a pro-British position. Elements within the American military firmly believed that Britain wished to draw the United States into the war for the purpose not just of defeating the Axis but also of saving the British Empire; as in World War I, America's sons would be used to pull England's imperial chestnuts out of the fire. British haughtiness and condescension added to the problem. Assistant Secretary of State Adolph Berle peevishly observed, "A British Imperial Englishman cannot easily get over the idea that no foreign government is entitled to a foreign policy without their OK, they of course reserving complete freedom." It was, Berle noted, "the survival of an old habit."[48] Even Roosevelt, despite the genuine warmth of his relationship with Churchill, found that he and the Prime Minister could not discuss the subject of British imperial rule in India without severely straining their relationship.

Not surprisingly, both countries were loath to exchange information on secret items that they perceived to be especially crucial to their security. Captain (later Vice Admiral) Alan Kirk was the United States Navy attaché in London and later the Director of the Office of Naval Intelligence. He recalled that "in no case was there what you might call wide-open exchange. Our side was very, very cautious, and so were they."[49] Such caution included the American denial of the Norden bombsight to the British, despite Neville Chamberlain's personal plea to the President.[50] In addition, the British had a strong concern that U.S. security was lax and that information furnished to America would find its way into German hands.[51] The British themselves had broken American diplomatic ciphers before the war and had regularly been listening in on U.S. diplomatic traffic, a fact of which William Bullitt had warned FDR back in 1938 and one which Churchill neglected to tell FDR until 1942.[52]

In the early days of the war, the United States had far more to gain from an exchange of information than Britain. Through combat Britain was gaining valuable military and technical experience that was unavailable to the United States. As a consequence, Roosevelt was advised that the British "will gradually outdistance us in many technical subjects." Thus, the United States should move toward "liberalizing our policies of exchange."[53]

The President understood this fact but it was not until the crisis brought on by the fall of France and by the fear of an encore in Britain that he took action. Very much in FDR's character, when he did act he used an unofficial, personal emissary who would report directly to him. In July 1940 Roosevelt picked William Donovan, a highly decorated former World War I army officer, to go to Britain. FDR had known him in law school at Columbia University, and the President had used him earlier for confidential intelligence-gathering tasks. Donovan's mission to London was to gain a "feel" for whether Britain would fight on or succumb.[54]

The latter prediction was the view of many American military and civilian officials, including the American ambassador on the scene, Joseph Kennedy. Hearing of Donovan's intelligence-gathering mission, Kennedy called to protest, claiming that the ill-conceived mission "will simply result in creating confusion and misunderstanding on the part of the British." Sumner Welles replied coolly that the President's decision had been made.[55]

The British suffered no confusion in the least. It was hardly difficult for them to deduce Donovan's mission, and what they failed to deduce the head of British intelligence in the United States, William S. Stephenson, apparently told them. Realizing that future American aid (including the destroyers for which Churchill had been pleading since May) and eventual participation in the war itself might well depend on Donovan's personal report to the President, the British welcomed Donovan's arrival and guaranteed that he met with all the right people and in all the right circumstances. As a Central Intelligence Agency study later described, "Donovan scurried about London and its environs visiting every important government office and inspecting many of the military, naval, and air installations then girding for the defense of the islands."[56] Along with demonstrating their determination to continue the fight no matter what the circumstances, the British made clear their willingness to share intelligence information.

Though only a first step, Donovan's trip was nonetheless an important first step. Not only did it result directly in increased Presidential confidence that Britain would survive, it also set the stage for a close personal working relationship between Donovan and Stephenson (referred to respectively as "Wild Bill" and "Little Bill"), for a steadfast and intimate Anglo-American intelligence collaboration (including the American gift to the British in late 1940 of one of the precious PURPLE machines used to decode Japanese diplomatic messages), and for the appointment of Donovan first as the Coordinator of Information (COI) and later as the Director of the Office of Strategic Services (OSS). Though it would be overstating the case to imply that all of these results were somehow what FDR intended to achieve when he made the decision to send Donovan, it also would be wrong to assume that the President did not understand the path that events might take.

When war first approached Europe during the late 1930s and then turned toward the United States in the early 1940s, a substantial portion of the intelligence assessments passing the President's desk concerned the economic resources of the Axis, for a common weakness of Germany, Italy, and Japan was their paucity in raw materials, especially oil. A confidential study by the Treasury Department, completed by early 1938, estimated that Japan imported 90 percent of its current petroleum needs, 64 percent of it coming from the United States. Japan also imported 100 percent of its rubber, 90 percent of its lead, 100 percent of its nickel, 80 percent of its iron ore, and 95 percent of its cotton; the list went on and on.[57] When the United States examined these figures, it had a difficult time contemplating a war with Japan. After all, how could Japan, so weak in resources, consider a war against the United States, a nation so strong in resources? Already at war with China, Japan surely would not seek an additional conflict with America.

Although Japan's need for imported oil was manifest, how the United States should use this fact to its advantage was not. If the United States cut off petroleum sales in order to force Japan into rethinking its expansionist foreign policy, would such an economic bludgeon change Japanese international behavior? Or might it instead accelerate Japanese thought of grabbing the oil-rich Dutch East Indies?

Germany's need for oil was of equal interest to Roosevelt, for petroleum not only represented a grave German strategic weakness, but for the same reason it provided a window into probable future German plans to ameliorate that condition. Anthony J. Biddle, the United States Ambassador to Poland, discussed possible German action with the President five months before Hitler's invasion of Poland. The iron ore of the Soviet Donetsk area and the oil of the Baku region would give Hitler what he needed. Although other sources of oil, such as Rumania, would be helpful, their production would not be enough. In terms of oil, Biddle observed, "Rumania may be marked down rather as a 'service station' on Hitler's envisaged route to Baku."[58]

In line with his usual *modus operandi*, Roosevelt also received unofficial economic assessments from private sources. Bernard Baruch served as one of Roosevelt's prime connections, and Baruch would request of experts in various economic fields that they contact FDR directly if Baruch himself did not have the information.[59] Economic data flowed to concerned agencies through the informal Interdepartmental Committee on Strategic Materials, which had representatives from the Navy, War, State, Commerce, and Interior departments.[60]

Additional information came to Roosevelt from his New York neighbor and friend, Vincent Astor. Owner of *Newsweek* magazine and a director of both the Western Union Telegraph Company and the Chase National Bank, this multimillionaire had an interest in intelligence matters that predated FDR's election, and he had used his business and social contacts to organize a loose informal intelligence circle marked by its Anglophile views. Through his contacts, Astor supplied political and economic data directly to FDR, including details on the movement of foreign funds passing through the Chase bank. Not only could this help in keeping track of foreign purchases of raw materials and other strategic goods within the country, but it also could assist in counterintelligence work. Astor reminded FDR that "espionage and sabotage need money, and that has to pass through the banks at one stage or another."[61] In providing his own intelligence system to the President, Astor did not limit himself to working within the country. In 1938 he sailed his private yacht *Nourmahal* to the Pacific to gather information on Japanese-controlled islands.[62] Roosevelt would later appoint Astor as the intelligence coordinator in the New York City area, where, as a Commander in the United States Naval Reserve, he would work with the FBI, ONI, MID, and William Stephenson.[63]

Once the European war had begun, the President continued to keep a close watch on economic resources. As Hitler's armies swept through Western Europe in the spring of 1940, Roosevelt received revised estimates that incorporated the effects of German success on its economic position. By the late summer of 1940, Anglo-American intelligence collaboration was becoming fact, and Treasury Department estimates now included British assessments of German, Italian, and Japanese oil stocks. Other studies investigated German food supplies, labor shortages, and finances.[64]

In July 1941 Roosevelt appointed Donovan Coordinator of Information and directed that he assist the President "in assembling and correlating information which may be useful in the formulation of basic plans for the defense of the Nation."[65] One of Donovan's first strategic estimates centered on Germany's military and economic position and its resources of manpower, agricultural products, minerals, transportation, and petroleum. Donovan also addressed the less easily quantified topic of morale. His twenty-one-page report concluded that in none of these categories, including the last two, was Germany likely to face a crisis in the coming year.[66]

Of equal or greater concern to Roosevelt during the late 1930s was the state of Axis and Allied aviation. Here the picture appeared gloomy in the extreme. Roosevelt understood that air power served as both a weapon of war and a truncheon of diplomacy. Few spectacles so effectively projected national power as the sight and sound of a sky laden with aircraft. As an astute politician, FDR must have looked with both anger and awe at the way Hitler's Luftwaffe had shaped European diplomacy before the war. If Britain and France had only had more aircraft, Roosevelt asserted, then "there would not have been any Munich."[67]

Six weeks after Munich, Roosevelt took steps to tend to America's air power frailty. He directed the War Department to plan a two-year program to construct ten thousand aircraft, as well as to provide for the establishment of manufacturing plants that could produce twenty thousand aircraft annually if needed.[68] This was a huge program. Not only does it represent one of the first steps toward American rearmament, but it also gives some insight into Roosevelt's thinking in the immediate post-Munich period.

As already noted, Roosevelt was only too well aware of the diplomatic power of aircraft. Hitler had proved it at Munich. FDR was determined that the United States should never be placed in a position similar to that of Britain and France. If the United States had a large force of aircraft in hand, American foreign policy would be enhanced and American national security protected. In fact, the sheer deterrent force of those aircraft might guarantee that they would never be used. Thus, Roosevelt's thoughts apparently rested on large numbers of aircraft and on getting them quickly, while at the same time he ignored the infrastructure that normally must support aircraft. There was no mention of a systematic expansion of training facilities, airfields, support units, and combat-ready pilots and crews. Deterrence was the President's purpose; an air force ready for war was not.

Although an increased air force would help to deter any threat to the nation, it might already be too late to arrest a European war. If so, America's large air program would then have the advantage of allowing the country, with proper modification or outright repeal of the neutrality law, to sell aircraft to Britain and France and, with the government aircraft plants that Roosevelt called for, to produce additional planes in large quantities.[69]

Yet there still remained the President's lingering hope that the mere knowledge of this air program and its possible availability to the Allies might act as a brake on Hitler's expansion. It was a hope that Congress destroyed when it failed to rethink the neutrality restrictions in the summer of 1939, though in hindsight it is hard to imagine any American action that would have influenced or stopped Hitler. Whatever the case, Roosevelt had no expectation at that time that his country would actually enter a war; hence, he saw little need to bring either air or ground units to a combat-ready status.

In the months before and immediately following Munich, the aviation assessments flowing to the Oval Office unanimously praised German aviation. From his position in Paris, Ambassador William Bullitt typed a steady stream of messages that warned of the patent superiority of German aircraft and production rates, bemoaned the disorganization of the French aviation industry, and complained of "ill-trained" British pilots.[70] In his apt words, the moral of recent European diplomacy was that "if you have enough airplanes you don't have to go to Berchtesgaden."[71] Ambassador Hugh Wilson's messages from Berlin seconded Bullitt's alarm.[72]

Private and industrial assessments reached the same conclusions. In early 1938 Joseph Kennedy, soon to be the American ambassador in London, forwarded to FDR a letter that he had received from Charles Lindbergh. Describing his recent two-week tour of Germany that included visits to Luftwaffe factories, aircraft, and research facilities, Lindbergh concluded that "German aviation development is without parallel."[73] Other firsthand evaluations of European aviation by Lawrence D. Bell of Bell Aircraft Corporation and G. L. Martin of Glenn L. Martin Company confirmed the extent of German superiority and French inferiority; Bell described French military aviation as "pathetic," and Martin saw it as "pitifully weak."[74]

At the end of 1938 Assistant Secretary of War Louis Johnson described world aviation strength to the President with both statistics and graphs; the latter, Johnson insisted, depict, "as mere words cannot do, the airplane situation of the major powers." Johnson was correct, for the graph representing Germany almost climbed off the chart. Not only did the figures estimate that total German aircraft numbered ten thousand, but also that the Reich's medium and heavy bomber strength numbered 3,400 at a time when no other world power deployed more than 960.[75]

Interestingly, the presentation ignored Japanese aircraft strength. This omission may have resulted from a lack of information, or perhaps it was simply symptomatic of the low regard the United States held of Japanese aviation. As this essay will explore later, Western racial perceptions of the Japanese colored the assessment of Japanese strength, especially regarding their aviation capabilities. National characteristics condemned that nation, so the United States believed, to perpetual weakness, since Japan depended on copies of Western designs, technology, and facilities. The Japanese "lack of originality is a national trait," an Army War Plans Division study confidently observed.[76] American estimates reflected these beliefs: A 1941 projection determined that Japan was producing aircraft at a current rate of barely two thousand a year; in reality, the actual production rate was then exceeding five thousand.[77] In fact, racial bias played both ways in America's assessment, and it helps to explain why the United States consistently overestimated Germany and underestimated Japan.

Other problems undermined American prewar assessments. U.S. military and naval attachés in foreign capitals provided a potentially vital source of information. Yet the services traditionally saw attaché assignments as "pink tea" duty that called primarily for excessive social graces and personal wealth. Secretary of State Hull understood that problem, and when he first proposed the Standing Liaison Committee to Roosevelt in 1938, he stressed the need to select "highly competent officers to serve as military and naval attachés."[78] While some capitals benefited from excellent officers, elsewhere the quality could be mediocre. In 1939 Chief of Staff Malin Craig had to admit to the President that the army attaché in Moscow "has been of no use to the War Department for approximately a year."[79] Other examples come to mind, including the military attaché in Rumania who wildly insisted that Hitler had stockpiled a reserve of forty thousand combat aircraft and crews.[80]

The same negative view of attaché duty extended to intelligence duty in Washington—it would drag down rather than lift up a career. After returning from attaché duty in London, Captain Alan Kirk took the assignment as the Director of Naval Intelligence. But he did not stay long (March–October 1941), for his friend Admiral Adolphus Andrews warned him that he needed to get sea duty, and get it quickly, if he expected to make rear admiral. Kirk took his friend's advice. Kirk recalled after the war:

The average tour of the Director of Naval Intelligence, in the ten years before we went in the war, was less than two years, always. Nobody was staying. It had very poor standing in the Navy Department, not because of the calibre of the officers, but everybody sort of thought Naval Intelligence was striped pants, cookie-pushers, going to parties and so on, abroad.[81]

Although continual turnover did not present quite the same problem within the army, there were defects nonetheless. The Military Intelligence Division, headed by Brigadier General Sherman Miles, did not represent a strength of the United States Army. General Marshall considered it one of the weakest areas of the service and later regretted that he had not pushed through reforms prior to Pearl Harbor. Eisenhower concurred in this negative estimate of MID, as did Stimson. In fact, the displeasure went all the way to the White House, for Roosevelt was upset with the performance of Miles but had not settled on a replacement before Pearl Harbor.[82]

Adding to the intelligence problem were bureaucratic rivalries and personalities. In August 1941 Major Haywood S. Hansell, Jr., had the priority task of collecting intelligence material for Air War Plans Division-1 (AWPD-1), which was the Army Air Corps estimate of aviation requirements necessary to defeat the Axis. In turn, AWPD-1 would be part of Roosevelt's larger "Victory Program" request of 9 July 1941 for the total production requirements needed for the United States to defeat its potential enemies. Hansell had just returned from gathering information in Britain on Royal Air Force bombing operations against Germany. When Hansell requested help from MID, he got none, for General Miles "was determined to preserve his turf." As a result, MID was "totally uncooperative." Blocked by MID, Hansell found much of the information he sought on German industrial targets in the financial and technical files of American banks and businesses that had lent money to build German power plants and factories during the 1920s.[83]

Similar rivalries hurt the navy. Rear Admiral Richmond Kelly Turner headed the Navy War Plans Division. Known within the navy as "Terrible Turner," the admiral displayed ample quantities of brilliance, energy, and arrogance. He quickly became involved in a jurisdictional dispute to increase his power as War Plans director at the expense of ONI. Turner's success, in the opinion of some, seriously weakened the pre–Pearl Harbor effectiveness and credibility of naval intelligence.[84] And still beyond these feuds within the services was the long-standing rivalry of MID and ONI with the FBI, to say nothing of their newer concern over Donovan, the Coordinator of Information.[85]

During much of the 1930s, information concerning espionage, counterespionage, and sabotage had been handled by an informal clearinghouse committee comprising representatives from the Departments of State, Treasury, War, Navy, Justice, and Post Office. In June 1939 Roosevelt terminated this arrangement and ordered instead that all such investigations be concentrated within the FBI, the MID, and the ONI. To prevent any misunderstanding, the President in a separate memorandum stressed that this did not mean that the intelligence efforts of the State Department should cease in any way. Instead, FDR directed that "it should be carried on as heretofore but the directors of the three agencies should be constantly kept in touch by the State Department with the work it is doing."[86] During the crucial 1940–41 period, Assistant Secretary of State Adolph Berle filled that intelligence liaison function with the FBI, MID, and ONI. At Berle's suggestion, a further organizational clarification came in June 1940 when the President directed that the FBI should be responsible for foreign intelligence within the Western Hemisphere, while MID and ONI would cover the remainder of the world.[87]

These efforts did not eliminate confusion and overlapping authority, however, for there were other players in the game. There was Stephenson, heading British intelligence in the United States; there was Donovan, the newly created COI; and there were Vincent Astor and John Carter, who operated independently of each other in their intelligence-gathering operations and reported directly to the President. Astor may have had a hand in prompting Roosevelt to make the FBI, rather than ONI or MID, the contact point with Stephenson. In Astor's opinion, the FBI was "the best equipped and trained, and the most alert and competent of our various intelligence agencies."[88] With this variety of formal and informal organizations, confusion and anger were inevitable as groups tripped over each other. Berle, the State Department liaison intelligence official, often found himself trying to salve hurt feelings or untangle knotted lines of authority, and this experienced diplomat admitted that he found these efforts "harder diplomacy than negotiating an inter-American agreement."[89] Even Roosevelt, who was normally so comfortable with jumbled bureaucracies, occasionally found himself confused as to what was happening or who was supposed to make it happen.[90]

Even if the country could look past these intelligence rivalries and weaknesses, there still remained the problem of commanders being unable to obtain a clear expression of national policy. Just as Ambassador Grew had asked Roosevelt to share his thoughts, so too did military commanders ask their superiors for the same information. In a letter of August 1940, Admiral Thomas C. Hart, commander of the U.S. Asiatic Fleet, plaintively wrote to the Chief of Naval Operations, "I will only add that I *still* feel very much out of touch with 'the management' and that does not make my lot easy."[91] Stark shared this letter with the President.

Two months later Stark received a similar plea from Admiral J. O. Richardson, Commander-in-Chief, U.S. Fleet. In a strongly worded message, Richardson stated that he must know the national policy: "the Commander-in-Chief [U.S. Fleet] finds himself . . . without an applicable directive. He cannot, in the absence of a clear picture of national policy, national commitments and national objectives, formulate his own plans."[92]

It was the fall of 1940. The United States wanted both to help Britain and to avoid war. The country moved in the midst of a heated presidential campaign. And President Franklin D. Roosevelt had no clear directive to give.

The war plans that the Joint Board prepared in the 1920s and early 1930s viewed Japan as the only possible enemy facing the United States. Japan had an impressive navy, and with the Versailles award of the mandated islands (Marshall, Caroline, and Mariana Islands) in the central Pacific to Japan, it sat astride the American lines of communication to the Far East. The Philippines, positioned seven thousand miles from the West Coast of America, now floated within a Japanese bathtub. The Joint Board faced a difficult if not impossible strategic problem: How could the United States defend the Philippines in light of the overwhelming regional Japanese superiority, especially within the political context of the naval reductions and fortifications freeze ordered by the Washington Naval Treaty, the low defense budgets of the post–World War I period, and the general American mood of pacifism, antimilitarism, and isolationism?

American war plans were color-coded, and the Joint Board plan for fighting Japan was ORANGE. In its various revisions, ORANGE envisaged primarily a naval war, with neither Japan nor the United States having allies. The Joint Board assumed that Japan would open hostilities with an overwhelming attack on the Philippines. In response the small

American army garrison was to withdraw into its prepared positions on Bataan and Corregidor and hold those positions so as to deny the Japanese invader the use of Manila Bay. Simultaneously the United States Navy was to fight its way through the Pacific, destroy the Japanese navy in a great fleet action en route, and come to the relief of the American forces in the Philippines. Once this rescue was accomplished, Japan probably would surrender. If not, using Manila Bay as a base, the navy would then force capitulation on Japan through a naval blockade.[93]

Understandably, the army lacked enthusiasm for the plan. It believed that its garrison would be doomed under ORANGE, for it would take the navy months, more probably years, to make its way through to the Philippines. The small American outpost could not be expected to hold off the enemy for so long. And ORANGE assumed that the navy could indeed fight its way through, a belief the army questioned, especially with the Japanese aviation as well as naval assets that would be confronted in the mandated islands.

Brigadier General Stanley Embick headed the Army War Plans Division in 1935. He had previously commanded the American forces at Corregidor. In communications to his military superiors, he made no effort to hide his beliefs regarding the planned navy role in ORANGE: "In the event of an Orange war under existing conditions, the early dispatch of our fleet to Philippine waters would be literally an act of madness."[94]

More importantly, the army questioned whether American interests in the Far East were vital or in any way commensurate with the probable cost of defending those interests. Military means and diplomatic obligations seemed woefully out of balance. In addition, there was a question as to whether American public opinion would support a war for the Philippines, especially a long-drawn-out conflict that might begin with a major American defeat. The army believed that public opinion would not. Thus, it proposed instead that military capabilities and vital interests be merged by pulling American forces back to an Alaska-Hawaii-Panama defense line.[95] Army officers, however, were loath to press their opinions forcefully on policy-makers. Their strong apolitical tradition and the lack of an effective structure to link military-diplomatic thought muted their protests.

Through the mid-1930s, the navy remained firm in its commitment to ORANGE. With the gospel of Mahan providing its commandments, the navy had a much more international outlook than the army. Foreign markets, geopolitical struggles, and colonial outposts seemed more natural to the navy than to the small and rather provincial army, which thought mainly in terms of continental or, at the most, hemispheric defense. In addition, ORANGE gave the navy a reason for being: For what did the United States need a large navy if not to fight Japan? Thus, ORANGE gave the navy primacy both in strategy and in budget demands.

The navy commitment to ORANGE, however, should not be construed as blindness to the difficulty that a real-life ORANGE entailed. In the interwar decades the Naval War College had tested ORANGE more than 120 times in its war games.[96] Where once the task had seemed difficult, by the late 1930s ORANGE seemed impossible. In any thrust across the Pacific the American navy would have to neutralize Japanese surface and submarine fleets as well as its land-based and carrier-based air forces. Advanced bases in the mandated islands would have to be seized, and neither the army nor the Marines had the necessary troops to seize them. Once taken, island facilities would have to be developed, demanding a profligate expenditure of time and money. Additionally, in its current peacetime status the navy lacked the vital support ships to implement the plan, and inevitable wartime attrition would weaken it further. Even if a bloodied and bruised American fleet fought its way through to the Philippines, from where would it operate? Manila would have long since fallen. Where would ships be repaired and resupplied? And, through it all, would the American public support so great an effort for so questionable a reward? The president of the Naval War College, Admiral Luke McNamee, warned the Navy General Board in early 1934 that a "war between Japan and the United States alone under present conditions would involve us in losses entirely out of proportion to any possible gain."[97]

Events in Europe forced a shift away from ORANGE. The United States no longer faced only the threat of Japan, but with the Japanese-German-Italian signing of the Anti-Comintern Pact in 1936, America saw the possibility of threats in the Atlantic and the Pacific simultaneously. With the possibility that the United States might become "involved in a general war" rather than in a regional conflict with Japan only, the navy began to move away from the idea of a power thrust through the Pacific that would culminate in a Jutland-style fleet action. Instead, the commander of the Asiatic Fleet, Admiral H. E. Yarnell, proposed in October 1937 that the navy should think in terms of an economic blockade. Yarnell assumed that the United States would be operating with allies; hence the coalition would control "roughly ninety per cent of the world's reserves of iron, coal and oil." Economic strangulation of Japan would be enough to bring victory. As a result, a fleet battle "would not be necessary nor justifiable."[98] Leahy shared this proposal with FDR, and the President replied, "Yarnell talks a lot of sense."[99]

At the same time that Yarnell wrote his letter to Leahy, the Joint Board was also reconsidering its position: The United States might have to fight a war in conjunction with allies over more than one ocean and against more than one enemy. It was time for strategic planning to think beyond the traditional ORANGE plan. The Joint Board soon after the Munich Crisis ordered its planning committee to consider the problem of a simultaneous war with Germany, Italy, and Japan in both the Atlantic and the Pacific. The following April the Planning Committee reported that if such a conflict occurred, the United States would have to fight a defensive war in the Pacific. America's main emphasis must come instead in the Atlantic and in the Caribbean approaches to the Panama Canal, for the European Axis were a greater threat to American interests and security than Japan. Using this general outline as a foundation, the Committee recommended that specific war plans be prepared that would be based on the primacy of the Atlantic-Caribbean area and that would incorporate a variety of geopolitical assumptions. The RAINBOW war plans resulted.[100]

Under RAINBOW 1, the United States assumed that it would fight the Axis without major allies. Defense of the United States, Central America, and the northern part of South America would have priority. Any offensive operations in the Pacific would have to wait for the successful conclusion of Atlantic operations. RAINBOW 2 called for the United States to fight the Axis with Britain and France as allies. As a result, some American forces would operate in Continental Europe, and the United States could undertake offensive operations in the Pacific. RAINBOW 3 expected the United States to fight without allies, but conditions in the Western Hemisphere would allow the country to undertake an early offensive in the Pacific. RAINBOW 4 assumed that the country would fight without allies and that Axis threats would force deployment of American troops throughout the Western Hemisphere. Again operations in the Pacific would wait for the conclusion of Atlantic operations. Finally, RAINBOW 5 anticipated that the country would be part of an alliance with Britain and France and that the nation would send major forces to operate in either Africa or Europe or in both. A defensive stance would be maintained in the Pacific until Germany and Italy had surrendered.

Roosevelt and the armed services were not the only national security participants, however. Congress had its role under the Constitution, and that body often differed with the President and the armed services over the interpretation of security needs. The previously mentioned neutrality restrictions presented one example. The need for naval bases west of Hawaii furnishes a second example. At the direction of Congress, in May 1938 Rear Admiral Arthur Hepburn and a navy board undertook a study of the need for additional naval bases for ship and air units in the United States and its territories. Presenting its findings in December of the same year, the Hepburn Report included extensive discussion of the need to develop Guam in the western Pacific. Guam, the report warned, was now "practically defenseless" against a Japanese attack. However, the development of the island with air and submarine facilities could change that situation dramatically, making Guam secure "against anything short of a major effort on the part of any probable enemy." In fact, such defense preparations would dramatically improve the American position in the entire region; "so long as Guam existed as a strong air and submarine base hostile operations against the Philippines would be a precarious undertaking." In short, as the report emphasized, funds spent for Guam would be a force multiplier, for the effective defense of Guam would "greatly simplify the military problem of the defense of the Philippines."[101] Since the fortification limitations mandated by the Washington Naval Treaty of 1922 had lapsed, no legal restrictions existed to the proposed construction. Isolationists within Congress, however, disagreed with the navy's findings, arguing instead that such a building program would be a provocation to Japan that would needlessly exacerbate tensions between the two countries. In February 1939 Congress voted to deny funds for the Guam project.

As with many issues before Pearl Harbor, the death of the Guam project was more complex than it appeared at first glance. Although Congress killed the proposal, the administration itself had a hand in the murder. The State Department had some of the identical fears of the isolationists, and it did not want to do anything to incite the militarists within Japan. Nor would the War Department lend the navy moral support, for the army believed that the United States should withdraw entirely from the western Pacific rather than entrench itself further. At the top, Roosevelt seemed hesitant and uncertain, apparently fearful of what both American and Japanese reaction might be. His solution was to keep himself at arm's length from the proposal.

Later that same year the navy began internal studies regarding its ability to prosecute a war successfully. In early August 1939 the Secretary of the Navy directed the Navy General Board to prepare an "Are We Ready?" study. The General Board found that especially critical deficiencies existed in seaplane tenders, fast tankers, anti-aircraft guns, naval bases west of Hawaii, enlisted personnel, and torpedoes.[102] Along with the aforementioned issue of Guam, the last two problems had previously been brought to the personal attention of the President on multiple occasions.[103]

Acting on the recommendation of the 1939 report that "Are We Ready?" studies be made "a continuing activity," the Board followed with 1940 and 1941 studies. Each of these reports identified specific weaknesses of the navy and outlined steps to alleviate or, "by hook or by crook," at least lessen problems. Despite the navy efforts, however, the 1941 study—like the previous two—concluded that "the Naval Establishment is not ready to meet a serious emergency." Included in the 1941 report, which the navy completed six months before Pearl Harbor, was the strong plea for the creation of a Joint Military General Staff responsible only to the President. The Board also found critical deficiencies in the Fleet Marine Force and pointed again to the still existing shortages in anti-aircraft guns, personnel, and torpedoes.[104]

The army undertook no similar studies. Perhaps it would have been superfluous, for the army certainly understood that it was not ready for an emergency—major, minor, or in between. When Germany invaded Poland, army strength totaled less than 200,000 men. In comparison to the armed forces of other nations, that figure placed the army nineteenth in the world, behind Portugal's land forces but ahead of Bulgaria's. A comparison of the percentage of population serving in the military placed the United States forty-fifth in the world. Much of the army's interwar period had been spent on merely surviving as an institution in the face of a hostile or indifferent populace and Congress. After all, the nation faced no enemies to its north or south, and neither the country nor the army expected ever again to send a large army overseas.

Even when the likelihood of a European conflagration became increasingly obvious, the President seemed surprisingly reluctant to expand and modernize the ground forces in conjunction with air and naval forces. The existing army plan developed to deal with a possible national emergency was the Protective Mobilization Plan (PMP), an outgrowth of army thinking during the 1930s. Designed for continental protection, it provided for the emergency expansion of the army to 1 million men through the activation of the National Guard and Reserves and the recruitment of volunteers. The Plan did not contemplate expansion beyond that number, instead providing for the freezing of the army at that total so that priority could be concentrated on producing a war-ready force through the emphasis on modernization and training.[105] In any national emergency, Army Chief of Staff Malin Craig (1935–39) realized that manpower could be acquired more readily than modern weapons; therefore, his periodic requests to Congress centered on the lead time necessary for any modernization. "The sums appropriated this year [1939]," the general stated in his annual report, "will not be fully transformed into military power for two years. Persons who state that they see no threat to the peace of the United States would hesitate to make the forecast through a two-year period."[106]

When Roosevelt met with the War Department officials in November 1938 to outline his desires on the expansion of air power, the army also expected support for a balanced expansion of the ground forces under the PMP. It planned accordingly and included an expected increase in the ground forces of nearly 100,000 troops and the acquisition of equipment to support a PMP force expanded to its planned size of one million men.[107] Roosevelt quickly let the army know that it was mistaken; he wanted planes and more planes, not ground troops. Even when the German invasion of Poland the next year brought the war that Roosevelt had been expecting, the President's response, along with proclaiming a "limited" national emergency, was to authorize a mere 17,000-man expansion of the army. He told the army that such a meager addition "was all the public would be ready to accept without undue excitement."[108] Roosevelt may have believed that was true, though in such a period of crisis it seems more likely that Congress and the public would have supported a larger expansion if the President had pressed for it vigorously. Roosevelt continued to be languid toward manpower expansion, as seen in his ambivalent approach toward selective service in 1940. Political reasons, including his reelection plans, undoubtedly played a part, but beyond those considerations was Roosevelt's judgment that America's role in the war would be limited to war matériel only or, at the very most, American matériel joined by naval and air units. In Roosevelt's mind, large American ground forces were neither needed nor wanted.

If the unexpected should occur, however, some of the immediate post–World War I planning of the army had examined the industrial mobilization that would be needed to build and deploy a major World War I–style expeditionary force. While the Army General Staff's role was to consider the military needs of a future mobilization, the Assistant Secretary of War was to concern himself with the business and industrial requirements of the mobilization. To help in this task, the Office of the Assistant Secretary received a Planning Branch whose work would be augmented by the creation of the Army Industrial College. Together the Assistant Secretary, the Planning Branch, and the Army Industrial College produced Industrial Mobilization Plans (IMP) in 1930, 1933, 1936, and 1939.

Bernard Baruch, the Wall Street financier who had headed American World War I mobilization, took particular interest in these plans and served as an important civilian reviewer and critic. As World War II approached, Baruch and Assistant Secretary of War Louis Johnson gave increasing attention to the plans and strongly encouraged Roosevelt to activate the necessary agencies to put the 1939 plan into operation. Roosevelt refused. To him, it seemed clear that Baruch wanted to regain his mobilization role of World War I, something Roosevelt did not wish. In addition, the IMP linked the military and business communities at the expense of other segments of society, such as labor. It is understandable that Roosevelt held back from granting possibly excessive powers to a proposed military–business War Resources Administration, especially given both the public's fear that mobilization plans meant that the country was actively preparing for war and the public's easy acceptance of the "merchants of death" theory regarding the cause of World War I. To their regret, Johnson and Baruch had ignored the political context in which any mobilization must take place. Additionally, Roosevelt had firm opinions on mobilization from his service as Assistant Secretary of Navy in World War I. And even more, the President had strong beliefs as to his power and role as the Commander-in-Chief. As with so many other items, he saw to it that the road to mobilization led to the Oval Office.

Until the spring of 1940, RAINBOW 2 (United States with Britain and France as allies fighting against the Axis) seemed the most likely scenario, and the Joint Board planners worked with that in mind. Hitler's stunning success in the west completely changed the strategic picture. France was now gone, and the fate of its battle fleet uncertain. Britain momentarily fought on but seemed likely to meet the same fate as France. If Germany gained control of both the French and British fleets, the Atlantic—long the protector of the United States—would become a German lake. Latin American nations would be forced to reach an economic accommodation with Hitler's Europe, for those countries traditionally exported their goods to Europe. Nor did democracy versus fascism seem an issue to the Latin Americans, since their democratic roots were shallow or nonexistent, while authoritarianism had a long and accepted tradition. Close to American borders lay Mexico and Central America. The former seemed unstable, and in the latter, Roosevelt admitted, the United States "could stage a revolution in any Central American government for between a million and four million dollars."[109] If the United States could do it, FDR believed, so could the Axis. Thus, it was not too difficult to envision a future in which the United States, cut off from its traditional markets and holding on to a political system that seemed ineffective and anachronistic, would find itself, at best, a single island in a hostile sea; at worst it would battle alone against an Axis invasion of the American hemisphere.

Roosevelt moved quickly to reevaluate America's strategic position, to strengthen security relations with Canada and Latin America, and to ascertain whether Britain could endure. He met almost daily with his military advisers in late May and throughout June 1940.[110] The military consensus was that Britain could not survive, that there was little or nothing that the United States could do to change that fact, and that the United States needed to keep all available military equipment for itself.[111] Brigadier General George Strong, head of the Army War Plans Division, cogently expressed that belief when, regarding the recommendation to withhold additional munitions to Britain, he stated:

> This is a recognition of the early defeat of the Allies, an admission of our inability to furnish means in quantities sufficient to affect the situation and an acknowledgement that we recognize the probability that we are next on the list of victims of the Axis powers and must devote every means to prepare to meet that threat.[112]

Marshall agreed with these views, as did Stark. At the same time, diplomatic reports from Britain were heavy with gloom, and Joseph Kennedy characterized England's military capacity to carry on the war as "pitiful."[113]

In contrast, Roosevelt displayed a characteristic—if admittedly cautious—optimism. On 13 June 1940 the President shared his thoughts with the heads of MID and ONI and sketched an alternate scenario for the remainder of 1940 in which both the British Isles and British Empire would survive to continue the fight against the European Axis. France, though occupied, would continue resisting through its colonial holdings. And while the Mediterranean might be lost to German or Italian forces, the Atlantic barrier from Greenland to Morocco would hold firm. Lastly, the United States now would have an active role in the war, but its participation would be limited to air and naval units only, and American industry would be moving to maximum aircraft production.[114]

While the Joint Board shifted its planning work to RAINBOW 4 (defense of the entire Western Hemisphere with no allies), Roosevelt sent Donovan to Britain for a personal inspection. At the invitation of Churchill, Roosevelt also dispatched General Strong and Major General Delos C. Emmons of the Air Corps to London. They would be joined a few weeks later by Rear Admiral Robert L. Ghormley. Donovan's report to the President came first and, as discussed earlier in this essay, was favorable toward the chance of Britain's survival in 1940. General Strong, who earlier had been deeply pessimistic, now agreed with Donovan, and the Strong–Emmons report in early October highlighted the spirited British morale, the nation's unity behind Churchill, and the relative strength of Britain's industry despite the German bombing. If the expected German invasion did not come by 15 October, Secretary of War Stimson related to the President, Britain's military position would be strengthened greatly. On the negative side, Britain's central weakness was its financial position, which was "dubious if not distinctly bad."[115] Soon afterward Churchill also made the economic plight clear to Roosevelt.[116] Convinced that Britain would and could resist, Roosevelt turned to the question of finances once his reelection was safely behind him. America, the President told the country, must become the "great arsenal of democracy." In March 1941 Roosevelt and Congress together eradicated the financial problem with Lend-Lease.

Though America had confirmed its aid to Britain, its military still lacked a clear expression of national policy. Where, under what conditions, and for what objectives should the United States fight? A few months before the enactment of Lend-Lease, Admiral Stark had tried to remedy that lack. Stark had served on the staff of Admiral William Sims in London during World War I and needed no one to convince him of the primacy of the Atlantic to American interests or the need for the nation to enter the war if the Axis threatened the security of that ocean. To clarify his own thoughts and, quite likely, to push Roosevelt to a clear expression of policy now that the President's reelection seemed assured, Stark produced his well-known "Plan Dog" memorandum of 12 November 1940.[117]

In the first paragraph of his twenty-six-page document, Stark drove home the importance of the Atlantic and Great Britain:

> If Britain wins decisively against Germany we could win everywhere; but that if she loses the problem confronting us would be very great; and, while we might not *lose everywhere*, we might, possibly, not *win anywhere*.

Although the United States did not desire war, Stark stressed that war might come at any time. Thus, the United States must examine its options so that it guaranteed that such a war best served the national interests. Outlining four possible courses of action, he recommended that the fourth—Plan D (or "Dog" in the military language of the period)—best served the country's interests. Under this plan America would enter the war with Britain as an ally and give priority to defeating the European Axis, including the deployment of extensive American ground troops to the European theater. In conjunction with this priority, the United States would assume a defensive stance in the Pacific. Assuring the survival of Britain and its empire was the best way to guarantee the security of the American hemisphere. Hence, the Chief of Naval Operations recommended that Plan D "is likely to be the most fruitful for the United States." Accordingly, Stark urged that American army and navy leaders initiate staff talks with their British counterparts as soon as possible.[118]

In organizing his thoughts and encouraging the President to do the same, Stark had produced the basic outline of American strategy for World War II. In the opinion of Louis Morton, Stark's memorandum constitutes "perhaps the most important single document in the development of World War II strategy."[119] Despite Stark's best effort, however, Roosevelt would not be pushed into a clear expression of national policy. He may yet have held out hope that U.S. aid would be enough to allow Britain to win the war without America's formal participation. By the summer of 1941 he would apparently lose that hope, though such thinking was still in the future.[120]

Roosevelt did move the country closer to the war, however, by approving the proposed Anglo-American military staff talks, which were held in Washington, D.C., from 29 January to 29 March 1941. These talks, known as ABC-1, confirmed the Europe-first priority of the Stark memorandum. Though U.S. entrance into the war was still uncertain (in Roosevelt's words it would happen if the country were "compelled"),[121] the conference clearly secured the mutual interests of the two nations. As the British historian David Reynolds declares, the ABC-1 conference recognized "the core of Anglo-American co-operation—a commitment to mutual control of the Atlantic as the key to both countries' survival."[122]

American planning had moved a long way from ORANGE. Plan Dog, RAINBOW 5, and ABC-1 expressed America's assessment of the world. Europe would have the priority. Britain must survive. The European Axis represented the greater threat. Despite America's later rage and frustration over Pearl Harbor—the compelling event of which Roosevelt had spoken—the country would not deviate from that strategic judgment.

In assessing the Axis threat, certain assumptions existed within the White House and within much of the administration. Even if the Axis somehow did not present a direct military threat to the United States—and that was not the perception from the Oval Office—there was little doubt as to the political and economic challenge facing the nation. Germany, the United States believed, would use its diplomatic success and military power to dominate world trade and to bully weaker countries, especially those in Latin America, into joining the German economic structure as satellite nations.[123] The result would be an economic crisis for the United States. If Germany were victorious in Europe and gained control of the British Empire, it "would cut American exports at least 50 percent in volume."[124] In the Pacific both official and informal sources left no doubt that Japan intended to drive all Western nations out of China and the Far East and to establish Asia as its own economic preserve.[125]

Cut off from both the traditional markets for American exports and the sources of such strategic materials as rubber and tin, America would face economic contraction, a lowered standard of living, and a weakened strategic position. Increasingly isolated in a threatening world, the United States would see its democratic values suffer as it moved toward a garrison state mentality. The survival of the nation would be at stake, and the result could be the ultimate irony for a democracy: "to fight totalitarianism we would have to adopt totalitarian methods."[126]

Although the United States correctly perceived that the German threat was greater than that of Japan, it magnified German danger to a size that was much larger than reality. Observers tended to believe that

Germany could do anything. A military attaché in Berlin warned: "Germany as a fighting nation is tremendously powerful. Under no condition should she be underestimated."[127]

The administration was already a true believer when it came to German military prowess. The American fear of a German military attack on Latin America presents an example of this conviction. The documents demonstrate how seriously the administration feared an attack from West Africa over to Brazil's Natal. From there, it seemed only a quick flight by bomber to Colombia (where Germany had been active in pre–World War II commercial aviation) and the Panama Canal. Although such German plans never existed, Roosevelt and his advisers took seriously their possibility, even to the point where FDR suffered nightmares of German bombers flying over his home in Hyde Park and inquired whether federal buildings along the Mexican border might be constructed with machine gun or anti-aircraft positions in case the Germans attacked through that nation.[128] Such ideas may seem far-fetched, but the concern was real. After all, the idea that Germany would conquer Norway, Denmark, Holland, Belgium, and France in a little over two months would have seemed equally farfetched in March 1940.

Another factor in America's view of Germany appears to be racial stereotyping. German efficiency, unity, and organization became racial maxims in American minds. Germany could do almost anything militarily, and partially for the same racial reasoning the American leaders suspected that Japan could do almost nothing. This assessment of the Japanese went all the way to the White House, for as late as 1942 Roosevelt optimistically believed that the "defeat of Germany means the defeat of Japan, probably without firing a shot or losing a life."[129]

There seemed to be facts to support this flawed assessment. Japan's weakness in raw materials was patent, and that flaw was coupled with a military that was suspect in quality. Though Japan had bested Russia in their war of 1904, Russia's military had been of questionable quality. In the more recent 1939 border clashes between the two countries, Russia had punished the Japanese ground forces. Nor had the Japanese armed forces been able to finish its war with a militarily weak and politically disunited China. Such a record hardly inspired Western awe.

The United States expressed particular doubt about Japan's aviation capabilities, a crucial component in modern war. Numerous commentators expressed the opinion that the Japanese as a race lacked creativity; thus, as a nation Japan had no choice but to copy Western aviation designs and to accept perpetual inferiority. "Japanese aviation and industrial development," the American naval attaché in Tokyo concluded, "will remain from two to three years behind that of the United States."[130]

When Japan took steps to ensure secrecy, the United States interpreted this action as Japan's dubious effort to hide its inferiority. The pages of the *United States Naval Institute Proceedings* asserted that the Japanese, bereft of originality, were imitators by nature. Aware of their national failings, the Japanese "seek to hide them from the world by every means in their power."[131] At the same time, however, military reports concerning Germany did not draw the same conclusion that the Third Reich's efforts toward secrecy had to represent an attempt to hide its inferiority.

Western observers consistently judged that Japanese training, pilots, and aircraft were inadequate. When Admiral Yarnell, commander of American naval forces in the Far East, first observed Japanese forces in the Shanghai area, he rated the Japanese navy quite highly. With their aircraft, however, he was "not greatly impressed," and he confidently predicted that "a few squadrons of our carrier planes would clear this river of Japs in 24 hours."[132] The British expressed the same confidence at the ABC-1 talks, where they indicated that warships based at Singapore would be completely safe from Japanese air power, which they rated at or below the quality of their Italian counterparts.[133] Occasional reports would discuss the considerable combat experience that Japanese pilots had amassed in China and warn that Japanese military aviation should not be derided, but these reports had little impact.[134]

Racial bias continued in the days following Pearl Harbor. Several American officers seemed unable to believe that the Japanese alone were responsible for Japan's success and wondered if Germany had provided help. In the early evening of 7 December 1941, Chief of Naval Operations Stark talked by telephone with Rear Admiral Claude Bloch at Pearl Harbor. When chronicling the damage, Bloch mentioned that a submarine had penetrated into the harbor and then had been sunk. Stark's first reaction was to ask if it were a German submarine.[135] In his original communication to the Atlantic Fleet and to SPENAVO (U.S. Special Naval Observer, London), Stark reported that two of the attacking aircraft at Pearl Harbor "had swastikas on their side."[136] Two days later General Marshall relayed to the White House General Douglas MacArthur's report that white pilots had flown some of the Japanese planes that bombed Clark Field.[137] A later intelligence report forwarded to Roosevelt identified German pilots as operating Japanese aircraft in the Java area.[138]

Despite the prevalent United States assumption of Japanese inferiority, Americans presumed that the Japanese would act and think in a way identical with their own. Perhaps this was a continuation of the American belief that the Japanese lacked originality, or perhaps it reflected American confidence that their way was the only way. Most likely it was a combination of factors, with racial bias added to the more traditional problem of one country's assumption that a potential adversary will behave as it would behave if in a similar situation. The war games that tested ORANGE at the Naval War College provide an example of this error, for throughout the exercises the officials presumed that Japan would react in the way American doctrine and thinking would have responded.[139]

Pearl Harbor presents another example of an incorrect assumption. In the administration's view, basing the fleet at Pearl Harbor served as a deterrent against war and as protection for Hawaii in case war came. As General Marshall told FDR, the "presence of [the] Fleet reduces [the] threat of major attack."[140] Ignored was the fact that the Japanese might take what to the United States was an illogical and even self-defeating action by making the fleet the target, attacking Hawaii, and bringing the United States into a war against them. Ambassador Grew in Tokyo had warned that American standards of logic could not be used in predicting Japanese action—"Japanese sanity cannot be measured by our own standards of logic"[141]—but it was a warning difficult for Americans to understand.

While the United States underestimated Japanese aviation, it overestimated its own, especially in the area of heavy bombers. Technical progress and doctrinal thinking in the 1930s produced an Air Corps belief in the independent offensive power of strategic bombing, with its instrument being the B-17 bomber. Much of this thinking germinated at the Air Corps Tactical School at Maxwell Field in Alabama. The air power prophecies of Billy Mitchell, Hugh Trenchard, and Giulio Douhet seemed about to be fulfilled. Technical limitations indicated, however, that a long-range single-engine fighter escort was an impossibility. Spurning the idea of inaccurate and inefficient area bombing at night, American bomber enthusiasts developed a doctrine of daylight precision strategic bombing without fighter escorts and tested the theory in prewar maneuvers. They claimed success.

Not all Air Corps officers agreed. Captain Claire Chennault argued that defensive fighters could intercept the bombers and charged that the Air Corps biased the tests against the intercepting fighters. Some bomber supporters would later agree that the "exercises may well have been prejudiced in favor of the bombers."[142]

At the same time, however, Chennault and others who favored the role of interceptors expressed no interest in having their fighters serve as escorts for bombers. They presumed that a single-engine fighter escort was a technical impossiblity. Even if it had seemed possible, they would have vehemently resisted the idea of using pursuit planes in the purely "defensive" mission of convoying a bomber formation. Thus, if strategic bombing were to become a reality, it would have to be done without fighter escorts. And the Air Corps was determined to make it a reality, because only through this independent strategic role could the Air Corps prove that it should be independent of and equal to the army. Without the doctrine of strategic bombing, the Air Corps feared that there would be no United States Air Force. Thus, Air Corps strategic doctrine for war rested, like many other issues, within a political context.

In the summer and fall of 1941 the administration and its advisers saw the B-17 and its alleged power as a possible solution to the defense of the Philippines within a region dominated by Japan. The B-17s could smash any Japanese invasion fleet. In fact, by the fall of 1941 the United States thought that it could turn the liability of the Philippines into an advantage by controlling the sea lanes to the east and west of the Islands through air power and by threatening Japan's "paper cities" with its Philippine-based B-17s. The mere location of the American bombers in those islands, General Marshall estimated, "has a better than 50% chance of forcing [the Japanese] to practically drop the Axis."[143] Here was heady wine, and Roosevelt and his advisers drank deeply.[144] As in the case of Pearl Harbor, however, the United States found at Clark Field that Japan did not react as it believed it should and that a deterrent could itself become the target.

There would be a final irony. Over Germany in 1943, the American air force found that deep-penetration daylight raids without fighter escorts resulted in prohibitive losses. To continue strategic bombing, a long-range fighter escort had to be developed. The answer came in 1944 with the use of jury-rigged disposable fuel tanks that would extend the range of the P-47 and P-51 fighters to equal that of the bombers. The fighters could then jettison the fuel tanks before going into combat. Here was the technical breakthrough that assured the defeat of the Luftwaffe. The irony is that the Japanese had used the idea earlier, and General "Hap" Arnold himself had brought that fact to the personal attention of the President. Arnold had passed along early combat experiences and lessons in a March 1942 memorandum:

> Japanese bombardment formations are often accompanied by Zero fighters, which carry a "belly-tank," constructed of plywood and canvas. This materially increases their range. On going into action they drop these "belly-tanks" in order to improve their maneuverability in combat. It is reported that Zero fighters with the "belly-tanks" and probably without bombs can accompany their bomber formations during their entire flights.[145]

Here was the solution to the agony of the bombers in 1943. But somehow the connection between 1942 experiences in the Pacific and possible 1943 losses in Europe was never made. The doctrine had been developed that bombing could be carried out without fighter escorts. The Air Corps believed—indeed for its future had to believe—that this doctrine would work. In effect, the doctrine had been developed because no long-range escort was thought possible. Then, when a technological solution to the escort problem became available, the doctrine was already in place and became an obstacle in itself. With it all, there is the lingering thought that if Arnold's report had concerned German combat experiences rather than Japanese, the crucial connection would have been made.

Other mistakes were committed, partially because of American trust in the accuracy of British intelligence assessments. Antisubmarine warfare (ASW) presents an example. During the interwar years, the United States Navy generally accepted the preeminence of the Royal Navy in the ASW field.[146] Britain assumed that the development late in World War I of its sonar-like device known as ASDIC (Allied Submarine Detection Investigation Committee) had solved permanently the submarine threat.[147] Thus, as World War II approached, the Royal Navy stated that the U-boats "should never again be able to present us with the problem we were faced with in 1917."[148] Instead, the British gave their attention to the German surface and air threat. American naval attaché accounts from London reflected the British perception. Although the notes described in copious detail such British anti-aircraft defenses as barrage balloons, reports of British ASW preparations were conspicuously missing. ASDIC, the British assumed, had won the U-boat war before it had even begun.[149]

British confidence continued into the early days of the war, for

German U-boats gained only limited early success. The Royal Navy gave the credit to ASDIC rather than to the possiblity that Germany was short of effective submarine bases or lacked adequate numbers of long-range U-boats. Nor did there appear to be any British thought that German captains might develop tactics that could neutralize ASDIC. Recalling the mutiny of the German navy in 1918, the Royal Navy blithely predicted that its current success would destroy the morale of the U-boat force.[150] It would be a repeat of World War I. In their conviction, the British ignored the possibility that the very memory and "stain" of that 1918 mutiny might make the German naval forces fight even harder in this new battle.[151]

Unfortunately for America, the Royal Navy was supposed to be the expert in the field. In 1939–40, England was also the prime source of firsthand naval combat experience for the United States. In addition, English confidence in ASDIC confirmed the optimistic findings of the U.S. Navy during the 1930s in its own efforts to develop an effective device for locating submerged submarines.[152] Thus, America gave little thought to a serious U-boat threat.[153] Here is a case where the acceptance of British intelligence assessments misled the nation, and both the United States and Great Britain would pay a dire toll for their errors.

Such mistakes were painful but ultimately not fatal. Other important technological issues were gauged correctly. Roosevelt's comprehension of the significance of the 1939 letter from Albert Einstein and the memorandum from Leo Szilard concerning the military implications of atomic energy presents a well-known example. There were others, and although they may lack the ultimate significance of atomic weapons, they demonstrate a crucial point: Anglo-American willingness to explore systematically and to cooperate closely in the military uses of science. Here was a key piece of the Allied victory.

Political instincts were even more important than scientific ones. In the case of Britain in 1940, Roosevelt correctly judged that it would survive, even while his more conservative military advisers counseled that it was doomed. A year later military advisers provided the same grim assessment of Russia's chance to endure under the massive onslaught of the German invasion. Stimson quickly advised that German victory would come within one to three months, and sources within the State Department during the next month agreed with the War Department prediction.[154]

Roosevelt refused to write off the Soviet Union. Instead, in a fashion reminiscent of the previous summer with Britain, he sent to Moscow his personal emissary Harry Hopkins, who reported back that Russia would hold.[155] As with England in 1940, the question of morale was crucial, and the President's envoy found it steadfast. "I feel ever so confident about this front," Hopkins observed. "The morale of the population is exceptionally good. There is unbounded determination to win."[156] Roosevelt took the risk that this former social worker was right and that his military advisers were wrong. Correct in both the summer of 1940 and the summer of 1941, Roosevelt's judgments led to the Grand Alliance and assured ultimate victory.

In the period before Pearl Harbor, FDR had understood that if the United States were to enter the war, the nation must be united in that action. To do otherwise in a democracy risked disintegration and disaster. Just as the unity of the country had been crucial if the nation were to enter the war, the unity of the alliance was crucial once the war was entered, and that meant working with the Soviet Union.

Roosevelt was quick to grasp the significance of the German invasion of Russia in June 1941. Within days of the German assault, FDR wrote Leahy: "Now comes this Russian diversion. If it is more than just that it will mean the liberation of Europe from Nazi domination."[157] Thus, the Soviet Union had to be helped with all available material, and it had to be helped quickly. Roosevelt made himself abundantly clear on this point, ordering aides to "use a heavy hand—act as a burr under the saddle and get things moving! . . . Step on it!"[158] Along with sustaining the Soviet armed forces, the United States needed simultaneously to allay Russian suspicion of the West. Without full Soviet participation in the east, there could be no later Anglo-American invasion in the west, a point well understood by the President.[159] As a result, Roosevelt put much of his wartime effort into trying to build that trust, for there was always the memory of Brest-Litovsk and the German-Soviet Nonaggression Pact to spur him on. At times, Roosevelt's efforts were assuredly egotistical and naïve, such as when he wrote to Churchill:

> I know you will not mind my being brutally frank when I tell you that I think I can personally handle Stalin better than either your Foreign Office or my State Department. Stalin hates the guts of all your top people. He thinks he likes me better, and I hope he will continue to do so.[160]

Silly as that statement may seem, the President's goal was correct, and he took very seriously what the historian Maurice Matloff would later call his role as the "guardian of the good relations of the coalition."[161]

Important to his emphasis on unity was Roosevelt's unlimited faith in American productive capacity. America would be an untouchable and inexhaustible factory. Its economic output would supply both its own and its allies' military forces with an abundance never before seen in warfare. Matériel rather than manpower would bury the nation's enemies and assure victory with a minimum loss of national blood. The President's concept of this "Arsenal of Democracy" furnished a fundamental part of his broad assessment of World War II and a basic part of America's military strategy. FDR told Stimson soon after Pearl Harbor that the war would be won "by our overwhelming mastery in the munitions of war."[162]

The Commander-in-Chief intuitively understood that as long as the Grand Alliance held firm, the Allies would win. The necessary elements would be in place, the formula for victory secure. The ingredient of Anglo-American superiority in the realm of air, sea, and science, added to the twin inexhaustibles of Soviet manpower and American productivity, would finally crush the Axis. Concerning this ultimate assessment the thirty-second President of the United States had no doubt.

8

Japanese Net Assessment in the Era Before Pearl Harbor

Alvin D. Coox

THE APPARATUS OF NET ASSESSMENT

JAPAN UNTIL 1945 was classified as a constitutional monarchy, though sovereignty resided entirely in the sacred and inviolable Emperor (Tennō), not in the bicameral legislature (Diet), whose function was only to give (or presumably to withhold) consent to legislation. Under the cabinet system, the Prime Minister was directly responsible to the Throne. Each cabinet minister was assisted by a vice minister, parliamentary vice minister, and counselor. As of mid-1941, under the Premier, Prince Konoe Fumimaro (in office from July 1940 to October 1941), the full cabinet included thirteen ministries, of which the most relevant for net assessment were those of Foreign Affairs, under Matsuoka Yōsuke; War, headed by Tōjō Hideki; and Navy, under Oikawa Koshirō.

Matsuoka held his post from July 1940 to July 1941. His Vice Minister was Ōhashi Chūichi (November 1940–July 1941). Among subordinate Foreign Ministry entities relevant to net assessment, the America Bureau was headed by Terasaki Tarō; the East Asia Bureau by Yamamoto Kumaichi; and the Euro-Asiatic Bureau by Sakamoto Tamao. These three bureau chiefs were brought in by Matsuoka in September 1940. They all "outlived" him, bureaucratically speaking, after he fell.

Apart from full cabinet meetings, called by the Premier, there were also periodic Four Ministers' meetings (Premier, War, Navy, Foreign) and Five Ministers' meetings (Finance added), bringing together core members of the cabinet to discuss specific issues for subsequent consideration by the whole body. The Cabinet Planning Board, which performed statistical and resources-estimating functions, was headed after April 1941 by Suzuki Tei'ichi, a retired general.

Theoretically, a Privy Council constituted the highest consultative body to the Emperor, advising him periodically on state matters of "grave importance." Under a president and vice president there were twenty-four councillors of the most senior rank. The Privy Council was unconnected with governmental administration. Retired Admiral Suzuki Kantarō became the President of the Privy Council in June 1940.

The Emperor directly appointed a state functionary of the Imperial Household with the ancient title of Lord Keeper of the Privy Seal. Charged with the innocuous duty of keeping the Imperial and State seals and of administering matters relating to Imperial decrees and documents, the Lord Keeper was in fact the most important civilian adviser to the Throne. In constant personal and confidential contact with the Emperor, the Lord Keeper also chaired meetings of the ex-premiers (*Jūshin*). Marquis Kido Kōichi held the post of Lord Keeper from June 1940 to 1945. His Chief Secretary was Matsudaira Yasumasa (1936–45).[1]

So far as the Japanese armed forces were concerned, the Emperor possessed supreme authority over the army and the navy (according to the Meiji Constitution of 1889), and all Imperial orders were issued in his name. Responsibility to the monarch for supreme command or operational guidance lay entirely outside the administrative purview of the ministers of state, including those of War and Navy, who handled matters of organization and military administration. It was the Chiefs of Staff of the two services who advised the Emperor about strategy and operations, and (like the service ministers) were privileged to be received directly by the monarch without going through civilian governmental channels such as the Premier, cabinet, or Diet.

As a matter of applied politics, the armed forces possessed life-and-death power over the formation of civilian cabinets by virtue of their ability to sanction or withhold approval of a Minister of War or of Navy. Since 1936, too, the services had obtained the restoration of a requirement that their cabinet ministers be selected only from active-duty general or flag officer rosters, e.g. lieutenant general or full general, vice admiral or full admiral.

With responsibility for handling matters pertaining to national defense and operational direction vested in the General Staffs of the Army and the Navy (AGS and NGS), under the direct command of the Emperor, the individual service Chiefs of Staff oversaw the necessary planning and attended His Majesty at periodic extragovernmental Throne Councils of War.

In November 1937, after the outbreak of hostilities with China, an Imperial General Headquarters (IGHQ) was established. Theoretically, IGHQ constituted a single instrumentality personally commanded by the Emperor. In practice it consisted of two autonomous organs: the army and the navy, under their respective Chiefs of Staff, there being no independent air force. The sphere of IGHQ was thus a function of command and not of administration. Contrary to the wish of civilian leaders who had hoped in vain that IGHQ would include the Premier and would be authorized to coordinate highest-level civil–military affairs, IGHQ itself proved to be a sheerly military symbol of operational guidance.[2]

To try to bridge the gap between the civilian authorities and the High Command, an IGHQ–Government Liaison Conference structure was devised and increasingly employed after 1940. Coordinated by the Chief Cabinet Secretary for the government and by the chiefs of the Military Affairs and Naval Affairs Bureaus for the two services, the extralegal Liaison Conference would assemble, as necessary, the Chiefs and/or Deputy Chiefs of Staff with the Premier, the Foreign Affairs, War, and Navy ministers, plus other cabinet members on occasion. Though the Liaison Conference was a very useful device and though the numerical balance of power was always tilted preponderantly in favor of the armed forces, a number of military and naval officers were less than enthusiastic about it, ever fearful of any civilian "instrusion" into the services' cherished prerogative of supreme command. Still, the Liaison Conference eventually became more important in foreign policy matters than the cabinet, which tended to devote itself mainly to domestic affairs.[3]

When ultimate legal sanction by the sovereign appeared necessary in the decision-making process above the Liaison Conference level, the Premier and the two chiefs of staff would call for an Imperial Conference—a full-scale meeting held in the presence of the Emperor at the Palace. By the time such an august conclave was convened, all preparatory discussions had been completed, and the pro forma seal of Imperial approval was all that remained to be elicited after an additional but indecisive period allotted for statements and for some questions by the Emperor's proxies.

THE KEY PLAYERS

Much of the Japanese net assessment apparatus was therefore of a disjointed, often ceremonial nature, and lacking in strong civilian input. Close students of the process have gone so far as to conclude that, to all intents and purposes, foreign policy questions were

> . . . answered almost exclusively by the armed services. It was largely the nucleus group within the army and navy who specified the program to be followed in the immediate future and who led the fight for its acceptance by the nonmilitary members of the government, who had to give their consent though they were otherwise powerless.[4]

According to officer veterans and to observers of the prewar Japanese net assessment process, there was a greater tendency in the army than in the navy for decision-making to work its way upward from the above-mentioned "nucleus" layer in the services.[5]

Heading the list of key players within the army's policy-making unit was Lieutenant General Tōjō Hideki, War Minister from July 1941. His Vice Minister, from April 1941, was Lieutenant General Kimura Heitarō. Major General Mutō Akira had headed the Military Affairs Bureau from September 1939, with Colonel Sanada Jōichirō as chief of the subordinate Army Affairs Section after February 1941. Other relevant War Ministry assessment elements included the Military Affairs Section under Colonel Satō Kenryō, the Military Administration Bureau of Major General Tanaka Ryūkichi, Colonel Yamazaki Masao's Military Administration Section, the Economic Mobilization Bureau led by Major General Yamada Seiichi, and the War Matériel Section under Colonel Okada Kikusaburō.

General Sugiyama Hajime had been Chief of the Army General Staff since October 1940 and Lieutenant General Tsukada Osamu his deputy from November of that year. The most important AGS net assessment units and their chiefs were the 1st (Operations) Bureau, Major General Tanaka Shin'ichi (October 1940); 2d (Operations) Section, Colonel Doi Akio (September 1940); and a 2d (Intelligence) Section, Major General Okamoto Kiyotomi (April 1941). The intelligence unit included the 5th Section (dealing with the U.S.S.R.) under Colonel Isomura Takesuke; the 6th Section (Europe–America), Colonel Amano Masakazu; and the 7th Section (China), Colonel Tokō Kitaru. Colonel Karakawa Yasuo commanded the 8th Section, dealing with propaganda and subversion matters. In October 1940 a 20th (War Guidance) Subsection was set up under Colonel Arisue Yadoru, reporting directly to the AGS Deputy Chief.

The Navy Minister since September 1940 was Admiral Oikawa Koshirō; Vice Admiral Sawamoto Yorio took over as Vice Minister in April 1941. The center for political policy-making in the navy reposed in the Naval Affairs Bureau. When Rear Admiral Oka Takazumi became chief of the Bureau in October 1940, he instituted a number of significant improvements. The main duties of the 2d Section were changed from administration to policy, and in November 1940 Oka assigned an old subordinate, Captain Ishikawa Shingo, to head the Section, which now became the counterpart of the Military Affairs Section in the War Ministry.

Naval Affairs Bureau chief Oka also formed an important National Defense Policy Committee made up of four subcommittees, the most influential of which was the 1st Subcommittee, dominated by Captain Ishikawa. The latter recruited experts on diplomacy and political strategy from the Naval Affairs Bureaus, notably his friends of long standing, Kami Shigenori and Shiba Katsuo. Other members of the 1st Subcommittee included the head of the Naval Affairs Bureau's 1st Section, Captain Takada Toshitane, and, from the NGS, the chief of the Operations Section and the officer in charge of War Guidance and International Relations. In the Navy Ministry too, from late 1940, a Naval Preparations Bureau existed under Rear Admiral Hoshina Zenshirō. His subordinate sections dealt with combat preparations, industrial mobilization, harbors, and labor.

Admiral Nagano Osami had become chief of the naval general staff in April 1941. Vice Admiral Kondō Nobutake still served as the Deputy Chief, since October 1939. Rear Admiral Fukudome Shigeru took charge of the 1st Bureau (Operations) in April 1941. Under him were Captain Tomioka Sadatoshi, 1st Section chief (Operations, October 1940), and Captain Okada Tameji, 2d Section chief (Defense, November 1939). Directly attached to the 1st Bureau chief as OIC for War Guidance and International Relations was Captain Ōno Takeji (since November 1939).

Rear Admiral Takagi Takeo directed the activities of the NGS 2d Bureau (Logistics and Mobilization) since November 1939. The 3d Section (Ships, Ordnance, and Facilities) came under Captain Yanagimoto Ryūsaku (November 1939); the 4th Section (Mobilization, Transportation, and Supplies), under Captain Kurihara Etsuzō (November 1940).

Rear Admiral Maeda Minoru commanded the NGS 3d Bureau (Intelligence) from October 1940. Its subordinate groups and their chiefs included the 5th Section (dealing with the United States and Latin America), Captain Yamaguchi Bunjirō (May 1940); 6th Section (China/Manchukuo), Captain Fujiwara Kiyoma (from October 1939, followed by Captain Kuwahara Shigetoh in June 1941); 7th Section (Europe and U.S.S.R.), Captain Kojima Hideo (May 1939); and 8th Section (U.K. and India), Captain Horiuchi Shigetada (November 1939). There was also an NGS War Preparations Analysis Committee (without a chairman *per se*), whose members were drawn from among the Naval Vice Ministers, Deputy Chief of Staff, and bureau and section chiefs as required.[6]

TESTING THE SYSTEM: THE SITUATION PRIOR TO SUMMER 1941

Five months before the European war broke out in 1939, the AGS Deputy, Lieutenant General Nakajima Tetsuzō, articulated the Japanese army's estimate of the situation and its prescriptions for dealing with envisaged international developments at the annual conference of chiefs of staff of all field armies held in Tokyo on 1 April:

> The recent European situation is changing rapidly, but in general we judge that around 1941–42 Germany will have acquired the full strength to take the offensive against other nations. England and the United

States, too, are aiming at the approximate date of 1941 for the buildup of their national strength and military preparations. Other countries are following their lead. As a result, worldwide changes can be expected around 1942.[7]

For the sake of Japan's independent national policy, the AGS Deputy continued, it was necessary to respond to the challenge of changes in the world arena by tackling two primary tasks: disposition of the China conflict and attainment of a full wartime footing. "We cannot attend to one of these tasks and ignore the other," Nakajima warned.

Japanese postwar critics have pointed out that the army's underestimation by three years of the advent of global crisis caused immeasurable harm to Japan's overall national defense readiness. Neither of the tasks identified as priorities by the AGS had been effectively addressed by 1941–42.[8] The Nakajima prospectus, however, is useful in suggesting the fuzzy prognostications and platitudinous exhortations that characterized what passed for net assessment at the upper levels of the prewar Japanese high command.

Even before the year 1939 had ended, and only nine months after General Nakajima's presentation, a series of cataclysmic events had already occurred on the international scene. First, Japan became involved in an undeclared but bloody war against the Russians on the border flatlands between Japan's puppet state Manchukuo and the Soviet satellite Outer Mongolia at Nomonhan/Khalkhin-gol (May–September).[9] Since the Japanese army was concurrently still bogged down in hostilities with China, the distracting conflict at Nomonhan added up to a one and one-half war situation unattractive to any strategist and taxing to any war guidance assessor.

Second, the Nazis and the Russians consummated an unlikely nonaggression pact on 23 August. Third, the Germans—freed from concern about Soviet interference—attacked Poland on 1 September. Fourth, England and France, which had done nothing to assist beleaguered Czechoslovakia in 1938, went to war with Germany over more distant Poland on 3 September. Fifth, the Poles were overrun and conquered by the Germans from the west and the Russians from the east in a matter of weeks. Sixth, at the end of November, the Soviet Union manufactured a pretext for invading and eventually defeating Finland.

Most of these events in Europe were not foretold accurately in Tokyo, causing problems of credibility for the incumbent Prime Minister and his cabinet. Minister of Home Affairs Hiranuma Kiichirō, for one, resigned amid the turmoil of August 1939 engendered by the "treacherous and unpardonable" Soviet-German nonaggression pact. Hiranuma admitted feebly that an "extremely complex if not baffling situation" had developed in Europe. His successor, the elderly retired General Abe Nobuyuki, was weak and ineffective, and lasted only four and one-half months. No foreign minister could even be recruited for almost a month, and the daily working of policy was left to career bureaucrats. For a while, according to one Japanese postwar critic, governmental and military estimates of the situation "lost objectivity and disarray grew."[10]

Some of the net assessment officials in Tokyo hoped that Europe's discomfiture might prove to be Japan's boon, whereby the China conflict could be solved and Chiang Kai-shek's stubborn regime brought down by a final ground offensive; by the breakoff of foreign assistance to China from such countries as England, France, and Russia; and by the creation of a pro-Japanese puppet regime in Nanking. Another approach, much debated in Tokyo, was to tighten military, economic, and political links with the European Axis powers. In due course, a Tripartite Pact was signed in Berlin with Germany and Italy on 27 September 1940.

Meanwhile, German armed forces had defeated Denmark, Norway, Belgium, Holland, and France in a ruthless Blitzkrieg campaign that achieved the pinnacle of victory when Paris fell on 13 June. Very much on Japanese minds now was the fate of the isolated yet resources-rich European colonies in the Far East—especially the Dutch East Indies and French Indochina. By September 1940 the Japanese had compelled the impotent Vichy French authorities to allow the establishment of the first Japanese beachheads in northern Indochina.

Germany next launched a mighty air offensive against the British home isles. Japanese net assessment officers now grappled with such issues as the prospects for German success in the air and in a land invasion of England. Then there was the question of whether the United States would enter the war on Britain's behalf or would be deterred by the Tripartite Pact, as hoped. Much centered on whether American interests were separable from those of the British, or whether the Anglo-Saxon powers would form a wartime coalition as in World War I.

The Soviet Specter

While a great deal of the discussion and cogitation occurring at the highest levels in Tokyo was devoted to matters involving Japan vis-à-vis the United States, England, France, the Netherlands East Indies,

China, and the Axis, thinking about one other country was always very near the surface, whether openly expressed or not: the Japanese Army's traditional main enemy, Russia.

Few Japanese officers would admit it, even today, but the thrashing that a goodly portion of the Kwantung Army incurred at Nomonhan in the summer of 1939 had caused Japanese Army leaders to become extremely apprehensive about the Russians afterward and to think twice about tangling with the U.S.S.R. Cocky Japanese estimates of the inferiority of the Soviet military had subsided after the experience at Nomonhan, and there was now a fear that, if the Russians chose to attack (as they might, once the Finnish war was over), they could overrun Manchukuo just as easily as the Germans had crushed Poland. By 1940, in fact, the number of infantry divisions in the Soviet Far East was thought to have increased ominously from 30 to 36. IJA operations analysts also estimated that if Soviet bombers based in Siberia attacked targets in Manchuria, it would prove impossible for the Kwantung Army to concentrate its forces in emergency.[11]

Three approaches to dealing with the Northern Problem (as the Soviet threat was called) seemed advisable: to lull the Russians into a condition of *détente;* to team up with the Germans (since the Japanese obviously could not go it alone at this stage) in case Hitler decided to strike the U.S.S.R. from the west; and, all the while, to build up military strength and the economic infrastructure inside Manchukuo. Even if the Japanese Army went into Southeast Asia to seize raw materials and to intercept foreign aid going to China, those operations would be merely temporary. As soon as the southern sphere had been secured, the Japanese Army intended to redeploy to the Manchurian theater to face off against the Russians, their chief hypothetical foe.

In the spring of 1941 Foreign Minister Matsuoka—voluble, tough-minded, experienced, and imaginative—decided on a grandiose scheme. He would visit not only Japan's Axis partners in Europe but also the Soviet Union. In Moscow he would strive to resolve tensions outstanding between Japan and Russia, to the extent of perhaps enticing the U.S.S.R. to join the Tripartite Pact, thereby forming a quadrilateral Continental Alliance that could be expected to restrain the United States and to help finish off England and China. In the event, on the way home on 13 April 1941 he settled for a surprising five-year Soviet-Japanese Neutrality Pact that took the pressure off the strategic rear of both countries. One astute AGS colonel wrote in his secret diary, as soon as he heard the news, that Stalin must have seized the chance to rush through the agreement with Matsuoka, out of dread of the unavoidability of hostilities with the Third Reich (despite the Soviet–German nonaggression pact).[12]

Early Signals of Russo-German Hostilities

Actually, the Japanese authorities were receiving a variety of authentic clues concerning a Nazi–Soviet war, months before the German invasion took place. Thus, when Kurusu Saburō, the departing Ambassador in Berlin, came to pay his respects to the Führer on 3 February, Hitler himself dropped an unmistakable hint about the deteriorating state of relations with the U.S.S.R. Four days later, an alerted Emperor shared his private concerns with Lord Keeper Kido in Tokyo. It was imperative, the monarch warned, to think very carefully about the current notion of taking action in Southeast Asia, for Japan would face a serious crisis if a simultaneous confrontation developed in the north as a result of obligations imposed by the Tripartite Pact.[13]

Kurusu's was not the only troubling indicator emanating from Europe. Disquieting and highly specific reports from Balkan listening posts such as Bucharest and especially Sofia noted the growing tension between the Third Reich and Russia and the steady eastward movement of German military forces. Vice Admiral Nomura Naokuni, a member of the Yamashita inspection mission to the Axis countries in Europe, insisted that the inevitability of a Russo-German war was the subject of conversation all over the Continent. In March in Berlin he told his old friend Admiral Raeder that if, as rumored, Germany was going to fight the Russians, the Tripartite Alliance was as good as dead.

An army member of the Yamashita mission, Major General Ayabe Kitsuju, was impressed by the technical excellence and coordination displayed by the German armed forces, yet he felt that German officers underestimated the Russians. Everybody told Ayabe that the U.S.S.R. could be defeated in a month, but already, in the spring of 1941, he believed that he could detect a "whiff of thought" among the Germans that the conquest of England was being abandoned and that the Germans were about to commence anti-Soviet operations. Ayabe often discussed with German officers the dangers of two-front operations; he became convinced that the German military was underestimating the problem and nurturing dangerous preconceptions.[14]

Reassuring messages about alleged quiescence on the Russo-German front, however, continued to reach Tokyo from the Ambassador to the U.S.S.R., retired Lieutenant General Tatekawa Yoshitsugu, and until around 1 April from Ōshima Hiroshi, the ardently Germanophile

retired lieutenant general who was the new envoy to Berlin. Typical of
IJA thinking at the time was the view expressed to Prince Higashikuni
by Ōshima's predecessor as military attaché in Berlin, Major General
Okamoto Kiyotomi, now the chief of the AGS Intelligence Bureau.
Germany, in Okamoto's view, was confronted by an untrustworthy
Russia on the east, by an undefeated England on the west, and by a
feeble Italian partner on the south. As Hitler, Ribbentrop, and the other
Nazi leaders had been telling Ōshima, the Germans could trust only the
Japanese and would leave Far Eastern matters entirely to them. It was
true that Germany had built up its army from 100 to 180 divisions since
the beginning of the European war, and that 130 to 140 of those
divisions were deployed on the Eastern Front. Still, Okamoto insisted,
the Nazi leaders seemed cautious about becoming involved in hostilities
with the Soviet Union and the United States, and they did not want
Japan to become involved either. Okamoto stressed that, while Japan
must remain loyal to its commitments, it should not rely excessively on
the Germans.[15]

In conversations with Hitler as well as Ribbentrop, Matsuoka heard
the "faithlessness" of the U.S.S.R. castigated, and he learned that the
Nazis were convinced the roots of trouble in Europe would never be
eradicated unless the Russians were dealt a blow once and for all.
Hitler's interpreter repeated the Führer's hint twice slowly: that a
Russo-German clash was "not necessarily unexpected."[16]

Uncertainties must still have been gnawing at Matsuoka as he
headed back to Moscow in early April. He may have been discouraged
by Germany's unilateral policy of an early preventive war against the
Soviet Union or may have been encouraged by the broadness of the
hints he had received in Berlin. Months later, when it was too late, he
admitted to his colleagues in Tokyo: "As a matter of fact, I concluded a
Neutrality Pact [with the U.S.S.R.] because I thought that Germany and
Soviet Russia would not go to war. If I had known . . . I would have
preferred to take a more friendly position towards Germany, and I
would not have concluded the Neutrality Treaty." Yet after the
signature of that pact in 1941, Ribbentrop is known to have said to
Ōshima in private: "We told [Matsuoka] unmistakably about the
inevitability of the Russo-German war."[17]

Based on his conversations with the Nazi leadership, Ōshima began
to dispatch reports to Tokyo suggesting that the Reich was moving in
the general direction of hostilities with the Soviet Union. On 10 April he
had an especially important talk with Ribbentrop, who asserted that,
depending on the attitude of the Russians, Germany might well fight the

U.S.S.R. that year. The Germans had ample strength now and could successfully terminate operations within several months of launching an invasion. It would be best to smash the Soviet Union before it could complete its own preparations. This statement was an even clearer expression of intent than Ribbentrop had recently voiced to Matsuoka.[18]

It is true that Ōshima had the advantage of possessing the single best entrée to Nazi policy-makers. He could chat face to face with Hitler without interpreters. Since the Führer did not customarily ask advice of his entourage concerning vital issues, the Japanese Ambassador could derive the earliest and most authentic intelligence and could often sense the hidden drift of Reich policy.

The subjective assets of Ōshima were, of course, counterbalanced by his natural tendency to ingest all information imparted to him as "gospel truth." He seemed unable to accept whatever cautionary views existed. In particular, he downplayed the pessimistic appreciations transmitted repeatedly to Tokyo by the excellent military attaché in Stockholm, Colonel Onodera Makoto, to the effect that Germany lacked the military and overall strength to overcome Russia in the long run. Perhaps it was not so much that Ōshima was being taken in by the Nazis as that he simply did not want to dwell on matters unfavorable to his beloved second homeland.[19]

Victims of Disinformation

Ōshima was particularly anxious to ascertain whether Germany had changed its stated policy and would instead conduct an assault against the U.S.S.R. before conquering Britain. Here he was the unwitting dupe of Hitler's secret ploy: to lull both foe and friend into believing that the vague plans for operation Sea Lion, the invasion of England, were both continuing and real. In this respect, Ōshima was in very good company; even Admiral Raeder and the German naval high command were among the last to learn about Hitler's true intentions for an offensive against the Soviet Union. As early as 1940 the Führer had disingenuously assured Raeder that German troop movements to the east were only feints designed to mask Sea Lion, although Hitler had already abandoned any serious idea about invading England.

Indeed, the Nazi command went so far as to perpetrate a crafty double bluff by spreading word, almost to the end, that Barbarossa was a deception concocted to divert the British from coping with Sea Lion. Senior German officers were secretly instructed by Marshal Keitel in February 1941 that, after mid-April, "the misdirecting measures meant for Barbarossa itself must not be seen as any more than misdirection and diversion for the invasion of England."[20]

That is exactly what Ōshima heard on the best authority and advised the net assessors in Tokyo. After consulting with army and navy colleagues in Berlin, on 16 April he wired his estimate of the situation to Premier Konoe, who shared it with Privy Seal Kido. The latter conveyed the information to the Emperor. It was Ōshima's impression that, sometime between May and October 1941 and undoubtedly before the winter of 1941–42, Germany might invade the Soviet Union simultaneously with an offensive against the British Isles. Such a war with Russia would arise not from the Reich's frustration in the struggle against England but from Soviet interference since the winter of 1940–41. The Germans seemed confident about their prospects and did not necessarily expect Japan to enter the war; they would be satisfied if the Japanese impeded Soviet troop transfers from Siberia. Ōshima did not want Japan to act hastily and strike north. Instead, the Japanese should seize the best opportunity and concentrate on reducing Singapore, the key to Anglo-American power in Southeast Asia.[21]

From Washington, Ambassador Nomura Kichisaburō, a retired admiral, also predicted the nearness of Russo-German hostilities. But whereas Ōshima pressed for a Japanese thrust to the south in force, Nomura argued for Japanese neutrality to the last. The contradictions in the situation vexed the more astute in Tokyo—notably the fact that, although the U.S.S.R. was the common enemy of Germany and Japan, the latter was still neutral, which meant that the vaunted intimacy between the Axis powers was out of kilter before summer 1941, apart from the matter of the timing. Colonel Tanemura Sakō, a general staff planner, recorded his private lament: "While epochal U.S.–Japanese negotiations are about to get under way [in Washington], our ally [Germany] and our Neutrality Pact co-signator [Russia] are going to fight. The world situation has become truly complicated."[22]

Soon afterward, on 13 May, the current Japanese military attaché in Berlin, Major General Sakanishi Kazuyoshi, reported on the basis of information from German army intelligence that Nazi-Soviet hostilities were inevitable, and he warned that the Yamashita mission ought to hurry home from Germany. Other IJA attachés in Europe reported various stages of German troop movement eastward. Japanese intelligence also knew that some redeployment of Soviet forces west from Siberia had begun from around March 1941.[23]

Despite the accumulating evidence, the civil and military net assessment analysts in Tokyo were clearly perplexed by the perennial challenge of weighing capabilities against intentions, Germany's in this case. Government officials agonized about an adjustment of national policy to deal with a possible Nazi-Soviet war. The general staff took Ōshima's and Sakanishi's reports with large doses of salt. Tantalized by the lure of the south, IJA leaders recognized that Russo-German relations had deteriorated but doubted Germany's seriousness about commencing all-out hostilities against the U.S.S.R.

From Moscow, Ambassador Tatekawa was still dispensing cheerful predictions. He had conferred in mid-May with Foreign Minister Molotov, who conveyed the impression that the Russians regarded the heavy concentration of German forces along their frontier as a mere "demonstration" designed to exert pressure on the Soviet Union to maintain the supply of essential commodities needed for the Reich's war machine, ranging from grain to oil and iron. Tatekawa expected no military clash between the Germans and the Russians unless the U.S.S.R. suddenly reversed its policy, which was unlikely, because Stalin had no real choice but to appease the Nazis. In short, Tatekawa judged that the likelihood of a full-scale war was slim.[24]

By the middle of May the thinking of the Japanese military had still not crystallized. Some felt that the concept of Sea Lion was very much alive but that no German cross-Channel landing would be launched until the English were reeling; in the meantime the Germans would rely on a counterblockade of the British Isles. There was also an opinion, held by such personages as Prince Higashikuni, that Japan should not allow itself to be exploited by Germany and enslaved by the Tripartite Pact. Like Okamoto, the Prince affirmed that Japan should use the treaty to its own advantage.[25]

With Sakanishi's most recent message from Berlin in hand, on 15 May the AGS convened a special meeting of bureau chiefs. They concluded that Nazi-Soviet hostilities would not break out soon. German troop movements to Eastern Europe were apparently intended to support foreign policy. The Reich would not be so foolhardy as to engage two major enemies—England and the U.S.S.R.—at the same time. Some effort was made to reopen the issue. Colonel Arisue's War Guidance Subsection wanted to know what stance the AGS and the War Ministry thought Japan should adopt in the event of a Russo-German war. From the War Ministry's Military Affairs Section, Lieutenant Colonel Ishii Akiho drafted a position paper, which he shared with his superiors and with the AGS. The consensus of net assessment, however, was that war was not imminent, and these activities stimulated little response.[26]

Much more on the military's mind was the increasing likelihood that the United States would go to war against Germany in order to save Britain. Kido discussed a number of related questions with Prince Higashikuni on 18 May: Was Japan bound to come in immediately to support the Reich in such an eventuality? Would the U.S.S.R. take the Anglo-Americans' side and fight Germany too? If Tokyo decided to go to war with the United States and Britain out of obligation to the Germans, would not the Japanese find themselves surrounded by enemies on all sides (America, England, and China) and left isolated in the Far East? Could Japan then withstand a protracted war? Dominating Kido's presentation was the desperate need for raw materials from the south, but he wanted Japan to assess the situation very carefully—entirely in terms of its own long-range perspective—and not to be railroaded into careless hostilities at such a decisive time in its history. The question of the probability of a Nazi-Soviet war did not figure in the discussion with Higashikuni.[27]

If Matsuoka had finally come round to the view that a Russo-German war was bound to erupt, at least he wanted it to be put off. On the basis of discussions in the cabinet and the high command, he sent a personal message to Ribbentrop on 28 May, requesting that hostilities be avoided and that he be given a candid response. Ribbentrop replied to the effect that hostilities were inevitable but that Germany was sure to be able to end operations successfully within two or three months of their start. The results of such a conflict would certainly benefit Japan. "Considering the fact that everything I have said in the past turned out the way I predicted," said Ribbentrop, "trust me now."[28]

Conflicting intelligence continued to confuse the Japanese government. Whereas the sources in Germany were predicting war, those in the Soviet Union were still denying it. In Moscow, at least two important persons did not share the general realization in the Russian capital that hostilities were coming: Stalin, who refused to believe it, and the Japanese military attaché, Colonel Yamaoka, who could not detect it, trapped as he was "like a bird in a cage." In Tokyo, it was Yamaoka's view that prevailed.

Nevertheless, the most able of the Soviet defectors—G. S. Lyushkov, the chief of the NKVD in Siberia until his flight to the Japanese in mid-1938—monitored Russian-language radio broadcasts, reached the conclusion that a Russo-German war was at hand, and warned the Japanese to be ready, a month before the German invasion. Japanese

Intelligence promptly issued a secret bulletin, distributed among the general staff. It elicited no reaction.[29]

The Murk Begins to Clear Slowly in Tokyo

Despite the accumulating evidence of the imminence of Nazi–Soviet hostilities, the net assessment people in Tokyo were still wallowing in bafflement as June dawned. Senior German military sources had been assuring Oshima that, once begun, the fighting against the Russians would probably be over in four weeks. "It should not, in fact, be called a war," these authorities boasted, "only a police action."

The Japanese wondered about the significance of Rudolf Hess's bizarre flight to England (11 May) but concluded that instead of heralding war between Germany and Russia, it might only imply a bilateral settlement between Germany and Britain. Even less was known about the implications of Hitler's conference with Mussolini at the Brenner Pass on 2 June.[30]

Some of the answers began to fall into place after Ōshima was invited to chat with Hitler and Ribbentrop at Berchtesgaden on 3–4 June. German–Soviet relations, said the Führer, had grown much worse, and war was probably unavoidable. Though the Russian attitude was ostensibly friendly, the facts belied it, especially with respect to the contest for Yugoslavia. Hitler found the Soviet activities unacceptable; he was the sort of person who drew his sword as soon as he discerned hostile intent in an opponent. It was imperative to crush the Communists for the sake of the final offensive against England. Operations against Russia would end swiftly, and neither Britain nor the United States could do a thing about it. From Hitler's tone, Ōshima judged that the Führer desired Japanese collaboration, yet would not demand actions that were not stipulated in the Axis alliance as obligations. In summary, Ōshima warned Tokyo that war was inevitable and that it was coming soon.[31]

Although Ōshima's access to the Nazi leadership was admired in Tokyo, the high command tended to question the objectivity of his reporting to a certain degree. But when a strong confirming message also arrived on 5 June from military attaché Sakanishi in Berlin, conveying his own impressions of Ōshima's most recent conversations with the Germans, the Japanese military authorities finally sat up and took notice. Judging from the atmosphere surrounding Ōshima's meetings, Sakanishi reported, hostilities were certain, and Tokyo should not err in reaching a decision as to national policy.

AGS Deputy Tsukada, for one, was jarred by the news. It was inexcusable, he told his staff, for Germany to go to war against the U.S.S.R. without consulting Japan beforehand. Under the circumstances, grumbled Tsukada, the Japanese might opt for neutrality. Meanwhile the general staff began serious consideration of national policy guidelines that ought to be adopted if the Reich did attack Russia. Colonel Doi's Operations Section, Major General Okamoto's Intelligence Bureau, and Colonel Arisue's War Guidance Subsection worked on the first drafts of a plan.[32]

The tenor of the thinking in the general staff at this time can be summarized as follows: While the Germans might be planning an attack, they might also be bluffing for political and strategic reasons bearing on the relations between Japan and the U.S.S.R. In fact, the Soviet Union had recently become more cooperative toward Japan, probably for the very reason that German-Russian relations had worsened. Germany's bluster might be a stratagem devised to mask a final offensive against the British Isles. Hints were one thing, but the Germans still had not revealed any specific time of action. Even Ōshima's reports indicated the following priorities of the German high command: (1) assault on England; (2) destruction of the Royal Navy in the eastern Mediterranean; (3) Iraq; (4) Egypt and Suez; (5) West Africa; (6) Gibraltar. In any event, most AGS officers concluded that, if a Soviet–German war did break out, Japan must consult its own interests with respect to the Axis and the U.S.S.R.[33]

Meanwhile, as soon as Premier Konoe received the latest information from Berlin, he communicated with Kido, who reported it to the Emperor. When the monarch's senior military aide de camp sounded out War Minister Tōjō, the latter responded that he did not regard the situation as urgent. Matsuoka himself went to the palace and, despite all of Ōshima's and Sakanishi's warnings, advised the Emperor that he regarded the chances for retention of the Russo-German status quo as 60 percent and assessed the prospect for war as only 40 percent.[34]

At a specially convened liaison conference, Matsuoka asserted that though he did not mean to contradict Ōshima, he wondered if Hitler was really willing to go to war to smash communism. Instead, might not Hitler be expecting the war in the west to drag on for twenty or thirty years, in which case he needed to be rid of the danger from the east? There was a distinct possibility that Germany and Britain would achieve a separate settlement. Matsuoka then indicated that he subscribed to the idea (planted by the Germans, we now know) that there would be some warning of events to come—that since Germany would need a pretext to declare war on the Russians, it would announce conditions in the form of an ultimatum before striking. Turning to the Army and Navy chiefs of staff, the Foreign Minister asked for their opinions. Those officers replied evasively that careful consideration should be given to the Russo-German question, but that (as Tōjō had told the Imperial ADC) they did not regard it as pressing. They deferred clarification of their attitudes for another occasion.[35]

Intelligence Bureau chief Okamoto was vexed by the dilly-dallying of the brass. "When the head of state says he will do something," Okamoto muttered (referring to Hitler's intimations to Ōshima), "he will do just that." To try to crystallize the nebulous net-assessment views and advance the process of developing an overdue national policy, the War Ministry's Military Affairs Section chief Satō and Army Affairs Section chief Sanada proposed conferring with AGS Operations Section chief Doi, Propaganda-Subversion Section chief Karakawa, and War Guidance Subsection chief Arisue.

What the War Ministry officers had in mind became apparent from the three draft plans that Satō placed on the table: Option 1, drive south by force; Option 2, tackle the Northern Problem while conciliating the United States; Option 3, let matters stand. Satō and Sanada pressed for Option 1. Doi and Karakawa concurred, but Arisue objected. Privately, he wondered what on earth the hawks were thinking, after War Guidance had been developing a measured policy vis-à-vis the south for the past six months. The navy would have to be induced to accept any radical new policy. Arisue was troubled that the atmosphere was still murky and that a unified and decisive national policy could not be formulated. Did Satō even know the background? The discussion grew heated, and no progress was made.[36]

Within the general staff, Arisue's subsection went back to the drawing board, trying to reconcile the discordant opinions. At the AGS conference next day, Doi argued for a contraction of Japanese operations in China immediately after war broke out between Germany and Russia. China Section chief Tokō disagreed. With the Chinese capacity to resist nearing collapse, why cut back the front? Euro-American Section chief Amano took issue with Tokō. China was not close to defeat, he argued, but even if the China problem could be solved, Japan could not survive without pushing south. What kind of fuzzy policy was it, asked Amano, when Japan would not push north, when the China option was no good, and when Japan would not push south either? Tokō did not seem to oppose a drive south, but Arisue did, apparently because of concern that the navy could not be won over.

Again, no consensus could be reached, despite vigorous discussion. Doi, however, did go to see his NGS counterpart in Operations, Captain Tomioka, and tried to get him to accept the southern option. The AGS diarist confided to his secret record on 6 June: "Now it is the turn for the Army and the Navy to be at loggerheads, while public opinion is not unified and national policy is not decided. What will be the fate of the nation? It truly is a source of anguish."[37]

Conference after conference ensued daily within and between the services. From one meeting between the AGS and NGS Operations Bureau chiefs and ministries' Military/Naval Affairs Bureau chiefs, the AGS diarist picked up contradictory signals.

> When we sounded out the Navy, our Military Affairs Bureau chief derived the impression that they were in agreement with us, but our Operations Bureau chief thought the opposite. The Navy's intentions are simply unclear to us.[38]

Particularly opaque to the army was the navy's attitude toward Japan's obligations under the Axis Pact and possible use of force against the United States and Britain. As for the proposed policy for dealing with a war between Germany and the U.S.S.R., the army staff deduced that the navy's position was far from unified internally and that the navy leaders themselves may have been confused and irresponsible. The army even feared that the navy might withdraw proposals that it had submitted as mere gambits to counter Matsuoka's "big talk." But some of the army staff officers railed privately against the so-called timidity and unclear outlook or their own superiors, such as Military Affairs Bureau chief Mutō and even AGS chief Sugiyama.[39]

As the days passed in early June, the net assessment officers in Tokyo were hung up on the question whether a Russo-German war would be good or bad for Japan. Clearly such a war would wreck the chances for a quadrilateral alliance designed to neutralize the United States and would upset the balance of power by pushing the U.S.S.R. into the Western camp. But could Germany knock out Russia as quickly as it claimed? Most IJA officers remained mesmerized by the German military, as could be seen in Intelligence Bureau chief Okamoto's attitude. There might be some quibbling over the speed of Germany's victory, but few doubted the eventual outcome. Instead, there was widespread concern lest Japan miss out on permanently eliminating the northern threat while it was pushing into the southern regions. Naval staff officers like Captain Ishikawa, however, dreaded a northern war, often asserting that there were no raw materials in Siberia and that operations to the north would have to be entirely an army show.[40]

From a rare IJN document (perhaps a working draft) that has survived, we know that on 7 June the navy devised its own approach to dealing with a Russo-German war: Japan should not intervene at present but should make preparations to respond to changes in the situation, meanwhile adopting a wait-and-see policy. The present setup of the army and navy should be maintained in general vis-à-vis the U.S.S.R., but this should not preclude the reinforcement of individual units. The preparations, coupled with hints of aggressive action when the time was ripe, should have the effect of not discouraging the Axis partners' hopes of seeing hostilities break out between Japan and Russia. Operations against China should be intensified; e.g. the Kunming campaign. In general terms, Japan should remain flexible for the time being, manifesting the effectiveness of the Triple Alliance by checking the United States, England, and the U.S.S.R. Intervention in a war against Russia would inevitably bring Japan into hostilities against the United States, Britain, China, and Holland as well—a confrontation for which Japan was not yet ready. Diplomacy should be used to accomplish the purchase of northern Sakhalin; force the Russians to stop helping Chiang Kai-shek; and get the U.S.S.R. to promise not to cooperate politically and militarily with the British and Americans in the Far East.[41]

On the army side, in the temporary absence of AGS chief Sugiyama and Operations Bureau chief Tanaka, Colonel Arisue came up with a strangely worded compromise called *junbijin taisei* (preparatory-formation setup) on 7 June. This plan called for Japan to be ready to strike either north or south, but the choice of direction would depend on circumstances. All-out preparations would be undertaken only after that decision was made. Arisue must have had various rationalizations for this opportunistic scheme. The northern hawks would be assuaged, while a southern advance depended on the navy anyhow. Though Okamoto and Doi interpreted the *junbijin* as sanctioning the southern notion, Arisue insisted that the plan reflected absolutely no commitment to go one way or another.

The AGS diarist was not charitable: Doi and Amano, he wrote, were star students; Arisue was a "dunce" who could not comprehend the problems of national strength and the handling of the China war. "Can't we devise a better plan? Do we have to settle for something inferior? This reflects the reality afflicting not only our War Guidance Subsection but also the nation."

When Sugiyama got back from Kyushu, a meeting of bureau chiefs was held on 8 June. Though the basic idea of *junbijin* was accepted, the Chief of Staff seemed dissatisfied, for the draft made no clear-cut choice between north and south. The conferees decided to put off the official decision until Tanaka had returned to Tokyo.[42]

As soon as Tanaka got back from his trip to Manchuria, the AGS called a meeting of bureau chiefs on 9 June. Tanaka expressed his displeasure with a plan that apparently envisaged war, whether in the north or in the south, only in the event of a "good chance." Did this mean that Japan would utterly avoid fighting if no such opportunity arose? Tanaka seemed not to oppose parallel operations northward *and* southward. Nevertheless, since the navy could not be expected to accept the new belligerent approach to the southern problem, the army might as well pursue the northern priority and de-emphasize the "good opportunity arising" prerequisite, at least where the south was concerned—a roundabout way of saying Japan should head north.

Sugiyama, however, seemed to be contemplating operations in the north without beefing up the Kwantung Army in Manchuria; in the south he was prepared to fight the United States and England as soon as the Japanese had established bases in French Indochina and Thailand. Though a protracted war should be avoided, Japan would inevitably have to engage in hostilities, without being unfaithful to the Axis alliance; it was merely a question of *when* to fight.

Put off by the chief of staff's "lack of resolve" and by his willingness to keep a watchful but pointless eye on both south and north, the Operations Bureau chief did not hesitate to speak his mind. Sugiyama flared up, in turn, intimating that a plan embodying Tanaka's strong language would only complicate matters for the conferees and wreck the possibility of agreement with all concerned. Indeed, the meeting on 9 June broke up without reaching a decision.[43]

After the bureau chiefs' meeting, Arisue went to see Tanaka to try to iron out the notion of the "good opportunity arising" that was stymieing the staff. Tanaka was adamant: A good chance had to be *manufactured* deliberately, not merely hoped for. The opportunity that resulted could then be exploited, and force could be used to the south and the north. These things had to be stated explicitly in the planning document, Tanaka insisted.

Arisue raised objections about the practicability of going that far in the language of a national policy paper. Tanaka "blew up" and, according to the AGS diarist, was on the verge of indulging in fisticuffs with Arisue. The latter gave in and reluctantly accepted the general's belligerent wording.[44] Such were a few of the perils and a glimpse into the subjectiveness of net assessment at the high command level in mid-1941.

Another one-on-one meeting between senior officers followed in the evening of 9 June—between AGS Major General Tanaka and War Ministry Major General Mutō. Interpreting what the navy really had in mind figured prominently in the discussion, but, as noted earlier, the navy's intentions remained obscure to both generals.

On the next day, 10 June, an additional bureau chiefs' conference took place. It was becoming apparent why Tanaka was opposing further contraction of the operations in China: Since he was so energetically contemplating drives north and south, Tanaka was concerned lest the army high command's freedom to conduct its own operational guidance might be curtailed if overt curbs were imposed on the China theater. The bureau chiefs also reviewed the question of how best to enunciate obligations within the spirit of the Axis alliance. Underlying the discussion of phraseology was the staff officers' inner conviction that, "though we would cling to the Pact, we were not going to commit double suicide because of it. We should make good use of it but decide the matter of waging war strictly on our own initiative." It is apparent that Tanaka's fundamental outlook was carrying the day so far.[45]

In the current discussions of strategic emphasis, questions bearing directly on the proposed advance into southern French Indochina and its implications distracted from and overlapped those concerning a hypothetical German–Soviet conflagration. On 13 June, however, a bit of progress was made in devising an overall policy. The War Ministry submitted a plan which was reviewed by the AGS War Guidance staff. Arisue then went back to convince Bureau Chief Tanaka that the idea of "deliberate manufacture" of a good chance should revert merely to prospects for an "opportunity arising" that Japan could seize. Tanaka finally gave in.

The plan now called for military preparations to be made against Russia, in concert with changes in the situation. If German–Soviet hostilities developed favorably from the standpoint of Japan, the latter would use force to solve the Northern Problem. Care should be taken to avoid dispersing Japanese national strength, and the domestic wartime setup should be reinforced, especially regarding defense of the homeland.

As for the stance that Japan should adopt for the time being in case of a German attack on the Soviet Union, the leadership of the two services reached a very cautious agreement: The government should make no statement whatsoever; public discussion should not be allowed; and requests from Germany should be answered in the spirit of the Axis alliance.

The AGS diarist was disgusted with the waffling nature of that policy: "In the event, our attitude is entirely unclear and 'wait-and-see.' The Intelligence Bureau is very unhappy with it. As for the AGS deputy chief, Lieutenant General Tsukada, he does not necessarily incline toward the Axis; his tone of guidance has been centering on disposition of the China conflict."[46]

Arisue briefed his navy counterparts concerning the IJA drafts on 14 June. There was considerable discussion of Japan's obligations to the Axis, about which the navy was not exactly enthusiastic, but there was no official IJN thought of abandoning the Alliance, since it was not believed that Japan's geostrategic position would be damaged by the outbreak of a German-Soviet war. In this sense, Arisue's greatest apprehensions about the IJN's attitude were assuaged.[47]

All of the many conversations in Tokyo from early to mid-June 1941 would have become moot unless the Germans did invade the U.S.S.R., but the signals were still so mixed that net assessment could not yet reach a definitive prognostication. From Berlin, Ōshima reported on 17 June that Ribbentrop had told him Germany had no intention of conducting negotiations with the Russians. Soviet armor could be annihilated in a month or two of combat. Ōshima, as usual, pressed for a definite time, to which Ribbentrop replied: "That is really a delicate question and I lack the authority to reply, but if it is necessary for Japan to get ready, kindly do so within the next two weeks at the latest."[48]

From Moscow, however, at much the same time, naval attaché Yamaguchi Suteji's report of 16 June reflected the wishful thinking of the Russians. There might be great tension between the two countries and some border clashes, but there would be no all-out war. Even the hitherto blinkered Japanese Ambassador in Moscow, General Tatekawa, at the last minute began to question Molotov's complacency and sanguine attitude. Tatekawa shared with the American ambassador, on 20 June, his own prediction as to Japanese policy in the event of a German-Russian war: "I do not think we will come in right away. We will probably wait to see what happens and if the outcome is what I think it will be, we will pick up the pieces." In the strictest confidence, Tatekawa revealed that both the Germans and the Japanese had begun to evacuate Embassy personnel from Moscow. War would probably come by the end of June, and operations would last through July and August, at which time the Red Army would crumble.[49]

The Japanese high command and Matsuoka remained inundated by concerns about the Southern Problem and the economic and political pressures being exerted by the Americans and the British. Amid the distractions, word suddenly reached Tokyo on 22 June that the Reich had indeed invaded Russia. The Foreign Ministry first heard about the war from International News Service in late morning. Matsuoka was at the Kabuki Theater with Wang Ching-wei, the head of the puppet regime in Nanking, when an urgent cable arrived from Ōshima. Ribbentrop had sent for the Ambassador at 4 A.M., an hour and a half before the German broadcast of Hitler's announcement, and had asked him to inform the Japanese government that the Reich had been provoked into going to war.

Premier Konoe had been away in the Kyoto area in mid-June and, most recently, had been involved in hosting Wang since 17 June. Kido, in the bath when the news was phoned to him on 22 June, promptly advised the Emperor. Ambassador Ott conveyed the information officially to Matsuoka in the evening. The duty officer at Kwantung Army headquarters in Hsinking heard about it from the Manchukuo National Press Agency. Yamashita's mission, aboard the train eastward from Moscow, was passing through Sverdlovsk when word reached it.[50]

Weeks and months of tantalizing speculation were at last at an end. Colonel Tanemura noted in his diary entry for 22 June:

> The Japanese people, who were shocked by the fact that a nonaggression agreement had been signed between the Germans and the Russians [in 1939], are stirred by deep emotion at the news of war between them. What should be done by Japan, linked to one party by the Tripartite Alliance and to the other by the Neutrality Pact?[51]

The Crisis in Net Assessment: The German-Soviet Nexus, June 1941

The befuddlement of Japanese net assessment concerning the German-Soviet relationship till mid-1941 was no longer tolerable after the Nazis invaded the U.S.S.R. on 22 June. The German action caused consternation in Tokyo. A mortified Premier Konoe felt that Hitler had betrayed Japan a second time, the first having been when he suddenly negotiated the nonaggression treaty with the Russians in 1939. For a while Konoe even considered the idea of Japanese withdrawal from the Tripartite Pact, but events had progressed too far to make such a reversal practicable.[52]

It had clearly become necessary to face up to the northern problem once and for all. At the governmental level Matsuoka performed a surprising and arbitrary flip-flop, with an alacrity that is still the subject of much controversy. Immediately after learning of the German assault on Russia, the architect of the Japanese–Soviet neutrality agreement of April rushed to see the Emperor, without first clearing matters with the cabinet. He told the monarch that Japan should now attack the U.S.S.R. in concert with the Germans. This would mean putting off the drive southward for a while, though eventually Japan would have to engage not only the Russians but also the Americans and the British simultaneously.

Astonished by the Foreign Minister's unexpected prognosis, the Emperor directed him to confer immediately with Konoe. The monarch then conveyed the thrust of Matsuoka's report to Kido for relay to Konoe. Yet even after the Foreign Minister came to see Konoe later that day, the Premier admitted in his diary that he could not fathom Matsuoka's true meaning. The most charitable interpretation was that the Foreign Minister must have wanted to share with the Emperor his personal assessment of the worst-case scenario.

On 23 June Konoe was received by the Emperor, whom he sought to reassure with respect to Matsuoka's unsettling presentation. Still uncertain, however, whether the Foreign Minister was submitting only an estimate or was pressing for a specific but unauthorized course of action, Konoe decided to put off further high-level deliberations until he and Kido could clarify the situation. On the basis of further probing, they surmised that Matsuoka meant the following: (1) Japan should definitely attack the Soviet Union; (2) war against the United States should be avoided; (3) if the Americans entered the war against Germany, Japan would have to fight the United States too.

Those might be Matsuoka's own opinions but, as Prime Minister, Konoe would have to decide the policy of the government as a whole. He therefore conferred with the War and Navy Ministers and proceeded to convene five IGHQ–Government Liaison Conferences in a row, culminating in a climactic Imperial Conference on 2 July.[53]

At the high command level, the War Ministry staff was generally less enthusiastic about the coming of the Russo-German struggle than was the AGS, whose diarist wrote as follows on 22 June: "Has Hitler overestimated Germany's national strength? If not, Germany is certain to win, in which case, 'Go ahead and do so!'" Asked later for his opinion of a possible negative impact of the Soviet-German war on Japan, Operations Bureau chief Tanaka replied in roundabout fashion:

> There is no simple answer. For a fact, the hostilities were bound to improve our defensive posture in the north, so I did think it would help our operations in the south. One had to assess the war in global terms, however, and on that count there was some uncertainty about the prospects for German success. The AGS Soviet Intelligence shop was particularly uncertain, in contrast to the views of AGS German Intelligence. In general, though, there was much expectation of a German victory; so, viewing matters from the larger standpoint, I felt that the developments were not necessarily disadvantageous for Japan.[54]

Typical of the more cautious AGS officers were Lieutenant Colonel Kumon Aribumi and Lieutenant Colonel Hayashi Saburō. Kumon, an air staff officer in the Operations Section, drew the attention of his sanguine colleagues when he reacted strongly to news of the German invasion. "Hitler has made a grievous error," he warned.

One of the AGS Soviet Intelligence officers to whom General Tanaka had alluded was Hayashi, an expert on the U.S.S.R. Originally, like the Operations staff, Hayashi had not expected the Reich to strike, out of concern for a two-front war. The most the Germans might do would be to conduct a feint designed to shift attention away from the main landing operations against England. But when Intelligence Bureau chief Okamoto ordered Soviet Section chief Isomura to come up with an estimate of the situation, it was Hayashi who prepared the draft. Two central questions concerned Hayashi: Had the German attack achieved surprise? Would the war be of long or short duration?

> I judged that the Germans did achieve surprise [Hayashi recollects], and I respected them highly for it. If the Germans did not win before winter set in, the Russians would revive, since space was their strength. Those who judged that the U.S.S.R. would not be defeated were low-ranking officers such as me. Bureau chief Okamoto tended to accept the Germans' statements because of his prior service as military attaché in the Reich. As a result, that tendency spread throughout the entire 2d Bureau.[55]

In the War Ministry, Military Affairs Section chief Satō Kenryō was displeased with the Germans for having attacked the Soviet Union without consulting Japan beforehand:

> I was concerned lest the Germans' eastern invasion become a carbon copy of Napoleon's campaign or of our experience in China, for I did not expect the U.S.S.R. to be defeated easily. Yet even if the Russians went down with little difficulty, I felt that the results would be bad for Japan, since England and America would still be unscathed. Army Affairs Section chief Sanada also said that Hitler had done an unwise thing.[56]

Those views were echoed by other War Ministry officers. Lieutenant Colonel Ishii, senior staff officer in Military Affairs, told his superior, Major General Mutō:

> The German forces may break through the Russians at first and push deeply to the east. But the Soviet territory is vast, the raw materials are plentiful, and the population is numerous—the same features embodied in the slogans of the resistance front in China. In addition, the political system under the one-party dictatorship of the Communist Party has been ensconced quite strongly. The U.S.S.R. will not give up easily, and I predict that a situation resembling the [protracted] China Incident will result.

To this, Mutō replied, "I agree with you completely. It would be disastrous if anybody was so optimistic as to think that the Soviet Union will collapse." None of Ishii's colleagues disagreed.[57]

In Moscow, however, Ambassador Tatekawa was very negative about the prospects for the Russians' survival. "Speaking as a military man," Tatekawa said to the American ambassador, "the Red Army . . . might make a creditable showing for a brief period of time but . . . when the break came it would be largely a question of the Germans collecting hundreds of thousands of prisoners." The Japanese envoy expected chaos and perhaps mob rule in Moscow; the Soviet government leadership would probably run away.[58]

Before Military Affairs Bureau chief Mutō and Operations chief Tanaka got together to coordinate their views, they received a detailed briefing by Intelligence chief Okamoto on 22 June. It soon became apparent that the Intelligence Bureau was of the opinion the Germans would knock out the Russians within a few months. If the Soviet forces had indeed been taken by surprise, then the U.S.S.R. as a whole was in grave danger; yet if the Russians managed to conduct retrograde operations, a prolonged war might well result. Okamoto backed away from espousing the latter hypothesis, however, by wondering whether it was really probable. Continuing to hedge his bets, the Intelligence chief balanced what he called the great likelihood that the hostilities would be quickly finished operationally against the problem that in overall terms the prospects were difficult to assess.

Okamoto then engaged in an interesting effort at quantification. Assuming that the war could not last more than two or three months and that in the process the Russians would have lost Leningrad, Moscow, Kharkov, the Donets Basin, and Baku, Japanese Intelligence estimated Soviet losses of national infrastructure as follows: electric power, 60 percent; iron ore, 50 percent; coal, 60 percent; oil, 75 percent; grain, 29 percent; and population, 75 percent.[59]

Armed with these rosy projections, Mutō and Tanaka agreed that the Japanese army's strategic thinking to date was sound. In this frame of mind, they participated in a four-hour meeting of IJA and IJN bureau chiefs in the afternoon of 23 June, with War Guidance chief Colonel Arisue and his navy counterpart, Captain Ono, in attendance too. According to Tanaka, though the navy voiced no particular dissent regarding the fundamental notion of "facing in two directions," it did not agree on details of implementation. The navy was worried that there would be a threat to its cherished strategy of advance to the south and defense in the north—a stance which implied "the navy first, the army second." Tanaka and his colleagues felt that the navy had some distrust of the army's objectives. The navy also struck the army chiefs as fuzzy in its own intentions, and devoid of firm resolve to commit itself to fight. As for the continental theater, the navy wanted to intensify the pressure on China by severing the land routes the Nationalists were using to bring in aid, but the army clung successfully to its insistence that the battle lines there not be expanded.

Tanaka was disappointed with the navy's stand. His skepticism regarding its alleged lack of true resolve went so far as to surmise that the navy was merely concerned with justifying its quest for national funding and resources needed to build up its own strength. Tanaka feared that Japan would lose a great opportunity to solve the northern problem if the army's attention was diverted southward by the "wishy-washy" navy. "I demanded that we use force in the north," Tanaka remembers, "but the navy did everything it could to prevent this." The army staff could not escape the impression that, no matter what the navy said openly, its planners were interested only in the south and nurtured the covert intention of checking the army from ever using force in the north. In the end, as Tanaka feared, the two services had to compromise on the vague principle of the "ripe persimmon."[60]

The metaphor about persimmons was much in vogue in Tokyo at the time, though interpretations of the exact meaning varied widely. An impatient person might knock persimmons off the tree with a pole when the fruit started to ripen. Others might say that persimmons were ripe only if they fell when the tree was shaken. Still others meant that persimmons should be picked off the ground only after they had fallen of their own weight.[61]

Matsuoka was not the only high-ranking official who wanted to knock persimmons off the tree. The more aggressive AGS staff officers were more than willing to use a pole against the ripening fruit. In the War Ministry, where there was a preference to wait for the persimmons to fall and to focus attention on the China conflict instead, stronger opinions also existed. A budget officer in the Army Affairs Section, Matsushita Yūzō, has said: "I thought the German–Soviet war would be a short one. I had the impression that Germany would be able to prevail. A number of us felt that Japan should not 'miss the bus' [another favorite phrase of the time] and ought to push north. . . . Regardless of our individual predictions, however, we were all devoted to the ripe-persimmon principle."[62]

Naturally, Konoe wanted to know what the military experts thought, especially after Matsuoka made his brazen foray to the Imperial Palace. Retired Lieutenant General Suzuki Tei'ichi, the head of the Cabinet Planning Board and an adherent of the hawkish old anti-Communist Imperial Way Faction (Kōdō-ha) within the army, had reputedly recommended the northern thrust to the Foreign Minister. To sound out the views of another Kōdō-ha confidant, retired Lieutenant General Obata Toshishirō, Premier Konoe sent his Chief Cabinet Secretary, Tomita. The latter reported Obata's unhesitant view that Germany would have the U.S.S.R. beaten by the end of September 1941. An unconvinced Konoe wondered if such an estimate was not much too optimistic, though General Okamoto's Intelligence briefing was even more positive: Hostilities would be over by the end of August.[63]

The navy's attitude was another matter. Naval Intelligence spoke of the advisability for Japan to maintain "benign neutrality" toward Germany for the time being while making the necessary preparations to respond quickly to changes in the situation. With specific reference to the Nazi–Soviet war, IJN Intelligence had a large number of points to make. First, the strategic timing for Germany's assault made good sense, for the Russians had been building up and reorganizing their military strength since only the autumn of 1940 and were at a very weak juncture at the moment. There were then two prospects for the campaign: If matters went well for the Germans (as was probable), the U.S.S.R. would be split, probably along the Volga River line, and would be neutralized for a while. Stalin's government might collapse, giving rise to a partisan resistance movement. On the other hand, the Germans might be quite successful militarily, but the Russians might be able to hold out too, maintaining the Stalin regime (or at least an anti-German structure), confronting the Germans far inland, and waging protracted hostilities.

As for the Soviet Far East, IJN Intelligence thought that the Russians would make every effort to transfer forces westward, especially air force units. Consequently, the U.S.S.R. would retain only minimum strength in Siberia, but what was left would be considerable. In particular, Soviet naval strength would not diminish. Depending upon the situation on the European front, the Russian Far East might break away from the Soviet Union and declare its independence. The military power of such a separate entity would be much weakened, however, because of Siberia's limited capability for self-sufficiency and small population, numbering only 2 million. To neutralize such a development, the U.S.S.R. could be expected to pursue a policy of appeasement toward Japan and cut aid to Chiang Kai-shek. The Japanese navy itself had no real interest in Siberia, though Japan might go so far as to contemplate acquiring northern Sakhalin, Kamchatka, and the Maritime Province.

Finally, the United States and England, much relieved by the German invasion of Russia, would make every effort to assist the U.S.S.R. logistically, militarily, and diplomatically. Of greatest immediate concern to the Anglo-Saxon "pseudo-alliance" was the stance of Japan, which they very much hoped would become enmeshed in war against the Soviet Union. But, in view of the diminished Japanese pressure to the north, the Americans and British were feeling greater pressure in the south and might pursue a reactive policy there. A prolonged German–Soviet war was what the Anglo-Saxon countries desired most, for they deemed that time was working in their favor.

It can be seen from the preceding assessment that, with respect to the larger picture, though not the matter of harvesting the persimmons, IJA and IJN prognostication was not particularly dissimilar. There can be no doubt that Army Intelligence, with its far superior capabilities of collection within the U.S.S.R., fed documentation and opinions to the navy and greatly influenced IJN analyses of the situation. Captain Ishikawa has summed up the navy's thinking at the time aptly:

> The idea of solving the Northern Problem was not at all on the minds of the Naval High Command. I told Matsuoka that I disagreed with his notion. We in the Navy had our hands full, even coping with the submarines based at Vladivostok. If we attacked northward, the United States would surely enter the war, leaving us helpless. I explained that we would end up in a situation where we would have to give up without a fight.[64]

Given the above outlook, the most that the navy might be expected to countenance would be the picking up of ripe persimmons already littering the ground in Siberia. Even Tsuji Masanobu, a Kwantung Army staff member and *enfant terrible* at Nomonhan in 1939, now an AGS Operations officer, was saying that Hitler had launched his attack on the U.S.S.R. too late. The snows would begin in European Russia in late October, by which time the ultimate German military objectives could not have been achieved. Only the "weaker-minded" members of the AGS were keen to follow the lead of those who favored a Japanese attack on the Soviet Union now: "Many advocates of the northern movement insisted on striking at the Soviet, not because they relied on the superior efficiency of their armies, but because they thought, according to the Hitler godhead, that at any moment Stalin would die mad." Tsuji added: "Should we side with Germany just because of Hitler's and Ribbentrop's bluster?"[65]

Weighing what he had learned from his sources in both the army and the navy, Konoe leaned in the direction of a short-term, unsatisfying wait-and-see policy, regardless of the well-known preferences of Matsuoka and the northern hawks. The latter had not at all abandoned hope of fighting Russia in 1941. When a certain Kwantung Army staff officer visited Tokyo and expressed views opposing a war with the Soviet Union, Operations Bureau chief Tanaka and Personnel Bureau chief Tominaga railed fiercely at him.[66]

The Final Week of Net Assessment in Japan

Very much on the minds of the Japanese leadership as soon as war broke out between the Nazis and the Russians was the question of what to tell friends and foes about Japan's future policy toward the belligerents. By 24 June the net assessment people decided that the Axis Powers should be notified that Japan would remain faithful to the terms of the Tripartite Pact regardless of the language of the Soviet–Japanese

Neutrality Agreement. There would be no mention of the possible use of force by Japan, and thus no revelation of geographical emphasis, either north or south.

On 25 June the 32d Government–IGHQ Liaison Conference was held, attended by Konoe, Matsuoka, Cabinet Secretary Tomita, and the following civilian officials and senior military officers: Hiranuma (Home Affairs), Tōjō (War), Oikawa (Navy), Sugiyama (AGS), Nagano (NGS), Mutō (Military Affairs), and Oka (Naval Affairs). AGS Deputy Tsukada and NGS Deputy Kondō also were present, by special invitation. At this meeting the military pressed Matsuoka to explain what he had said to the Soviet Ambassador in particular and what the latter's reaction had been. "I suppose he may have thought, from what he told me," replied the Foreign Minister, "that Japan's stance seemed calm but not particularly clear-cut." Asked whether the Russian envoy may have deduced that Japan intended to be loyal to the Axis but disloyal to the Neutrality Pact, Matsuoka remarked that he did not think his words had exerted such a great effect. Despite Matsuoka's rationale, AGS Deputy Tsukada drew the conclusion that the Soviet Ambassador must have interpreted the Foreign Minister's evasive wording to mean the Neutrality Pact was as good as dead.

As for German Ambassador Ott, Matsuoka stated that he had not spoken officially to him. The Foreign Minister wanted a definitive national policy to be determined soon, however, for Ott was talking a lot about the westward movement of Soviet Far Eastern forces. Tōjō and Tsukada discounted the Nazi Ambassador's comments. While reports of Russian troop transfers undoubtedly exerted a great effect on the Germans, it was only natural that Japan should not be particularly exercised. Indeed, it was not advisable to pay heed to everything the Germans were saying.

Admiral Oikawa then voiced the unsolicited opinion of the navy, obviously directed to Matsuoka, regarding future Japanese diplomatic efforts:

> The past is the past, but now, when international relations are at such a very sensitive stage, you should not speak about the far-off future without consulting the High Command. The Navy is confident in the event of war against the United States and England, but not if the U.S.S.R. is added to the lineup. If America teamed up with the Russians and was able to set up naval and air bases, radio observation posts, etc., in the Soviet Far Eastern territory; and if the Russian submarines stationed at Vladivostok were turned over to the United States—such developments would render our naval operations very difficult.

In what amounted to a reprimand, Oikawa then told Matsuoka not to talk about striking the Soviet Union as well as heading south: "The Navy does not want the U.S.S.R. riled up."

Matsuoka asked Oikawa why the navy was opposed to fighting the Russians since it said it was not fearful of a war against America and England. The question must have struck the admiral as sophomoric; wouldn't war with Russia mean the increase of major enemies from two to three? "Anyhow," Oikawa grumbled, "don't talk too much about the future." Matsuoka retorted that that was not his style, but that the discussion itself pointed up the urgent need for the conferees to nail down the basic principles of national policy.

Having ironed out and approved the agenda item calling for acceleration of the advance to the south (specifically Indochina), the conference examined the text of the draft document that had been the product of army and navy discussion for weeks—the important but rather inconclusive "Outline of National Policy in Terms of the Changes in the Situation." Sugiyama reviewed the main points, with which Matsuoka seemed to be in basic agreement although he wanted a more decisive stance. Since neither the army nor the navy was ready for war, their service chiefs voiced a number of uncertainties involving China, the north, and the south. With respect to the Russians, the chiefs warned of the necessity to keep an eye on the transfer of Soviet forces from Siberia to Europe and on the survivability of Stalin's government. In particular, the chiefs warned against engaging the U.S.S.R. prematurely, lest it bring about American entry into the hostilities.

Matsuoka was not convinced that the United States would intervene in the event of a Japanese attack on the Soviet Union. He pointed out another consideration: When Germany knocked out the U.S.S.R., Japan could not very well pluck the persimmons without having done a thing in return. It was necessary either to shed blood or to engage in diplomacy, preferably the former. What exactly would Japan do after the Soviet Union had been finished off by the Nazis? The Germans must be wondering too. Shouldn't Japan at least undertake a diversion?

The service ministers retorted that there were a variety of ways to create a diversion. The very fact that Japan stood firm could be regarded as one such move. Failing to be mollified by this response, which was not what he wanted to hear, Matsuoka called for a quick decision regarding Japan's course of action. This exhortation evoked a demand by an unidentified conferee that, in any case, nothing hasty be done.

Following a discussion that had lasted for two hours, the liaison meeting ended without agreement as to the national policy draft under review. A one-hour Cabinet conference had already been scheduled to examine the southern-advance document thrashed out that day at the liaison meeting (exclusive of high command matters). Thereupon the Premier and the two chiefs of staff would report directly to the Emperor. Consideration of the national policy that needed to be adopted in terms of the new international situation was put off until 10 A.M. next day.[67]

The participants in the 33d Government–IGHQ Liaison Conference were the same as those of the 32d, but they came no closer to resolving the question of how to respond to the Soviet–German war. First, AGS Deputy Tsukada read aloud the army–navy draft document; next, AGS chief Sugiyama explained the text, working from a background paper that had been prepared for an eventual Imperial audience and had been signed by Konoe and both chiefs of staff. Matsuoka then conducted what might be called a cross-examination. The Foreign Minister had no objection, he said, to the pursuit of efforts to settle the China conflict or to the establishment of a basis for the self-sufficiency and self-defense of the country. Nevertheless, he could not understand what was meant about taking steps to move to the south or the language about solving the northern problem.

Sugiyama knew what Matsuoka was getting at—the unspecified relative importance of the south versus the north. "There is no difference in emphasis," the AGS chief asserted. "Matters will be decided on the basis of changes in the situation." Did this mean, Matsuoka wondered, that the southern advance would not be undertaken soon? Nonplussed, NGS chief Nagano called on NGS Deputy Kondō to bail him out. Kondō whispered to Nagano that it was the south that took precedence (by which he really meant the thrust into southern Vietnam).

The Foreign Minister was disturbed (or elated?) by this evidence of a lack of unity in the views of the army and navy. AGS Deputy Tsukada tried to plug the gap by "speaking more clearly":

> There is no difference in weight between the South and the North. The sequence and the method depend on the circumstances. It is not possible to do both at the same time, however. We simply cannot make a decision now whether to go North or South.

After some further discussion of matters involving China, Matsuoka returned to his favorite subject: the meaning of Japan's "deciding independently" whether or not to fight Russia. A lengthy debate ensued between the Foreign Minister and Lieutenant General Tsukada about the need to consult with Germany concerning the use of force. Tsukada, abetted by Tōjō and Sugiyama, made the point that Germany had gone ahead and done what it wanted to do arbitrarily. The military requirements for speed and secrecy dictated that Japan do what it thought best too.

When Matsuoka spoke of the advisability of faithfulness to the spirit of the alliance with Germany, Tsukada replied that matters of high policy must be separated from those involving the prerogatives of high command. Using military force, after all, was a matter of national victory or defeat. The Foreign Minister attempted a new tack: What did the military mean when it spoke of circumstances *not* developing "extremely favorably" for Japan? Tsukada's response was a model of the military net assessor's patronizing of a presumably ill-informed civilian:

> We would proceed if we deemed the situation to be very advantageous; we would not proceed if we did not think it was very favorable. That is why we used the wording "extremely favorable."

Matsuoka did not desist. What was meant by the military's wording about insuring that there must be "no great obstacles" to the maintenance of the country's basic stance vis-à-vis the South? Tsukada supplied a short explanation no less patronizing than his earlier lecture:

> "Great" means "great." Small obstacles are to be expected. The High Command lacks optimal strength. Whether that will prove to be a "great obstacle" cannot be determined until the time comes.

Following a short statement by Nagano, who sought to reconcile the views of Tsukada and Matsuoka on several counts, the Foreign Minister asserted that, though he still entertained a number of reservations, he basically agreed with the army–navy draft. This encouraged Bureau chief Mutō to leap into the fray with the suggestion that Matsuoka signify his concurrence in writing. The Foreign Minister bluntly refused to do so. On this note, the meeting ended, still with no decision as to the document titled "Outline of National Policy in Terms of the Changes in the Situation."[68]

At 1 P.M. on 27 June the 34th Government–IGHQ Liaison Conference was convened, again with the same cast of characters, to endeavor to reach a decision on national policy. Matsuoka proceeded to offer a long disquisition on his views of the world scene from the standpoint of diplomatic strategy, and he tried once more to get the armed forces to reconsider their wait-and-see attitude. Basically, he wanted Japan to resolve right away to intervene in the German-Soviet war, attacking northward first and then heading south, while disposing of the China conflict in the meantime. As he had noted earlier, Matsuoka stressed, he was in general agreement with the army-navy draft, but he wanted an immediate decision on the question of fighting the Soviet Union. All the reports from Ōshima in Berlin pointed to the fact that the Germans would defeat the Russians soon, and also would end the war with England by autumn or at least by year's end. Japan should therefore not tarry too long.

It was at this meeting that Matsuoka claimed he had been estimating the chances of a German-Soviet war at 50–50. (Kido's diary, however, says the Foreign Minister had put the probability of hostilities at 40 percent.) In any case, Matsuoka spoke of his efforts to devise plans that combined diplomacy and operations. Judging that there was no hope of dealing directly with the Chungking regime to achieve a far-reaching peace settlement, he had sought to contain China from all sides and had gone so far as to conclude the Neutrality Pact with the U.S.S.R. Although the Germans' assistance had not been requested, Matsuoka asserted that he had been able to join hands with them. The only remaining stumbling block to the Foreign Minister's grand design was the United States.

Matsuoka now warmed to his incessant theme of fighting Russia. While Japan could pursue a wait-and-see policy in the short term, it would be necessary to face up to the difficult situation with great resolve, sooner or later. If it was thought that the German-Soviet fighting would end shortly, Japan could not afford to stay out, going neither north nor south; it should clearly opt to strike north. To talk about solving the Northern Problem only after Germany had knocked out the Soviet Union would be meaningless from the standpoint of diplomacy.

If Japan took action to engage the Russians quickly, Matsuoka insisted, the United States would not intervene. For one thing, the Americans could not assist the U.S.S.R. in point of fact; for another, the United States customarily disliked Russia. In case Japan did attack the U.S.S.R., Matsuoka expressed confidence that he could hold off the Americans by diplomatic means for three or four months. Deferring a decision, as IGHQ proposed, would not help. Such a course would only allow the United States and Britain time to team up with the Soviet Union and surround Japan. Though Matsuoka admitted there might be some flaws in his assessment, he insisted that the main thing was to strike north before thrusting south, for (as an old Japanese proverb put it) "if you do not enter the tiger's den, you cannot seize the tiger's cub."

NGS chief Nagano reverted to the point about three enemy powers ganging up on Japan. During the discussion on the preceding day, he had admittedly mentioned the possibility of America's intervening in the German–Soviet war. What he had meant to say was that he wanted Matsuoka to conduct diplomacy designed to prevent the Americans from entering, and thus to avoid a situation whereby Japan would have to fight three countries at the same time. "Fine," said the Foreign Minister.

War Minister Tōjō then asked Matsuoka to address the connections with China. The Foreign Minister admitted that, until the end of 1940, he had been thinking that Japan should head south before striking north. In that way, the China problem might have been disposed of effectively—an approach that no longer seemed viable. Now Matsuoka had come round to the view that the best way to exert pressure on Chiang Kai-shek was to push north, to invade Russia as far as Irkutsk. Even if the Japanese got only halfway there, it might be enough to force all-out peace with China.

Thereupon Tōjō asked a very logical followup question—whether Matsuoka meant that Japan should go north even if the conflict in China would have to be abandoned. The Foreign Minister replied, without particular vehemence, that that was indeed the better course, even if Japan had to give up on China "to a certain degree." Not unexpectedly, the War Minister demurred; the China incident had to be pursued to the end.

At this point, Navy Minister Oikawa injected a confusing assessment that must have been intended to appease the different parties: The world war could be expected to drag on for a decade, during which time the China conflict would "evaporate" (presumably with a Japanese victory). In the meantime—a statement not further defined by Oikawa —Japan could engage Russia.

These remarks induced Matsuoka to reaffirm his devotion to "moral diplomacy." He would not hear of quitting the Tripartite Pact, though he had no compunctions about suspending the Neutrality Agreement with Russia. There was also a pragmatic advantage for Japan to drive against the U.S.S.R. now: At this juncture the Germans had not yet won the war. In other words, the Japanese possessed important leverage that might be lost later.

The Minister of Home Affairs, Hiranuma, asked Matsuoka to think carefully about the problems confronting Japan. Had the Foreign

Minister really meant to say that, as a matter of national policy, Japan should attack the U.S.S.R. immediately? Matsuoka replied in the affirmative. Thereupon Hiranuma went on to observe that speed was not the only prerequisite; so was excellent preparation. Indeed, implementing national policy and using force of arms both demanded preparation, didn't they? Matsuoka did not respond directly. The main concerns, he insisted, were to reach a decision to head north first and to forewarn Germany.

The recurring subject of notifying the Germans agitated General Sugiyama. While morality and honor were admirable elements of diplomacy, the army faced problems that militated against exclusive reliance on righteousness at a time when large forces were deployed in China. Though the high command would certainly make preparations, it was impossible at this point to decide whether or not to strike. It would take 40–50 days for the Kwantung Army alone to get ready. Additional time would be needed to convert to an overall wartime footing and to prepare to assume the offensive. By that point, the outcome of the German–Soviet hostilities ought to have become clearer. If the situation seemed very favorable, then and only then would Japan take action.

This was not good enough for Matsuoka, who objected to the terminology "very favorable" and wanted the military to opt for an outright attack on the Soviet Union. To this, Sugiyama bluntly replied, "No." Once more the navy, in the person of Nagano, tried to bridge the gap by assuring the Foreign Minister that the high command would consider the "rather big problem" he was raising. Matsuoka, in turn, repeated his earlier assertion that he had no objections to the IGHQ draft in general, but he wanted to know if his opinion would be accepted or not. Sugiyama offered to mention diplomacy in the document. Though Matsuoka willingly accepted the addition, he was pessimistic about the prospects for the negotiations with the United States. Hiranuma closed out the day's proceedings with a request that the Tripartite Alliance be regarded as the basis for policy insofar as Germany was concerned, an idea that continued to be dear to Matsuoka's heart.

In reviewing the discussion of 27 June, the AGS diarist noted that the army utterly disagreed with the Foreign Minister's argument. While it could sympathize with Matsuoka's feelings, the army could not agree with the notion of going to war right away and clung to its old concept of the "favorable opportunity." Indeed, the military was impaled on the horns of a dilemma: To start preparations only after a decision was made would preclude the chances of fighting successfully; but if no decision was made at all, full-scale preparations would be impossible. The truth, the diarist admitted, was that the army simply lacked the confidence to reach the immediate, definitive decision Matsuoka was demanding.[69]

The sequential workings of the day-to-day Japanese net assessment process are revealed by the activities that immediately followed the Liaison Conference of 27 June. At 6:30 P.M. on the same day, an IJA bureau chiefs' conference was held at the War Minister's official residence. The agenda centered on the best way to deal with Matsuoka's stubborn opinions. At the core of the chiefs' discussion was reconciliation of the need to reach a definitive decision to use force. It is known that Mutō suggested wording that would authorize secret armed preparations against the Russians. The sources, however, do not agree on whether such action was to be accompanied by a decision to use force immediately, or indeed whether the conferees were opposed to both ideas: preparations plus resolve to fight. In any case, Naval Affairs Bureau chief Oka did not go along with Mutō's notion, and Tanaka apparently had some other reservations at first.

One of the things that was bothering Tanaka, he later explained, was the fact that, although preparations surely had to get started right away, it was impossible at the moment to persuade the navy to resolve on war. To Tanaka it seemed that time would work in favor of striking north—once the persimmon grew ripe. Meanwhile, he nourished the covert intention of building up to fight the Russians—the old desire of the Japanese army, exploiting the current opportunity "whether or not we actually did go north."

Ultimately, the bureau chiefs agreed to suggest proceeding with the agreed-upon plans to establish bases in the south, with a view to reining in the United States and England, but also reinforcing preparations against the Russians and thus checking them too. Notification to the Germans about the specific method and the exact time that Japan intended to dispose of the Northern Problem would be determined later. These recommendations were to be submitted to the next IGHQ-Government Liaison Conference, scheduled for the following day.[70]

First, on the morning of 28 June, the Military Affairs and Naval Affairs Bureau chiefs discussed with Matsuoka and his Vice Minister, Ōhashi, the various matters bearing on diplomacy discussed by the bureau chiefs the preceding evening. Basic agreement on addenda was reached, though the Foreign Minister retained some reservations.

In the afternoon of the 28th, the scheduled IGHQ–Government Liaison Conference was convened, with the same participation as on previous days. Matsuoka had still another opportunity to voice the same old concerns, centering especially on his fear that a drive to the south would involve Japan not only in distracting hostilities against the United States and England but also against Japan's priority foe, Russia, to boot. Such an unselective course, he argued, was like playing with fire. Though the time was not quite ripe to begin actual operations against the Soviet Union alone, the Foreign Minister remained convinced that the decision to do so in due course had to be made right now. Since Germany had to be told sooner or later, why should Japan wait to be asked?

Already, Admiral Nagano had informed General Sugiyama privately that the navy was utterly opposed to telling the Germans about Japanese intent to attack Russia. Consequently neither the IJA nor the IJN leaders said a word when Matsuoka was exhorting them to make up their minds to engage the U.S.S.R. once and for all and to alert Germany accordingly. Exasperated by the high command's silence, the Foreign Minister finally asked Sugiyama for his direct opinion. The army chief of staff did not budge from his oft-expressed insistence that Germany could not very well be told about a decision that was not yet clear to the Japanese military themselves. Indeed, it would be strange if premature notice was given to Berlin but then things did not turn out as desired. To this, Nagano spoke up that the navy was in full agreement with Sugiyama's stand.

After a week of haggling and indecision, the net assessors and the decision-makers had basically reached a dead end. Unable to allay every concern, they finally declared their adoption of the "Outline of National Policy in Terms of the Changes in the Situation." There would be another Liaison Conference on 30 June, at which time the conferees were to decide upon the text of a government communiqué and of a notification to be sent to the Germans. The following morning, on 1 July, the full Cabinet would discuss the Outline. After that, a rubber-stamp Imperial Conference would be convened, to which the Finance Minister and the heads of the Privy Council and the Planning Board would be invited. Till then, the Japanese diplomats abroad would be told nothing about the substance of the high-level deliberations in Tokyo.

Two noteworthy features had characterized the whole convoluted process: Never had there been so many Government–IGHQ Liaison Conferences in succession; and the Prime Minister, Konoe, apparently spoke not a word throughout the discussions that surged around him.[71]

Sheer opportunism, fashioned by a consensus of the lowest common denominator, had won out over the preferences of either the hawks or the doves.

CONCLUSIONS

The Japanese system of net assessment in the period prior to the attack on Pearl Harbor in 1941 was relatively unsophisticated, parochial, fragmented, adamantine, spasmodic, and often vague or waffling to boot. Many reasons contributed to this unsatisfactory state of affairs, beginning with the independence of the supreme command prerogative and the nature of the monarch, who reigned but did not rule. Other factors were the tradition of military supremacy over civil rule, a consensual approach to decision-making, ideological inflexibility, psychological hangups at the national level, and idiosyncratic educational patterns nurturing leadership. To the cultural and historical differences from Western practice must be added problems stemming from an often nonspecific, ideographically couched language of expression and circumlocutory modes of communication.

Specifically, in the crisis year of 1941 there was no single, full-blown decision for war or peace, but instead a series of interlinked sequential decisions. One particular option originally transcended all others in importance—the so-called Go-North Option, which has never received the attention it deserves for the simple reason that, although very seriously considered at the time, as we have seen, it was a choice that was ultimately not adopted, a "road not taken" (to borrow the imagery of Robert Frost). Finally, for all its faults, preconceptions, and weaknesses, Japanese net assessment was nonetheless rationally driven and deliberate.

Notes

1. Net Assessment on the Eve of World War II

1. Sun Tzu, *The Art of War,* trans. Samuel B. Griffith II, rev. ed. (New York and London, 1963), p. 71.

2. The implications of "chaos theory" for the social sciences are beginning to emerge. It is interesting to note that economists have initially proved receptive to this line of mathematical inquiry, while political scientists have largely ignored its implications, perhaps because most economists have *solid* mathematical training. The same cannot be said for most political scientists.

3. Astonishingly, with all the ink spilt over the Munich crisis, only one author in English has attempted to calculate the actual correlation of forces. See Williamson Murray, *The Change in the European Balance of Power, 1938-1939* (Princeton, NJ; 1984).

4. For an egregious example of the confusion that can result from reading too many documents on one side of the balance, see Robert J. Young, *In Command of France: French Foreign Policy and Military Planning, 1933-1940* (Cambridge, MA, 1978). Young attempts to rehabilitate the reputations of General Maurice Gamelin and the French high command by placing most of the blame for the 1940 disaster on the shoulders of civilian leaders.

5. Again the Munich crisis provides examples. On the side of those who have argued that Britain and France could easily have won a war against Germany in 1938, see the analysis in Telford Taylor, *Sword and Swastika* (Chicago, 1969), p. 223. For an analysis of how Chamberlain "saved" Britain at Munich that posits a chain of events running in a pattern similar to those of the 1939 conflict and then argues that Fighter Command could not have defended the British Isles against the Luftwaffe in summer 1939, see Keith Eubank, *Munich* (Norman, OK, 1963).

6. With the exceptions of MacGregor Knox, Paul Kennedy, Holger Herwig, and John Erickson, the essays in Ernest R. May (ed.), *Knowing One's Enemies: Intelligence*

Assessment Before the Two World Wars (Princeton, NJ, 1984), rarely move beyond national intelligence organizations to the process of national net assessment.

7. In terms of the present-day analysis of intelligence organizations it is worth noting that the Defense Intelligence Agency by law cannot study "blue" forces but instead only calculates "red" strength. Consequently it is incapable of estimating the Soviet "correlation of forces"; obviously it cannot engage in any coherent effort at net assessment.

8. Paul M. Kennedy, "Great Britain Before 1914," in May, *Knowing One's Enemies*, p. 194.

9. Williamson Murray and Barry Watts, "Net Assessment," a memorandum for Dr. Andrew Marshall, Director of Net Assessment, Office of the Secretary of Defense, 1987.

10. Kenneth Macksey, *Tank Warfare* (New York, 1981), pp. 70–107; Field Marshal Lord Carver, *The Apostles of Mobility: The Theory and Practice of Armoured Warfare* (New York, 1979), pp. 31–54.

11. Ernest R. May, "Capabilities and Proclivities," in May, *Knowing One's Enemies*, pp. 503–42.

12. For our analysis of net assessment in the 1930s, we have relied principally on the essays in this study but also upon our earlier edited work: Allan R. Millett and Williamson Murray (eds.), *Military Effectiveness*, 3 vols. (London and Boston, 1988). The observations on current organization theory are drawn from Paul S. Goodman, Johannes M. Pennings, and associates, *New Perspectives on Organizational Effectiveness* (San Francisco and London, 1977), and Jay M. Shafritz and Philip H. Whitbeck (eds. and comps.), *Classics of Organization Theory* (Oak Park, IL, 1978).

13. In addition to our own judgments, we have profited by a memorandum, "Conclusions and Reflections," drafted by one of our authors, Professor Paul Kennedy of Yale University, in 1988.

2. British "Net Assessment" and the Coming of the Second World War

1. For details of the British system, see John Ehrman, *Cabinet Government and War, 1890–1940* (Cambridge, UK, 1958); N. H. Gibbs, *Grand Strategy*, vol. 1, *Rearmament Policy* (London, 1976), ch. 20; Franklyn A. Johnson, *Defense by Committee: The British Committee of Imperial Defence, 1885–1959* (London, 1960).

2. Ronald Robinson and John Gallagher, with Alice Denny, *Africa and the Victorians: The Official Mind of Imperialism* (London, 1961), pp. 19–20 and *passim*.

3. This refers to my critique in Paul Kennedy, *The Realities Behind Diplomacy: Background Influences on British External Policy, 1865–1980* (London, 1981), pp. 59–65, 236–57.

4. Apart from Ehrman, *Cabinet Government*, see Donald C. Gordon, *The Dominion Partnership in Imperial Defence, 1870–1914* (Baltimore, 1965).

5. The literature on this point is summarized in Kennedy, *Realities Behind Diplomacy*, chs. 1 and 2, and Aaron Friedberg, *The Weary Titan* (Princeton, NJ, 1989).

6. Ehrman, *Cabinet Government and War*, traces these developments, as does Gibbs, *Grand Strategy*, vol. 1, ch. 20.

7. Correlli Barnett, *The Collapse of British Power* (London and New York, 1972), provides a good account of these procedures. There is also a useful summary in

Williamson Murray, *The Change in the European Balance of Power, 1938-1939* (Princeton, NJ, 1984), ch. 2.

8. The Secret Intelligence Service's flow of information, by contrast, was much more uneven. See Francis H. Hinsley *et al., British Intelligence in the Second World War,* vol. 1 (London, 1979), chs. 1 and 2.

9. See Public Record Office, London (hereafter, PRO), War Office (hereafter, WO) 106/5422, "Visit to German Tank Corps by Military Attaché Berlin" (1938); note by Captain Vivian, "Difficulties Encountered by the Naval Attaché in Tokyo in Visits to Naval and Industrial Establishments," 1936, cited in Wesley K. Wark, "In Search of a Suitable Japan: British Naval Intelligence in the Pacific Before the Second World War," *Intelligence and National Security,* 1, no. 2 (May 1986): 189-211.

10. Wesley K. Wark, "Three Military Attachés at Berlin in the 1930s: Soldier-Statesmen and the Limits of Ambiguity," *The International History Review,* 9, no. 4 (November 1987): 588-94; Wark, "In Search of a Suitable Japan."

11. PRO, Cab. 27/625, Proceedings of the Cabinet Committee on Foreign Policy (F.P. 36), 51st Meeting, 13 June 1939.

12. *Ibid.,* 52d Meeting, 19 June 1939, remarks by Hoare, Halifax, and Chatfield.

13. Wesley K. Wark, *The Ultimate Enemy: British Intelligence and Nazi Germany, 1933-1939* (Ithaca, NY, and London, 1985), ch. 6.

14. For examples, see the 1930 and 1931 *Progress in Tactics* reports, which were produced after the fleet maneuvers each year by the Naval Staff's Tactical Division. I am grateful to Professor Jon Sumida for supplying me with copies.

15. Wark, "In Search of a Suitable Japan"; Arthur J. Marder, *Old Friends, New Enemies: The Royal Navy and the Imperial Japanese Navy* (Oxford, 1981), pp. 341-62.

16. Stephen W. Roskill, *Naval Policy Between the Wars,* 2 vols. (London, 1968 and 1976), is best here. See also G. Till, *Air Power and the Royal Navy, 1914-1945* (London, 1979).

17. Wark, *Ultimate Enemy,* ch. 6; Lawrence R. Pratt, *East of Malta, West of Suez: Britain's Mediterranean Crisis, 1936-1939* (Cambridge, UK, 1975).

18. PRO, Air 9/76 (Plans), "Comparison of the Strengths of Great Britain with That of Certain Other Nations 1938," Final Air Staff memo (no title), copy, 10 September 1937.

19. Wark, *Ultimate Enemy,* pp. 68-69; and PRO, Cab. 104/37, "Germans, Estimated Scale of Air Attack on England in the Event of War With," note by Dykes of 25 November 1937.

20. PRO, Air 9/90, Air Staff memo of 24 August 1938, enclosed in Fraser to Slessor note of 29 August 1938.

21. *Ibid.* See also Hore-Belisha's similar point in PRO, Cab. 21/521, "Air Force, Allotment of, to the Field Force in War."

22. This is well covered in Brian Bond, *British Military Policy Between the Two World Wars* (Oxford, 1980), as well as in Michael Howard, *The Continental Commitment* (London, 1972), chs. 4 and 5.

23. Bond, *British Military Policy,* pp. 118-19, reproduces a war office map of "Distribution of British Troops, 1 January 1938." The far greater British concern about Russia rather than Germany for most of the interwar years emerges in Christopher Andrew, *Secret Service: The Making of the British Intelligence Community* (London, 1985).

24. Bond, *British Military Policy*, chs. 2, 7-9; Barnett, *Collapse of British Power*, ch. 5.

25. Bond, *British Military Policy*, ch. 9; Murray, *Change in European Balance of Power*, chs. 5-7.

26. PRO, Cab. 21/544, "Note on the Question of Whether It Would Be to Our Military Advantage to Fight Germany Now or to Postpone the Issue," by General Ismay, 20 September 1938; and see Murray's comments in *Change in European Balance of Power*, p. 210. For the contrary opinions about the strength of the Czech army, see Wark, "Three Military Attachés in Berlin," pp. 604-7.

27. Wark, *Ultimate Enemy*, p. 115.

28. See especially the papers in PRO, WO 216/189; Wark, *Ultimate Enemy*, pp. 93-99; Bond, *British Military Policy*, chs. 6 and 9.

29. Roy F. Holland, *Britain and the Commonwealth Alliance, 1918-39* (London, 1987), is best here. PRO, Cab. 104/19, "Position of the Dominions in the Event of War," contains interesting discussions of whether the Dominions would join a European war.

30. See A. L. Goldman, "Two Views of Germany: Nevile Henderson vs. Vansittart and the Foreign Office, 1937-1939," *British Journal of International Studies*, 6 (1980): 247-77.

31. The text is in PRO, Cab. 53/45, COS Paper 843, Chiefs of Staff Sub-Committee, *European Appreciation, 1939-40*, 20 February 1939.

32. For good examples, see D. Cameron Watt, *How War Came: The Immediate Origins of the Second World War, 1938-1939* (New York, 1989), ch. 6; Andrew, *Secret Service*, ch. 13; David Dilks, "Appeasement and Intelligence," in Dilks (ed.), *Retreat from Power*, 2 vols. (London, 1981), 1: 136-69.

33. Apart from Wark, *Ultimate Enemy*, ch. 7, see also R. Young, "Spokesmen for Economic Warfare: Industrial Intelligence Centre in the 1930s," *European Studies Review*, 6 (1976): 473-89.

34. See also the coverage in Reginald W. Thompson, *Churchill and Morton* (London, 1976).

35. Wark, *Ultimate Enemy*, ch. 7.

36. *European Appreciation*, paras. 3-5, 250-68.

37. G. C. Peden, *British Rearmament and the Treasury, 1932-1939* (Edinburgh, 1979), chs. 4-6; Barnett, *Collapse of British Power*, ch. 5; Murray, *Change in European Balance of Power*, pp. 58-59, 72-73, 295-96.

38. PRO, Air 9/86 [Plans], Foreign Office Comments on Up-dating the "German Appreciation," Annex II of Hollis to Slessor, 26 April 1938.

39. *Ibid.*, "Future Work of the Joint Planning Sub-Committee," attached to Hollis to Slessor, 17 January 1938.

40. Barnett, *Collapse of British Power*, pp. 345-50, and, more specifically, Peter Lowe, *Britain in the Far East* (London, 1981), chs. 8 and 9.

41. Marder, *Old Friends, New Enemies*, and Wark, "In Search of a Suitable Japan," are best here.

42. PRO, Cab. 106/5680, "Japan . . . Warfare Under Special Conditions," minutes on.

43. Wark, *Ultimate Enemy*, is fundamental here.

44. This is perhaps best expressed in Simon's observation that "the arrangements made by Germany in peace could only be adopted in this country if we had a 'Hitler' and

a population which would accept a 'Hitler,'" made at the 330th Meeting of the CID, 31 July 1938, in PRO, Cab. 64/14.

45. Wark, *Ultimate Enemy*, pp. 203–10; Murray, *Change in European Balance of Power*, pp. 504–46; and Telford Taylor, *Munich: The Price of Peace* (London, 1979), are best here.

46. There is some important correspondence on these points in PRO, Air 9/90, "Group-Captain Slessor: Special Papers in Connection with the GERMAN EMERGENCY" (i.e., Munich Crisis). More generally, see Murray, *Change in European Balance of Power*, pp. 245–53; and Williamson Murray, "German Air Power and the Munich Crisis," in Brian Bond and I. Roy (eds.), *War and Society* (London, 1977), 2: 107–18.

47. Arthur J. Marder, "The Royal Navy and the Ethiopean Crisis of 1935–36," *American Historical Review*, 75, no. 5 (1970): 1327–56; Pratt, *East of Malta, West of Suez*, chs. 1 and 2.

48. Pratt, *East of Malta, West of Suez*, pp. 173ff.

49. *Ibid.*, p. 197.

50. Well argued in Murray, *Change in European Balance of Power*, pp. 314–21.

51. PRO, Adm. 1/1085, Alexander to Halifax, 29 November 1940.

52. C. A. MacDonald, *The United States, Britain and Appeasement, 1936–1939* (London, 1980); David Reynolds, *The Creation of the Anglo-American Alliance, 1937–1941* (London, 1981).

53. In addition to the studies of MacDonald and Reynolds, see also the coverage of Chamberlain's views on the United States in Maurice Cowling, *The Impact of Hitler: British Politics and British Policies, 1933–1940* (Cambridge, UK, 1975).

54. Max Beloff, *Imperial Sunset*, vol. 1, *Britain's Liberal Empire, 1897–1921* (London, 1969), chs. 5 and 6; Howard, *Continental Commitment*, chs. 2 and 3.

55. Murray, *Change in European Balance of Power*, pp. 274–90; Howard, *Continental Commitment*, pp. 128–33.

56. Wark, *Ultimate Enemy*, p. 115.

57. F. S. Northedge and Audrey Wells, *Britain and Soviet Communism: The Impact of a Revolution* (London, 1982); G. Niedhart, *Grossbritannien und die Sowjetunion, 1934–1939* (Munich, 1972).

58. This is best covered in J. S. Herndon, "British Perceptions of Soviet Military Capability, 1936–39," in Wolfgang J. Mommsen and Lothar Kettenacker (eds.), *The Fascist Challenge and the Policy of Appeasement* (London, 1983), pp. 297–319.

59. Herndon, "British Perceptions," p. 309. See also PRO, Cab. 53/48, COS paper 887, "Military Value of Russia."

60. Barnett, *Collapse of British Power*, pp. 558–70.

61. Howard, *Continental Commitment*, pp. 120–21.

62. PRO, Cab, 27/624, Proceedings of the Cabinet Committee on Foreign Policy (FP 36), 38th Meeting, 27 March 1939, observation by the Minister for the Coordination of Defence (Chatfield).

63. Quoted in Howard, *Continental Commitment*, p. 105.

64. Gibbs, *Grand Strategy*, 1: 102–27.

65. Marder, *Old Friends, New Enemies*, ch. 1; Stephen Pelz, *Race to Pearl Harbor* (Cambridge, MA, 1972); Ann Trotter, *Britain and East Asia, 1933–37* (Cambridge, UK, 1975).

66. See Marder, "Royal Navy and Ethiopean Crisis"; Pratt, *East of Malta, West*

of Suez; R. Meyers, "British Imperial Interests and the Policy of Appeasement," and W.
R. Louis, "The Road to Singapore: British Imperialism in the Far East, 1932–1942,"
both in Mommsen and Kettenacker, *Fascist Challenge.*

67. Barnett, *Collapse of British Power,* pp. 382*ff;* Bond, *British Military Policy,* pp.
225*ff;* Wark, *Ultimate Enemy,* pp. 195*ff.*

68. Wark, *Ultimate Enemy,* pp. 202–11.

69. This is Wark's term; see *ibid.,* pp. 227–31.

70. See the powerful critiques in Murray, *Change in European Balance of Power,*
and in Barnett, *Collapse of British Power.*

71. There is a good summary of this position in D. Dilks, "Appeasement
Revisited," *University of Leeds Review,* 15 (1972): 28–56.

72. As argued in Cowling, *Impact of Hitler;* and, more recently, John Charmley,
Chamberlain and the Lost Peace (London, 1989).

73. This now notorious phrase comes, of course, from Chamberlain's (near-
exhausted) radio broadcast on the evening of 27 September 1938; see Taylor, *Munich:
Price of Peace,* p. 884.

74. See the coverage of the Chiefs of Staff's advice in Wark, *Ultimate Enemy,* pp.
104–10, 202–11; Taylor, *Munich: Price of Peace,* pp. 629–33, 832–37; Murray,
Change in European Balance of Power, pp. 156–62, 209–10.

75. Chamberlain's ruthless utilization of the military appreciation is best covered in
Barnett, *Collapse of British Power,* pp. 517*ff.*

76. Compare, for example, the assessment in I. McCleod, *Neville Chamberlain*
(London, 1961), with the much more critical analysis in Murray, *Change in European
Balance of Power.*

77. The document is discussed in Wark, *Ultimate Enemy,* pp. 211–24; Murray,
Change in European Balance of Power, pp. 311–14.

78. The differences between the first draft and the final version can be seen by
comparing PRO Cab. 53/44 (draft) and Cab. 53/45 (final). Generally, the planners
became a little more cautious over naval weaknesses and more pessimistic over the
attitude of Spain, but slightly more confident over the long-term effects of a maritime
blockade upon the German economy.

79. Gibbs, *Grand Strategy,* 1: 666*f.*

80. Paul Kennedy, "The Tradition of Appeasement in British Foreign Policy,
1865–1939," in Paul Kennedy (ed.), *Strategy and Diplomacy, 1870–1945* (London,
1983), pp. 33–36; Watt, *How War Came,* pp. 86–108.

81. Bond, *British Military Policy,* pp. 295–306; Howard, *Continental Commitment,* pp. 128–33.

82. Their work can be followed in, respectively, PRO, Cab. 27/657, Cab. 21/532,
and Cab. 27/662.

83. Watt, *How War Came;* Murray, *Change in European Balance of Power;* and
Mommsen and Kettenacker, *Fascist Challenge.*

84. *European Appreciation,* para. 27.

85. Murray, *Change in European Balance of Power,* pp. 314–21.

86. Pratt, *East of Malta, West of Suez,* pp. 170–80; Gibbs, *Grand Strategy,* 1:
420–31.

87. Cited in Arthur J. Marder, "Winston Is Back: Churchill at the Admiralty,
1939–40," *The English Historical Review,* supplement 5 (London, 1972), p. 55.

88. Keith Feiling, *The Life of Neville Chamberlain* (London, 1957), p. 426; William K. Hancock and M. M. Gowing, *British War Economy* (London, 1949), p. 72.

89. Compare the scanty remarks in paras. 381–85 of *European Appreciation* with the details in paras. 319–80.

90. Cited in Robert P. Shay, Jr., *British Rearmament in the Thirties: Politics and Profits* (Princeton, NJ, 1977), p. 243.

91. Quoted in Barnett, *Collapse of British Power*, p. 564.

92. *Ibid.*, p. 569.

93. Murray, *Change in European Balance of Power*, chs. 1, 7–10.

94. PRO, Cab. 16/147, Sub-Committee on the Vulnerability of Capital Ships to Air Attack. I am grateful to Professor Jon Sumida for providing me with details of this file.

95. Marder, "Winston Is Back," p. 55.

96. Stephen W. Roskill, *The War at Sea*, 3 vols. (London, 1954–61); John Winton, *Convoy* (London, 1983), p. 127 ff.

97. PRO, Cab. 21/521, "Air Force, Allotment of, to the Field Force in War."

98. The British inability to come to grips with this form of warfare is detailed in Shelford Bidwell and Dominick Graham, *Fire-Power: British Army Weapons and Theories of War, 1904–1945* (London, 1982), chs. 12 and 13; and Williamson Murray, "British Military Effectiveness in the Second World War," in Allan R. Millett and Williamson Murray (eds.), *Military Effectiveness*, 3 vols. (London and Boston, 1988), 3: 107–30.

99. See PRO, WO 106/5423, "German Methods of Providing Bomber Support," (November 1939–September 1941), which has some very prescient and revealing documents.

100. See the analysis in Max Hastings, *Overlord: D-Day and the Battle for Normandy* (London, 1984), pp. 14, 370, and *passim;* Martin Van Creveld, *Fighting Power: German and U.S. Army Performance, 1939–1945* (Westport, CT, 1982); T. N. Dupuy, *A Genius for War* (Englewood Cliffs, NJ, 1977).

101. Stanley W. Kirby, *The War Against Japan*, 5 vols. (London, 1957–60), vol. 1.

102. John Lukacs, *The Last European War* (London, 1977), and William Carr, *Poland to Pearl Harbor* (London, 1985).

103. Winston S. Churchill, *The Second World War* (London, 1959), 3: 539–40.

3. Net Assessment in Nazi Germany in the 1930s

1. Fritz Stern, *The Politics of Cultural Despair: A Study in the Rise of the Germanic Ideology* (Berkeley, CA, 1961).

2. Walter Goerlitz, *The German General Staff* (New York, 1962), p. 210.

3. For an outstanding examination of this campaign to distort the historical record and the impact this effort had, see Holger H. Herwig, "Clio Deceived, Patriotic Self-censorship in Germany after the Great War," *International Security*, 12, no. 2 (Fall 1987).

4. For Delbrück's contributions to military thought and history, see the outstanding article by Gordon Craig, "Delbrück, the Military Historian," in Edward Mead Earle (ed.), *Makers of Modern Strategy* (Princeton, NJ, 1943).

5. Letter from General Geyer von Schweppenberg to B. H. Liddell Hart, 3.8.49, Liddell Hart papers, King's College Library, London.

6. Final report of Captain Albert C. Wedemeyer on his tour at the Kriegsakademie, German General Staff School, Report 15, 999, dated 11 July 1938, from the Military Attaché, Berlin, 1kb, 23 February 1939, National Archives.

7. For the most thorough examination of the increasing role that the military played in German strategy, see Gerhard Ritter, *The Sword and The Scepter: The Problem of Militarism in Germany*, 4 vols. (Coral Gables, FL, 1969).

8. I am indebted to my former graduate student Bradley Meyer for this point.

9. See in particular Holger Herwig, *The Politics of Frustration: The United States in German Naval Planning, 1889-1941* (Boston, 1976).

10. Holger Herwig, "The Dynamics of Necessity: German Military Policy During the Great War," in Allan R. Millett and Williamson Murray (eds.), *Military Effectiveness*, vol. I, *The First World War* (London and Boston, 1988), p. 99.

11. See the essay by Allan R. Millett and Williamson Murray, "The Constraints on Waging War: Military Effectiveness in the Twentieth Century," *The National Interest*, no. 14 (Winter 1988).

12. The most important contribution to the rethinking of the role of ideology in the dynamism of the Nazi regime in reaction to A. J. P. Taylor's claims that Hitler was only an opportunistic statesman came with the appearance of Eberhard Jäckel's *Hitlers Weltanschauung* (Tübingen, 1969), published in English as *Hitler's Weltanschauung* (Middletown, CT, 1972). The most sophisticated examination of Nazi ideology is MacGregor Knox, "Conquest, Foreign and Domestic, in Fascist Italy and Nazi Germany," *The Journal of Modern History* (March-December 1984). The discussion of Nazi ideology here is largely drawn from these two sources.

13. Quoted in Jäckel, *Hitler's Weltanschauung*, p. 60.

14. *Documents on German Foreign Policy* (hereafter, *DGFP*), series D, vol. I, no. 19, "Memorandum of the Conference in the Reich Chancellery," 5 November 1937.

15. *DGFP*, series D, vol. VII, no. 192, "Unsigned Memorandum," speech by the Führer to the Commanders-in-Chief on 22 August 1939.

16. "Aufzeichnung Liebmann," *Vierteljahrshefte für Zeitgeschichte*, vol. 2, no. 4 (October 1954).

17. Knox, "Conquest, Foreign and Domestic," p. 8, no. 18.

18. For a discussion of the diplomatic and strategic policies of the British in the 1930s, see Williamson Murray, *The Change in the European Balance of Power, 1938-1939* (Princeton, NJ, 1984), ch. 2.

19. Public Record Office (hereafter, PRO) CAB 23/95, Cab 37(38), meeting of the Cabinet, 12 September 1938, pp. 8-10.

20. I am indebted to Professor Gerhard Weinberg of the University of North Carolina for this formulation of the Soviet misapprehensions, which he enumerated at the Air Force Academy's 1988 colloquium on military intelligence.

21. Herwig, "Dynamics of Necessity," p. 82.

22. John W. Wheeler-Bennett, *The Nemesis of Power: The German Army in Politics, 1918-1945* (New York, 1964), p. 44.

23. Michael Geyer, *Aufrüstung oder Sicherheit: Die Reichswehr in der Krise der Machtpolitik, 1924-1936* (Wiesbaden, 1980), p. 80.

24. For a description of how the British system functioned in the 1930s, see Murray, *Change in European Balance of Power*, pp. 55-57.

25. See Gaines Post, *The Civil-Military Fabric of Weimar Foreign Policy* (Princeton, NJ, 1973), pp. 197*ff*.

26. Wilhelm Deist, *The Wehrmacht and German Rearmament* (London, 1981), p. 16.

27. *DGFP,* series D, vol. I, no. 19, "Memorandum of the Conference in the Reich Chancellery," 5 November 1937 (emphasis added).

28. Telford Taylor, *Munich: The Price of Peace* (New York, 1979), p. 698, and Wheeler-Bennett, *Nemesis of Power,* p. 404.

29. Walter Warlimont, *Inside Hitler's Headquarters* (New York, 1964), p. 54.

30. Geyer, *Aufrüstung oder Sicherheit,* pp. 110–12.

31. Michael Geyer, "National Socialist Germany: The Politics of Information," in Ernest R. May (ed.), *Knowing One's Enemies: Intelligence Assessment Before the Two World Wars* (Princeton, NJ, 1984), p. 317.

32. *Ibid.*

33. There are a number of examples that can be given of the products of the British assessment system; one of the most interesting, whatever its defects, is "Military Implications of German Aggression Against Czechoslovakia," PRO, CAB 53/37, COS 698 (Reuse). See also paper DP[P] 22, CID, COS Sub-Committee, 28 March 1938. For a discussion of the bureaucratic origins of this study, see Murray, *Change in European Balance of Power,* pp. 157–62.

34. For the most important of Beck's studies see Bundesarchiv/Militärarchiv (hereafter, BA/MA), N 28/3, Nachlass Generaloberst Ludwig Beck, "Betrachtungen zur gegenwärtigen mil. politischen Lage," 5.5.38; "Bemerkungen zu den Ausführungen des Führers am 28.5.38," 29.5.38; Report an den Herrn Oberbefehlshaber des Heeres, 3.6.38; "Vortrag," 16.7.38; and Vortragsnotiz vom 29.7.38.

35. For the Heye Memorandum see BA/MA, K 10-2/6, Captain Heye, "Beurteilung der Lage Deutschland-Tschechei, Juli 1938"; for Guse's analysis see BA/MA, K 10-2/6, Admiral Guse 17.7.38; and for Weizsäcker see *Akten zur deutschen auswärtigen Politik,* vol. II, Doc. 259, 20.6.38, "Aufzeichnung aus dem Auswärtigen Amt, 8.6.38 an R.M. v. Ribbentrop gegeben."

36. *DGFP,* series D, vol. I, no. 19, "Memorandum of the Conference in the Reich Chancellery," 5 November 1937.

37. A. J. P. Taylor, *The Origins of the Second World War* (London, 1962), pp. 28–132.

38. *DGFP,* series D, vol. VII, no. 192, "Unsigned Memorandum, Speech by the Führer to the Commanders in Chief on August 22, 1939." See also the entry in the Halder Diaries for 22 August 1939.

39. *DGFP,* series D, vol. I, no. 19, "Memorandum of the Conference in the Reich Chancellery," 5 November 1937.

40. For the most thorough discussion of the Fritsch–Blomberg crisis, see Harold C. Deutsch, *Hitler and His Generals: The Hidden Crisis, January–June 1938* (Minneapolis, 1979). See also Robert J. O'Neill, *The German Army and the Nazi Party, 1933–1939* (New York, 1966).

41. Indeed Hitler's intuitions were not far off the mark. At a Cabinet meeting shortly after the demise of the Austrian Republic, Chamberlain admitted that the German methods had shocked and distressed the world "as a typical illustration of power politics, while unfortunately making international appeasement more difficult." PRO, CAB 23/92, Cab 12(38), Meeting of the Cabinet, 12 March 1938, pp. 349–50.

42. *DGFP,* series D, vol. VII, no. (K) (i), "Directive by the Commander-in-Chief of the Wehrmacht," 21 December 1937.

43. *DGFP*, series D, vol. II, no. 132, "Notes Made by the Führer's Adjutant (Schmundt) on Observations Made by the Führer on the Contemporary Strategic Situation," April 1938.

44. *Ibid.*, no. 175, "Letter from the OKW to the Führer, Enclosing Revised Draft Directive for Operation Green," 20 May 1938.

45. *Ibid.*, no. 220, "Directive for Operation 'Green,' from the Führer to the Commander-in-Chief, . . . " 30 May 1938.

46. *Ibid.*, no. 133, "Memorandum on Operation 'Green,' initiated by the Führer's Adjutant," 22 April 1938.

47. *Ibid.*, "Directive for Operation 'Green,' from the Führer to the Commander-in-Chief," 30 May 1938.

48. For an analysis of the military and strategic factors involved in the confrontation in late September 1938, see Murray, *Change in European Balance of Power*, ch. 7.

49. BA/MA, Beck Nachlass: "Betrachtungen zur gegenwärtigen mil. politischen Lage," 5.5.38. For the most thorough discussion of Beck's analysis and opposition see Klaus-Jürgen Müller, *General Ludwig Beck, Studien und Dokumente zur politisch-militarischen Vorstellungswelt und Tätigkeit des Generalstabs Chefs des deutschen Heeres, 1933-1938* (Boppard am Rhein, 1980).

50. *Ibid.*, "Bemerkungen zu den Ausführungen des Führers am 28.5.38."

51. Beck's quarrel was not with the larger design of European conquest; rather, it was with Hitler's timing.

52. *DGFP*, series D, vol. II, no. 259, Memorandum 20.6.38. The German version of *DGFP* notes that the memorandum was given to Ribbentrop on 8.6.38. For other Weizsäcker memoranda see *DGFP*, series D, vol. II, no. 304, 21.7.38, no. 374, 19.8.38, and no. 409, 30.8.38. It is also worth nothing that there was considerable unease at the highest levels of the German navy in 1938. See particularly the two following strategic sketches: BA/MA, K 10-2/6, Captain Heye, "Beurteilung des Lage Deutschland—Tschechei, Juli 1938," and BA/MA, K 10-2/6, Admiral Guse 17/7 (38).

53. Gerhard Engel, *Heeresadjutant bei Hitler, 1938-1945*, ed. Hildegard von Kotze (Stuttgart, 1975), pp. 27-28.

54. Wolfgang Foerster, *Generaloberst Ludwig Beck* (Munich, 1958), p. 141.

55. Wilhelm Deist *et al.*, *Das Deutsche Reich und der Zweite Weltkrieg*, vol. I, *Ursachen und Voraussetzungen der deutschen Kriegspolitik* (Stuttgart, 1979), p. 645.

56. Taylor, *Munich*, p. 697.

57. *Ibid.*, p. 698.

58. International Military Tribunal, *Trials of Major War Criminals*, vol. XXVIII, no. 1780-PS, Jodl Diary, entry for 10.8.38, p. 374.

59. Quoted in Taylor, *Munich*, p. 684.

60. Klaus-Jürgen Müller, *Armee, Politik und Gesellschaft in Deutschland, 1933-1945* (Paderbon, 1979), pp. 96-99.

61. BA/MA, N 28/3, letter from Manstein, Kommandeur der 18. Division, to Beck, 21.7.38.

62. *DGFP*, series D, vol. VII, no. (K) (iii), memorandum by Colonel von der Chevallerie of the OKH.

63. Murray, *Change in European Balance of Power*, pp. 225-29.

64. *DGFP*, series D, vol. VII, no. 192, "Speech by the Führer to the Commanders in Chief on August 22, 1939."

65. *Ibid.*

66. For the reaction of the Western Powers to the *Anschluss* as well as the internal German conflicts over the strategic situation, see Murray, *Change in European Balance of Power,* pp. 155–94.

67. Galeazzo Ciano, *The Ciano Diaries, 1939–1943* (Garden City, NY, 1946), p. 286, entry for 20 August 1940.

68. Francis K. Mason, *Battle Over Britain* (Garden City, NY, 1969), Appendix K, OKL, 16.7.40, Operations Staff Ic.

69. Franz Halder, *Kriegstagebuch,* ed. Hans Adolf Jacobsen (Stuttgart, 1964), III: 170.

70. This was exactly the opposite of what this author's experience was in the USAF during the late 1960s.

71. Williamson Murray, "The German Response to Victory in Poland: A Case Study in Professionalism," *Armed Forces and Society* (Winter 1981), pp. 294–95.

72. Telford Taylor, *The March of Conquest: The German Victories in Western Europe, 1940* (New York, 1958), pp. 53–54.

73. For the most thorough examination of the German navy's undervaluation of the military power of the United States and the role that the misevaluation played in German strategy, see Holger Herwig, *The Politics of Frustration: The United States in German Military Planning, 1889–1941* (Boston, 1976).

74. About the best that can be said for the German navy's rationale is that with the British break into the German naval codes in July 1941, the sinkings by the German submarines had precipitately declined. Nevertheless, the weighing of the short-time advantages of declaring war on the United States against the long-range disadvantages was distinctly absent from German discussions. For the impact of Ultra on the Battle of the Atlantic, see Patrick Beesley, *Very Special Intelligence: The Story of the Admiralty's Operational Intelligence Centre, 1939–1945* (Garden City, NY, 1978), pp. 92–106.

75. Horst Boog, "Higher Command and Leadership in the German Luftwaffe, 1935–1945," in Alfred F. Hurley and Robert C. Ehrhart (eds.), *Airpower and Warfare* (Washington, DC, 1979), p. 129.

76. Müller, *Armee, Politik und Gesellschaft in Deutschland,* pp. 96–99.

77. See Taylor, *March of Conquest,* pp. 174–75, for a discussion of the war game and the argument within the German high command over its implementation; Heinz Guderian, *Panzer Leader* (New York, 1957), pp. 70–71, also gives a highly colored account of the war game.

78. See George E. Blau, *The German Campaign in Russia: Planning and Operations (1940–42)* (Washington, DC, 1955), pp. 14–15.

79. See particularly the outstanding article by David M. Glantz, "The Red Mask: The Nature and Legacy of Soviet Military Deception in the Second World War," in Michael J. Handel (ed.), *Strategic and Operational Deception in the Second World War* (London, 1987).

80. *DGFP,* series D, vol. VII, no. 192, "Speech by the Führer to the Commanders in Chief on August 22, 1939."

81. For a discussion of Britain's rearmament program from 1937 through 1938 and the constraints that the Chamberlain government placed on that effort, see Murray, *Change in European Balance of Power,* pp. 71–78.

82. See Peter Dennis, *Decision by Default: Peacetime Conscription and British Defence, 1919–1939* (London, 1972).

83. For a discussion of Hitler's strategic and economic survey that led to the creation of the "Four Year Plan," see Wilhelm Treue, "Hitlers Denkschrift zum Vierjahrsplan, 1936," *Vierteljahrshefte für Zeitgeschichte*, no. 2 (1955), p. 184.

84. Reichswirtschaftsminister, Berlin, 10.8.40, Betr: "Sicherung von Ausfuhrfragung," National Archives and Records Service (hereafter, NARS) T-71/118/621477.

85. Hans-Erich Volkmann, "Aussenhandel und Aufrüstung in Deutschland, 1933 bis 1939," in Friedrich Forstmeier and Hans-Erich Volkmann (eds.), *Wirtschaft und Rüstung am Vorabend des Zweiten Weltkrieges* (Düsseldorf, 1975), p. 91.

86. Reichsverteidigungsausschuss, 15.12.38, NARS T-1022/3048/PG 33272.

87. International Military Tribunal, *Trial of Major War Criminals*, vol. XXXII, no. 3575 PS, p. 413.

88. Jost Dülffer, *Weimar, Hitler und die Marine: Reichspolitik und Flottenbau, 1920–1939* (Düsseldorf, 1973), p. 504.

89. For a discussion of the economic decisions taken in 1940–41, see Williamson Murray, *Luftwaffe* (Baltimore, MD, 1985), pp. 92–94. For the air battles of 1943–44 and the contribution that Allied numerical superiority made, see chs. 6 and 7.

90. Telford Taylor, *Sword and Swastika* (Chicago, 1969), pp. 325–26.

91. For this fact I am indebted to Wilhelm Deist of the Militärgeschichtliches Forschungsamt.

92. For a discussion of Beck's memoranda see Murray, *Change in European Balance of Power*, pp. 174–84.

93. Treue, "Hitlers Denkschrift zum Vierjahrsplan, 1936," p. 184.

94. PRO CAB 63/14, letter from Sir A. Robinson to Sir Thomas Inskip, Minister for the Coordination of Defence, 19 October 1936.

95. "Bericht des Herrn Professor Dr. C. Krauch über die Lage auf dem Arbeitsgebreit der Chemie in der Sitzung des Generalrates am 24.6.41"; NARS T-84/217/1586749.

96. See Murray, *Luftwaffe*, pp. 92–104.

97. Chef WFA, 30.6.40, "Die Weiterführung des Krieg gegen England," IMT, *TMWC*, 28: 301–3.

98. Josef Goebbels, *The Goebbels Diaries, 1942–1943*, ed. L. Lochner (New York, 1948), pp. 41, 65, 104, 169, 251.

99. Asher Lee, *Goering, Air Leader* (New York, 1972), p. 58.

100. There is considerable irony here, for it was entirely due to Polish intelligence efforts and mathematicians that the basis was created in the 1930s that allowed British signals intelligence to break into the German enigma enciphering system.

101. Horst Boog, Jürgen Förster, Joachim Hoffman, Ernst Klink, Rolf-Dieter Müller, and Gerd R. Ueberschär, *Das Deutsche Reich und der Zweite Weltkrieg*, vol. 4, *Der Angriff auf die Sowjetunion* (Stuttgart, 1983), p. 29, fn. 13.

102. Quoted in Klaus Reinhardt, *Die Wende vor Moskau: Das Scheitern der Strategie Hitlers im Winter 1941/1942* (Stuttgart, 1972), p. 27.

103. *Ibid.*, p. 21.

4. The Impatient Cat

1. Giuseppe Bottai, *Diario 1935–1944* (Milan, 1982), p. 188.

Notes 311

2. Renzo de Felice, *Mussolini il duce*, II: *Lo stato totalitario, 1936–1940* (Turin, 1981), pp. 15–44.

3. Badoglio's career is traced in Piero Pieri and Giorgio Rochat, *Pietro Badoglio* (Turin, 1974), and Giovanni De Luna, *Badoglio: Un militare al potere* (Milan, 1974).

4. Adrian Lyttelton, *The Seizure of Power: Fascism in Italy, 1919–1929*, 2d ed. (New York, 1988), pp. 244–50, 293–307, 429–32; Philip V. Cannistraro (ed.), *Historical Dictionary of Fascist Italy* (Westport, CT, 1982), pp. 585–89; Renzo de Felice, *Mussolini il fascista*, II: *L'organizzazione dello Stato fascista, 1925–1929* (Turin, 1968), pp. 3–381; *idem, Mussolini il duce*, I: *Gli anni del consenso, 1929–1936* (Turin, 1974), pp. 127–322.

5. Guido Neppi Modona, "La magistratura e il fascismo," in Guido Quazza (ed.), *Fascismo e società italiana* (Turin, 1977), p. 149; Herman Finer, *Mussolini's Italy* (New York, 1965), pp. 270–73; Allan Cassels, *Italian Foreign Policy, 1918–1945: A Guide to Research and Research Materials* (Wilmington, DE, 1981), pp. 13–15; Brian R. Sullivan, "A Thirst for Glory: Mussolini, the Italian Military, and the Fascist Regime, 1922–1936," Ph.D. dissertation, Columbia University, 1984, pp. 271–84, 352–57.

6. Archivio Centrale dello Stato (hereafter, ACS), Ministero dell'Africa Italiana, busta (hereafter, b) 9, Commissione suprema di difesa, segretaria generale, verbali delle XII, XVI, XVII sessioni (hereafter, CSD, followed by session number); Mario Missori, *Gerarchie e statuti del P.N.F. Gran consiglio, Direttorio nazionale, Federazioni provinciali: quadri e biografie* (Rome, 1986), pp. 49–53.

7. Mario Montanari, *L'esercito italiano alla vigilia della 2a guerra mondiale* (Rome, 1982), p. 544.

8. Sullivan, "A Thirst for Glory," p. 135; CSD, XII, pp. 17–21, 55–57; *idem*, XVI, pp. 118–32; *idem*, XVII, pp. 9–15, 24–25, 35–41, 79–80, 116–18, 128–34; Galeazzo Ciano, *Diario 1937–1943* (Milan, 1980), pp. 95–96, 395–96.

9. Bottai, *Diario*, pp. 115–92; Ciano, *Diario*, pp. 47, 68, 100, 102, 129, 142, 172, 209–10, 290, 340, 388–90, 439–40.

10. De Felice, *Mussolini il duce*, II: 274–86; John T. Whitaker, *We Cannot Escape History* (New York, 1943), pp. 62–63.

11. Bottai, *Diario*, pp. 111, 178, 481; De Felice, *Mussolini il duce*, II: 49–69, 269–74; Margherita Sarfatti, "Mussolini: Cómo lo Conocí," IX: "El Duce Fué un Hombre Huraño y sin Amigos, que Huyó de la Multitud," and X: "La Tragedia del Conde Ciano, el Titere que Quiso Ser Hombre," *Critica* (Buenos Aires), 27 and 28 June 1945; Giordano Bruno Guerri, *Galeazzo Ciano: Una vita 1903/1944* (Milan, 1979), pp. 174–75, 275–76.

12. Dino Grandi, *Il mio paese: Ricordi autobiografici* (Bologna, 1985), p. 380; CSD, XVII, pp. 79–80.

13. Mario Roatta, *Otto milioni di baionette* (Milan, 1946), p. 21.

14. MacGregor Knox, "Fascist Italy Assesses Its Enemies, 1935–40," in Ernest R. May (ed.), *Knowing One's Enemies: Intelligence Assessment Before the Two World Wars* (Princeton, NJ, 1984), pp. 349–52.

15. Sullivan, "A Thirst for Glory," pp. 352–53, 367–68; Public Record Office (hereafter, PRO), FO 371/20418, R 1724/458/22 ("Records of Leading Personalities in Italy"), pp. 3, 7–8, 16, 22–23.

16. Cesare Amé, *Guerra segreta in Italia, 1940–43* (Rome, 1954), p. 50; Sullivan, "A Thirst for Glory," pp. 639–45; Vladeta Milicevic, *A King Dies in Marseilles: The*

Crime and Its Background (Bad Godesberg, 1959), pp. 52–75; Carte Pariani, Civiche Raccolte Storiche di Milano (hereafter, CP), quaderno (hereafter, q) 1, Pariani to Roatta, 6 October 1934; Luigi Goglia, "Un aspetto dell 'azione politica italiana durante la campagna d'Etiopia 1935–36," *Storia contemporanea,* December 1977; Clara Conti, *Servizio segreto* (Rome, 1945), pp. 32, 38, 70–73, 87–93, 137–43, 195–201, 212–46, 273; *idem* (ed.), *Il processo Roatta: I documenti* (Rome, 1945), pp. 30, 45–47, 82; Emilio Canevari, *La guerra Italiana: Retroscena della disfatta,* 2 vols. (Rome, 1948), II: 381–82; Emilio Faldella, *L'Italia nella seconda guerra mondiale: Revisione di giudizi, 1941–1943* (Rome, 1978), pp. 97–98.

17. CP, q 12, Pariani to Angioy, 14 October 1936; *idem,* q 18, Pariani to Angioy, 20 and 23 July 1937; *idem;* q 21, Pariani to Tripiccione, 26 November and 7 December 1937; *idem,* q 24, Pariani to Tripiccione, 9 March 1938; *idem,* q 27, Pariani to Tripiccione, 25 August 1938; *idem,* q 28, Pariani to Ciano, 8 September 1938, Pariani to Tripiccione, 10 September 1938, Pariani to Mussolini, 27 September 1938; *idem,* q 31, Pariani to Tripiccione, 22 November 1938; *idem,* q 34, Pariani to Tripiccione, 27 December 1938; *idem,* q 35, Pariani to Tripiccione, 9 January 1939; *idem,* q 37, Pariani to Tripiccione, 7 April 1939; *idem,* q 38, Pariani to Mussolini, (early) May 1939; *idem,* q 41, Pariani to Tripiccione, 1 September 1939.

18. Sullivan, "A Thirst for Glory," pp. 408–542.

19. National Archives (hereafter, NA), T586, reel 24, *passim;* Knox, "Fascist Italy Assesses Its Enemies," p. 364; *Documents on German Foreign Policy* (hereafter, *DGFP*), series D, vol. VIII, p. 908; Alberto Pirelli, *Taccuini 1922/1943* (Bologna, 1984), pp. 260, 263–64; Claudio Segre, "Italo Balbo," in Ferdinando Cordova (ed.), *Uomini e volti del fascismo* (Rome, 1980), p. 25.

20. Dorello Ferrari, "Dalla divisione ternaria alla binaria," *Memorie storiche militari 1982* (Rome, 1983).

21. Lucio Ceva and Andrea Curami, *La meccanizzazione dell'esercito italiano dalle origini al 1943,* 2 vols. (Rome, 1989), I: 234–46.

22. *Ibid.,* I: 191–212.

23. Ciano, *Diario,* pp. 98, 174, 184, 254, 333; Ministero della Guerra, Direzione del servizio chimico militare, *Note sull'impiego degli aggressivi* (Rome, 1936); *idem, Note sull'impiego dell'yprite* (Rome, 1936); NA T78, reel 364, frames 6325825–28, 6326069–70, 6326285–89, reel 365, frames 6326712–4; NA T1022, reel 2519, PG 45170, p. 2; CP, q 31, "Riunione per servizio chimico," 9 and 21 November 1938; *idem,* q 36, "Riunione," 18 February 1939; *idem,* q 38, "Riunione chimica," 21 June 1939, "La Guerra (appunti per Duce)," p. 50, n.d. (but mid-1939); *idem,* q 40, "Riunione chimico," 23 August 1939; Hungarian National Archives, K100, Foreign Ministry Archives, László Szabó, Military Attaché Papers (hereafter, SP), 1938, report 671/443, "Presentation to the Duce."

24. Giancarlo Garello, "The Air Force During Italian Fascism," in *Colloque international: Adaptation de l'arme aérienne aux conflits contemporains et processus d'indépendance des armées de l'Air des origines à la fin de la Seconde Guerre mondiale* (Paris, 1985), p. 291; Fortunato Minniti, "Il problema degli armamenti nella preparazione militare italiana dal 1935 al 1943," *Storia contemporanea,* February 1978, pp. 29–33.

25. James J. Sadkovich, "The Development of the Italian Air Force Prior to World

War II," *Military Affairs* (January 1987); Virgilio Ilari, "L'intervento fascista nella guerra civile spagnola," in Virgilio Ilari and Antonio Sema (eds.), *Marte in orbace: Guerra, esercito e milizia nella concezione fascista della nazione* (Ancona, 1988), p. 260; PRO, FO 371, 1938, 22435/R1821, R5206, R5351, R8414, and R10066.

26. Fortunato Minniti, "Aspetti territoriali e politici del controllo sulla produzione bellica in Italia (1936-42)," *Clio* (January-March 1979); *idem*, "La politica industriale del Ministero dell'Aeronautica: Mercato, pianificazione, sviluppo (1935-1943)," part two, *Storia contemporanea*, April 1981, pp. 286-89; Nicola della Volpe, *Difesa del territorio e protezione anitaerea (1915-1943)* (Rome, 1986), pp. 32-40, 204-18.

27. Lucio Ceva, "L'evoluzione dei materiali bellici in Italia," in Ennio Di Nolfo, Romain Rainero, and Brunello Vigezzi (eds.), *L'Italia e la politica di potenza in Europa (1938-40)* (Milan, 1985), pp. 359-79; Fortunato Minniti, "La politica industriale," part one, *Storia contemporanea*, February 1981, p. 36.

28. Brian R. Sullivan, "A Fleet in Being: The Rise and Fall of Italian Sea Power, 1861-1943," *The International History Review* (February 1988), pp. 114-20; Ufficio Storico della Marina Militare (hereafter, USMM), *La marina italiana nella seconda guerra mondiale*, 21 vols. (Rome, 1950-75), vol. XIV, *I mezzi d'assalto*, pp. 5-28, 288-89, and vol. XVIII, *La guerra di mine*, pp. 14, 30-31.

29. Ezio Ferrante, *Il pensiero strategico navale in Italia* (Rome, 1988) (supplement to *Rivista marittima*), pp. 56-58; NA T78, reel 364, frames 6325967-68; Luigi Sansonetti, "The Royal Italian Navy," *Brassey's Naval Annual 1938* (London, 1938), pp. 83-84.

30. Lucio Ceva, "Appunti per una storia dello Stato Maggiore generale fino alla vigilia della 'non-belligeranza' (giugno 1925-luglio 1939)," *Storia contemporanea*, April 1979, pp. 222-26, 235-45; Giorgio Rochat, *Militari e politici nella preparazione della campagna d'Etiopia: Studio e documenti, 1932-1936* (Milan, 1971), pp. 226-29; *idem*, *Italo Balbo* (Turin, 1986), pp. 277-80; Alberto Pariani, *Chiacchiere e realtà. lettera agli amici* (Milan, 1949), pp. 23-25; Montanari, *L'esercito*, pp. 410-29, 442-54.

31. Sullivan, "A Thirst for Glory," pp. 476-500; John Coverdale, *Italian Intervention in the Spanish Civil War* (Princeton, NJ, 1975), pp. 212-75; Mario Montanari, *Le truppe italiane in Albania (Anni 1914-20 e 1939)* (Rome, 1978), pp. 273-78, 419-31; Ciano, *Diario*, pp. 278-85; Pariani, *Chiacchiere*, p. 16.

32. NA T586, reel 405, frames 000045-46; De Felice, *Mussolini il duce*, II: 319-30; Ciano, *Diario*, pp. 292-93, 299; Malcolm Muggeridge (ed.), *Ciano's Diplomatic Papers* (London, 1948), p. 284; Pirelli, *Taccuini*, pp. 216-17; Grandi, *Il mio paese*, pp. 462-68; Ceva, "Appunti," p. 247; Domenico Cavagnari, "La marina nella vigilia e nel primo periodo della guerra," *Nuova antologia*, August 1947, p. 374.

33. Ubaldo Soddu, "Mussolini e Badoglio," pp. 7-14 in "Memorie e riflessioni di un generale (1933-1941)" typescript, 1948.

34. NA T586, reel 405, frames 000039-46; De Felice, *Mussolini il duce*, II: 319-30, 589 ff; Canevari, *La guerra Italiana*, I: 211-12; Romeo Bernotti, *Storia della guerra in Mediterraneo* (Rome, 1960), p. 18.

35. Ciano, *Diario*, p. 250; François Bedarida, "La 'gouvernante anglaise'," in Rene Remond and Janini Bourdin (eds.), *Edouard Daladier, Chef de gouvernement, avril*

1938–septembre 1939 (Paris, 1977), pp. 236–37; *Documents on British Foreign Policy* (hereafter, DBFP), 3d series, vol. V, no. 255.

36. Yvon De Begnac, *Palazzo Venezia; storia di un regime* (Rome, 1950), p. 617; De Felice, *Mussolini il duce*, II: 615–39; Ciano, *Diario*, pp. 294–300, 308–9; Muggeridge, *Ciano's Diplomatic Papers*, pp. 284–95; Pirelli, *Taccuini*, p. 231; Enzo Collotti, "L'Italia dall' intervento alla 'guerra parallela'," in Francesca Tosi, Gaetano Grassi, and Massimo Legnani (eds.), *L'Italia nella seconda guerra mondiale e nella resistenza* (Milan, 1988), pp. 16–17; Montanari, *L'esercito*, pp. 430–32; Ramón Serrano Súñer, *Entre Hendaya y Gibraltar* (Madrid, 1947), pp. 94–99; William Garzke, Jr., and Robert Dulin, Jr., *Battleships: Axis and Neutral Battleships in World War II* (Annapolis, MD, 1985), pp. 437–40.

37. Montanari, *L'esercito*, pp. 379–409.

38. Ciano, *Diario*, pp. 320–26; Bottai, *Diario*, p. 147; Pirelli, *Taccuini*, pp. 217, 221.

39. NA T821, reel 384, frames 377–97; Silvio Bertoldi, *Vittorio Emanuele III* (Turin, 1971), pp. 388–89; De Luna, *Badoglio*, p. 171; Canevari, *La guerra italiana*, I: 570; L. Ceva, "Un intervento di Badoglio e il mancato rinnovamento delle artigliere italiane," *Il Risorgimento* (June 1976), pp. 165–66; Ciano, *Diario*, p. 333; Camillo Caleffi, "Elogio dell'armata Po," *L'illustrazione italiana*, 20 August 1939; Rodolfo Corselli, "Vita e problemi dell'esercito," *Nuova antologia*, 1 September 1939; Thomas B. Morgan, *Spurs on the Boot: Italy Under Her Masters* (New York, 1941), p. 159.

40. Enrico Serra, "Leonardo Vitetti e una sua testimonianza," *Nuova Antologia*, September–December 1973, pp. 494–96; Ciano, *Diario*, pp. 292–93, 327–35, 349; Grandi, *Il mio paese*, pp. 523–38; Bottai, *Diario*, pp. 152–53; Montanari, *L'esercito*, pp. 439–40; Giuseppe Bastianini, *Uomini, cose, fatti* (Milan, 1959), p. 69; Guerri, *Galeazzo Ciano*, pp. 416–39; CP, q 40, Pariani to Soddu, 17 August 1939, "Riunione 22-8-39-XVII," and q 41, "Riunione 28-8-39-XVII"; Pariani, *Chiacchiere*, pp. 16–17; DGFP, series D, vol. VIII, no. 489; SP, 1939, notes on conversation with Pariani, 18 July 1939; DBFP, series 3, vol. VII, no. 96.

41. MacGregor Knox, *Mussolini Unleashed, 1939–1941: Politics and Strategy in Fascist Italy's Last War* (New York, 1982), p. 55; CP, q 41–42, *passim*; q 43, Pariani to Morso, 25 September 1939, Pariani to Bancale, 25 September 1939, and Pariani to Sorice, 26 September 1939; and q 45, Pariani to Rossini, 15 October 1939.

42. Pirelli, *Taccuini*, pp. 187, 206–7, 230; Grandi, *Il mio paese*, p. 544; Ciano, *Diario*, pp. 336, 340; De Felice, *Mussolini il duce*, II: 594–97; Donatella Bolech Cecchi, *Non bruciare i ponti con Roma* (Milan, 1986), p. 514.

43. Guerri, *Galeazzo Ciano*, pp. 442–45; Massimo Legnani, "Sul finanziamento della guerra fascista," in Tosi, Grassi, and Legnani, *L'Italia nella seconda guerra mondiale e nella resistenza*, pp. 293–95; De Felice, *Mussolini il duce*, II: 676–97; Knox, *Mussolini Unleashed*, pp. 44–54.

44. CP, q 39, "Note per Consiglio Esercito," 2 May 1939, Pariani to Ciano, 16 June 1939; q 42, Pariani to Commanders of First and Fourth Armies, 6 September 1939, "Riunioni 11-9-39,"; q 43, Pariani to Bancale and Cappa, 24 September 1939, "Riunione artigl. 28-9-39-XVII,"; q 44, Pariani to Basso and Sarracino, 29 September 1939, Pariani to Soddu, 30 September 1939, Pariani to Robotti, 6 October 1939, "Riunione 9-10-39-XVII," Pariani to Sorice, 17 October 1939, Pariani to Bancale, 18

October 1939; q 46, Pariani to Manera, 26 October 1939, "Riunione 30-10-XVIII"; Ufficio Storico, Stato Maggiore Esercito (hereafter, USE), *L'esercito italiano tra la 1a e la 2a guerra mondiale* (Rome, 1954), p. 142; Lucio Ceva, *Le forze armate* (Turin, 1981), p. 260; NA T821, reel 107, frames 160–63.

45. Ciano, *Diario,* pp. 254, 290, 333, 334, 345, 347, 349, 351, 359, 361, 362–63; Bottai, *Diario,* pp. 153–54, 160–61, 173; Montanari, *L'esercito,* p. 29; De Felice, *Mussolini il duce,* II: 702–3; *DGFP,* series D, vol. VIII, no. 406; Soddu, "Mussolini e Badoglio," pp. 4–5.

46. Knox, "Fascist Italy Assesses Its Enemies," p. 349.

47. Montanari, *L'esercito,* pp. 367–73; Knox, *Mussolini Unleashed,* pp. 56, 314, n. 59; Giuseppe D'Avanzo, *Ali e poltrone* (Rome, 1981), pp. 880–83, 886.

48. Montanari, *L'esercito,* pp. 441–54; Knox, *Mussolini Unleashed,* pp. 57–58.

49. Montanari, *L'esercito,* pp. 282–84, 515–22; Angela Raspin, "The Italian War Economy, 1940–43, with Particular Reference to Italian Relations with Germany," Ph.D. dissertation, London School of Economics, 1980, pp. 113–14.

50. *I documenti diplomatici italiani* (hereafter, *DDI*), series 9, vol. I, nos. 285, 755; NA T821, reel 109, frames 1–106; Knox, "Fascist Italy Assesses Its Enemies," pp. 355–56.

51. NA T821, reel 109, frames 108–16; reel 23, frames 98–111.

52. SP, "Promemoria," 7 September 1939, and handwritten notes, 9–28 September 1939; CP, q 42, Pariani to commanders of First and Fourth Armies, 6 September 1939, and "Riunione 13-9-XVII"; Carlo De Risio, *Generali, servizi segreti e fascismo: La guerra nella guerra, 1940-1943* (Milan, 1978), p. 21; De Felice, *Mussolini il duce,* II: 685.

53. Bottai, *Diario,* p. 170; Pirelli, *Taccuini,* p. 248; USMM, vol. XXI, *L'organizzazione della Marina durante il conflitto,* tomo I, *Efficienza all'aperatura delle ostilità* (Rome, 1972) p. 349; SP, report no. 288/40, 26 February 1940; DDI, 9th series, vol. III, no. 689; Ubaldo Soddu, "Un anno di sottosegretaria alla guerra," pp. 24–28 in Soddu, "Memorie e riflessioni di un generale"; Knox, *Mussolini Unleashed,* pp. 36–37, 61; Pietro Badoglio, *Italy in the Second World War* (Westport, CT, 1976), p. 7.

54. Bottai, *Diario,* pp. 169–70.

55. Ciano, *Diario,* pp. 372–75; Bottai, *Diario,* p. 176; Grandi, *Il mio paese,* pp. 557–58; Pirelli, *Taccuini,* pp. 238–39; De Felice, *Mussolini il duce,* II: 744–48; Knox, *Mussolini Unleashed,* pp. 62–63.

56. *DGFP,* series D, vol. VIII, no. 504; Knox, *Mussolini Unleashed,* pp. 67–69; Collotti, "L'Italia dall'intervento," pp. 22–23.

57. *DDI,* series 9, vol. I, nos. 122, 211, 240, 244, 321, 328, 755, 762, 797, 817 and pp. 599–600; vol. II, nos. 275, 298, 443, 490, 570, 582, 591, 588, 602, 628, 661, 711, 751; vol. III, nos. 60, 196, 264, 398, 408, 419; CP, q 44, Pariani to Soddu, 19 October 1939; SP, 1940, report no. 288/40, 26 February 1940; Giuseppe Santoro, *L'aeronautica italiana nella seconda guerra mondiale,* 2 vols. (Rome, 1957), I: 39; Minniti, "La politica industriale," part one, pp. 45–51; Aldo Fraccaroli, *Italian Warships of World War II* (London, 1968), pp. 42, 85; William Shorrock, *From Ally to Enemy: The Enigma of Fascist Italy in French Diplomacy, 1920-1940* (Kent, OH, 1988), pp. 273–74; Knox, *Mussolini Unleashed,* p. 71.

58. *DDI,* series 9, vol. III, nos. 102, 144, 254, 300; *DGFP,* series D, vol. VIII, no.

599; Knox, *Mussolini Unleashed,* pp. 72–81, 294; MacGregor Knox, "1940: Italy's 'Parallel War,' Part I: From Non-Belligerance to the Collapse of France," Ph.D. dissertation, Yale University, 1976, pp. 175–204; Raspin, "Italian War Economy," pp. 163–72.

59. CSD, XVII, pp. 74–81, 128–35; Bottai, *Diario,* p. 176; Ciano, *Diario,* pp. 395–96; Badoglio, *Italy in Second World War,* pp. 12–13.

60. *DGFP,* series D, vol. VIII, nos. 627, 634, 665, pp. 883–84, 669, n. 12; Knox, *Mussolini Unleashed,* pp. 82–84.

61. *DGFP,* series D, vol. VIII, nos. 665, 669, 670; Ciano, *Diario,* pp. 405–6; Muggeridge, *Ciano's Diplomatic Papers,* pp. 339–59.

62. *DGFP,* series D, vol. IX, no. 1; Muggeridge, *Ciano's Diplomatic Papers,* pp. 361–65; Ciano, *Diario,* p. 408; Siegfried Westphal, *The German Army in the West* (London, 1951), p. 78; Walter Warlimont, *Inside Hitler's Headquarters* (London, 1964), pp. 23, 55, 64; Knox, *Mussolini Unleashed,* p. 94.

63. *DDI,* series 9, vol. III, nos. 567, 581, 611, 614, 617, 640, 657, 661, 704; Ciano, *Diario,* pp. 409–12; Bottai, *Diario,* pp. 180–83; Pirelli, *Taccuini,* pp. 255–57; Enrico Serra, "Leonardo Vitetti e una sua testimonianza," *Nuova antologia,* September–December 1973, p. 499.

64. Ciano, *Diario,* pp. 412–15; Bottai, *Diario,* pp. 183–85; Massimo De Leonardis, "La monarchia e l'intervento dell'Italia in guerra," in Di Nolfo, Rainero, and Vigezzi, *L'Italia e la politica,* pp. 51–52; *Opera Omnia di Benito Mussolini,* 44 vols. (Florence, 1952; Rome, 1978–80), XLIII: 31–32; Knox, *Mussolini Unleashed,* p. 90.

65. *DDI,* series 9, vol. III, nos. 658, 689; Ciano, *Diario,* p. 412.

66. De Risio, *Generali,* pp. 21–57; Amé, *Guerra segreta in Italia,* pp. 9–13, 21–24, 32–34; Santoro, *L'aeronautica italiana,* I: 91; Minniti, "La politica industriale," pp. 5–6; Knox, *Mussolini Unleashed,* p. 99.

67. U.S. Army Military History Institute, William Donovan Papers, box 74B (hereafter, WDP), "A Study by General Roatta to the Chief of Army Staff," 6 April 1940; De Leonardis, "La monarchia," p. 56; Knox, *Mussolini Unleashed,* pp. 94–95; Montanari, *L'esercito,* pp. 457–77 (quotes by Cavagnari, pp. 461, 468).

68. Luigi Romersa, "La vita di Amedeo di Savoia il duca di ferro," *Tempo,* 6 February 1958; Edoardo Borra, *Amedeo di Savoia, terzo duca d'Aosta e vicere d'Etiopia* (Milan, 1985), pp. 142–43; Angelo Del Boca, *Gli italiani in Africa Orientale,* 4 vols. (Bari, 1976–84), III: *La caduta dell'Impero,* pp. 352–53; Montanari, *L'esercito,* pp. 151–52, 469–70; Rochat, *Balbo,* p. 288; Ciano, *Diario,* pp. 416–17.

69. *DGFP,* series D, vol. IX, nos. 68, 69, 82, 84, 92; *DDI,* series 9, vol. III, no. 726, and vol. IV, no. 71; Montanari, *L'esercito,* p. 485; Ciano, *Diario,* pp. 417–18.

70. Bottai, *Diario,* pp. 186–87; De Felice, *Mussolini il duce,* II: 696–97.

71. De Risio, *Generali,* pp. 58–60; Knox, *Mussolini Unleashed,* p. 99; Ciano, *Diario,* pp. 292, 343, 370, 393, 463; *DDI,* series 9, vol. III, nos. 581, 611, 614, 617, 640, 657, 661, 694, 704, and vol. IV, nos. 100, 153.

72. Ciano, *Diario,* p. 419; Bottai, *Diario,* p. 188; *DDI,* series 9, vol. IV, no. 190; *DGFP,* series D, vol. IX, nos. 164, 165; NA T821, reel 126, frames 995–99.

73. *DDI,* series 9, vol. IV, nos. 163, 186, 192, 193, 195, 205, 224, 233, 241, 269, 278, 311, 314; SP, 1940, Szabó to Hungarian Army Chief of Staff, 19 April 1940; SP

"Promemoria," 20–26 April 1940; and SP, Szabó to Hungarian Army Chief of Staff, 9 May 1940; WDP, Graziani to Badoglio and Soddu, 21 April 1940; Montanari, *L'esercito,* pp. 478–81 (quote by Badoglio, p. 479); Pirelli, *Taccuini,* p. 260.

74. Ciano, *Diario,* pp. 427–30; Soddu, "Un anno di sottosegretario alla guerra," pp. 58–60.

75. Grandi, *Il mio paese,* p. 580; Dino Grandi, *25 luglio: Quarant'anni dopo* (Bologna, 1983), pp. 188–89; Ciano, *Diario,* p. 441.

76. Shorrock, *From Ally to Enemy,* pp. 282–84; *DDI,* series 9, vol. IV, nos. 549, 565, 589, 627, 644, 652, 657, 659, 661, 664, 665; Raffaele Guariglia, *Scritti "storico-eruditi" e documenti diplomatici (1936–1940)* (Naples, 1981), pp. 401–8.

77. Soddu, "Un anno di sottosegretario alla guerra," pp. 60–62; Montanari, *L'esercito,* pp. 486, 503–8; SP, 1940, report no. 10.351/1940, and handwritten notes 8 May–10 June 1940.

78. Ciano, *Diario,* pp. 430–36; NA T821, reel 126, frames 998–99; Bottai, *Diario,* pp. 191–92; Pirelli, *Taccuini,* p. 263; Knox, *Mussolini Unleashed,* pp. 106–7; Simona Colarizi, "L'opinione pubblica italiana di fronte all'intervento in guerra," in Di Nolfo, Rainero and Vigezzi, *L'Italia e la politica,* pp. 300–301.

79. De Leonardis, "La monarchia," pp. 57–58, 65–66; Ciano, *Diario,* pp. 438, 440; Knox, *Mussolini Unleashed,* pp. 104–5.

80. Montanari, *L'esercito,* pp. 485–88; *DDI,* series 9, vol. IV, no. 567; *DGFP,* series D, vol. IX, no. 356; Ciano, *Diario,* pp. 435–36; Bottai, *Diario,* p. 192.

81. Montanari, *L'esercito,* pp. 500–502; *DGFP,* series D, vol. IX, no. 387.

82. Fortunato Minniti, "Il 'Diario storico del Comando supremo': Considerazioni e ipotesi sul ruolo del capo di Stato Maggiore Generale nell'estate del 1940," *Storia contemporanea,* February 1987, p. 182.

83. Edward Crankshaw (ed.), *Khrushchev Remembers* (Boston, 1970), p. 134.

84. Ceva, *Le forze armate,* pp. 263, 270, 274; D'Avanzo, *Ali e poltrone,* pp. 885–86.

85. Montanari, *L'esercito,* pp. 358–60; Bottai, *Diario,* pp. 192–93; Claudio Segrè, *Italo Balbo: A Fascist Life* (Berkeley, 1987), pp. 378–81; Alberto Aquarone, "Nello Quilici e il suo 'Diario di guerra'," *Storia contemporaneà,* June 1975, pp. 355–57; Ciano, *Diario,* p. 597; Alfredo Ferruzza, "Il diario del viceré dell'Impero," *Gente,* 12 March 1969.

86. NA T821, reel 109, frames 341–46; De Risio, *Generali,* pp. 26–39, 50–51; Lucio Ceva, "I servizi segreti italiani nella seconda guerra mondiale," *Il Risorgimento* (June 1978), p. 111; David Hunt, "Sea of Troubles: Conflicting Pressures in the Mediterranean Theater," paper delivered at the First International Conference on Strategy, Army War College, Carlisle Barracks, PA, 8 February 1990, p. 6.

87. Pirelli, *Taccuini,* p. 261; *DDI,* series 9, vol. IV, no. 829; *DGFP,* series D, vol. IX, no. 408; Fortunato Minniti, "Profilo dell'iniziativa strategica italiana dalla 'non-belligeranza' alla 'guerra parallela'," *Storia contemporanea,* December 1987, pp. 1157–58; Ciano, *Diario,* p. 84; Leopoldo Nuti, "I problemi storiografici connessi con l'intervento italiano nella seconda guerra mondiale," *Storia delle relazioni internazionali,* 2 (1985): 386–87.

88. Nicola Caracciolo, "Su facciamo una guerra facile facile," *La Repubblica Mercurio,* 26 May 1990.

5. French Net Assessment

1. J. B. Duroselle, *Politique étrangère de la France, 1871-1969: La Décadence, 1932-1939* (Paris, 1979), p. 169.

2. Cited in L. Mysyrowicz, *Autopsie d'une défaite: Origines de l'effondrement militaire français de 1940* (Lausanne, 1973), pp. 337-38.

3. Among the most vigorous proponents of this view is the excellent study by A. Adamthwaite, *France and the Coming of the Second World War, 1936-1939* (London, 1977).

4. Cited in William E. Scott, *Alliance Against Hitler: The Origins of the Franco-Soviet Pact* (Durham, NC, 1962), p. 103.

5. Frederic Pottecher, *Le procès de la défaite: Riom fevrier-avril 1942* (Paris, 1989), p. 122.

6. France, Ministère des affaires étrangères, *Documents diplomatiques français, 1932-1939, 2e série, 1936-1939* (Paris, 1966), XIX: 9-10.

7. André François-Poncet, *The Fateful Years: Memoirs of a French Ambassador in Berlin, 1931-1938* (New York, 1949), p. 279.

8. *Documents diplomatiques*, XIX: 312-18.

9. Duroselle, *Politique étrangère*, ch. 9.

10. *Ibid.*

11. Robert Young, "French Military Intelligence and Nazi Germany, 1938-1939," in Ernest R. May (ed.), *Knowing One's Enemies: Intelligence Assessment Before the Two World Wars* (Princeton, NJ, 1984), pp. 274-77.

12. *Ibid.*

13. *Ibid.*, pp. 278-80.

14. *Ibid.*, pp. 280-82.

15. *Ibid.*

16. Henri Dutailly, *Les problèmes de l'armée de terre française, 1935-1939* (Paris, 1980), pp. 27-33.

17. *Ibid.*

18. *Ibid.*, p. 73.

19. Robert Frankenstein, *Le prix du réarmement français* (Paris, 1982), p. 238.

20. T. Kemp, *The French Economy, 1919-1939: The History of a Decline* (New York, 1972), p. 160.

21. Frankenstein, *Le prix du réarmement*, p. 35.

22. Robert J. Young, *In Command of France: French Foreign Policy and Military Planning, 1933-1940* (Cambridge, MA, 1978), pp. 19-21.

23. Brian Bond, *France and Belgium, 1939-1940* (Newark, NJ, 1975), pp. 23-28.

24. 2d Bureau report on meeting with the head of Polish military intelligence, Service historique de l'armée de terre (hereafter, SHA) Carton 7N3006.

25. SHA Carton 7N3143.

26. SHA Carton 7N3184.

27. SHA Carton 7N3143.

28. Frankenstein, *Le prix du réarmement*, pp. 305-7.

29. Robert A. Doughty, "The French Armed Forces," in Allan R. Millett and Williamson Murray (eds.), *Military Effectiveness*, 3 vols. (London and Boston, 1988), II: 50.

30. Robert A. Doughty, *The Seeds of Disaster: The Development of French Army Doctrine, 1919-1939* (Hamden, CT, 1985), p. 177.

31. Doughty, "French Armed Forces," p. 50.

32. CPDN discussion of 5 December 1938, in SHA Carton 2N25.

33. Doughty, "French Armed Forces," p. 51.

34. *Ibid.*

35. Doughty, *Seeds of Disaster*, pp. 23-24.

36. Doughty, "French Armed Forces," pp. 53-59.

37. Doughty, *Seeds of Disaster*, p. 152.

38. *Ibid.*, pp. 155-56.

39. *Ibid.*, pp. 164-65.

40. SHA Carton 7N2292.

41. On light armored divisions, see Doughty, *Seeds of Disaster*, pp. 161, 170-74.

42. See the Army Staff study of 15 April 1939 in SHA Carton 7N2524.

43. Paul Reynaud, *In the Thick of the Fight, 1930-1945* (New York, 1955), p. 91.

44. *Documents diplomatiques*, III: 19, 20-23.

45. *Ibid.*, III: 23.

46. Mark Jacobsen, Robert Levine, and William Schwabe, *Contingency Plans for War in Western Europe, 1920-1940* (Santa Monica, CA, 1985), pp. 15-23.

47. *Ibid.*, pp. 23-27.

48. François-André Paoli, *L'armée française de 1919 à 1939: La fin des illusions* (Paris, 1980), pp. 48-49.

49. SHA Carton 7N2524.

50. Maurice-Henri Gauché, *Le deuxième bureau au travail (1935-1940)* (Paris, 1953), pp. 39-40, and Paoli, *L'armée française*, p. 155.

51. SHA Carton 7N2292.

52. François-Poncet, *Fateful Years*, pp. 172-73.

53. Gamelin makes this claim. See M. Gamelin, *Servir: Le prologue du drame* (Paris, 1940), p. 194.

54. France, Assemblée Nationale, *Les événements survenus en France de 1933-1945* (Paris 1989), II: 475-76.

55. *Documents diplomatiques*, II: 37-38, 89-91, 91-92, 107-8, 113.

56. SHA Carton 7N3434.

57. SHA Carton 1N43. See also *Documents diplomatiques*, II: 291-92.

58. Dutailly, *Les problèmes de l'armée*, pp. 48-49.

59. SHA Carton 1N43; *Documents diplomatiques*, II: 301.

60. Gamelin, *Servir*, p. 202.

61. *Ibid.*, pp. 205-6, 211; *Documents diplomatiques*, II: 697-700. Young points out that the government did not ask the army for contingency plans until after the German move into the Rhineland; see Young, *In Command of France*, p. 122. For a general view of the French reaction, see Donald C. Watt, *Too Serious a Business: European Armed Forces and the Approach to the Second World War* (Berkeley, CA, 1975).

62. *Documents diplomatiques*, II: 141-42; Gauché, *Le deuxième bureau*, p. 54.

63. Gauché, *Le deuxième bureau*, p. 133; SHA Carton 7N7076.

64. *Documents diplomatiques*, IV: 484.

65. *Documents diplomatiques*, V: 79–82. For additional views of Soviet power see the attaché reports contained in SHA Carton 7N3184.

66. SHA Carton 5N579.

67. SHA Cartons 7N2515 and 5N579.

68. SHA Carton 5N579.

69. *Documents diplomatiques*, VIII: 821.

70. SHA Carton 2N25.

71. Dutailly, *Les problèmes de l'armée*, pp. 59–60.

72. *Documents diplomatiques*, IX: 251–56, 665.

73. Dutailly, *Les problèmes de l'armée*, p. 62.

74. *Documents diplomatiques*, XI: 426.

75. *Ibid.*, XI: 576.

76. *Ibid.*, IV: 185.

77. *Ibid.*, XI: 205–6.

78. SHA Cartons 7N2290, 7N7575, and 7N2601.

79. *Documents diplomatiques*, VI: 79–82.

80. SHA Carton 7N3110.

81. *Ibid.;* SHA Carton 7N2506.

82. *Documents diplomatiques*, XI: 106–7, 570–71.

83. *Ibid.*, XI: 613.

84. SHA Carton 7N3110 contains reports of 22 March, 13 June, 18 August, and 9 September from the French military mission in Prague.

85. *Documents diplomatiques*, IX: 393–94.

86. *Ibid.*, IX: 8.

87. *Ibid.*, IX: 393–94.

88. *Ibid.*, IX: 409.

89. Adamthwaite, *France and Coming of Second World War*, p. 204. Reynaud claims that as early as September 1937 King Carol of Rumania told General Gamelin that he would permit the passage of Soviet forces. See Reynaud, *In the Thick of the Fight*, pp. 52–53. See also J. Paul-Boncour, *Entre deux guerres: souvenirs sur la IIIe république* (New York, 1946), p. 112, and Assemblée Nationale, *Les événements*, IX: 2625.

90. Philippe Henriot (ed.), *Carnets secrets de Jean Zay* (Paris, 1942), pp. 3–5.

91. SHA Carton 5N579.

92. SHA Carton 1N43.

93. SHA Cartons 7N2676 and 7N2516.

94. SHA Carton 7N2524.

95. SHA Carton 7N2602.

96. SHA Cartons 7N2524 and 7N2516.

97. Dutailly, *Les problèmes de l'armée*, p. 83.

98. SHA Carton 7N2516.

99. SHA Carton 2N25.

100. *Documents diplomatiques*, XVI: 795–96.

101. *Ibid.*, XVII: 356–59.

102. Claude Paillat, *Le désastre de 1940: La guerre immobile, avril 1939–10 mai 1940* (Paris, 1984), pp. 74–75.

103. SHA Carton 5N579.

104. *Ibid.*

105. SHA Carton 7N2523.
106. Dutailly, *Les problèmes de l'armée*, pp. 310–11.
107. SHA Carton 7N2523.
108. SHA Cartons 1N43 and 5N579.
109. SHA Carton 2N25.
110. Williamson Murray, *The Change in the European Balance of Power, 1938–1939* (Princeton, NJ, 1984), p. 211; *idem, Luftwaffe* (London, 1985), p. 20.
111. Gauché, *Le deuxième bureau*, pp. 133–37.
112. SHA Cartons 7N2680 and 7N2506.
113. SHA Carton 7N2695.
114. SHA Carton 7N2506.
115. SHA Carton 7N2692.
116. SHA Carton 7N2506.
117. Doughty, *Seeds of Disaster*, p. 89.
118. SHA Carton 7N2506.
119. Doughty, *Seeds of Disaster*, p. 89.
120. *Ibid.*, p. 220.
121. SHA Carton 7N2515.
122. SHA Carton 7N2290.
123. SHA Carton 7N2506.
124. *Ibid.*
125. SHA Carton 7N3006.
126. *Ibid.*

6. Soviet Net Assessment in the 1930s

1. Hajo Holborn, *A History of Modern Germany* (New York, 1969), 3: 667.
2. Robert A. Hoover, *Arms Control: The Interwar Naval Limitation Agreements* (Denver, 1980), pp. 95–98; Erich Gröner, *Die deutschen Kriegsschiffe, 1815–1945* (Munich, 1966), 1:124.
3. J. Stalin, *Political Report of the Central Committee to the Sixteenth Congress of the CPSU(B)* (Moscow, 1951), pp. 7–39, 91.
4. Ministerstvo Oborony SSSR, Institut Voyennoi Istorii, *Sovetskaya voyennaya entsiklopedia* (Moscow, 1976–79), 4: 266 (hereafter, *SVE*).
5. On Voroshilov, see V. S. Akshinsky, *Kliment Yefremovich Voroshilov* (Moscow, 1976); John Erickson, *The Soviet High Command* (London, 1962), esp. pp. 200–201.
6. Ministerstvo Oborony SSSR, Institut Voyennoi Istorii, *Istoriya vtoroi mirovoi voiny, 1939–1945* (Moscow, 1973–79), 1: 258 (hereafter, *IVMV*).
7. *SVE,* 2:272.
8. Erickson, *High Command*, pp. 366–70.
9. *IVMV*, 2:204.
10. *SVE,* 8: 151.
11. S. A. Tyushkevich *et al., The Soviet Armed Forces: A History of Their Organizational Development* (Washington, DC, 1978), pp. 195, 500; Erickson, *High Command*, p. 845.
12. The Soviet literature does not say what became of the 1934 Military Council. Tyushkevich, *Armed Forces*, p. 501; Erickson, *High Command*, p. 478.
13. Biographical information on these persons is found in *SVE* under their name

entries. See also G. K. Zhukov, *The Memoirs of Marshal Zhukov* (New York, 1971), pp. 76–146 *passim;* K. A. Meretskov, *Serving the People* (Moscow, 1971), pp. 119–22.

14. A main military council also existed from 1950 to 1953, during the Korean War. *SVE,* 2: 566*f.*

15. Nikolai Kondratyev, *Marshal Blyukher* (Moscow, 1965), p. 292; Aleksandr Zolotrubov, *Budenny* (Moscow, 1983), p. 300.

16. *IVMV,* 2: 172.

17. Meretskov, *Serving,* p. 95.

18. *SVE,* 2: 238, 242; 3: 321; 4: 511; 5: 294, 295, 448; 6: 115*f;* 7: 393. Michael Morozow, *Die Falken des Kreml* (Munich, 1982), pp. 153, 167; Jurg Meister, *Soviet Warships of the Second World War* (New York, 1977), p. 7; N. Kuznetsov, "Before the War," *International Affairs* (January 1967), p. 103.

19. S. P. Ivanov *et al., The Initial Period of War* (Washington, DC, 1986), p. 57.

20. K. Y. Voroshilov, *Stalin and the Armed Forces of the USSR* (Moscow, 1951), p. 50.

21. N. S. Khrushchev, *Khrushchev Remembers* (Boston, 1970), pp. 18, 20.

22. See their biographical entries in *SVE.*

23. Dmitri Shostakovich, *Testimony* (New York, 1979), p. 96.

24. A. I. Todorsky, *Marshal Tukhachevsky* (Moscow, 1963), pp. 61*f,* 66*f.*

25. *Ibid.,* p. 82*f.*

26. N. I. Koritsky, *Marshal Tukhachevsky* (Moscow, 1969), p. 131.

27. In *Knowledge and Power: The Role of Stalin's Secret Chancellery* (Copenhagen, 1978), Niels Erik Rosenfeldt compiled a comparative analysis of the existing published evidence that confirms the secret chancellery's importance and demonstrates how little is known about it.

28. John J. Dziak, "The Study of the Soviet Intelligence and Security System," in Roy Godson (ed.), *Comparing Foreign Intelligence* (New York, 1988), p. 65*f.*

29. On the secret chancellery and the OGPU/NKVD see Rosenfeldt, *Secret Chancellery;* Walter Laqueur, *A World of Secrets* (New York, 1985), pp. 234–37; Simon Wolin and Robert Slusser (eds.), *The Soviet Secret Police* (New York, 1957), pp. 10–17.

30. N. Lomov and V. Golubovich, "Ob organizatsii i metodakh raboty general novo staba," *Voyenno-istorichesky Zhurnal* (February 1981), p. 12 (hereafter, *ViZ*).

31. Ivanov, *Initial Period,* p. 173.

32. Laqueur, *Secrets,* pp. 240, 242.

33. German intelligence collected Soviet military literature during World War II, which passed into United States military intelligence libraries after 1945 and to the National Archives in the early 1980s.

34. M. V. Zakharov (ed.), *Voprosy strategii i operativnovo iskustva v sovetskikh voyennykh trudakh, 1917–1940* (Moscow, 1965), pp. 29–44; F. N. Petrov (ed.), *M. V. Frunze* (Moscow, 1962), pp. 233–37.

35. I. A. Korotkov, *Istoria sovetskoi voyennoi mysli* (Moscow, 1980), p. 98.

36. *KPSS o vooruzhennykh silakh sovetskovo soyuza* (Moscow, 1981), p. 263.

37. *Bolshaya sovetskaya entsiklopedia* (1928), 12: 576–98.

38. V. K. Triandafilov, "Karakter operatsii sovremennykh armii," in Zakharov, *Voprosy strategii,* pp. 291–345.

39. Helm Speidel, "Reichswehr und Rote Armee," in *Vierteljahreshefte für Zeitgeschichte,* 1 (1953): 18.

40. B. Perrett, *Fighting Vehicles of the Red Army* (London, 1969), pp. 15, 26.

41. *IVMV*, 1: 262, 263; V. A. Anfilov, *Proval blitskriga* (Moscow, 1974), p. 117.

42. Olaf Groehler, *Geschichte des Luftkriegs* (Berlin, 1980), p. 135.

43. Zakharov, *Voprosy strategii*, pp. 374-84.

44. J. Stalin, *Report to the Seventeenth Congress of the CPSU(B) on the Work of the Central Committee* (Moscow, 1951), pp. 29-37.

45. Lev Nikulin, *Tukhachevsky* (Moscow, 1964), p. 177.

46. Tyushkevich, *Armed Forces*, pp. 187-91; Perrett, *Fighting Vehicles*, pp. 24-30, 45-47; Bill Gunston, *Combat Aircraft of World War II* (New York, 1978), pp. 184-88, 191.

47. Korotkov, *Voyennoi mysli*, pp. 178-82; *IVMV*, 1: 262, 269; *SVE*, 1: 144, 2: 230, and 3: 599.

48. V. S. Shumikhin, *Sovetskaya voyennaya aviatia, 1917-1941* (Moscow, 1986), p. 185; Groehler, *Luftkriegs*, p. 301.

49. Candidates had all the rights of membership in the Central Committee but could not vote.

50. On the current significance of deep operations, see Earl F. Ziemke, "The Soviet Theory of Deep Operations," *Parameters* (June 1983), pp. 23-40.

51. *IVMV*, 2: 171.

52. A. A. Grechko, *The Armed Forces of the Soviet State* (Washington, DC, 1975), p. 261.

53. Ivanov, *Initial Period*, p. 40*f.*

54. Tyushkevich, *Armed Forces*, p. 150.

55. M. N. Tukhachevsky, *Zadachi oborony SSSR* (Moscow, 1936), pp. 6-16.

56. A. Nikonov and I. Lemin (eds.), *Vooruzhenia kapitalisticheskikh stran v 1935g* (Moscow, 1936), pp. 3-10.

57. The Academy of Science analysis concentrated mainly on economic matters. The first chapter, which has been used here, appears to be an expanded and updated version of a critique Tukhachevsky wrote in 1930 as the introduction to the Russian translation of J. F. C. Fuller's 1923 book, *The Reformation of War*. See M. N. Tukhachevsky, *Izbrannye proizvedenia* (Moscow, 1964), 2: 147-56, and Richard Simpkin, *Deep Battle* (London, 1987), pp. 125-34 (for an English translation).

58. M. V. Zakharov, *50 let vooruzhennykh sil SSSR* (Moscow, 1968), p. 198.

59. A. I. Yeremenko, *The Arduous Beginning* (Moscow, 1964), pp. 7-10; G. S. Isserson, "Razvitiye teorii sovetskovo operativnovo iskustva v 30-te gody," *ViZ* (January 1965), pp. 44-46; *SVE*, 5: 121*f.*

60. Yeremenko, *Beginning*, pp. 11, 12.

61. On this see Maurice Tugwell, *Airborne to Battle: A History of Airborne Warfare, 1918-1971* (London, 1971), pp. 17-26.

62. Ronald R. Rader, "Anglo-French Estimates of the Red Army," in David R. Jones (ed.), *Soviet Armed Forces Review Annual, 1980* (Gulf Breeze, FL, 1980), p. 266.

63. Giffard Martel, *The Russian Outlook* (London, 1947), pp. 17-21.

64. Todorsky, *Tukhachevsky*, p. 89*f.*

65. Zakharov, *Voprosy strategii*, p. 22; *idem*, "O teorii glubokoy operatsii," *ViZ* (October 1970).

66. For a different evaluation see Simpkin, *Deep Battle*, which also (pp. 177-246) gives excerpts from PU 36 in English translation.

67. See Narodny Kommissariat Oborony, *Vremenny polevoi ustav RKKA 1936* (Moscow, 1936), and Chef der Heeresleitung, *Truppenführung* (Berlin, 1936), Teil I.

Although the German army was still under the restrictions imposed by the Treaty of Versailles, the 1933 field service regulations were written as if they applied to an army that possessed the full range of modern weapons and equipment.

68. Zakharov, "O teorii," p. 14.

69. G. S. Isserson, *Novye formy borby* (Moscow, 1940), excerpted in Zakharov, *Voprosy strategii*, p. 425.

70. M. N. Tukhachevsky, "O novom Polevom ustave RKKA," in Zakharov, *Voprosy strategii*, pp. 13–15; Simpkin, *Deep Battle*, pp. 161*f.*, 163.

71. S. Lubarsky, "Nekotorye vyvody iz opita voiny v Ispanii," *Voyennaya Mysl* (October 1938), pp. 12–31; (November 1936), pp. 95–108.

72. S. Lyubarsky, *Nekotorye operativno-takticheskiye vyvody iz opita voiny v Ispanii* (Moscow, 1939), pp. 16, 33*f.*, 37, 47, 62.

73. *Ibid.*, pp. 10, 12, 14, 15, 19, 24, 49, 53, 57*f.*

74. A. N. Lapchinsky, *Vozdushnaya armia* (Moscow, 1939), pp. 94, 144.

75. *IVMV*, 2: 211–13. See also Alvin D. Coox, *The Anatomy of a Small War* (Westport, CT, 1977), p. 111. The relative strengths and the casualties at Khalkhin-Gol are uncertain.

76. N. F. Kuzin, *Na strazhe minovo truda* (Moscow, 1959), p. 208*f.*

77. *IVMV*, 2: 215.

78. Zhukov, *Memoirs*, pp. 168–71; Meretskov, *Serving*, p. 93*f.;* N. N. Voronov, *Na sluzhbe voyennoi* (Moscow, 1963), p. 110*f.*

79. J. Stalin, *Report to the Eighteenth Congress of the CPSU(B) on the Work of the Central Committee* (Moscow, 1951), pp. 22, 28.

80. Jost Dulffer, *Weimar, Hitler und die Marine* (Düsseldorf, 1973), p. 570; Roger Chesneau (ed.), *All the World's Fighting Ships, 1922–1946* (New York, 1980), p. 178; N. G. Kuznetsov, "Before the War," *International Affairs* (December 1966), p. 95.

81. N. G. Kuznetsov, *Nakanune* (Moscow, 1969), p. 227.

82. Donald W. Mitchell, *A History of Russian and Soviet Sea Power* (New York, 1974), p. 366; Meister, *Soviet Warships*, pp. 20*f.*, 22, 39–43, 59–65, 184–208.

83. Shumikhin, *Aviatsia*, p. 185; *SVE*, 1: 259.

84. Korotkov, *Voyennoi mysli*, p. 174*f;* Gunston, *Combat Aircraft*, p. 175; Igor Andreyev, "The Plane That Joined Two Continents," *Soviet Life*, July 1987, p. 35.

85. Anfilov, *Proval*, p. 117*f.*

86. *GVE*, 7: 405.

87. Narodny Komissariat Oborony SSSR, *Polevoi ustav RKKA 1939* (Moscow, 1939), pp. 9, 11 (hereafter, *PU 39*).

88. Institut Marksizma-Leninizma, *Istoria velikoi otechestvennoi voiny sovetskovo soyuza* (Moscow, 1960–65), 1: 441.

89. *PU 39*, pp. 20–22, 24.

90. Carl Mannerheim, *The Memoirs of Marshal Mannerheim* (New York, 1954), pp. 350–67.

91. *IVMV*, 3: 409.

92. A. V. Anfilov, *Bessmertny podvig* (Moscow, 1971), p. 128.

93. *IVMV*, 3: 430*f.*

94. *Krasnaya Zvezda*, 2 October 1940.

95. A. M. Vasilevsky, *Delo vsei zhizni* (Moscow, 1976), p. 106; Ivanov, *Initial Period*, pp. 174, 175.

96. Department of State, *Foreign Relations of the United States* (Washington, DC, 1959), Vol. 1, *1940*, p. 611 (hereafter, *FRUS*).

97. Isserson, *Novye formy*, pp. 423, 437, 438.

98. G. S. Isserson, "Razvitie teorii sovetskovo operativnovo iskustva," *ViZ* (March 1965), pp. 54, 55.

99. Anfilov, *Proval*, p. 118, 123; I. E. Krupchenko *et al.*, *Sovetskie tankovye voiska* (Moscow, 1973), p. 13.

100. Narodny Komissariat Oborony SSSR, *Polevoi ustav Krasnoy Armii 1940 g* (Moscow, 1940), pp. 10, 15–22, 25, 26.

101. Korotkov, *Voyennoi mysli*, p. 137.

102. Meretskov, *Serving*, p. 124*f.;* M. I. Kazakov, *Nad Kartoi bylykh srazhenny* (Moscow, 1971), p. 52.

103. Ivanov, *Initial Period*, p. 72; Anfilov, *Proval*, p. 162.

104. Korotkov, *Voyennoi mysli*, p. 156.

105. Anfilov, *Proval*, p. 167.

106. Korotkov, *Voyennoi mysli*, p. 172*f.;* Yeremenko, *Beginning*, p. 31*f.;* Anfilov, *Proval*, p. 121.

107. Anfilov, *Proval*, p. 170.

108. *Ibid.*

109. Louis Rotundo, "War Plans and the 1941 Kremlin War Game," *Journal of Strategic Studies* (March 1987), pp. 84–97, gives a detailed analysis of the war games and the Kremlin meeting.

110. Yeremenko, *Beginning*, p. 34; Kazakov, *Nad kartoi*, p. 59.

111. Yeremenko, *Beginning*, p. 35; Kazakov, *Nad kartoi*, p. 60. A. I. Yeremenko, *Pomny voiny* (Donetsk, 1971), p. 129*f. Pomny voiny (War Recollections)*, the last of Yeremenko's three memoirs, in some respects contradicts the account of the Kremlin meeting he gave in *The Arduous Beginning*. See E. F. Ziemke, "Stalin as a Strategist, 1940–1941," *Military Affairs* (December 1983), p. 176.

112. Meretskov, *Serving*, p. 125.

113. Zhukov, *Memoirs*, p. 198.

114. *IVMV*, 3: 439.

115. *IVMV*, 3: 435, 438.

116. Zhukov, *Memoirs*, p. 215; Vasilevsky, *Delo*, p. 101; Ivanov, *Initial Period*, p. 106; V. D. Sokolovsky, *Soviet Military Strategy* (Englewood Cliffs, NJ, 1963), p. 232.

117. Ivanov, *Initial Period*, p. 174.

118. Gabriel Gorodetsky, *Stafford Cripps' Mission to Moscow, 1940–1942* (New York, 1984), p. 125*f.*

119. Department of State, *Nazi-Soviet Relations, 1939–1941* (Washington, DC, 1984), p. 324.

120. *FRUS*, 1941, 1:149.

121. G. A. Deborin and B. S. Telpukhovsky, *Itogi i uroki velikoi otechestvennoi voiny* (Moscow, 1975), p. 102.

122. Winston S. Churchill, *The Gathering Storm* (Boston, 1949), p. 367.

123. *Khrushchev Remembers*, p. 588.

124. See Earl F. Ziemke, *The German Northern Theater of Operations, 1940–1945* (Washington, DC, 1959), p. 138; Ivanov, *Initial Period*, p. 165*f.*

125. F. H. Hinsley *et al.*, *British Intelligence in the Second World War* (New York, 1979), 1:463–81.

126. Zhukov, *Memoirs*, p. 230.

127. Vasilevsky, *Delo*, p. 119; *IVMV*, 3: 440*f.*

128. Llewellyn Woodward, *British Foreign Policy in the Second World War* (London, 1970), 1: 623.

129. Zhukov, *Memoirs*, p. 223.

130. Ivanov, *Initial Period*, p. 179; *IVMV*, 3:438.

131. See Ivanov, *Initial Period*, p. 184, or any other comparable Soviet account.

132. Zakharov, *50 let*, p. 252; *IVMV*, 3:440; B. S. Telpukhovsky (ed.), *Velikaya otechestvennaya voina sovetskovo soyuza* (Moscow, 1984), p. 50; Ivanov, *Initial Period*, pp. 181, 184.

133. Earl F. Ziemke, *Moscow to Stalingrad: Decision in the East* (Washington, DC, 1987), p. 7. See also Horst Boog *et al.*, "Der Angriff auf die Sowetunion," in *Das Deutsche Reich und der Zweite Weltkrieg* (Stuttgart, 1983), 4: 271, 312.

134. Ivanov, *Initial Period*, p. 184.

135. P. N. Bobylev *et al.*, *Velikaya otechestvennaya voina* (Moscow, 1984), p. 75.

136. Tyushkevich, *Armed Forces*, p. 231.

137. Ivanov, *Initial Period*, p. 184.

138. *Ibid.; IVMV*, 3: 441.

139. *IVMV*, 3: 415.

140. *IVMV*, 12: 156, 157, 161.

141. Shumikhin, *Aviatsia*, p. 241; Boog, *Angriff*, pp. 653–55; Anfilov, *Proval*, pp. 207, 220; Morozow, *Falken*, p. 262*f.*

142. *IVMV*, Vol. 3, p. 427; Kuznetsov, "Before the War," pp. 94–96; Meister, *Warships*, pp. 22*ff.*, 26*f.*, 38–45.

7. Roosevelt and the Craft of Strategic Assessment

1. The author would like to thank the Franklin D. Roosevelt Library (hereafter, FDRL), Hyde Park, New York; the Franklin and Eleanor Roosevelt Institute; and the Four Freedoms Foundation for their help in this study.

2. Letter, Franklin D. Roosevelt (hereafter, FDR) to Antonio C. Gonzalez, Minister to Ecuador, 16 October 1937, in Donald B. Schewe (ed.), *Franklin D. Roosevelt and Foreign Affairs* (hereafter, *FDR & FA)* (New York, 1979), 7:111.

3. Quoted in Arthur Bryant, *The Turn of the Tide* (New York, 1957), p. 234.

4. Astor was a multimillionaire friend of FDR, while Carter was a journalist. See President's Secretary's File (hereafter, PSF), Subject: Vincent Astor; PSF, Subject: John F. Carter; and Official File (hereafter, OF) 4514, J. Franklin Carter files—all FDRL.

5. Roberta Wohlstetter, *Pearl Harbor: Warning and Decision* (Stanford, CA, 1962), p. 180, uses this word to describe government use of MAGIC information, but it is an apt description of Roosevelt's use of non-MAGIC material as well.

6. Quoted in J. Garry Clifford, "Both Ends of the Telescope," *Diplomatic History*, 13, no. 2 (Spring 1989): 220.

7. *The United States Strategic Bombing Surveys: Summary Reports* (Reprint, Maxwell Air Force Base, AL, 1987), pp. 111–12.

8. *FDR & FA* 4:v.

9. FDR, confidential conference with the Senate Military Affairs Committee, 31 January 1939, *FDR & FA*, 13: 214.

10. Letter, FDR to Anthony J. Biddle, Jr., Ambassador to Poland, 10 November 1937, *FDR & FA*, 7:196.

11. Letter, FDR to John Cudahy, Minister to the Irish Free State, 16 April 1938, *FDR & FA*, 9:423.

12. Letter, FDR to William Phillips, Ambassador to Italy, 17 October 1938, PSF, Diplomatic: Italy: Phillips, FDRL. Although it appears that FDR was speaking specifically about the Munich settlement when he made that comment, it is also possible that his statement referred to other concerns which Phillips mentioned in his messages of 29 September and 1 October 1938.

13. Letter, Arthur Murray to FDR, 15 December 1938, PSF, Diplomatic: Great Britain: Arthur Murray, FDRL.

14. Letter, FDR to Arthur Murray, 24 August 1939, PSF, Diplomatic: Great Britain: Arthur Murray, FDRL.

15. Memorandum, FDR to Swanson, 12 February 1938, PSF, Departmental: Navy: Claude Swanson; letter, FDR to Admiral William Leahy, 10 November 1937, PSF, Departmental: Navy Department, October 1936–37; memorandum, FDR to Captain Callaghan, 1 July 1939, OF 18, Department of the Navy: July–December 1939; see the Navy files in the Secret, Confidential, and Departmental files, PSF, and OF, FDRL.

16. FDR, confidential conference with the Senate Military Affairs Committee, 31 January 1939, *FDR & FA*, 13:200.

17. Quoted in William L. Langer and S. Everett Gleason, *The Challenge to Isolation* (New York, 1964), p. 597.

18. Robert Dallek, *Franklin D. Roosevelt and American Foreign Policy, 1932–1945* (New York, 1979), p. 16.

19. PSF, Diplomatic: Great Britain: Arthur Murray, *passim*, FDRL.

20. FDR, confidential conference with the Senate Military Affairs Committee, 31 January 1939, *FDR & FA*, 13: 199.

21. Letter, FDR to William Phillips, 15 September 1938, *FDR & FA*, 11:172.

22. Letter, R. Walton Moore, Counselor of the Department of State, to FDR, 12 May 1939, PSF, Neutrality, 1939–41; letter, Moore to FDR, 19 May 1939, PSF, Subject: Neutrality, 1939–41, both FDRL.

23. Memorandum, FDR to Hull and Welles, 28 March 1939, PSF, Subject: Neutrality, 1939–41, FDRL.

24. Letter, FDR to Representative Caroline O'Day, 1 July 1939, *FDR & FA*, 16:47; also see letter, O'Day to FDR, 7 July 1939, PSF, Subject: Congress, 1932–40 (Folder I), FDRL.

25. Letter, FDR to Frank Knox, 29 December 1939, PSF, Departmental: Navy: Frank Knox, FDRL.

26. Letter, FDR to Arthur and Faith Murray, 2 June 1941, PSF, Diplomatic: Great Britain: Arthur Murray, 1940–44, FDRL.

27. Louis Morton, "Interservice Co-operation and Political–Military Collaboration," in Harry L. Coles (ed.), *Total War and Cold War* (Columbus, OH, 1962), pp. 132–39.

28. Quoted in Ernest R. May, "The Development of Political–Military Consulta-

tion in the United States," *Political Science Quarterly*, 70, no. 2 (June 1955): 167.

29. *Ibid.*, p. 168.

30. Memorandum, Captain Adolphus Staton, USN, to the Assistant Commandant, the Army War College, 25 February 1932, GB 425, Record Group (hereafter, RG) 80, National Archives (hereafter, NA).

31. Quoted in Vernon E. Davis, *The History of the Joint Chiefs in World War II*, vol. 1, *Origin of the Joint and Combined Chiefs of Staff* (Washington, DC, 1972), p. 31.

32. Letter, Joseph C. Grew to FDR, 14 December 1940, PSF, Confidential: State Department, 1939–40, FDRL.

33. *Hearings Before the Joint Committee on the Investigation of the Pearl Harbor Attack, Congress of the United States*, 79th Cong., 1st Sess., Part II, p. 455.

34. Letter, Hull to FDR, 28 March 1938, *FDR & FA*, 9: 250; memorandum, FDR to Hull, 4 April 1938, *FDR & FA*, 9:319.

35. Memorandum, Local Joint Planning Committee to Rear Admiral H. E. Yarnell, Commandant, Fourteenth Naval District, and Major General H. A. Drum, Commanding General, Hawaiian Department, 25 May 1936, PSF, Departmental: War Department, 1934–36, FDRL.

36. Memorandum, FDR to the Chief of Naval Operations, 10 August 1936, PSF, Departmental: War Department: Harry Woodring, FDRL.

37. Letter, Harry Woodring, Secretary of War, to FDR, 17 November 1937, and memorandum, FDR to Woodring, 26 November 1937, *FDR & FA*, 7: 242–44, 315.

38. Memorandum, FDR to Woodring, 22 May 1937, PSF, Departmental: War Department: Harry Woodring, FDRL.

39. Memorandum for the Secretary of War and the Acting Secretary of Navy, 25 August 1939, PSF, Departmental: Navy Department: Charles Edison, FDRL; Eric Larrabee, *Commander in Chief* (New York, 1987), pp. 16–17; Davis, *Origin of Joint Chiefs*, pp. 40–41.

40. Morton, "Interservice Co-operation," p. 156.

41. Morgenthau Presidential Diaries, 22 May 1941, FDRL; Morton, "Interservice Co-operation," p. 156.

42. Forest C. Pogue, *George C. Marshall*, Vol. 2, *Ordeal and Hope, 1939–1942* (New York, 1966), p. 26; Henry L. Stimson and McGeorge Bundy, *On Active Service in Peace and War* (New York, 1947), p. 334.

43. Letter, FDR to Winston Churchill, 11 September 1939, in Warren Kimball (ed.), *Churchill & Roosevelt: The Complete Correspondence* (hereafter *C & R*), (Princeton, NJ, 1984), 1:24.

44. Memorandum, Ambassador Ronald C. Lindsay to FDR and Cordell Hull, 28 February 1939, *FDR & FA*, 14: 32.

45. Quoted in Christopher Andrew, *Her Majesty's Secret Service* (New York, 1986), p. 467.

46. Letter, Arthur Murray to FDR, 4 March 1940, PSF, Diplomatic: Great Britain: Arthur Murray, 1940–44, FDRL.

47. Letter, Lord Lothian to FDR, 19 May 1940, PSF, Diplomatic: Great Britain, Reports from London on Military Situation by Lord Lothian, May–August 1940, FDRL; letter, Lord Halifax to FDR, 28 February 1942, PSF, Diplomatic: Great Britain, Daily Reports, 1942, FDRL. The FDRL never received the reports from 1941.

48. Adolph Berle, Jr., Papers, Diary, 13 February 1941, FDRL.

49. "The Reminiscences of Alan Goodrich Kirk," Oral History Research Office, Columbia University, 1962, p. 133. A copy is in the Operational Archives, Naval Historical Center (hereafter, OA, NHC), Washington Navy Yard, Washington, DC. Also see telegram, Ambassador John Winant to FDR, 3 April 1941, PSF, Safe: Winant, FDRL.

50. "Reminiscences of Kirk," p. 144; letter, Chamberlain to FDR, 25 August 1939, and letter, FDR to Neville Chamberlain, 31 August 1939, *FDR & FA*, 16: 299–301, 400.

51. "Reminiscences of Kirk," p. 143.

52. Letter, William C. Bullitt, Ambassador to France, to FDR, 10 January 1938, *FDR & FA*, 8:64–65; letter, Churchill to FDR, 25 February 1942, *C & R*, 1:371.

53. Letter, Captain Alan Kirk to Rear Admiral W. S. Anderson, Director, Naval Intelligence, 3 November 1939, PSF, Departmental: Navy Department, October–December 1939, FDRL. This letter was brought to FDR's attention; memorandum, Captain D. J. Callaghan, USN, Naval Aide to the President, to FDR, 8 December 1939, PSF, Departmental: Navy Department, October–December 1939, FDRL.

54. Thomas Troy, *Donovan and the CIA* (Washington, DC, 1981), pp. 31–32.

55. Letter, Sumner Welles to FDR, 12 July 1940, PSF, Departmental: Navy Department: Frank Knox, FDRL.

56. Troy, *Donovan*, p. 32.

57. "Some Pertinent Data on Restrictions on Japanese Trade," PSF, Departmental: Treasury Department: Henry Morgenthau, Jr., 1938, no date (late 1937 or early 1938), FDRL.

58. Letter and memorandum, Anthony J. Biddle, Jr. to FDR, 7 April 1939, *FDR & FA*, 14:276–82.

59. Memorandum, Bernard Baruch to FDR, 29 April 1938, PSF, Confidential: War Department, 1933–41, FDRL; memorandum, Baruch to FDR, 28 June 1938, PSF, Departmental: War Department: Louis Johnson, FDRL; letter, Baruch to FDR, 31 July 1939, *FDR & FA*, 16: 175–78; letter, Edward R. Stettinius, Jr., Chairman, U.S. Steel Corporation, to FDR, 5 July 1938, *FDR & FA*, 10:369.

60. Memorandum, Louis Johnson, Assistant Secretary of War, to FDR, 16 January 1939, PSF, Departmental: War Department: Louis Johnson, FDRL.

61. Letter, Astor to FDR, no date (summer 1940?), PSF, Subject: Vincent Astor, FDRL.

62. Letter, Astor to FDR, no date (spring 1938), PSF, Subject: Vincent Astor, FDRL.

63. Memorandum, (March 1941), PSF, Subject: Vincent Astor, FDRL.

64. Memorandum, Harry Hopkins, Secretary of Commerce, to Marguerite LeHand, private secretary to the President, 7 May 1940, PSF, Subject: Harry L. Hopkins, FDRL; and memorandum, 6 September 1940, PSF, Departmental: Treasury Department: Henry Morgenthau, Jr., 1940, Part II, FDRL; PSF, Safe: Germany, FDRL; letter, Sumner Welles to FDR, 21 February 1941, PSF, Departmental: State Department: Welles, January–May 1941, FDRL.

65. Letter, FDR to Secretary of the Navy, 14 July 1941, OF 4485, Office of Strategic Services, 1940–October 1941, FDRL.

66. Coordinator of Information, "The German Military and Economic Position:

Summary and Conclusion," Monograph no. 3, 12 December 1941, PSF, Safe: Germany, FDRL.

67. FDR, confidential conference with the Senate Military Affairs Committee, 31 January 1939, FDR & FA, 13: 203.

68. Memorandum, Major General H. H. Arnold to Chief of Staff, 15 November 1938, OF25T: War Department: Chief of Staff (Army), 1935–39, FDRL.

69. FDR, confidential conference with the Senate Military Affairs Committee, 31 January 1939, FDR & FA, 13: 7–8, 12–17, 26–27; press conference, 31 January 1939, FDR & FA, 13: 224–26.

70. Letter, Bullitt to FDR, 16 September 1939, PSF, Safe: William C. Bullitt, FDRL; letter, Bullitt to FDR, 12 May 1938, FDR & FA, 10:87–95; letter, Bullitt to FDR, 23 November 1937, FDR & FA, 7: 280–93.

71. Letter, Bullitt to FDR, 20 September 1938, FDR & FA, 11:194.

72. Letter, Wilson to FDR, 11 July 1938, FDR & FA, 10:383.

73. Memorandum, Joseph P. Kennedy, Chairman, U.S. Maritime Commission, to FDR, 9 February 1938, FDR & FA, 8:250.

74. "Report on Military Aircraft, Plants, and Production . . . ," 12 September 1938, PSF, Departmental: War Department, 1938, FDRL; memorandum, Colonel J. H. Burns, Ordnance Department, to Louis Johnson, 23 June 1938, PSF, Departmental: War Department: Louis Johnson, FDRL.

75. Letter, Louis Johnson to FDR, 7 December 1938, with accompanying material, PSF, Confidential: War Department, 1933–41, FDRL; also see "Joint Annual Army–Navy Aviation Report on Germany, as of July 1, 1938," PSF, Departmental: Navy Department, March–December 1938, FDRL.

76. "Aircraft Production: Germany-Italy-Japan," no date (fall 1941?), WPD 4494, RG 165, NA.

77. Ibid.; Alvin D. Coox, "The Rise and Fall of the Imperial Japanese Air Forces," Aerospace Historian, 27, no. 2 (June 1980): p. 81.

78. Letter, Hull to FDR, 28 March 1938, FDR & FA, 9:254.

79. Memorandum, General Malin Craig to FDR, 1 February 1939, FDR & FA, 13:229.

80. Dwight Eisenhower, Crusade in Europe (Garden City, NY, 1950), p. 33.

81. "Reminiscences of Kirk," p. 183.

82. Pogue, Ordeal, pp. 200–201; Eisenhower, Crusade, pp. 32–34; Berle Papers, Diary, 8 March 1941, FDRL.

83. Letter, Hansell to Robert F. Futrell, 5 July 1988 (copy sent to Calvin L. Christman by Hansell), and letter, Hansell to Calvin L. Christman, 27 September 1988, both in author's possession; Haywood S. Hansell, The Air Plan That Defeated Hitler (Atlanta, 1972), pp. 49–56.

84. Edwin T. Layton, "And I Was There:" Pearl Harbor and Midway—Breaking the Secrets (New York, 1985), p. 96; "Reminiscences of Kirk," pp. 179–80; Gordon W. Prange, Pearl Harbor: The Verdict of History (New York, 1986), pp. 294–95.

85. "Reminiscences of Kirk," p. 181; Troy, Donovan, pp. 43–70.

86. Letter, Attorney General to FDR, 17 June 1939, and memorandum, FDR to Secretary of State, 26 June 1939, OF10A-10B, Department of Justice: FBI, 1939, FDRL.

87. Memorandum, Francis Biddle, Attorney General, to FDR, 22 December 1941, OF10A-10B, Department of Justice: FBI, 1941-42, FDRL.

88. Letter, Astor to FDR, 7 June 1940; and letter, Astor to FDR, 14 March [1941], both in PSF, Subject: Vincent Astor, FDRL.

89. Berle Papers, Diary, 12 February 1941, FDRL.

90. Memorandum, FDR to the Attorney General, the Under Secretary of State, Donovan, MID, and ONI, 30 December 1941, OF10A-10B, Department of Justice: FBI, 1941-42, FDRL.

91. Letter, Hart to Stark, 20 August 1940, PSF, Departmental: Navy Department, July-October 1940, FDRL. Emphasis in original.

92. Memorandum, Richardson to Stark, 22 October 1940, SEC NAV CNO 1940-41, Secret, A16/FF1, CINCUS to CNO, RG 80, NA.

93. Records of the Joint Board, JB 325, Serial 533, 533 (a), 546, 617 and 618, RG 225, NA; Louis Morton, *Strategy and Command* (Washington, DC, 1962), ch. 1.

94. "The Defense of the Philippine Islands by the United States," War Plans Division, 2 December 1935, WPD 3389-29, RG 165, NA.

95. *Ibid.;* memorandum, Chairman of the General Board to the Secretary of the Navy, 4 May 1932, GB 425, Serial No. 1502, RG 80, NA.

96. John Keegan, *The Price of Admiralty* (New York, 1989), p. 171.

97. Quoted in Michael K. Doyle, "The U.S. Navy and War Plan Orange, 1933-1940: Making Necessity a Virtue," *Naval War College Review*, 23 (May-June 1980): 56.

98. Letter, Yarnell to Leahy, 15 October 1937, PSF, Departmental: Navy Department, October 1936-37, FDRL.

99. Letter, FDR to Leahy, 10 November 1937, PSF, Departmental: Navy Department, October 1936-37, FDRL. FDR had given his Chicago "quarantine speech" on 5 October. Yarnell had written his letter to Leahy from Shanghai on 15 October 1937.

100. Records of the Joint Board, JB 325, Serial 642-1, RG 225, NA; Morton, *Strategy and Command*, pp. 67-72; Maurice Matloff and Edwin M. Snell, *Strategic Planning for Coalition Warfare, 1941-1942* (Washington, DC, 1953), pp. 3-8.

101. Memorandum, Hepburn Report to the Secretary of the Navy, 1 December 1938, PSF, Subject: Aviation (Folder I), FDRL.

102. "Are We Ready?" 31 August 1939, GB 425, Serial 1868, PSF, Departmental: Navy Department, January-September 1939, FDRL.

103. See the following files: Departmental: Navy: Claude Swanson; Confidential: Navy Department, 1933-39; Departmental: Navy Department, January-February 1938; Departmental: Navy Department, July-October 1940; Departmental: War Department Draft (1940); Departmental: Navy Department, November-December 1940, all PSF, FDRL.

104. "Are We Ready-III," 14 June 1941, GB 425, Serial 144, RG 80, NA; memorandum from Stark, 2 June 1941, GB 425, RG 80, NA.

105. Christopher R. Gabel, "The U.S. Army GHQ Maneuvers of 1941," Ph.D. dissertation, The Ohio State University, 1981, ch. 1.

106. Quoted in Mark S. Watson, *Chief of Staff: Prewar Plans and Preparations: The War Department* (Washington, DC, 1950), p. 30.

107. Letter, Louis Johnson to General Craig, 10 December 1938, PSF, Subject: Aviation (Folder I); memorandum, General Craig to Johnson, 19 December 1938, both FDRL.

108. Quoted in Watson, *Chief of Staff*, p. 157.

109. FDR, confidential conference with the Senate Military Affairs Committee, 31 January 1939, *FDR & FA*, 13:207.

110. PPF1-0 (3), President, *Diaries and Itineraries (Combined)*, 1937–40; PPF1-0 (2), President, *Appointment Diary*, 1940; *Usher's Diary*, 1940, all FDRL.

111. Tracy B. Kittredge, "United States–British Naval Cooperation, 1940–1945," unpublished manuscript, chs. 7 and 8, OA, NHC; Stetson Conn, "Changing Concepts of National Defense in the United States, 1937–1947," *Military Affairs*, 28 (Spring 1964): 3–5; Louis Morton, "Germany First: The Basic Concept of Allied Strategy in World War II," in Kent R. Greenfield (ed.), *Command Decisions* (New York, 1959), pp. 18–24; David Reynolds, *The Creation of the Anglo-American Alliance, 1937–1941* (Chapel Hill, NC, 1982), pp. 124–27; Matloff and Snell, *Strategic Planning*, pp. 11–25.

112. Quoted in Matloff and Snell, *Strategic Planning*, p. 19.

113. Telegram, Kennedy to Hull, 12 June 1940, PSF, Safe: Kennedy, FDRL.

114. Matloff and Snell, *Strategic Planning*, pp. 13–15.

115. Memorandum, Henry L. Stimson to FDR, 9 October 1940, PSF, Departmental: War Department: Henry L. Stimson, 1940–41, FDRL.

116. Letter, Churchill to Roosevelt, 7 December 1940, in Kimball, *C & R*, 1:108–9.

117. Mark M. Lowenthal, "The Stark Memorandum and the American National Security Process, 1940," in Robert William Love (ed.), *Changing Interpretations and New Sources in Naval History: Papers from the Third United States Naval Academy History Symposium* (New York, 1980), pp. 352–59.

118. Stark to Frank Knox, 12 November 1940, PSF, Safe: Navy Department: Plan Dog, FDRL, emphasis in the original; Stark's draft memorandum of 4 November is in PSF, Departmental: Navy Department, November–December 1940, FDRL.

119. Morton, "Germany First," p. 26.

120. FDR probably reached this conclusion in late spring 1941, as Germany seemed everywhere victorious. Although intelligence reports pointed toward a forthcoming German attack on the Soviet Union, these same reports also speculated that Moscow might accede to Berlin's demands. In that case, Germany might proceed with an assault on Britain or make a move against Iceland or Greenland. Other reports indicated that Germany might push into Spain and Gibraltar. From there, the administration feared, Germany might jump to the Azores and Cape Verde Islands, West Africa, and then to Brazil. See Berle Papers, Diary, Spring 1941, *passim*, FDRL, and Waldo Heinrichs, *Threshold of War: Franklin D. Roosevelt and American Entry into World War II* (New York, 1988), chs. 3–4, *passim*.

121. Memorandum, FDR to Knox, 26 January 1941, PSF, Departmental: Navy Department, January–June 1941, FDRL.

122. Reynolds, *Alliance*, p. 184.

123. Letter, George S. Messersmith, Assistant Secretary of State, to Cordell Hull, 29 September 1938, *FDR & FA*, 11:272–77; memorandum, unsigned, 11 October 1938, *FDR & FA*, 11: 346–52; FDR, confidential conference with the Senate Military Affairs Committee, 31 January 1939, *FDR & FA*, 13:197–223; summary, prepared by U.S. Embassy in London, 3 March 1939, *FDR & FA*, 14: 5–25; report, naval attaché,

Berlin, 10 July 1941, PSF, Estimates of Potential Military Strength, Berlin, FDRL.

124. Summary, prepared by U.S. Embassy in London, 3 March 1939, *FDR & FA*, 14:18.

125. Report, naval attaché, Tokyo, No. 236-38, 28 November 1938, PSF, Estimates of Potential Military Strength, Tokyo, FDRL; letter, Captain Evans Carlson, USMC, to Marguerite LeHand, private secretary to the President, 29 November 1938, *FDR&FA*, 12:219; memoranda, Leahy to FDR, 6 January 1938, *FDR&FA*, 8:30-33, and Leahy to FDR, 15 December 1938, *FDR&FA*, 12:328-29.

126. Summary, prepared by U.S. Embassy in London, 3 March 1939, *FDR & FA*, 14:20.

127. Report, military attaché, Berlin, 24 January 1941, PSF, Estimates of Potential Military Strength, Berlin, FDRL.

128. Adolph Berle, Jr., Papers, Diary, 26 May 1941, FDRL; memorandum, FDR to Henry Morgenthau, Jr., 1 April 1941, PSF, Departmental: Treasury Department: Henry Morgenthau, Jr., 1941-42, FDRL.

129. Memorandum, Roosevelt to Hopkins, Marshall, and King, 16 July 1942, PSF, Safe: Marshall, FDRL.

130. Report, naval attaché, Tokyo, No. 178-39, 9 August 1939, PSF, Estimates of Potential Military Strength, Tokyo, FDRL.

131. "Professional Notes," *United States Naval Institute Proceedings*, 67 (June 1941): 880.

132. Quoted in memorandum, Admiral Leahy to FDR, 11 October 1937, PSF, Departmental: Navy Department, October 1936-1937, FDRL.

133. Minutes, British-United States Staff Conversations, 31 January 1941, WPD 4402-89, part VI, RG 165, NA.

134. Report, naval attaché, Tokyo, No. 236-38, 28 November 1938, PSF, Estimates of Potential Military Strength, Tokyo, FDRL; letter, Captain Riley F. McConnell, Chief of Staff, Commander-in-Chief, Asiatic Fleet, to Admiral James O. Richardson, Office of the Chief of Naval Operations, 27 January 1938, *FDR & FA*, 8: 339. Also see Howard Young, "Racial Attitudes and the U.S. Navy's Unpreparedness for War with Japan," in *New Aspects of Naval History: Selected Papers from the 5th Naval History Symposium* (Baltimore, 1985), pp. 177-82, and William M. Leary, "Assessing the Japanese Threat: Air Intelligence Prior to Pearl Harbor," *Aerospace Historian*, 34, no. 4 (Winter 1987): 272-77.

135. Telephone conversation, Stark and Bloch, 7 December 1941, OPNAV Telephone Records, 1941-42, OA, NHC.

136. Message, OPNAV to CINCLANT and SPENAVO, 7 December 1941, Pearl Harbor Liaison Office, RG 80, NA.

137. Memorandum, E. M. Watson to FDR, 9 December 1941, PSF, Diplomatic: Philippines, 1941, FDRL.

138. Interview, 20 March 1942, PSF, Safe: War Department, FDRL.

139. Doyle, "Navy and Orange," p. 53.

140. Memorandum, Marshall to FDR, 22 September 1941, PSF, Departmental: War Department, 1941, FDRL.

141. Telegram, Grew to Hull, 3 November 1941, PSF, Confidential: Japan, 8 May 1939 to 17 November 1941, FDRL.

142. Captain Claire Chennault, "The Role of Defensive Pursuit," Air Corps Tactical

School, [1933] 248.282-4, United States Air Force Historical Research Center (Maxwell AFB, AL); memorandum, Chennault to Commandant, Air Corps Tactical School, 7 March 1935, 248.282-27, USAFHRC; Letter, Haywood S. Hansell, Jr., to Calvin L. Christman, 27 September 1988.

143. Telephone conversation between Marshall and Lieutenant Commander W. R. Smedberg, III, 25 September 1941, OPNAV Telephone Records, 1941-42, OA, NHC.

144. Charts showing bombing radius from Philippine airfields, September 1941, PSF, Departmental (no file folder), FDRL; memorandum, Brigadier General Gerow to Stimson, 8 October 1941, WPD 3251-60, RG 165, NA; letter, FDR to Stimson, 14 October 1941, PSF, Departmental: "War Department 1941," FDRL; letter, Stimson to FDR, 21 October 1941, PSF, Departmental: War Department: Henry L. Stimson, 1940-41, FDRL; and memorandum, Lieutenant Colonel George to General Arnold, 21 October 1941, pp. 145.94-2 (WP-I) bk. 2, USAFHRC.

145. Memorandum, Lieutenant General H. H. Arnold to FDR, 23 March 1942, PSF, Departmental: War Department: General Henry H. "Hap" Arnold, FDRL.

146. Interview, Calvin L. Christman with Edward L. Beach, World War II American submarine captain, 23 September 1987.

147. Stephen Roskill, *Naval Policy Between the Wars*, Vol. 2, *The Period of Reluctant Rearmament, 1930-1939* (Annapolis, 1976), pp. 226-29, 336-37; Wesley K. Wark, "Naval Intelligence in Peacetime: Britain's Problems in Assessing the German Threat, 1933-39," in Daniel M. Masterson (ed.), *Naval History: The Sixth Symposium of the U.S. Naval Academy* (Wilmington, DE, 1987), p. 201.

148. Quoted in Roskill, *Reluctant Rearament*, p. 337.

149. "Estimate of Potential Military Strength," Documents A, Naval Attaché, London, Documents Numbers 1-141 (12 January 1937-2 August 1939), PSF, FDRL. Out of 141 reports from London, only one mentioned British ASW preparations, and that was a brief comment in August 1939 on trawlers being acquired for ASW work.

150. Naval attaché report, London, 11 March 1940, PSF, Departmental: Navy Department, January-April 1940, FDRL. His naval aide brought this report to FDR's attention.

151. Interview, Calvin L. Christman with Erich Topp, World War II German submarine captain, 25 March 1988.

152. Letter, Swanson to FDR, 3 December 1935, PSF, Departmental: Navy: Claude Swanson, FDRL.

153. General Board, memorandum, "Lessons from the current war and their effect . . . ," 9 May 1940, General Board 429-4, RG 80, NA.

154. Letter, Stimson to FDR, 23 June 1941, PSF, Departmental: War Department: Henry L. Stimson, 1940-41; Berle Papers, Diary, 19 July 1941; telegram, Greene to Hull, 27 July 1941, PSF, Safe: Germany, all FDRL. Heinrichs, *Threshold of War*, chs. 5-7, *passim*, provides a detailed discussion of the various reports flowing into Washington and of the swings in opinion during the summer and fall of 1941 as to whether or not the Soviet Union would still exist by winter.

155. Conference held at the Kremlin between Stalin and Hopkins, with interpreter Litvinov, 31 July 1941, Part I, PSF, Safe: Russia, FDRL.

156. Telegram, Hopkins to FDR, Hull, and Welles, 1 August 1941, PSF, Safe: Russia, FDRL.

157. Letter, FDR to Leahy, 26 June 1941, in Elliott Roosevelt (ed.), *F.D.R.: His Personal Letters* (New York, 1950), 2: 1177.

158. Memorandum, FDR to Wayne Coy, 2 August 1941, in *ibid.*, 2:1195–96.

159. Memoranda, FDR to Hopkins, Marshall, and King, 16 and 24 July 1942, PSF, Safe: Marshall, FDRL.

160. Letter, FDR to Churchill, 18 March 1942, Kimball, *C & R*, 1:421.

161. Maurice Matloff, "Mr. Roosevelt's Three Wars," Harmon Memorial Lectures, no. 6 (Colorado Springs, 1964), p. 5.

162. Letter, Roosevelt to Stimson, 3 January 1942, PSF, Confidential: War Department, 1942 (Folder I), FDRL.

8. Japanese Net Assessment in the Era Before Pearl Harbor

1. Foreign Affairs Association of Japan, *The Japan Year Book 1944–45* (Tokyo, 1945), ch. 4. In keeping with Japanese usage, surnames precede given names in this chapter, except in cases of books in English by Japanese authors cited herein.

2. See Morimatsu Toshio, *Daihonei* (Tokyo, 1981), pp. 209–10.

3. The format and nomenclature of the Liaison Conference underwent considerable modification by 1941. For details see Morimatsu, *Daihonei*, p. 210.

4. Robert J. C. Butow, *Tojo and the Coming of the War* (Princeton, NJ, 1961), p. 214.

5. Author's interviews with Colonel Suginoo Yoshio, JGSDF (Japan Ground Self-Defense Force), and Rear Admiral Hirama Yōichi, JMSDF (Japan Maritime Self-Defense Force). The war-related destruction of many primary records makes reconstruction of events within prewar and wartime Japan difficult, but the author has been able to supplement extant Japanese-language documentation with numerous personal interviews conducted in Japan with knowledgeable survivors of the period.

6. Nihon Kindai Shiryō Kenkyūkai (eds.), *Nihon Riku-Kaigun no Seido Soshiki Jinji* (Tokyo, 1971), pp. 130ff.

7. Bōeichō Bōeikenshūsho Senshi Shitsu (hereafter, BBSS), *Daihonei Rikugunbu (2)* (Tokyo, 1968), pp. 1–2.

8. *Ibid.*, p. 2.

9. See Alvin D. Coox, *Nomonhan: Japan Against Russia, 1939*, 2 Vols. (Stanford, CA, 1985).

10. Author's interview with Hata Ikuhiko.

11. BBSS, *Daihonei Rikugunbu (2)*, p. 34.

12. Author's interview with Tanemura Sakō.

13. BBSS, *Daihonei Kaigunbu: Daitōa Sensō Kaisen Keii (4)* (Tokyo, 1975), pp. 139–40.

14. Author's interview with Ayabe Kitsuju. See also Alvin D. Coox, "Japanese Foreknowledge of the Soviet-German War, 1941," *Soviet Studies*, 23 (April 1972): 554–55, 558–59.

15. Higashikuni Naruhiko, *Ichikōzoku no Sensō Nikki* (Tokyo, 1950), p. 42.

16. Coox, "Japanese Foreknowledge," pp. 555–56.

17. *Ibid.*, pp. 556–57.

18. *Ibid.*, p. 560.

19. Author's interviews with Onodera Makoto and Kohtani Etsuo; Endō Etsuo in Nakamura Kikuo, *Shōwa Rikugun Hishi* (Tokyo, 1968), pp. 223–24.

20. See Barton Whaley, *Codeword BARBAROSSA* (Cambridge, MA, 1973), pp. 172–74, 247–51.

21. Nishi Haruhiko (ed.), *Ni-So Kokkō Mondai 1917–1945*, in *Nihon Gaikōshi* series (Tokyo, 1970), 15: 227–28; Yabe Teiji, *Konoe Fumimaro* (Tokyo, 1952), 2:294.

22. Tanemura Sakō, *Daihonei Kimitsu Nisshi* (Tokyo, 1952), pp. 54–55; author's interviews with Tanemura and Kohtani Etsuo.

23. Tanemura, *Daihonei*, p. 57; author's interviews with Takei Seitarō and Yabe Chūta.

24. BBSS, *Daitōa Sensō Kaisen Keii (2)*, p. 320 (16 May 1941).

25. Higashikuni, *Ichikōzoku*, p. 47.

26. Nishi, *Ni-So*, 15: 228; *Kido Kōichi Nikki* (Tokyo, 1966), 2:875 (15 May 1941); author's interview with Takei.

27. BBSS, *Daitōa Sensō Kaisen Keii (4)*, pp. 140–42; Higashikuni, *Ichikōzoku*, pp. 49–51; *Kido Nikki*, 2:875 (18 May 1941).

28. Saitō Yoshie, *Azamukareta Rekishi: Matsuoka to Sangoku Dōmei no Rimen* (Tokyo, 1953), p. 195; Nishi, *Ni-So*, 15: 228; Yabe, *Konoe*, 2:294.

29. Author's interview with Yabe. See also Alvin D. Coox, "L'Affaire Lyushkov: Anatomy of a Defector," *Soviet Studies*, 19 (January 1968): 405–20.

30. Yabe, *Konoe*, 2:295.

31. Nishi, *Ni-So*, 15:229.

32. BBSS, *Daitōa Sensō Kaisen Keii (4)*, p. 142.

33. Higashikuni, *Ichikōzoku*, pp. 57–59; Yō Isshū, *Taiheiyō Sensō Zenya* (Tokyo, 1970), p. 206; Yabe, *Konoe*, 2:295; Akisada Tsuruzō, *Tōjō Hideki* (Tokyo, 1968), p. 376; Kase Toshikazu, *Journey to the Missouri* (New Haven, CT, 1950), p. 160.

34. *Kido Nikki*, 2:879; Yabe, *Konoe*, 2:296; Nishi, *Ni-So*, 15:229.

35. *Sugiyama Memo* (Tokyo, 1967), 1:218; Nobutaka Ike (trans. and ed.), *Japan's Decision for War: Records of the 1941 Policy Conferences* (Stanford, CA, 1967), pp. 46–47; Whaley, *Codeword*, p. 175.

36. BBSS, *Daitōa Sensō Kaisen Keii (4)*, pp. 143–44, and *(2)*, p. 326.

37. *Ibid. (2)*, p. 327.

38. *Ibid.*, p. 329.

39. *Ibid. (4)*, pp. 144–45, 150–51.

40. *Ibid.*, pp. 157–59.

41. *Ibid.*, pp. 147–48.

42. *Ibid.*, pp. 150–54.

43. *Ibid.*, p. 154.

44. *Ibid.*, pp. 154–55.

45. *Ibid. (2)*, pp. 329–30; *ibid. (4)*, pp. 155–56.

46. *Ibid. (4)*, p. 159.

47. *Ibid. (2)*, p. 322.

48. *Ibid.*

49. U.S. Department of State, *Foreign Relations of the United States: Diplomatic Papers, 1941*, Vol. 4, *The Far East* (Washington, DC, 1956), pp. 977–78 (hereafter, *FRUS*); author's interview with Ayabe; Oki Shūji, *Yamashita Tomoyuki* (Tokyo, 1968), p. 170; and *Ugaki Kazunari Nikki* (Tokyo, 1971), 3:1455.

50. *Kido Nikki*, 2:884; Kase, *Journey*, pp. 160–61; Yabe, *Konoe*, 2:296; Higashikuni, *Ichikōzoku*, p. 60; author's interviews with Kohtani and Ayabe.

51. Tanemura, *Daihonei*, p. 64.

52. Yabe, *Konoe*, 2:297–98; BBSS, *Daitōa Sensō Kaisen Keii (4)*, pp. 172–73.

53. *Ibid. (2)*, pp. 339–40; *ibid. (4)*, pp. 169–71.

54. *Ibid. (4)*, p. 146.

55. Author's interview with Hayashi Saburō; BBSS, *Daitōa Sensō Kaisen Keii (4)*, pp. 146–47.

56. BBSS, *Daitōa Sensō Kaisen Keii (4)*, p. 149.

57. *Ibid.*, pp. 148–49.

58. *FRUS*, p. 978.

59. BBSS, *Daitōa Sensō Kaisen Keii (4)*, p. 165.

60. *Ibid.*, pp. 162–64, 166.

61. Alvin D. Coox, *Tojo* (New York, 1975), p. 76.

62. BBSS, *Daitōa Sensō Kaisen Keii (4)*, p. 150.

63. *Ibid.*, p. 173.

64. *Ibid.*, pp. 159–63; *ibid. (2)*, pp. 341–42.

65. Masanobu Tsuji, *Singapore: The Japanese Version*, trans. M. E. Lake (New York, 1960), pp. 15–21 *passim*.

66. *Ibid.*, p. 17.

67. BBSS, *Daitōa Sensō Kaisen Keii (4)*, pp. 174–75; Ike, *Japan's Decision*, pp. 56–60.

68. BBSS, *Daitōa Sensō Kaisen Keii (4)*, pp. 177–79; Ike, *Japan's Decision*, pp. 60–64.

69. BBSS, *Daitōa Sensō Kaisen Keii (4)*, pp. 179–81; Ike, *Japan's Decision*, pp. 64–67.

70. BBSS, *Danitōa Sensō Kaisen Keii (4)*, p. 182.

71. *Ibid.*, p. 184; Ike, *Japan's Decision*, pp. 68–70.

About the Contributors

Calvin L. Christman is Professor of History at Cedar Valley College and Adjunct Professor at the University of North Texas. He has published articles on the United States in World War II in *Military Affairs, Diplomatic History, Mid-America,* and *The Americas.* He is currently an Associate Chairman and Southwestern Regional Coordinator of the Inter-University Seminar on Armed Forces and Society.

Alvin D. Coox served as a historian and analyst with the Army and Air Force in Japan from 1955 to 1963 and is currently Professor of History at San Diego State University. He is author of *Year of the Tiger* (1964); *The Anatomy of a Small War: The Soviet-Japanese Struggle for Changkufeng/Khusan, 1938* (1977); and the two-volume *Nomonhan: Japan Against Russia, 1939* (1985). He was also a contributor to *Military Effectiveness* (1988).

Paul Kennedy has been J. Richardson Dilworth Professor of History at Yale University since 1983. His numerous publications include *The Rise and Fall of British Naval Mastery* (1976); *The Rise of the Anglo-German Antagonism, 1860-1914* (1981); *The Realities Behind Diplomacy: Background Influences on British External Policy, 1865-1980* (1981); and *The Rise and Fall of the Great Powers: Economic Change and Military Conflict from 1500 to 2000* (1988).

Allan R. Millett is Professor of History and Associate Director of The Mershon Center at The Ohio State University. A specialist in the

history of American military policy and institutions, he is the author
of *The Politics of Intervention: The Military Occupation of Cuba,
1906-1909* (1968); *The General: Robert L. Bullard and Officership
in the United States Army, 1881-1925* (1975); and *Semper Fidelis:
The History of the United States Marine Corps* (1980). His latest
book, *For the Common Defense: A Military History of the United
States, 1607-1983,* written in collaboration with a former student,
Dr. Peter Maslowski, was published in 1984. He is co-editor and a
contributor to *Military Effectiveness,* an acclaimed three-volume
history of military affairs, 1900-1945 (1988).

Williamson Murray has been Professor of History at The Ohio State
University since 1977 and has been a visiting professor at the Air
War College, West Point, and the Naval War College. He has written
two books, *The Change in the European Balance of Power,
1938-1939* (1984); and *Luftwaffe* (1985); and was co-editor of
Military Effectiveness (1988) with Allan R. Millett. Presently a
reserve officer assigned to the Doctrine and Concepts Branch of
HQ/USAF, Professor Murray has just completed editing a collection of his articles for publication titled *German Military Effectiveness* (forthcoming).

Steven Ross has served on the faculty of the U.S. Naval War College
since 1973. Professor Ross has authored numerous articles and
books on the French Revolution and Napoleon, including *Quest for
Victory: French Military Strategy, 1792-1799* (1973); *From Flint-
lock to Rifle: Infantry Tactics, 1740-1866* (1979); and *French
Military History, 1661-1799: A Guide to the Literature* (1984).

Brian R. Sullivan is Senior Fellow at the National Defense University
in Washington, D.C. He is the author of articles on Italian military
and naval history and was a contributor to *Military Effectiveness*
(1988). Dr. Sullivan and Philip V. Cannistraro are currently
completing a biography of Margherita Grassini Sarfatti, the intimate adviser and confidante of Mussolini.

Earl F. Ziemke worked for the U.S. Army's Office of the Chief of
Military History from 1955 to 1967 and has been Professor of
History at the University of Georgia since 1967. Dr. Ziemke is
author of *The German Northern Theater of Operations, 1940-1945*
(1959); and *Stalingrad to Berlin: The German Defeat in the East*
(1968). He also co-authored *Moscow to Stalingrad: Decision in the
East* (1985) and has contributed to numerous publications, including *Military Effectiveness* (1988).

Index